D0385209

THE AMERICAN SELF

THE AMERICAN SELF

Myth, Ideology, and Popular Culture

Edited by Sam B. Girgus

UNIVERSITY OF NEW MEXICO PRESS
Albuquerque

Library of Congress Cataloging in Publication Data
Main entry under title:

The American self.

Includes bibliographical references.
1. United States—Civilization—Addresses, essays,
lectures. 2. United States—Popular culture—
Addresses, essays, lectures. 3. National character-
istics, American—Addresses, essays, lectures.
I. Girgus, Sam B., 1941–
E169.1.A482   973   80-52281
ISBN 0-8263-0557-1

To Scottie

Contents

Acknowledgments   ix

1. Introduction: American Studies and the American Self
   Sam B. Girgus   1

2. The Rites of Assent: Rhetoric, Ritual, and the Ideology
   of American Consensus
   Sacvan Bercovitch   5

3. Fiction and the American Ideology: The Genesis of Howells'
   Early Realism
   Henry Nash Smith   43

4. Cultural Revisions in the Twenties: Brooklyn Bridge as
   "Usable Past"
   Alan Trachtenberg   58

5. Some Varieties of Howells' Religious Experience
   George Arms   76

6. The American Quest for Religious Certainty, 1880–1915
   Ferenc Szasz   88

7. The New Covenant: The Jews and the Myth of America
   Sam B. Girgus   105

8. The "Limitless" Freedom of Myth: Paul Laurence Dunbar's
   The Sport of the Gods and the Criticism of Afro-American
   Literature
   Houston A. Baker, Jr.   124

9. American Values and Organized Crime: Suckers and Wiseguys
   Peter A. Lupsha   144

10. Frontier Families: Crisis in Ideology
    Lillian Schlissel   155

11. Rawhide Heroines: The Evolution of the Cowgirl and the
    Myth of America
    Shelley Armitage   166

12. Pornography, Catastrophe, and Vengeance: Shifting Narrative
    Structures in a Changing American Culture
    John Cawelti   182

13. *Ball Four* with Epilogue
    William C. Dowling and James Barbour   193

14. God and Man in Bedford Falls: Frank Capra's
    It's a Wonderful Life
    Robert Sklar   211

15. The Penitente Brotherhood in Southwestern Fiction: Notes
    on Folklife and Literature
    Marta Weigle   221

16. Mark Twain and the Mind's Ear
    Walter Blair   231

17. American Studies: The Myth of Methodology
    Joel Jones   240

Acknowledgments

Two people—Hamlin Hill of English and American Studies and William E. Davis, President of the University of New Mexico—were especially important to the development of both this book and the American Studies lecture series out of which it grew. I, therefore, would like to thank Hill for not only encouraging and supporting me in both projects but also for playing an instrumental role in making it possible for several of the participants in the lecture series to visit the university. Funding for Hill's National Endowment for the Humanities Seminar on American Humor enabled us to invite John Cawelti to teach for a semester at the university. In addition, Hill also encouraged Davis to sponsor a series of miniseminars that brought Henry Nash Smith and Walter Blair to campus. Through these and many other ventures both Hill and Davis have done much to promote American Studies and other interdisciplinary endeavors at the university. I also would like to thank Elizabeth Hadas of the University of New Mexico Press for her enthusiastic support of the book. In addition, several graduate students in American Studies worked on this book during various stages of its development. I thank them all. I also would like to acknowledge the many friends and colleagues from New Mexico and elsewhere who have worked with me and the department over the years in important and supportive ways. These include Lawrence Buell, Leonard Kriegel, Eddie O'Neil, Marshall Berman, Sanford Pinsker, Ed Hotaling, Joe Fashing, Dieter Schulz, Joan Girgus, and John Raeburn. At New Mexico the support of Peter White, Patrick Gallacher, Michael Hogan, McAllister Hull, Chris Garcia, Ernest Baughman, Nathaniel Wollman, Robert Fleming, Nancy Magnuson, Hugh Witemeyer, Bernard Spolsky, James Thorson, Mary Power, Rudolfo Anaya, Mary Bess Whidden, Harold Rhodes, David Benedetti, Howard Rabinowitz, Vera John-Steiner, Richard Tomasson, Janet Roebuck, and Jane Slaughter has been invaluable to the success and growth of both the graduate and undergraduate programs. Also, Trisha Black, Dr. Robert Michael, Angela Boone, David and Judith Bennahum, Brian Jones, Ken Darling, and Bill Jones remain true friends of American Studies faculty and students. I especially wish to thank the "core" faculty in American Studies who have provided the foundation for the department including Helen Bannan, Charles Biebel, and Vera Norwood. I once again would like to acknowledge my mother for her continuing support and encouragement. My greatest appreciation and thanks go to my wife Scottie for all her help, support, patience, and encouragement. I could never find the words to adequately express my feelings for all she has done and continues to do for me, our family, and for the community of students, colleagues, and friends that make up our life in New Mexico.

1

Introduction: American Studies and the American Self

American Studies was born in controversy and nurtured in dissent. From the beginning the legitimacy of studying American culture and character as a separate and distinct subject area was challenged. Nevertheless the idea of studying America as a special culture and the American as a unique "self" or character type gained momentum during the 1920s. Throughout the twenties and thirties this attitude toward American culture grew as scholars worked within their own disciplines. Thus, the founding of *American Literature* and the writing of the *Literary History of the United States* helped pave the way for what would become another controversy over the acceptance of a need to study the culture from an interdisciplinary perspective. With the growth of an interdisciplinary way of thinking and working, many scholars went into American Studies with a vision of themselves as academic renegades and rebels working on the new frontiers of culture studies and scholarly thought. At a national convention one former president of the American Studies Association described American Studies as a tribe of nomads whose tents could be found outside established disciplines and departments. Others saw the movement less dramatically but as still inherently innovative and somewhat irreverent because of its nature as the interdisciplinary study of a dynamic and pluralistic culture and society.

While interdisciplinary studies grew in respectability in the early 1950s, the use by American Studies scholars of symbol and myth and of intellectual history as ways of studying the culture generated new academic debate. Such debate developed interest in American Studies while also encouraging members of traditional disciplines and departments to alter and expand their own intellectual horizons and academic methodologies. Later changes in the culture during the 1960s and 1970s were reflected in

1

new methods and approaches involving ethnic, regional, and women studies. These developments along with the emergence of social history and
popular culture have caused something of a renaissance of interest in
American Studies and a revolution of traditional methodologies.

Accordingly, the essays collected here demonstrate the development of
both American culture and American Studies. While they indicate how
American Studies has developed a diversity of approaches, methodologies, and concerns, the essays also show how many scholars in the field
have retained their original interest in myth and ideology as a means for
understanding American culture and character. The first group of essays
in the collection reflects more traditional approaches to American Studies. Using sources primarily from literary and intellectual history, Sacvan
Bercovitch of Columbia University establishes the tone for the collection
with his opening essay on the myth of America and the ideology of consensus. The essay constitutes a new look at the Puritan experience as a
whole and offers new insights into the impact of the Puritans upon American culture and history. In many ways, including its conclusions about the
myth and ideology of America and contemporary culture, the essay
expands upon Bercovitch's celebrated and seminal earlier works on the
Puritan experience. In addition, it also includes detailed bibliographical
material. Thus the essay is a new statement from Bercovitch and an
important contribution to scholarship that provides an introduction and
background to themes about American culture and character that are
developed in the other original essays in the collection. Henry Nash
Smith of the University of California, Berkeley, expands on the idea
of an American ideology through his argument that Howells' commitment
to "the standard American ideology" as represented by middle-class values
and perspectives impeded his ability to create truly modern fiction. In
Smith's study the work of Howells exemplifies Bercovitch's thesis concerning the significance of ideological consensus to the American imagination.
By the twenties, according to Alan Trachtenberg of Yale University, modernism in America was presenting "an alternative way of life." In an
article that demonstrates the importance of myth and symbol to the history of American Studies, Trachtenberg reexamines "the subjective features" of the Brooklyn Bridge and how it influenced the poetry, painting
and photography of the period. However, even in this explosive time,
American artists often seemed to see their work in terms of a unique
American self and vision that related to a common cultural tradition and a
"usable past."

George Arms, who has represented American Studies at the University
of New Mexico for several decades, broadens the concept of ideology by
introducing the element of religion into the discussion with his analysis of
the complexity of Howells' religious thought and experience. Arms' view
of Howells provides an interesting contrast with the earlier picture pre-

sented by Smith and demonstrates how different critics can view one writer's ideology in widely different ways. Through his use of intellectual history, Ferenc Szasz of the Department of History of the University of New Mexico shows that in America religious belief does not come from just the cultural and intellectual elite but from all elements of the society. In his delineation of the explosion of religious movements at the grass-roots level, Szasz develops a fascinating social and cultural portrait of America from 1880 to 1915.

In recent years many scholars have focused their interests on ethnic, regional, and women studies. My essay concentrates on the impact of Jewish writers and thinkers upon the myth of America, while Houston Baker, Jr., of the University of Pennsylvania argues that an understanding of works of Afro-American literature in terms of mythic and symbolic potency can significantly improve our understanding of these works. Baker's essay is an attempt to free black literature from the misconceptions that have been imposed upon it. Peter Lupsha of the University of New Mexico Department of Political Science asks, "What's American about American crime?" He answers that what is perceived as a basically lawless American environment creates a "sucker" mentality in which the fear of the confidence man becomes a self-justification for crime as a form of defense.

In an essay that relates women studies and oral history to the social history of the frontier, Lillian Schlissel of Brooklyn College adds another dimension to our study of ideology by analyzing the connection between the expectations of Victorian ideology and the need for women on the frontier to change their traditional roles and self-images. Another picture of women on the frontier is presented by Shelley Armitage, a University of New Mexico graduate student in American Studies, who uses a methodology derived from popular culture studies, literary analysis, and social history to argue that the cattle frontier inspired the creation in the popular imagination of "perhaps the only true American heroine"—the cowgirl or "rawhide heroine."

The importance of popular culture studies to American Studies is further demonstrated by John Cawelti of the University of Kentucky. Cawelti believes that recent shifts in patterns of popular narrative in the media of print, film, and television may indicate significant changes in popular values and consciousness. He discerns the emergence of new mythic patterns centering on sexual liberation and domination, catastrophe and vengeance. Such shifts may signal the beginning of a final breakdown of the long-lasting American consensus that Bercovitch's opening essay addressed. Robert Sklar of New York University traces the evolution in Frank Capra's movies of the hero figure, especially as it culminates in *It's A Wonderful Life*. In the movie (which Sklar does not discuss in his book *Movie-Made America*), Sklar says, Capra felt the need for divine intervention to save the hero as opposed to the usual populist solutions in his films. According to Sklar, the movie indicates Capra's sense of the decline of liberty and individualism in America. For James Barbour and William Dowling of the New Mexico Department of English, sports, myth, and popular culture come together in the genre of the baseball autobiography. In *Ball Four* the writer's life and his relationship to his culture become the major game. For Barbour and Dowling, Jim Bouton represents aspects of American life and character for his time and place. Sources from popular culture are integrated into Marta Weigle's study of the folklore of New Mexico. Her article continues her examination of one of the most fascinating aspects of the culture of New Mexico—the mysterious brotherhood of the Penitentes. Weigle holds a joint appointment in the Departments of English and Anthropology at New Mexico.

The essay by Walter Blair of the University of Chicago relates Mark Twain the writer and humorist to Twain the public entertainer and demonstrates how reading Twain aloud can serve as an important "key to appreciating him" by helping the listener to train "the mind's ear" to understand more fully the complexity of Twain's artistry. Blair's approach to American culture through the study of American humor has been a basic element of American Studies for the past fifty years. The final essay by Joel Jones of American Studies deals primarily with the question of methodology and offers his perspective on the pluralistic, eclectic, and experimental philosophy of American Studies. The essay indicates how American Studies evolved into the diversity of approaches and interests that are reflected in this book. The convergence in this collection of a multiplicity of perspectives and methods on basic American themes and issues demonstrates the growth of American Studies as an academic tradition. However, like a modern painting, the collection also renders through its many parts a coherent view of the culture as a whole.

Finally, it should be noted that the book grew out of a lecture series and other presentations sponsored by the Department of American Studies. The quality of the lectures and the enthusiastic response to them led me to invite contributions from others who also have worked in-depth on a prolonged basis with our students. Accordingly, the book indicates something of the nature and history of American Studies at the University of New Mexico. It demonstrates a commitment over a span of generations that continues today as younger scholars and students open and explore new fields for learning and research.

Sam B. Girgus
University of New Mexico

2

The Rites of Assent:
Rhetoric, Ritual, and the Ideology of
American Consensus

Sacvan Bercovitch

the semiological definition of myth in a bourgeois society: *myth is depoliticized speech*. One must naturally understand *political* in its deeper meaning, as describing the whole of human relations in their real, social structure, in their power of remaking the world; one must above all give an active value to the prefix *de-*: here it represents an operational movement . . . it is the bourgeois ideology itself, the process through which the bourgeoisie transforms the reality of the world into an image of the world . . . [so that] the basic idea of a perfectible mobile world produces the inverted image of an unchanging humanity, characterized by an indefinite repetition of its identity.

Roland Barthes, *Mythologies*

My first encounter with American consensus was in the late sixties, when I crossed the border into the United States and found myself inside the myth of America. Not of North America, for the myth stopped short at the Canadian and Mexican borders, but of a country that despite its arbitrary frontiers, despite its bewildering mix of race and creed, could believe in something called the True America, and could invest that patent fiction with all the moral and emotional appeal of a religious symbol. It was as though a special lunacy had stormed the general optimism of the land. Here was the Jewish anarchist Paul Goodman berating the

5

Midwest for abandoning the promise; here, the descendant of American slaves, Martin Luther King, denouncing injustice as a violation of the American Way; here, an endless debate about national destiny, full of rage and faith, conservatives scavenging for un-Americans, New Left historians recalling the country to its sacred mission. Their problem was not what's usually called identity. These people never asked "Who are we?" but, as though deliberately avoiding that commonsense question, "When is our errand to be fulfilled? How long, O Lord, how long?" And their answers invariably joined celebration and lament in reaffirming the dream.

Nothing in my Canadian background had prepared me for that spectacle. I say this gratefully, to acknowledge the benefits of cultural shock in American studies. It gave me something of an anthropologist's sense of wonder at the symbols of the tribe. Mexico may have been the land of gold, and Canada might be the Dominion of the North; but America was a venture in exegesis. You were supposed to discover it as a believer unveils scripture. America's meaning was implicit in its destiny, and its destiny was manifest to all who had the grace to discover its meaning. To a Canadian skeptic, a gentile in God's Country, it made for a breathtaking scene: a pluralistic, pragmatic people openly living in a dream, bound together by an ideological consensus unmatched by any other modern society.

Let me repeat that mundane phrase: *ideological consensus*. For it wasn't the idea of exceptionalism that I discovered in '68. That I *had* heard about in Canada, through the works of "consensus historians." What I discovered had to do not with historiography, but (in Roland Barthes' sense of the word) with mythology. It was a hundred sects and factions, each apparently different from the others, yet all celebrating the same mission; a vast *Pequod's* crew of self-declared isolatoes, joined together in a deafening *concordia discors*. Ideology in this sense is perhaps a narrower concept than those usually associated with "America," but a more helpful one. It speaks of the day-to-day *uses* of myth. It reminds us that myth gains substance from its relation to facts, that it reflects and affects particular social needs, and that it persists through its capacity to influence people in history. Thus, although the consensus I refer to is not a measure of what census-takers call society, and although its function has been to mystify or mask social realities, nonetheless it denotes something equally "real": a system of values, symbols, and beliefs, and a series of rituals designed to keep the system going. So, it seemed to me, the rhetoric of mission served ten years ago. What was lost, I realized, in that endless debate about America was the fact that the debate itself was part of a long-ripened mode of socialization. And in trying to make sense of my discovery, I found myself back in the rhetoric of the antebellum North.[1] It was there the myth was established; there the rituals of God's country were completed and sanctified.

My purpose here is to explore, so as to expose, the nature of that consensus. I use the terms ritual and ideology, accordingly, in their broadest sense, to mean the forms and strategies through which the culture justified its ways and sought to enforce its norms. My major landmarks are the Revolution and the Civil War; but part of the terrain is the long foreground to revolution. I assume, with many recent historians, that the Civil War was the result of a gradual consolidation of ideological forces, a process that reflected the steady (if often turbulent) growth of middle-class American culture. I assume, further, that the meaning of America was not God-given but man-made, that the men who made it were not prophets but spokesmen for a certain social order, and that the rhetoric of consensus, which helped sustain and mold the social order, originated in colonial New England. A long foreground, as I said, but crucial to an understanding of my subject, and so I begin with a brief account of New England's errand into free enterprise.

I trust that this view of the Puritan errand won't seem to overstrain the worn links between Protestantism and the rise of capitalism. What I would suggest is simply that certain elements in Puritanism lent themselves powerfully to that conjunction, and precisely those elements came to the fore when the Massachusetts Bay emigrants, a group drawn mainly from the entrepreneurial and professional middle classes (tradesmen, lawyers, artisans, clerics, and merchants) severed their ties with the feudal forms of Old England and set up a comparatively fluid society on the American strand—a society that devalued aristocracy, denounced beggary, and, despite its traditions of deference, opened up political and economic opportunities to a relatively broad spectrum of the population. All this has been amply documented. A recent *New Yorker* cartoon has one Puritan emigrant say to another, as they disembark from the *Arbella*, "My immediate goal is freedom of religion, but my long-range plan is to get into real estate." No doubt Tocqueville had something like that in mind when he wrote, in a famous passage of 1835, that the "whole destiny of America is contained in the first Puritan who landed on these shores, as that of the whole human race in the first man."[2]

Tocqueville was making the point by hyperbole, but the point itself is valid enough to suggest a general difference between New England and other modern communities. In Europe, capitalism evolved dialectically, through conflict with earlier and persisting ways of thought and belief. It was an emerging force in a complex cultural design. Basically, New England bypassed the conflict. This is by no means to say that conflict was avoided altogether. The first century of New England was a remarkable instance of rapid social change, involving widespread social and moral tensions. But by and large those tensions marked transitional stages in the growth of the dominant culture. They signified not a contest between an established and an evolving system, as in Europe, but a troubled period of maturation. There were overlays of earlier agrarian patterns of life, but these did not offer the obstacles to modernization that peasant culture did (say) in pre-Revolutionary France. There were vestiges of folk customs, and assertions of aristocratic privilege, but these found no soil in which to take root; they showed none of the stubborn and substantive resistance to bourgeois values that Keith Thomas has found among the lower classes—or Christopher Hill among the aristocracy—of seventeenth-century Britain. Conflict there was in Puritan New England, but no place or period better illustrates Eric Hobsbawm's dictum that "the value of studies of major aspects of society are inversely proportional to our concentration on brief moments of conflict."[3]

For in all major aspects, New England was an outpost of the modern world from the start. Capitalism came there, in Carl Degler's phrase, "in the first ships"; or as Max Weber put it, "the spirit of capitalism . . . was present [there] before the capitalistic order," and "no medieval antecedents or complicating institutional heritage [intervened] to mitigate the impact of the Protestant Ethic on American [middle class] economic development."[4] On the contrary, in their revolt against Old World antecedents, the Puritans brought with them a sense of purpose that facilitated the process of modernization in crucial ways. They were only one of many groups of emigrants, from Jamestown to Philadelphia, that brought the spirit of capitalism to the New World; but more than any others it was they who gave that spirit a distinctive New World identity—gave it a local habitation, America, and a name, the New England Way, and an ideology that would in time fuse both terms in providing a distinctive rhetoric for the major free enterprise culture of the modern world. New England evolved from its own origins into the American Way, because from the start the colony was knit together, ideologically, by the concept of an errand into the wilderness.

It's that ideological function of the errand I want to stress. Considered as theology, the Puritan errand was a radical skewing of Christian tradition to fit the fantasies of a particular sect. Considered as ideology, it was a mode of consensus designed to fill the needs of a certain social order. Let me take a moment to explain the basic tenets of consensus in the Puritans' own terms. By errand they meant, first of all, *migration*—not simply from one place to another, but from a depraved Old World to a New Canaan. Properly speaking, they explained, the "new-ness" of their New World was prophetic: it signaled the long-awaited new heaven and new earth of the millennium. The desert land they were reclaiming had its past in Bible promises: America was there so that in due time they could make it blossom as the rose. In other words, they used the biblical myth of exodus and conquest to justify imperialism before the fact. The Puritans sometimes appear as isolationists, but basically they were as eager as any other group of emigrants for land and gain. The difference was that they managed more effectively to explain away their greed. Other peoples, as John Cotton put it, had their land by providence; *they* had it by promise.[5] Others might stake their colonial claims on royal patents or racial superiority or missionary rights. For the Massachusetts Bay Puritans it was a matter not of claiming rights but of reclaiming ownership. The wilderness belonged to their errand before the errand belonged to them.

That was one tenet of their consensus: migration as a function of prophecy, and prophecy as an unlimited license to expand. A second tenet of consensus centered on the problem of discipline. For on the whole the Puritans were an unruly lot—a volatile group of dissenters, "militant, apocalyptic, radically particularistic." In effect, the emigrant leaders were confronting what was to become a focal issue of free enterprise society: how to endorse individualism without promoting anarchy. They found a variety of solutions at hand: a doctrine of calling that linked private and public identity; a series of interlocking covenants that transformed congregational "polity from an instrument of rebellion to one of control"; a concept of preparation for grace that "generated both a respect for individual freedom and a need for external discipline." All these methods, as various scholars have shown, helped to "harness the turbulent force of [Puritan] individualism."[6] They found a common framework in the concept of representative selfhood.

The concept derived from what might be called the spiritual, as distinct from the prophetic, sense of the errand. I refer now to the concept of errand as pilgrimage. For each Puritan saint, the venture into the wilderness had an inward and private end. It was a journey of the soul to God, the believer's pilgrimage through the world's wilderness to redemption. In this sense, the Puritan venture was above all a matter of personal self-assertion. It built upon a series of free and voluntary commitments, and it made for a community grounded not in tradition or class status, but in private acts of will. Yet not merely private, for in a larger sense, as the Puritans never tired of saying, every one of those acts was part of a communal venture. To assert oneself in the right way, here in the American wilderness, was to embody the goals of New England. And let me say again that these goals were secular as well as sacred. The errand presupposed the actual flowering of the wilderness. It was a rare thing, the Puritans knew, for piety and prosperity to grow together; but New England was a rare place. Whatever furthered the errand hastened the kingdom. Every sign of an individual's success, moral or material, made New England's destiny visible.

As migration, then, the errand rationalized the expansive and acquisitive aspects of settlement. As pilgrimage, the errand provided for internal control by rooting personal identity in social enterprise. The third tenet of consensus spoke directly to the dynamics of the enterprise at large. By definition, the errand meant progress. It implied a teleology reaching from Genesis to the Apocalypse. As a community on an errand, New England was a movement from sacred past to sacred future, a shifting point somewhere between migration and millennium. Its institutions were geared not so much to maintain stability as to sustain process and growth. Problems of order were characteristically framed in such questions as "How far have we come?" and "Where are we headed?" Hierarchy remained, but it was increasingly subsumed in what amounted to a daring re-vision of social norms. The Old World ideal of society was vertical, a model of class harmony. Ideally, New England was a "way," a road into the future. Virtually all its rituals of control—its doctrines of calling and preparation, its covenants of church, state, and grace—were directed toward that ideal. They were rites of assent designed at once to yoke the forces of individualism and to spur the venture forward to completion. Even the legend of the fathers, as the Puritans construed this, was a summons onward. It was not enough for them to conform to the past; or rather to conform in their case was to dedicate oneself to constant improvement. That's why their sermons rose to a pitch of indignation and shrill excess unmatched in the European pulpit. The Puritans' vision fed on the distance between fact and promise. Anxiety became their chief means of establishing control. The errand, after all, was a state of *un*fulfillment, and only a sense of crisis, properly directed and controlled, could guarantee the outcome.

What I've been suggesting is that, in essence, the New England Way was not theocracy. It was the ideology of a new culture encased in outmoded, quasi-biblical forms. To the extent that the Puritans confused theocracy with ideology, their errand was no more than a tribal vision. Migration was defined by a certain locale, New England; pilgrimage expressed the outlook of a certain sect, Nonseparating Congregationalism; and progress was limited to an exclusive group, the visible saints and their offspring. But considered in its own terms, both symbolic and functional—considered, that is, as the ideology of a nascent free enterprise culture—the errand was as boundless as the wilderness. For to the Puritans, Congregationalism was not just another sect. It was the vanguard of the Protestant movement; and Protestantism was not just another creed, but the last stage of the world-wide work of redemption. So, it was, too, with their locale. The Puritans took possession first by imposing their own image on the land, and then by seeing themselves reflected back in the image they had imposed. The wilderness became their mirror of prophecy. What they saw revealed there was not a geographical entity, but a chosen nation in progress—a New Israel whose constituency was as numerous, potentially, as the entire people of God, and potentially as vast as America.

It was that larger, American vision which the Puritans bequeathed to the culture. This was their legacy: a system of sacred-secular symbols

(New Israel, American Jerusalem) for a people intent on progress; a set of rituals of anxiety and control that could at once encourage and confine the energies of free enterprise; a rhetoric of mission so broad in its implications, and so specifically American in its application, that it could facilitate the transitions from Puritan to Yankee, and from errand to manifest destiny and the dream. That these transitions effected changes in rhetoric and ritual goes without saying. But the capacity to accommodate change is proof of *vitality*, in symbolic no less than in social systems; and through the eighteenth century the rhetoric of errand remained a major vehicle of social continuity. Elsewhere, I've described various aspects of continuity in some detail.[7] Here I want briefly to note the changes, particularly during the Great Awakening and the French and Indian War, which expanded, deepened, and finally Americanized the rhetoric of consensus.

To begin with, the concept of representative selfhood took on a broad Anglo-American meaning. The Great Awakening opened the gates of New Canaan to any evangelical, North and South; and the French and Indian War opened them wider still, to include any loyal colonist, evangelical and nonevangelical. Between 1740 and 1760, then, the benefits of the errand as pilgrimage—the special sense of oneself as representing God's New Israel—were extended to every patriotic Protestant American. Of course, this involved a general redefinition of the self. It also reflected a tendency of the age toward what we have come to term individualism. Eighteenth-century America offered brave new vistas for private enterprise, provided higher incentives for self-assertion, and fortified self-interest with a new theological and philosophical rationale for self-love. To some extent, these liberal attitudes paralleled, or could be made to parallel, the tenets of Puritan ideology. And most of them contributed in some way to loosen and enlarge the concept of representative selfhood. But the concept itself, we recall, was intended as a strategy of control. It was designed to keep self-assertion within cultural bounds. So it was used, in effect, by the leaders of the Great Awakening. Significantly, the revivalist emphasis on the self issued in the first major rituals of intercolonial unity. So also the spokesmen for the French-Indian War appealed to conscience and self-interest, only to make these synonymous with Protestant patriotism, and the Protestant cause inseparable from the rising glory of America. Both in revival and in war, representative selfhood bound the rights of personal ascent to the rites of social assent.

In both cases, too, the terms of assent extended the meaning of the Puritan migration. Indeed, the legend of the founding fathers was virtually transformed during this period, from a tribal legend to a legend of cultural origins. This is not to say that the Puritan vision was substantially altered. The transformation I speak of involved a process of revision, not replacement. It was a means of providing for continuity in change even as it allowed for change through continuity. On the one hand, the epic of the

Puritan exodus became the common property of all Anglo-American settlers. Long after the theocracy had failed, after Puritanism itself had faded
theologically, the heroes of 1630 were being ritually invoked—not just in
New England, but in Pennsylvania, New York, and the South—to unite
colonial Americans in their sense of heritage and purpose. On the other
hand, the meaning of the Puritan exodus was adjusted to the conditions of
a new age. For revivalists, the Great Migration was a herald of the Great
Awakening, an image or type of the "blessed unions" of converts that
would soon knit together, as one city on a hill, the whole of Anglo-
America. For leaders of the French and Indian War, the Puritan emigrants were heroes in the cause of liberty. Their mission was Protestantism
and liberalism entwined. Freedom was their motive, and a New Eden of
industry and free trade their sacred legacy.

These revisions of meaning had far-reaching consequences. Eventually, they were to provide a civic base for religion and a religious base for
liberalism in America. And they could have such broad effect only because the rhetorical and social implications of the New England Way
reflected the tendencies of the dominant culture. Most dramatically, this
applies to the eighteenth-century re-vision of the errand as progress. The
crucial change here came with the revivalist doctrine of postmillennialism.
Technically speaking, the Puritans were premillennialists. That is, they
believed that the millennium was still to come, and accordingly they
expected that their errand would terminate in the miracles of the apocalypse. Edwards and his followers had an idea better suited to the Enlightenment and the New Science. They envisioned a continual increase of
moral, spiritual, and material goods in this world—an age of sacred-
secular wonders within history. They inherited the hope of supernatural
things to come, and they altered this to mean an indefinite course of
human progress. The glories of the coming of the Lord, they explained,
were to be the last act in the conquest of the New World wilderness. For
the Edwardsians, those glories centered on revival and conversion. For
the clergy of 1760, the millennial hope centered on the defeat of French
Canada. Clothing imperialism as holy war, they described Catholic Quebec
as the last bastion of evil. A golden age of peace and prosperity, they
promised, would follow the Protestant American victory. In short, the
errand for them was not just the way to the millennium. It was millennialism as the American Way.

In all this, the rhetoric of the errand contributed to the Revolution.
And let me repeat that it expressed a developing ideological mode. During the Great Awakening, it helped both to elicit and to direct the energies
of economic growth. During the French and Indian War, it was used both
to mobilize the colonists for invasion and to fortify their civic institutions.
That ritual of anxiety and control the patriotic Whigs put to effective
use—first, in their propaganda war against England, and then, even more

conspicuously, in their struggle for internal control. The nature of that struggle is well known. The Revolution had inspired what the Whig leaders termed a dangerous upsurge of egalitarian demands. Antiauthoritarianism was abroad in the land, and the men of wealth and property who ran the republic had a great deal at stake in the status quo. They could not afford a breakdown of established forms of deference. They found the order they sought in the ideology of errand. Elsewhere, they pointed out, revolution was a threat to society. It meant hiatus, discord, the dysfunction of class structure. But revolution in America was a different matter. Here it meant the unfolding of a redemptive plan. It required progress through conformity, the ordained succession from one generation to the next. What the Puritan fathers had begun, their sons were bound to com-plete—*bound* by covenant and precedent. The War of Independence signaled America's long-prepared-for, reverently *ordered* passage into nationhood.

In other words, the Whig leaders brought the violence of revolution under control by making revolution a controlling metaphor for national identity. In a sense this was simply the product of anticolonial struggle. The rhetoric that prepared the colonists for revolution provided their leaders with a vehicle of social control: the pattern has become so familiar as to seem a condition of modern nationalism. What distinguishes the American Revolution within this pattern is the rhetorical mode it brought to fruition. When the patriot Whigs expanded the concept of the errand into an apologia for independence, they gave full and final sanction to the ideology of consensus. Once and for all, the errand took on a special, self-enclosed *American* form. Independence from England completed the separation of the New World from the Old. Henceforth, Americans could direct the process of migration toward its proper goal, the conquest of a continent. Independence became the norm for representative selfhood: independence of mind, independence of means, and these twin blessings, sacred and secular, the mirror of a rising nation—what could better dem-onstrate the bond of personal and social identity? Elsewhere, to be inde-pendent was to challenge society. In the United States, it was to be a model of consensus. Above all, independence gave a distinctive national shape to the idea of progress. The sacred origin was the Puritan migra-tion; the telos was the Revolution. Drawing out the logic of the errand to a point undreamed of by their forebears, the patriot Whigs announced that the long-awaited apocalyptic moment had arrived on July 4, 1776.

It took another generation or so before all the details could be worked out—before Washington could be enshrined as savior, his apostles ranked, the Judas in their midst identified, and the Declaration of Independence adequately compared to the Sermon on the Mount. But the ritual plot, the narrative frame of the ideology of errand, had at last found its focus.

With the Revolution, the Puritan vision flowered into the myth of America. For the errand itself was rooted in biblical myth. However eccentric their interpretations, the Puritans had relied on the authority of scripture. No matter how flagrantly they distorted sacred history to justify their experience, they were appealing, finally, to Christian tradition. The Revolutionary Whigs took the justification, rather than the tradition behind it, as their authority. No matter how piously they invoked scripture they were appealing not to Christian tradition, but to the series of recent events through which they defined the American experience. Their symbology centered on the act of migration; their text was the progress from theocracy to republic; their source of prophecy, the pilgrimage of the representative American.[8]

The story they told was broadcast through the land every July Fourth, the high holy day of American civil religion. A new era, so the story went, had begun with the discovery of the New World, and the Revolution confirmed it, just as Christ had confirmed the new era of faith. In both cases, the event was at once definitive and heuristic. Christ had invoked the authority of the prophets, but it was His mission that verified their prophecies. Such too was the relation between Old and New Israel. As the patriot spokesmen put it, the Revolution "is indissolubly linked with the Redeemer's mission." It is "the wonder and the blessing of the world," the moment "from which the new order of things is to be reckoned," the epoch-making "accomplishment of all . . . the great events, designed from eternal ages" to "promote *the perfection and happiness of mankind.*" "Here, from the analogy of reason and providence, we can expect God's greatest works." With the Revolution, God has shown that "The UNITED STATES OF AMERICA are to be His vineyard"—"the principal Seat of [His] glorious kingdom"—wherein the promises of the past "are to be brought to harvest," for "the benefit of the whole world."[9]

What a harvest! The flight of Abraham, the desert wanderings of Israel, the revival of the church, its war of independence against Catholic Rome, and the march of civilization from Greece and Rome through Renaissance, Reformation, and Enlightenment: to all these the Revolution stood as fulfillment to promise. And as fulfillment, it obviated the need for any further American uprisings. In the cliché that George Bancroft made famous, it was a revolution to end revolutions. Revisions and cleansings there would have to be, but fundamentally the direction was set. Hereafter, the spirit of progress was the spirit of '76. And the converse was equally true. As the fulfillment of promises past, the Revolution was the guarantee of better things to come. "The American war [against England] is over," the Whig leaders explained in 1787; "but this is far from being the case with the American revolution. On the contrary, nothing but the first act of the great drama is closed." Now that we have "made good our fathers' covenant," the *magnalia Christi Americana* will continue, in the image of the Revolution "to the end of time."[10]

The leaders of Puritan New England had devised the errand to bring a group of potential revolutionaries under control. The patriot Whigs took control of the republic by translating the errand into the rhetoric of continuing revolution. In doing so, they set forth the one myth patterned specifically to the needs of liberal middle-class society. Protestantism may have given modern culture its ethic, but Puritanism gave it the myth of America. And no culture, let me add, ever stood more in need of a myth. From the seventeenth century on, modernism has meant a world where the self was cut loose in a marketplace of other independent selves; where no theory of government could offer a ready way to impose community; where the guiding philosophers were the masters of *Realpolitik*—not Plato or Aristotle, but Bacon and Machiavelli; not Aquinas or Calvin, but Hobbes and Locke. The Constitution-makers had no substitute except nature's laws for the divine right of kings. "Neither Philosophy, nor Religion," they recognized, "nor Morality, nor Wisdom, nor Intellect will ever govern nations or parties, against their Vanity, Pride, Resentment or Revenge, or their Avarice and Ambition. Nothing but Force and Power and Strength can restrain them. . . . [Therefore,] power must be opposed to power, force to force, strength to strength, [and] interest to interest."[11] What they offered, accordingly, was a pragmatic federalism: division of powers, self-protective multiplicity. It was a model of modern statecraft, embracing the open competition of values (as of goods) and encouraging discrepant views to coexist in the same society even as they challenged each other's priorities. In effect, the Constitution-makers provided the first full-scale rationale for the forces of secularization and pluralization that shaped the postfeudal West.

It was not enough. Modern communities, as we have come to learn, have as much need for spiritual cohesion as did the communities of the past. The citizens of a republic, no less than the subjects of a monarchy or the members of a church-state, require some means of consecrating their way of life—a set of metaphysically (as well as naturally) self-evident truths; a moral framework within which a certain complex of attitudes, assumptions, and beliefs can be taken for granted as being right; a super-empirical authority to sustain the norms of personal and social selfhood. And those needs were particularly strong in the new republic. One has only to consider the traumatic effects of the break with monarchy, or Crèvecoeur's charges at the end of his *Letters from an American Farmer*, in a chapter rarely cited by Americanists, where he explains his preference for the "primitive" order of Indian society to the chaos of independence. The charges were reasonable enough. To all appearances, the country in the late 1770s *was*, as the Loyalists said, "anarchy set loose":[12] a nation without a past, a people of diverse customs, a territory without clear boundaries, an economy without a stable center—variously agrarian, urban, preindustrial, and in transition toward industrialism—and a free enterprise system that was endangered by the very doctrine of self-interest it sought to encourage, as well as by the values of independence and revolt upon which the nation was founded.

One major reason for the Whigs' success was that the rhetoric of consensus filled the need for a communal myth. It gave the country a past and a future in sacred history, rendered its civic institutions a fulfillment of prophecy, elevated its so-called true inhabitants, the Anglo-Saxon Protestants who had immigrated within the past century or so, to the status of God's chosen, and declared the vast territories around them to be their promised land. Above all, it grounded the myth in a central symbol, "America," that joined the Hobbist and figural poles of the social order. The effects of this fusion can hardly be overestimated. Translated into the terms of modern anthropology, they imply the basic dynamics of socialization, the "deep structure" ("normative" and "oretic") of the ritual process itself:

> At the ideological [or normative] pole . . . there is a cluster of meanings referring to moral values, principles of social organization, rules of social behavior, the ideals of corporate groups, in short all the obligatory elements in the social order. At the sensory [or oretic] pole . . . there are gross sensations, desires, and feelings. The norms, values, principles and rules at the ideological pole are abstract and remote and [so] . . . not sufficient to induce [a person] to action. It is only when he is emotionally agitated . . . that he will be moved to action. In the action situation of the ritual . . . the ritual symbol effects an interchange of qualities between the two poles of the symbol. Norms and values become saturated with emotion, while . . . basic emotions become ennobled through contact with social values. The irksomeness of moral constraint is transformed into the love of goodness. Ritual thus becomes a mechanism which periodically converts the obligatory into the desirable. [13]

This analysis applies in some degree to any cohesive culture. But its applicability to the new republic has special significance. Nowhere has constraint (social or moral) been more "irksome," potentially, than in the formative stages of free enterprise capitalism; nowhere has "gross desire" more directly challenged the status quo; and nowhere in the modern world were those threats more firmly converted into voluntary allegiance than in the formation of the United States. In a ritual procession of speeches and sermons that made oratory a high American art form, the spokesmen for the republic invested "America" with a binding ritual double meaning. As the dominant symbol of the myth, interchangeably sensory and ideological, it came to signify both self-gratification and the self-evident good, the most pragmatic of communities and the most abstract of ideals. Social organization, if *American*, was by definition noble. To be noble in the *American* grain was ipso facto the practical way to get things done.

On that basis, the Federalist leaders channelled the volatile emotions of revolt into the structures of a (rhetorically) homogeneous nation. Their rituals of crisis proved a decisive moral mechanism in the war against excessive self-interest. Their invocations to continuing revolution effectually barred the influence of unsettling "foreign ideologies," particularly those of revolutionary France. Their summons to independence magnified the "pursuit of happiness" from a merely private enterprise into an enterprise that entailed not only the common good but the redemption of mankind. In virtually every area of life, the rhetoric of American consensus served to consecrate the practice and theory of democratic capitalism. Mediating between "gross feelings" and "remote abstraction," the felt rights of ascent and the imposed duties of assent, it gave contract the sanctity of covenant, free enterprise the halo of grace, progress the assurance of millennium, and chauvinism the grandeur of typology. In sum, it wed modernism to the errand, conferred on both the blessings of continuing revolution, and certified the union with the Great Seal of the United States: *Annuit Coeptis, Novo Ordus Seclorum*—"God prospered this undertaking; it shall be the new order of the ages."

The union was a fruitful one. Its success is attested by the fact that the United States not only usurped American identity but retained its exclusive meaning. Elsewhere during this period, the Enlightenment rhetoric of "the people" proved to be a major obstacle for revolutionaries. The vagueness of Robespierre's appeal to "the people" forced him, in George Rudé's words, to fall "victim to his own ideals," trapped between the bourgeois who controlled the French Republic and the sans-culottes he thought he represented. Similar ambiguities in Hidalgo's rhetoric undermined the 1810 revolution in Mexico. Preaching the parallels between the gospels, Rousseau, and Adam Smith, Hidalgo had hoped to forge a coalition of Creoles and Indians against Spanish colonists. Instead, he incited a more basic conflict in which all the upper classes, alarmed at the threat to property rights, allied themselves against the dispossessed majority. The same conflicts worked to destroy Bolivar's dream of a South American Republic. Having made himself the Liberator of too many of "the people"—blacks, Indians, and mulattoes, as well as the aspiring middle class he came from—having succeeded too well, that is, with the liberal rhetoric of equality, Bolivar too, like Robespierre and Hidalgo, found himself betrayed by the realities of class conflict.[14]

The leaders of New Israel simply sidestepped those pitfalls. They could endorse universalism and yet exclude from it whatever then hindered their progress. The American was not (like the Frenchman or the Latin American) a member of "the people." He stood for a mission that was limitless in effect, because it was limited in fact to a "peculiar" nation. Thus (in the notorious paradox of the Declaration) he could denounce servitude and oppression while concerning himself least, if at all, with the most enslaved and inadequately represented groups in the land. Those groups were part of "the people," perhaps, but not the *chosen* people; they were in America, but not of it. I think here not only of moderates and conservatives, like Adams and Hamilton, but of so-called radicals like Tom Paine. If at first Paine "manipulated" the rhetoric of consensus, as some historians claim, eventually he became himself an instrument of the rhetoric, a missionary to Europe for the Constitution and the American Way. Thus in direct contrast to French radicals, who used "the language of the people" to stress class divisions, Paine appealed in that language for "social harmony" and the "spirit of reconciliation." The basis for his appeal, throughout the 1790s, was America—the one true "Republic in the world," a "veritable utopia" where "the poor are not oppressed, the rich are not privileged . . . government is just, and . . . there is nothing to engender riots and tumults"—a New Canaan charged "by the design of Heaven" with "the cause of all mankind."[15]

Paine was to change his mind, reluctantly, upon his return to New Canaan. But the consensus he espoused continued to gather strength during the Federalist period. Through the rituals of continuing revolution, the middle-class leaders of the republic recast the Declaration to read, "all propertied, white, Anglo-Saxon Protestant males are created equal." Through those rituals they confined the meaning of revolution to American progress, American progress to God's chosen, and God's chosen to people of their own kind. It's no accident that under Jefferson's administration, the Revolution issued in an increasing violation—for blacks and Indians—of life, liberty, and the pursuit of happiness. Nor is it by accident that so many of the electoral debates through the Middle Period turned on which party was the legitimate heir to the title of American Israel, and which candidate the true son of the Revolutionary fathers and Puritan forefathers. Nor is it by accident, finally, that while France and Latin America degenerated into factional pandemoniums, the United States generated a conformist spirit that foreign observers termed a "tyranny of the majority."

A *tyranny of the culture* would have been more precise. Nationalism served elsewhere during this period to unify modern communities, but it brought with it the archaic myths and mystiques of the communal past. This was the case in post-Revolutionary France, where the old pantheon of regal heroes remained intact—Charlemagne, Roland, Henry IV, the Sun King Louis XIV—just as the term *aristocrat* retained its honorific meaning and *bourgeois* its pejorative meaning, despite the triumph of the middle class. This was also the case in nineteenth-century Germany, where nationalism helped equally to modernize the state and to conjure up an atavistic *Volksgeist*, fired by feudal legends and profound anti-libertarian sentiments. A similar clash of interests attended the rise of Russian nationalism. Westernization and Pan-Slavism both contributed to that development, but the myth of Pan-Slavic destiny provided a wholly different basis for community from that offered by the progressivists, whether liberal, socialist, or communist.

The American rhetoric of consensus showed no such conflicts. Here, the ideals of community wholly supported the goals of free enterprise. Even when these ideals seemed to conflict, as between Jefferson and Adams, agrarian and entrepreneur, Jacksonians and bankers, even then the conflicts bespoke a single organic process of development. Here only, the invocation of the past enhanced the values of progress. Hadn't Puritan simplicity led *upward* toward the events of '76? And weren't the Revolutionary heroes all independent self-made men, the models of a *rising* nation? The Russian Church denounced secular reform in the name of sacred history, peasant tradition, and the "Russian soul." German and French Romantics arraigned themselves against the Enlightenment.[16] But in the United States, all three movements, Christian, Deist, and Romantic, fused in the national symbol. By 1840, America was the land of prophecy, reason, and nature entwined. Here as nowhere else, the very hope of improvement led social critics to reject the idea of alternative systems (not to mention class conflict) since improvement was the American Way, and "American," after all, was a consensual term. Ritually and ideologically, it embodied the promise of the New World, and therefore of the future at large.

It was a tyranny not of the majority but of middle-class thought. The United States has never had what Tocqueville called a "universal middling standard," nor was it ever a nation of "similar participants in a uniform way of life," a people "all of the same estate," as Louis Hartz claimed. Rather, it was a culture bound by an extraordinary ideological hegemony. How else can we explain so many major writers bewailing the lack of history and diversity in the land? "I have never seen a people so much alike in my life, as the Americans," marveled James Fenimore Cooper in 1828. He knew well enough about differences between whites and Indians or blacks, about differences between urban socialites, immigrant laborers, and rural gentry, and for that matter about the different customs in the North, South, and West. So, too, did Hawthorne when in 1860, on the eve of civil war, he described the United States as "a country where there is no antiquity, no mystery, no picturesque and gloomy wrong, nor anything but a commonplace prosperity, in broad and simple daylight.[17] It was not ignorance or insensitivity that led to these wry complaints. It was merely, astonishingly, that in terms of the myth such differences did not count. Nation meant *Americans*, *Americans* meant *the people,* and *the people* meant those who, thanks to the Revolution, enjoyed a *commonplace prosperity:* the simple sunny rewards of American middle-class life.

It's really beside the point to speak here of evasions or distortions of the facts. Those evasions or distortions express a fundamental truth about the culture. They reveal a dominant pattern of belief, reaching from Ben Franklin's Poor Richard to Horatio Alger's Ragged Dick. Of course, the pattern I speak of yields only one sort of truth. Seen from outside the consensus, mid-nineteenth-century America had a very different look. It was a stratified, pluralistic society, rife with ethnic and class divisions. One of every five Americans was a black or an Indian; one of every eight whites was a recent immigrant; in the urban centers, where $1,000 a year was an average middle-class income, only 1 percent of the population earned over $800. During this so-called era of the common man, fewer than 2 percent of the rich were not born rich. Jacksonian democracy was a less egalitarian state than Puritan theocracy. Consider these recent statistics: in 1670, when Samuel Danforth delivered his famous sermon on New England's errand, 5 percent of the saints owned one-quarter of the wealth. In 1770, when Franklin praised the colonies' "general Mediocrity of Fortune," 3 percent of the colonists owned one-third of the wealth. In the 1830s, when Tocqueville wrote his myth of egalitarian democracy, 1 percent of Americans owned almost half the wealth of America.[18]

Hence the importance of the rhetoric of consensus. It served then, as always, to blur such discrepancies. But in doing so, the rhetoric provides us with a map of social reality that is no less accurate in its way than any quantitative chart. It locates the sources of social revitalization and integration. It helps explain how the majority of people kept the faith despite their day-by-day experiences. It reveals the basis on which the most heterogeneous people in the world was molded into what remains (even after the Marxist revolutions) the most monolithic of modern cultures. For the fact is that what Cooper and Hawthorne said about the country may be found throughout the popular literature. Virtually every one of the hundreds of mid-nineteenth-century biographers of "great Americans" insisted that his subject was not someone unique, but the emblem of American enterprise. So it was, too, in the countless rags-to-riches stories. However humble their origins, these heroes were not members of the working class, nor were they, after their success, bourgeois or *nouveau riche*, and certainly they never became aristocrats. They were rather, every fatherless son of them, aspiring, self-motivated (even when, like Whitman's Walt, they were motivated by the idea of America), self-reliant (even when, like Alger's Sam Barker, they depended on employers), self-educated (even when, like Thoreau, they were Harvard graduates), mobile (even if they decided, like Hawthorne's Holgrave, to settle down), and independent. And independence, of course, signified not so much an economic state as a state of mind and being, an entire system of moral, political, and religious values. In short, the American hero could represent no particular class because he represented all classes—which is to say, a cultural myth. To be self-made in 1850 was more than to make one's own fortune; it was to embody a metaphysics.

By and large, it was a metaphysics for men, but women found their own ways of joining the consensus. One way was through motherhood. As Catherine Beecher, the high priestess of the cult of domesticity, put it in 1841: "The shaping of the people" has been "committed mainly to the female hand." As mothers, we mold the characters of our children; and as American mothers, we mold the character of those who are to continue the errand. We are therefore "agents in accomplishing the greatest work ever entrusted to human responsibility." "To *American* women, more than any others on earth, is committed the exalted privilege of extending over the world the blessed influences that are to renovate degraded man." Another way was militant feminism. We appeal to "principles cherished by all Americans," wrote Elizabeth Cady Stanton. The cause we fight for is no "foreign import." It is the "legacy of the Fathers," augmented now by "a new spirit of energy"—open competition, free labor, equal opportunity, and the sanctity of private property, especially the property of the self. That was 1848, the year of the first Paris Commune and the Communist Manifesto; the year also of the first women's rights convention, at Seneca Falls, whose manifesto followed the form and phrases of the Declaration of Independence, and whose goal, in the words of Antoinette Brown, was to "remove the [last] stigma resting on this republic."[19]

Of course, these feminists may have been using patriotism for propaganda effect. But if so, they were miscalculating the relation of ends and means. In effect, they were conforming to a ritual of consensus that defused all issues in debate by restricting the debate itself, symbolically and substantively, to the meaning of America. In this, the feminists were like most American radicals of their time. William Lloyd Garrison, for example, organized the American Anti-Slavery Society as "a renewal of the nation's founding principles" and of the "national ideal." Frederick Douglass based his demands for black liberation on America's "destiny," the "sacred meaning" of July Fourth, and "the genius of American institutions," which would one day, he hoped, transform the world (including "darkest Africa") in "all-pervading light." In that faith, Robert Rantoul defended his "left-wing programs" as expressing the "national errand" for "the renovation of mankind." With that prospect in view, Adin Ballou organized his "experiment in radical reform" at Hopedale. Like the transcendentalist founders of Brook Farm, he expected the venture in utopia to "provide 'types' for the millennium" in America. Similar examples abound in every area of the country. As a leading historian of the period has remarked, "the typical reformer, for all his uncompromising spirit, was no more alienated—no more truly rebellious—than the typical democrat. . . . [He] might sound radical while nevertheless associating himself with the fundamental principles and underlying tendencies of America."[20]

Nothing more clearly attests to the continuing power of the myth than does the proliferation of "radical" manifestoes in antebellum America.

For (once the Revolution was secured) the rhetoric of consensus not only allowed for but actually elicited social criticism. After all, what higher defense could one offer for middle-class society than an American Way that *sui generis* evoked the free competition of ideas? And what could make things safer for middle-class society than to define freedom in terms of the American Way? In mid-nineteenth-century Europe, the summons to "the people" exposed the pretense of unity; there, revolution bared the dialectics of historical change. In America at this time, the summons to dissent, because it was grounded in prescribed ritual forms, ruled out the threat of basic social alternatives. It was a means of containing radicalism, we might say, in the double sense of *containment*, as sustenance and restriction. It facilitated process in such a way as to enlist radicalism itself in the cause of continuing revolution.

I don't mean by this to belittle the struggle of those reformers. Garrison, Rantoul, and Ballou payed a high personal price for their dissent. Douglass and Stanton claimed to be true Americans, and Thoreau called John Brown "the most American of us all," but to most of their neighbors they were three more in a long list of un-Americans, along with the other abolitionists, feminists, and utopians (not to mention such blatant outsiders as Chief Black Hawk, Rabbi Meyer Isaac Wise, and John England, the Catholic Bishop of Charleston, South Carolina). In this sense, the ritual meant consensus through negation: garden versus wilderness, chosen people versus the nations of the earth. One major characteristic of the period was its astonishing variety of official or self-appointed committees to keep America pure: "progressivists" for eradicating the Indians; "American Christians" for deporting the Catholics; "benevolent societies" for returning the blacks to Africa; "Young Americans" for banning European culture; "temperance societies" for purging the backsliders. "In America," thundered the popular revivalist Albert Barnes in 1834, "every drunkard opposes the millennium."[21]

But in the long run exclusion was a strategy for absorption. Like the Puritan concept of errand, it was a way of saying "not yet" so that finally one could say "you, too." The conflict between garden and wilderness implied that what was wilderness now would soon be a greater New Canaan. So it was also in the case of the chosen people versus the world (including European culture); so also in the case of true versus false Americans. The American consensus *could* absorb feminism, if feminism would lead into the middle-class American Way. Blacks and Indians could also learn to be True Americans, when in the fullness of time they would adopt the tenets of black and red capitalism. On that provision, Jews and even Catholics could eventually become sons and daughters of the Revolution. On those grounds, even such unlikely candidates for perfection as Alaska and Hawaii could become America.

All of these recent developments are implicit in the rhetoric of errand;

and the implications help define what I called a cultural, as distinct from a national, mode of consensus. The biblical Hebrews were nationalists. Although they claimed their land by promise, Canaan itself was a country (like any other) with fixed boundaries; and though they called themselves a "peculiar people," their peculiarity was based (like that of any other people in their time) upon genealogy and a certain form of religion. Genealogy, boundaries, and a certain form of religion were precisely what American nationhood has *not* meant. American genealogy was simply the idea of mission brought up to date. As a community, New Israel was the heir of the ages; its representative citizen was independent, unbound by any public or personal ties, except the ties of culture that required him to be self-made. As for boundaries, political leaders dissolved that barrier to progress by reversing the meaning of frontier. Traditionally, a frontier was a border dividing one people from another. It implied differences between nations. In a sense, antebellum Americans recognized such differences—their frontier separated them from the Indians—but they could hardly accept the restriction as permanent. This was God's Country, was it not? So they effected a decisive shift in the meaning of frontier, from barrier to threshold. Even as they spoke of their frontier as a meeting ground between two civilizations, Christian and pagan, they redefined it, in an inversion characteristic of the myth-making imagination, to mean a *figural* outpost, the outskirts of the advancing kingdom of God.

The inversion has become so familiar by now as to seem an inevitable outgrowth of the Westward movement. But the fact is that other immigrant groups responded in entirely different ways. I think here not only of the Spaniards, who had the whole run of the West from the Mississippi Valley to California, but primarily of the Anglo-Canadians, who had the same cultural heritage as the Americans, including a common set of dominant racial and religious traits, WASP, a common liberal ideology, and a common commitment, virtually from the start, to the process of modernization.[22] They also defined themselves in relation to the Western frontier, yet their definition issued in a decidedly un-American outlook. To Canadians, the frontier has always meant "antagonism," the clash of cultures, the "loneliness of a huge and thinly settled country," the problems of "carving out" a community "in the face of 'hostile' elements." The most widely accepted image of the Canadian West, "the bush country," derives directly from the commonsense meaning of frontier as barrier, dividing line, or state of separation. To be a Canadian pioneer in the nineteenth century was to be "surrounded with a physical or psychological frontier," separated from . . . cultural sources"; it was to join (for purposes of commerce and survival) in "small and isolated communities: communities . . . that [were] compelled to feel a great respect for the law and order that [held] them together, yet confronted with a huge unthinking, menacing and formidable physical setting."[23] In short, the Canadians' errand was grounded in history, not rhetoric. Whether it denoted the Northland, the prairie, or the far West, their concept of frontier conveyed the conditions of colonization, the contradictions inherent in the very notion of a *Canadian* wilderness.

The American rhetoric of frontier was designed precisely to obviate such contradictions. As Northrop Frye remarked, "Robert Frost's line, 'The land was ours before we were the land's . . .' does not apply to Canada." Nor does the Turner thesis, nor the idea of nature's nation or virgin land or American Adam—not because Canada had no vast tracts of uninhabited land, not because it lacked idealists or Edenic vistas, not because it couldn't offer immigrants the prospect of a fresh start, but because (as the Canadian poet Douglas Le Pan put it) Canada is "a country without a mythology." And lacking a mythology, how could the Canadian frontiersman see, as his American counterpart did, that the "open territory" was "a holy text"? How could he draw the map of Alberta, as John Filson drew the map of Kentucky, in a series of prophecies, each "voicing a more sweeping vision of American glory"? Even when Canadians transgressed boundaries, they retained the relativisitic, *dialectic* meaning of the term. The myth of America eliminated the very issue of transgression by changing the meaning of the New World (in Cotton Mather's phrase) "from geography to Christianography." From being a dividing line, "frontier" became a prophetic summons to expand, a reminder to a people in covenant that (in Melville's famous passage of 1849) "we Americans are the Israel of our time; we bear the ark . . . God has given to us, for a future inheritance, the broad dominions of the political pagans. . . . We are the pioneers, the advance-guard, sent on through the wilderness . . . to break a new path in the New World that is ours."[24] And as the holy commonwealth spread across the continent, the Westward movement came to provide a sort of serial enactment of the ritual of consensus. It was a moving stage for the drama of exodus and conquest, a continuing act of self-vindication by a remnant of visible saints become a host of visible WASPs—a new chosen people that had broadened, in proportion to the broadening American landscape, to include all denominations of the American Protestant faith.

I refer here, of course, to the doctrine of multidenominationalism, which became national policy after the Revolution. National, however, in that peculiar sense I mentioned: it revealed the absence, in this nation, of any traditional form of religion. Multidenominationalism came clothed in the brightest rhetoric of the millennium, but what it amounted to was a more or less spiritual version of free enterprise. It issued in a religious identity that was as open-ended—as vague in scope and theological content—as was the concept of pilgrimage, migration, or progress. As the clergy kept insisting, the American churches were together carrying the ark of Christ and the Constitution. Like standard-bearers of the twelve separate tribes of Israel, they all stood for one sacred-secular cause. In effect, the midcentury clerics turned the pulpit openly into a platform for the American Way. The great crusades of Lyman Beecher and Charles Grandison Finney brought the "Gospel tidings" that "rugged individualism in business enterprise, laissez faire in economic theory, [and] constitutional democracy in political thought" would "usher in the millennial morning." These were the tidings, too, of Francis Wayland in 1825, urging the parallels between piety, self-help, and the Second Coming; of Albert Barnes in 1832, explaining that "this land has been preserved [so] that there might be here furnished [through] . . . enterprise and liberty . . . the fairest civilization that the world has ever seen of pure Christianity"; of William Sprague in 1833, declaring that religion had made America the universal "model of social and civil renovation"; of Mark Hopkins in 1850, offering evidence for the approaching kingdom in the "liberty and rights of the individual"; of William Conant in 1858, explaining that "truly to be self-made" was to unite "the intensity of individual force with the majority of multitude and the spirit of Eternal Love. . . . We certainly witness at present a revival of unprecedented power, in which *the people are the preachers* . . . in beautiful harmony with the nature of modern American existence."[25]

The nature of modern American existence: under that banner "the hope of Revival," as Perry Miller has observed, "cut across denominations." In reply to all criticisms, the "defense again and again insisted that [revivalism] was an *American* method." Thus "while the religious leaders were ostensibly talking about harmony among the churches, they were actually charting the way toward a homogeneous America." Through the various associations they founded—"The American Education Society (1815), The American Bible Society (1816), The American Sunday School Union (1824), The American Tract Society (1825), The American Home Missionary Society (1826)"—the revivalists "were not [just] preaching nationalism, they were enacting it." I would add to Miller's analysis that they were not just enacting nationalism, they were transforming it into cultural consensus. "The Spirit of the Lord," they declared, "was mightily at work," fusing "Protestantism and American patriotism, capitalist economics and Christian morality"; "free enterprise, bent upon the creation of a Christian commonwealth," was establishing "the millennium through the hallowing of America."[26] The Great Awakening has been called the last Calvinist offspring of the New England Way; the nineteenth-century revivals may be seen as the Frankenstein's monster of the Puritan errand. What they undertook, in effect, was a nationwide cooption of the conversion experience—a wholesale reversal of spiritual communitas into a rite of socialization.

Naturally, none of this (including all the talk "about harmony among the churches") discouraged sectarian acrimony. Following the logic of consensus, the belief in a common cause nourished dissent and debate. Since every truly American church was ipso facto a true church, each of them was by definition the one true interpreter of the American public order. The result was a deafening *concordia discors*—revivalists against Unitarians, premillennialists against postmillennialists, Methodists against Baptists, Calvinists against anti-Calvinists, Beecher against Finney, Wayland against Sprague against Hopkins against Conant—a thousand aggressively independent individuals and sects all saying the same thing. For if in some ways the American public order proved to be a more ambiguous text than even the Protestant Bible, the ambiguities it spawned, like those of the Bible, were self-enclosed: in all cases the true way was defined a priori by the meaning of America.

Let me illustrate how the clergy went about defining it by extracting one voice from the chorus. Philip Schaff was born in Switzerland, and educated in Stuttgart, Halle, and Berlin. He came to the United States in 1844, in his early twenties, to save emigrant Pennsylvania Lutherans from the dangers of Americanization. He stayed to join the consensus. Ten years later he explained why:

> When history shall have erected its central stage of action on the magnificent theatre of the new world, the extreme ends of the civilized world will be brought together in the achievements of modern science, the leveling influences of the press and public opinion, and the workings of the everlasting Gospel. Then . . . [will come] the millennium of righteousness. This . . . [is] the distinctive mission of the American nation, to represent a compact, well defined and yet world-embracing. As the children of the sturdy Puritans, we are the nation of the future. . . . The first Adam was a type and prophecy of the second Adam; the very name of Abraham pointed to the Messianic blessings that should flow from . . . [our] seed upon the nations of the earth. . . .
>
> Such high views ought to humble us with a deep sense of our responsibility . . . [but] there are fearful tendencies in our national life. There is a false Americanism as well as a true one. I need only remind you of the wild and radical tendencies of our youth; the piratical schemes of our manifest-destinarians who would swallow in one meal, Cuba, all Central America, Mexico and Canada. . . . [Still, these various signs of degeneracy are] merely the wild oats of the young giant who will in due time learn better manners and settle down upon the sober discharge of his proper duties. God delivered us from greater dangers and will not forsake us until He has accomplished His purposes through our instrumentality.[27]

I've quoted this passage at length because it so vividly demonstrates what it meant to become acculturated into the antebellum North. Philip Schaff was perhaps the greatest church historian of his time, an emigrant deeply rooted in the traditions of European thought, and an outspoken opponent of some of the more outrageous forms of Americanism. Nonetheless, by 1854 he could not imagine a viable alternative to the American Way. The very terms of his denunciation—the sweeping antithesis he asserts between true and false Americans—remind us how far the consensus reached, and how enveloping were its powers. It was a web spun out of scriptural myth and middle-class ideology that allowed virtually no avenue of escape. Technology and religion, individualism and social progress, spiritual, political, and economic values—all the fragmented aspects of life and thought in this pluralistic society flowed into "America," the symbol of cultural consensus, and then, in a ritual balance of anxiety and control, flowed outward again to each independent unit of society. To celebrate the future was to criticize the present. To denounce American life was to endorse the national dream. Whether one felt "humble," "fearful," or "hopeful," the sense of crisis that attended those feelings affirmed a single, omnivorous mission. As an exponent of the errand, the Swiss-born, German-educated Philip Schaff had no more hesitation in calling the Puritans *his* fathers than did the "manifest-destinarians" he despised. Ten years later, in fact, he joined them in acclaiming the Civil War as the full and final proof of America's mission.[28]

It would be easy to show the gathering force of this outlook through the 1850s. It would be easier still to document the persistent rhetoric of consensus on the part of abolitionists and gradualists alike, on both sides of the Lincoln-Douglas debates, and to some extent even in the Confederate stand.[29] But my point is not that the Civil War was inspired by a certain mode of rhetoric. It's that the rhetoric reflected and shaped a broad ideological movement which, for a variety of reasons, issued in civil war. Chief among these reasons, as John Higham has shown, was the coalescence of three separate "adhesive forces," each of them inherent in "the process of modernization": "a collective mission, a dispersal of power, [and] an individual locus of opportunity." It's tempting to see these forces in terms of the errand, as progress, migration, and pilgrimage; but that would probably be excessive on my part. Let me simply present Higham's analysis as a summary statement of the development I've been exploring:

> ideology . . . links social action with fundamental beliefs, collective identity with the course of history. This combination of generality with directional thrust has enabled ideology to function as an important unifying force . . . in America [because here Puritanism] . . .

arrived not as a subversive or divisive force [as it was in England], but as a bedrock of order, purpose, and cohesion. . . . The Puritans had needed the discipline of ideology to . . . stave off fragmentation. Their descendents . . . put their ideological inheritance to expanded uses. What had been a discipline became also an incitement . . . [one that] offered Americans a collective task and a sustaining hope. . . . [With the Revolution,] Protestant ideology . . . attached itself to American nationalism . . . [and thereby] forged the strongest bonds that united the American people during the nineteenth century. . . . As the desire for ideological unity increased, slavery—a flat denial of the American ideology—became less and less tolerable. In that broad sense the Civil War, like the expansionism that preceded it, was the result of a general intensification of ideological forces.[30]

Ironically, then, what made conflict irrepressible was the irrepressible growth toward ideological unity. It's a fitting climax to what might be considered the major irony of colonial history, when the Puritans set out a rhetoric and ritual for a new culture, and so facilitated the growth from the New England to the American Way.

The movement toward consolidation permeated all levels of the culture. On the broadest scale, it issued in what Alan Trachtenberg calls "the incorporation of America"; it found its most dramatic expression, in the decade prior to the Civil War, in the American Renaissance. To see how indebted our classic writers were to the national symbol, how deeply engaged they were in the rhetoric of consensus, is to recognize the native grounds of American Romanticism. Both the American and the European Romantics presented themselves as isolatoes, prophets crying in the wilderness. But our classic writers were *American* prophets, at once lamenting a declension and celebrating a national dream. Directly or indirectly, their works formed part of the same ritual that enveloped (and transmuted) all forms of antebellum dissent. The European Romantics took a different course. Even for the nationalists and conservatives among them, "high literature" was (in Northrop Frye's words) "a conscious mythology: it create[d] an autonomous world" that stood apart from the "kind of mythology . . . produced by society." In this they were of course modern artists, representing a recent and far-reaching change in the relation between literature and society. Traditionally, "the same work could belong to both mythologies at once"; literature in premodern societies was intrinsic to "the work of culture," and often designed to perpetuate existing social values. The European Romantics, on the contrary, tended toward a divisive, even subversive "play of the imagination." Directly or indirectly, they express the separation of "high art" from "popular culture" that remains "a perspective of our own revolutionary age."[31]

It seems a paradox that in the United States—the land of the modern, a nation self-consciously founded on revolution, a culture committed to diversity and fragmentation—that here of all places the national myth should preempt the growth of "conscious mythology." But it's the sort of paradox upon which the entire mechanism of consensus was built. Precisely because the United States was the land of the modern, the symbol of America could subsume the "autonomous worlds" of Romantic (and post-Romantic) art. The same factors obtain here that I mentioned earlier with regard to American nationality. Modernization brought with it a distinctive set of free enterprise ideals, but in Europe the old ideals lingered, like deposed rulers or kings in exile, offering themselves at every opportunity as the solution to what appeared to be a world run out of control. Hence the power and profusion of "conscious mythologies." Ever since the Romantic period, high art has flourished through a symbolic play between cultural options—a sort of creative mediation between competing value systems which were still imaginatively (if not actually) available, and through which, therefore, the artist could offer a genuinely different perspective—whether radical, reactionary, or purely aesthetic—from that of the dominant culture.

None of our classic writers conceived of imaginative perspectives other than those implicit in the vision of America. Their works are characterized by an *unmediated* relation between the facts of American life and the ideals of American free enterprise. Confronted with the inadequacies of their society, they turned for solace and inspiration to its social ideals. It was not that they lacked radical energies, but that they had invested these in a vision which reinforced (because it emanated from) the values of their culture. Their quarrels with America took the form of intracultural dialogues—as in Thoreau's *Walden*, where "the only true America" beckons to us as a timeless image of the country's time-bound ideals (minimal government, extravagant economics, endless mobility, unlimited self aggrandizement); or in Whitman's *Leaves of Grass*, which offers the highest Romantic tribute, the process of poetic self-creation, as text-proof of America's errand into the future. In these and other key instances, the autonomous act that might have posed fundamental alternatives, imaginative or actual, became instead a mimesis of cultural norms. The works of our classic writers show more clearly than any others I know how American radicalism could be turned into a force against radical change. If the nineteenth-century revivals were the Frankenstein's monster of Puritan rhetoric, the American Renaissance was its aesthetic masterpiece, the creative *summum et ultimum* of a social myth designed to meet the exigencies of modern society in the New World.

I realize that in saying this I may offend just about everybody: those who see our classic writers as champions of the absolutes embodied in the American Way; those who dismiss them, quantitatively, as an unrepresentative elite; those who believe that they "transcended" their time and place; and especially those who seek in them a source of moral or political protest. So I should at least point out that what I've said by no means reduces their achievement to ideology. Indeed, it may be no more than to speak of (say) Chaucer's debt to medieval Christianity—except for two things. First, Chaucer wrote openly from within his culture. Our classic writers wore the Romantic mask of defiance. They have been called the first modernists, and so they were—the traditionalists of modern society, doing the "work of culture" in terms appropriate to their culture, as individualists, isolatoes, and self-made prophets. Second, Chaucer assumed a qualitative difference between temporal and spiritual ideals. He believed that Christianity supported the forms of feudal England; but he believed, too, that ultimately Christianity was not of this world. It was largely to obviate the division between secular and sacred that the errand was launched. The social myth (which the errand fostered) fused eschatology and geography, nationhood and religion. When, therefore, our classic writers invested their ideals of art and the self in the symbol of America, they were doing more than echoing cultural commonplaces. Elizabeth Stanton invested women's rights in the concept of errand as progress. Philip Schaff rendered himself the example of the errand as migration. But the American Romantics enlisted the pilgrimage in that cause. I mean pilgrimage now in its highest sense, as signifying the absolute claims of the spirit within. Those claims inspired our classic writers to oppose the status quo in many ways; but it also compelled them to speak their opposition as keepers of the dream. Damning or affirming, their writings offer the most striking testimony we have to the power of American consensus.

Appropriately, the testimony is clearest in the case of Emerson. No one made larger claims than he did for the individual, no one has been more influential upon the American literary tradition, no one was more centrally *the* American Romantic, no one more passionately denounced injustice in America, and no one more firmly upheld the metaphysics of the culture. "I dedicate this book to the Spirit of America," he wrote at the start of his journals. He might have begun all his books that way. When he felt himself exiled for his religion, he remembered that America was bound to shape the religion of the future. Distrustful of the "raw multitudes" of the West, he invoked the frontier landscape to justify "America's errand of genius and love." Confronted with a "riot of mediocrities" in politics and art, he listened all the more intently to his prophetic inner voice, speaking of "the pilgrimage of American liberty," revealing (through "the healthy sentiment of the American people") "the promise of better times and of greater men." "The history of America," he wrote in 1823, " is meagre because it has been . . . under better government, better circumstances of religions, moral, political, commercial prosperity than any nation ever was before. History . . . grow[s] less interesting as the world grows better." Fifteen years later, increasingly troubled by the complexities of history—in the face of public discouragement and personal tragedy—he found solace in recalling that "Asia, Africa, and Europe [are] old, leprous, & wicked. . . . My birthright in America is a preferable gift to the honors of any nation that breathes upon the earth."[32]

Note the variety of meanings. America was a state of soul for Emerson. But it was also a civic identity and a place. In particular, America served, as symbol, to root the ideals of individualism and of history, pilgrimage, and progress, in a certain way of life. Self-reliance was the standard by which Emerson gauged social failure or success. And self-reliance, he wrote, has its "true basis" in a political economy of free enterprise: "freedom of trade," a "self-adjusting meter of supply and demand," "noninterference" by the state. "The less government we have the better,—the fewer laws and the less confided power"—for "there is always a reason, *in the man*, for his good or bad fortune, and so in making money." Indeed, "money . . . is in effects and laws as beautiful as roses. Property keeps the accounts of the world, and is always moral." What is the "merchant's economy," after all, but "a coarse symbol of the soul's economy [?] . . . The merchant has but one rule, *absorb and invest:* he is to be capitalist. . . . Well, the man must be capitalist. Will he spend his income, or will he invest?" For these reasons, Adam Smith's *Wealth of Nations* is "a book of wisdom"; for such purposes, "the Constitution is the best book in the world next to the New Testament." As "a nation of individuals," a community of capitalists, America stands for an economic and political system that has "all nature behind it." It is proof to the world that "all great men came out of the middle classes."[33]

Emerson, to repeat, was not an ideologue. Far from being an apologist for the middle class (in any debased sense of the phrase), he was often its severe critic. But his criticisms were couched in terms that reaffirmed the structures and beliefs of his society. To the extent that those terms were economic, they reflected an intraclass dispute between the bourgeois Brahmins and the new-rich, "the pushing middle class" which Emerson felt had "contaminated American culture with its . . . vulgarity and . . . false standards." To the extent that his terms were political, they were free enterprise slogans directed against feudalism on the one hand (as in his arguments with Carlyle or his disparagement of European aristocracy) and against socialism on the other hand: "Thoreau was in his own person a practical answer, almost a refutation, to the theories of the socialists"; "In the question of Socialism . . . one has only this guidance: you shall not so arrange property as to remove the motive to industry. If you refuse rent and interest, you make all men idle and immoral." But above all, of course, the terms of Emerson's social criticism were transcendental. There were many false standards, as he said over and again, but only one true one, and that for him was synonymous with the spirit of America. Thus the many disparities he saw between social and ultimate values were not

defects of the American Way. They were aberrations, like the backslid-
ings of a de facto saint or the stiff-necked recalcitrance of a chosen people.
Emerson's denunciations, like those of Whitman and Thoreau, were part
of a ritual attempt to wake his countrymen up to the potential of their
culture.[34] The sun of the good that Emerson saw reflected in the pond,
the bare common, or the leaf of grass was the same sun that warmed
Boston and all the antebellum North.

This was the public Emerson. Privately, we know, he could sound the
depths of despair. But despair in this case was simply the other side of
consensus. For the faith that magnified the culture into a cosmos carried
with it an ominous prospect. If America failed, then the cosmos itself—
the laws of history, nature, and the mind—had failed as well. Millennium
or doomsday, American heaven or universal hell: it was the choice demanded by the rhetoric of consensus. Either way it served to obviate
social alternatives, and on those grounds the leaders of American society,
from Winthrop through Lincoln, have invoked the threat of doomsday,
formulaically, as a rallying cry for cultural revitalization. In one form or
another, they have always insisted that America is the last, best hope of
mankind—meaning by *last* both telos (as in the Puritan sense of "latter
days" or the Whig notion of a revolution to end revolutions) and final
choice, one last chance to redeem humanity. Both versions carried the
same message. *Last* plus consensus meant *best; last* without consensus
meant catastrophe. The point was not to offer alternatives but to induce a
state of anxiety, an apocalyptic sense of urgency, that would enforce
compliance. And generally, through the nineteenth century, the American middle class (including, as we've seen, the middle class "radicals")
responded by embracing the covenant.

Those who did not join in hope conformed in desperation. Thus the
Populist Ignatius Donnelly, confronted with what he thought were the
consequences of America's "betrayal of promise" ("utter social destruction," "world cataclysm"), found a way out of "perpetual nihilism" by
rededicating himself to the "unfathomed reservoir of virtue . . . within all
Americans." Edward Bellamy made the same sort of Pascal's wager on the
side of America. *"Let us bear in mind,"* he cautioned his militant followers,
*"that if it be a failure, it will be a final failure. There can be no more new
worlds to be discovered";* and on that premise he summoned them (along
with all other "true nationalists") "forward to the American Jerusalem."
The young Whitman was even more direct in his reasoning. On 24 November 1846, as the left-wing republican editor of *The Brooklyn Daily
Eagle*, he reminded his readers that

> The time will surely come—that holy millennium of liberty—when
> the "Victory of endurance born" shall lift the masses . . . and make
> them achieve something of that destiny which we may suppose God

intends eligible for mankind. And this problem is to be worked out through the people, territory, and government of the United States. If it should fail! O, dark were the hour and dreary beyond description the horror of such a failure—which we anticipate not at all!

When he did dare to anticipate it, decades later, Whitman promptly recoiled from the horror into what remains the most impassioned paean in the literature to the nation's "Democratic Vistas." The excesses of business and technology, he explained, the greed of politicians and "this almost maniacal appetite for wealth prevalent in the United States," all these were "parts of amelioration and progress, indispensably needed to prepare" for America's "assur'd" and "unparrallel'd success." The very "darkness of the hour" cast figural shadows, intimating "imperial destinies, dazzling as the sun."[35]

Most major writers did not enlist so readily in the party of hope. A few, like Henry Adams, grimly settled for the doomsday option. Others, like Mark Twain, seem to have slid into it, as it were, against their will and with unresolved ambivalence. Still others, like Melville, vacillated between extremes ("the political Messiah has come in *us*"; "Columbus ended earth's romance"). But by and large our classic writers found the prospect of final failure too painful to sustain. Here as elsewhere, Emerson's reaction is representative; it constitutes a major testament not only to the doomsday trap of the rhetoric of consensus—the double bind of best and/or last—but to the ideology that links high literature and popular culture in the United States. Having alternated often and long between euphoria and despair, Emerson finally opted outright for the culture. "My estimate of America," he confided in his journals, "is all or nothing." Beyond America, *nothing*: it was the errand internalized, and made an avatar of the Self. And since Emerson refused to abandon hope, since for him the Self was center and circumference of the spirit, he gave *all* to America. "Those [who] complain about the flatness of American life," he decided, "have no perception of its destiny. They are not Americans." They cannot see that America is "a garden of plenty, . . . a magazine of power. . . . Here is man in the Garden of Eden: here, the Genesis and the Exodus," and here is to be the Revelation.[36]

In that spirit, Emerson greeted the Armageddon of the Republic. He had been slow to endorse abolitionism. He continued to believe in the inferiority of the blacks (as well as of the Chinese, the Irish, and the Indians); and he had recently defended states rights. But he had no qualms about the war. By 1860 he was the oracle of an ideology fully matured, a ritual of crisis and control that had virtually assumed a dynamic of its own. America was in covenant with the future—it was consecrated, that is, to progress, unity, and the middle class—and the South was not. Hence, once again, Americans had to rally to the task of fulfilling

God's will. The fathers had provided the pattern and set the direction. It was time for the sons to complete their work. When the South would conform, it too could join the errand toward the American City of God. Meanwhile, Emerson concluded, destiny left the North no alternative: "We must realize our rhetoric and our rituals."[37]

Well, the rhetoric and rituals were still being realized in the late 1960s; and under the aegis, by then, of a third set of fathers, among them Lincoln and Emerson. But it may be that 1860 marks the real climax of the story. I refer in general to the widening rift or fissure in the house of consensus, to the cultural schizophrenia that has intensified steadily ever since the Civil War. In particular, I refer to the recent incursions of history upon the myth of America. The rhetoric of consensus was built on the rejection of limits; it inspired its adherents to reshape reality in accordance with prophecy and vision; it thrived on the perils of Gog and Magog; but it may not be able to survive the reduction of "America" to the level of common sense. And by all accounts, common sense has been impinging on the American Way. Apparently, the summons to the great society and new frontiers, the cries of millennium or doomsday, have had a hollow sound of late. Of course all this has happened before, and the rhetoric has always risen to the challenge. Over and again it has managed to absorb the lament (or celebration) over the passing of the myth. The ideological pressures that forced late-nineteenth-century radicals to recast socialism in "the framework of progressive liberalism" (Dorothy Ross) also prevented the "muckrakers" from challenging "the premises . . . of progress in its American guise" (Rush Welter); these were the pressures that led Frederick Douglass, on "Colored People's Day" in 1893, to renounce all basic alternatives to the system ("There is no Negro problem. The problem is whether the American People have . . . patriotism enough to live up to their own Constitution"), and "the radical social critic" William Dean Howells to center his hopes upon "his own 'home' . . . the true, the real America" (Alan Trachtenberg); under these pressures, the labor leaders of the Gilded Age defined unionization as the "Good Old American Way" ("we mean no conflict with legitimate enterprise, no antagonism to necessary capital"); these pressures explain why American Stalinists enrolled "Washington, Jefferson, and Franklin . . . posthumously in the popular front, under the slogan 'Communism is twentieth-century Americanism' " (Edmund Morgan); these pressures account for the failure of our New Left historians to deal adequately with the question of American consensus (Aileen Kraditor), and the "utter incapacity" of Berkeley student dissidents even to "conceive of [some] alternative ascendant polity, in this world or any other," to the American Way (Paul Sniderman). The most recent bit of evidence in this line was the "birth" in Cleveland in 1980 of a new "Citizens Party," which *The New York Times* reporter

laconically termed "the latest in a historic series of left-wing progeny."
His report is worth citing as a testament to the astonishing tenacity of
the myth, and (ironically in this case) as a sort of state-of-the-consensus
address:

> Some 275 delegates represented 30 states at the founding of what
> they call a "second party" rather than a third, on the frequently
> stated contention that the Republicans and Democrats and their
> prospective candidates were one indistinguishable mass.
>
> Delegates included old radicals of the Socialist era, young envi-
> ronmentalists, ardent feminists and labor union activists; almost
> everyone was a "ist" of some kind. . . . Speaker after speaker em-
> phasized how different the Citizens Party convention would be from
> those of the major parties. . . .
>
> Keynoting the convention . . . Studs Terkel, the Chicago writer,
> predicted that the new party would "reclaim the American dream
> from the predators who've stolen it—that's what this meeting is all
> about."[38]

So for the time being the myth is alive and well, at least in Cleveland,
Ohio. But not *as* well, I think, as it was in '68, and certainly not as alive as
it was for Emerson in 1860. During the past two or three decades—after
Hiroshima, Vietnam, and Watergate—the efforts to reclaim the American
dream have come to seem increasingly strained. The encroachments of
history appear to be more substantial; the contradictions of capitalism
more transparent; the ideals of free enterprise less self-evident, even in
the context of "America." It's hard to imagine the United States, like
Canada, as a country without a mythology. How can a society accustomed
to thinking of itself in absolutes accept the limitations of analysis? How can
a "peculiar people" that took their land by promise come to believe, with
the Canadian frontierswoman Susanna Moodie, that "whether the wilderness is/real or not/depends on who lives there"? Still, there are grounds
for hope. "Myth is a type of speech chosen by history," as Roland Barthes
remarked; "it is human history which converts reality into speech, and it
alone rules the life and death of mythical languages."[39] And history has
been making it clear for some time that the hazards of living out the
dream outweigh the advantages. The antebellum period brought to harvest
the figural discovery of America. This may be the age of discovery of
America as a cultural artifact. Who knows, the errand may come to rest,
where it always belonged, in the realm of the imagination; and the United
States recognized for what it is, not a beacon of mankind, as Winthrop
proclaimed in his *Arbella* address of 1630, not the political Messiah, as
the young Melville hymned in *White-Jacket*—not even a covenanted people robbed by un-American predators of their sacred trust—but simply
goy b'goyim, just one more profane nation in the wilderness of this world.

NOTES

1. The question of Southern ideology lies outside the scope of this paper, but it may be pertinent to note that "except for the institution of slavery, the South had little to give it a national identity" (Kenneth Stampp, "The Southern Road to Appomattox," in *The National Temper*, ed. L. W. Levine and R. Middlekauff [New York, 1972], pp. 216–17). To be sure, "the peculiar institution" gave the South a strong *regional* identity, but as a mode of cultural cohesion that identity was undermined by a basic commitment from the start to the tenets of free enterprise. This applies to the question of slavery (e.g., Richard B. Davis, *Intellectual Life in the Colonial South* [Knoxville, Tenn., 1978], III, 1586, and especially Edmund S. Morgan, *American Slavery, American Freedom* [New York, 1975]) as well as to the ideals of the yeoman farmer and even (in practice and effect) to the "plantation legend," where Cavalier norms and "the appeal of the medieval manor as a model" were contradicted by the actual "commercial role" of the "gentleman planter" (Theodore Marmon, "Anti-Industrialism and the Old South: The Agrarian Pespective of John C. Calhoun," *Comparative Studies in Society and History*, 9 [1967]: 377–406). On the general importance of laissez-faire republicanism in Southern thought, see Marcus Cunliffe, *Chattel Slavery and Wage Slavery* (Athens, Ga., 1979), and John McCardell, *The Idea of a Southern Nation* (New York, 1979).

2. Timothy H. Breen and Stephen Foster, "Moving to the New World: The Character of Early Massachusetts Immigration," *William and Mary Quarterly* 30(1973):189–222; B. Katherine Brown, "The Controversy Over the Franchise in Puritan Massachusetts, 1654 to 1674," *William and Mary Quarterly* 33(1976):212–41; Alexis de Tocqueville, *Democracy in America*, ed. J. P. Mayer, trans. G. Lawrence (Garden City, N.Y., 1969), p. 279.

3. Robert Mandrou, "Cultures ou niveaux culturels dans les sociétés d'Ancien Régime," *Revue des études Sud-Est européennes* 10(1972):415–22; Keith V. Thomas, *Religion and the Decline of Magic* (London, 1971), pp. 26 ff.; Christopher Hill, *Century of Revolution* (Edinburgh, 1961), p. 102; Eric J. Hobsbawm, *Primitive Rebels* (New York, 1959), p. 69. For a general contrast in these terms between Old and New England, compare Lawrence Stone, "Social Mobility in England, 1500–1700," *Past & Present*, 33(1966):16–55, with James Henretta, "Families and Farms: Mentalité in Pre-Industrial America," *William and Mary Quarterly* 35(1978): 6–9, and Richard D. Brown, "Modernization and the Modern Personality in Early America, 1600–1865: A Sketch of a Synthesis," *Journal of Interdisciplinary History* (1972): 201–28.

4. Carl Degler, quoted in Stuart Bruchey, *The Roots of American Economic Growth* (New York, 1968), p. 44 (see also Bruchey's commentary on this matter, and his summary [p. 200] of colonial economic growth); Max Weber, *The Protestant Ethic*, trans. Talcott Parsons (New York, 1930), pp. 55–56; Gabriel Kolko, "Max Weber on America: Theory and Evidence," in *Studies in the Philosophy of History*, ed. G. N. Nadel (New York, 1965), p. 181.

5. John Cotton, *God's Promise to His Plantations* (1630), in *Old South Leaflets* (Boston, 1896), vol. III, no. 53, p. 17.

6. Emery Battis, *Saints and Sectaries* (Chapel Hill, N.C., 1962), p. 255; Bruchey, *Roots*, p. 47; Richard L. Bushman, *From Puritan to Yankee* (New York, 1967), p. 147; Kai T. Erikson, *Wayward Puritans* (New York, 1966), p. 53; Hill, *Century*, p. 97.

7. Sacvan Bercovitch, "The Typology of America's Mission," *American Quarterly* 30 (1978):135–55.

8. The development I trace in the preceding paragraphs is presented in expanded form in my book, *The American Jeremiad* (Madison, 1978), and in a previous essay, "How the Puritans Won the American Revolution," *Massachusetts Review* 17(1976):597–630.

9. Samuel Williams, *A Discourse on the Love of Country* (Salem, 1775), p. 22; Ebenezer Baldwin, *The Duty of Rejoicing* (New York, 1776), pp. 38–40; Thomas Blockway, *America Saved* (Hartford, 1784), p. 24; Thomas Barnard, quoted in Ernest L. Tuveson, *Redeemer Nation* (Chicago, 1968), p. 31.

10. George Bancroft, *History of the United States* (Boston, 1876), IV, 16; Benjamin Rush, *Address to the People of the United States* (Boston, 1787), p. 1; Timothy Dwight, *A Sermon Preached at Northampton* (Hartford [1781], p. 27.

11. John Adams to Thomas Jefferson, Oct. 9, 1787, in *The Adams-Jefferson Correspondence*, ed. L. J. Cappon (Williamsburg, 1959), p. xliv. See Alexander Hamilton, Federalist 6, and James Madison, Federalist 51, in *The Federalist Papers*, ed. C. Rossiter (New York, 1961), esp. pp. 57, 59, 322, 324; and cf. Peter Berger, "A Sociological View of the Secularization of Theology," *Journal for the Scientific Study of Religion* 6(1967): 9, 11–12.

12. J. Hector St. Jean de Crèvecoeur, *Letters from an American Farmer*, ed. W. Blake (New York, 1957), pp. 192–226; Camillo Querno [pseudonym], "The American Times," in *The Loyalist Poetry of the Revolution* ed. W. Sargent (Philadelphia, 1957), pp. 1–37. See also C. S. Crary, ed. *The Price of Loyalty* (New York, 1973).

13. Victor Turner, *Dramas, Fields, and Metaphors* (Ithaca, 1974), p. 55; Abner Cohen, "Symbolic Action and the Structure of the Self," in *Symbols and Sentiments*, ed. I. Lewis (London, 1977), p. 121. Cf. Turner, *Forest of Symbols* (Ithaca, 1967), especially pp. 19–58. In this context, I use the term *myth* in tandem with ideology to suggest the scope of the rhetoric of American consensus. My point is not just that the myth was clearly the product of ideology; it's that the ideology was, in basic ways, endowed with the traditional qualities of myth. This subject is too complex to consider here. Let me simply observe that "America," as a cultural symbol, bridges the antinomies that are often used by political scientists to distinguish between myth and ideology: sacred and secular, nostalgic and progressivist, millennial and utopian, prophetic and situational, holistic and particularistic, and especially rational and prerational or irrational. See Ben Halpern " 'Myth' and 'Ideology' in Modern Usage," in *History and Theory* 1(1960):129–49. I might also add, at the risk of stating the obvious, that "America" is not used in this way elsewhere in North, Central, or South America. That's basically the rationale for my emphasis on the *rhetoric* of consensus. My approach reflects my special interest as a literary critic; but more than that, it expresses my belief in the extraordinary importance of language to the country's development.

14. George Rudé, *Robespierre* (Englewood Cliffs, N.J., 1967), p. 173; Luis Villoro, "Hidalgo: Su violencia y libertad," *Cuadernas Americanos* 2(1952):223–39; John J. Johnson, *Simon Bolivar and Spanish American Independence* (New York, 1968), pp. 3–8 ff. For other Latin American examples, see Kenneth Maxwell, "The Generation of the 1790's and the Idea of the Luso-Brazilian Empire," in *Colonial Roots of Modern Brazil*, ed. D. Alden (Berkeley, 1973), pp. 120–40.

15. Eric Foner, *Tom Paine and Revolutionary America* (New York, 1976), pp. 217, 242, 253; Thomas Paine, *Common Sense*, ed. N. F. Adkins (Indianapolis, 1953), pp. 27, 3, 23. Louis Hartz makes a telling contrast in this connection between the "populist liberalism" of the American rebel Daniel Shays and the "proletarian economics" that lay behind the French rebel Babeuf's "community of wealth" (*The Liberal Tradition in America* [New York, 1955], pp. 76–77), but part of the contrast involves what I consider Hartz's mistaken notion of the "clash" in American liberalism between Lockean cosmopolitanism and what he calls "a curiously Hebraic kind of separatism"—a provincial "pride of inheritance, not a pride of achievement," which opposed the ideals of "Christian universalism" and Enlightenment progress (p. 37). What I would suggest is that the figural concept of New Israel allowed Americans to take pride simultaneously in their inheritance and in their achievement (present and to come). As the *figura* itself implied, the national covenant was a vehicle for something larger: an expanding and potentially universalist community of shared values and ideals.

16. Hans Kohn, "Romanticism and the Rise of German Nationalism," *Review of Politics* 12(1950):443–72; Robert M. Berdahl, "New Thoughts on German Nationalism," *American Historical Review* 77(1972): 65–80; Franco Venturi, *Roots of Revolution* (New York, 1966), pp. 122 ff. For a contrast in these terms between American and other national forms of millennialism, see for example Francis R. Hill, "Nationalist Millenarians and Millenarian

Nationalists: Conflicts and Cooperation in New Jersualem," *American Behavioral Scientist* 16(1972): 269–88.

17. Tocqueville, *Democracy*, p. 56; Hartz, *Liberal Tradition*, p. 131 (citing General Root); James Fenimore Cooper, *Notions of the Americans* (Philadelphia, 1828), II, 143; Nathaniel Hawthorne, *The Marble Faun*, ed. M. Krieger (New York, 1961), p. vi.

18. Benjamin Franklin, *Writings*, ed. A. H. Smyth (New York, 1905–7), vol. VIII, pp. 603–14; Edward Pessen, "The Egalitarian Myth and the American Social Reality: Wealth, Mobility, and Equality in the 'Era of the Common Man,' " in *The Many-Faceted Jacksonian Era*, ed. E. Pessen (London, 1977), pp. 7–46; J. D. B. DeBow, *Statistical View of the U.S.* (Washington, 1854); U.S. Census Office, *Sixth Census* (Washington, 1841); Peter Temin, *The Jacksonian Economy* (New York, 1969).

19. Catharine Beecher, quoted in Kathryn K. Sklar, *Catharine Beecher* (New Haven, 1973), p. 159; Catharine Beecher, *A Treatise on Domestic Economy* (1841), ed. K. K. Sklar (New York, 1977), p. 13; Stanton and Brown, quoted in Susan P. Conrad, *Perish the Thought* (New York, 1976), pp. 123–24, 150.

20. William Lloyd Garrison, "No Union with Slave-Holders," *Liberator* (1837), in *Slavery Attacked*, ed. J. R. Thomas (Englewood Cliffs, N.J., 1965), pp. 76–77; Garrison, quoted in William A. Clebsch, *From Sacred to Profane America* (New York, 1968), pp. 93–94; Frederick Douglass, "Oration" (1854), in *Black Writers of America*, ed. K. Kinnamon and R. Barksdale (New York, 1972), pp. 89–93, 99–101; Rantoul, quoted in Rush Welter, *The Mind of America* (New York, 1975), p. 49; Lewis Perry, "Adin Ballou's Hopedale Community and the Theology of Antislavery," *Church History* 39(1970): 16–17 (quoting Ballou); O. B. Frothingham, *George Ripley* (Boston, 1882), p. 111; John Higham, *From Boundlessness to Consolidation* (Ann Arbor, Mich., 1969), p. 13.

21. Henry David Thoreau, *Reform Papers*, ed. W. Glick (Princeton, 1972), p. 124; Albert Barnes, quoted in Perry Miller, *The Life of the Mind of America* (New York, 1965), p. 86.

22. I refer here specifically to David Potter's critique (following that of George Wilson Pearson) of the Turner thesis: "What about the Spaniards . . .? Did the Mississippi Valley make them democratic . . .? In a word, do not the level of culture and the 'fitness' of a society for the wilderness, matter more than the wilderness?" Potter's argument is that "the Anglo-Americans . . . were particularly apt at exploiting the new country" (*History and American Society*, ed. D. E. Fehrenbacher [Oxford, 1973], p. 133). Their aptness, I would suggest, like the "fitness" of their society and culture, was due in considerable measure to the rhetoric and rituals they inherited. Indeed, the writings of Turner himself testify to that legacy.

23. Douglas G. Jones, *Butterfly on Rock* (Toronto, 1970), pp. 57, 87–88; Brian Parker, "Is There a Canadian Identity?" in *The Canadian Imagination*, ed. D. Staines (Cambridge, Mass., 1977), p. 154; Northrop Frye, *The Bush Garden* (Toronto, 1971), p. 138; Margaret Atwood, *Survival* (Toronto, 1972), pp. 31–33; Northrop Frye, "Conclusion" to vol. II of *The Literary History of Canada*, ed. C. F. Klinck (Toronto, 1976; 2d ed.), pp. 220–21, 225–26. The image of the "bush country" in effect links Frye's "bush garden" with two other widely accepted definitions of Canadian identity: the special conditions of geography and trade which, according to the classic "Laurentian thesis," shaped the course of Canada's development (see Donald Creighton, *The Commerical Empire of the St. Lawrence* [Toronto, 1937]), and the concept of the "mosaic," a "society of allegiance" as opposed to America's "society of compact," a nation of diverse groups loosely joined by their common faith in free enterprise (Ramsay Cook, *The Maple Leaf Forever* [Toronto, 1971], p. 142). For the importance of the frontier experience in shaping the concept of the mosaic, see John A. Porter, *The Vertical Mosaic* (Toronto, 1965). Summarizing that experience, Margaret Atwood remarks that in the United States "the West was something to be conquered and claimed. The West, or the wilderness, is in Canadian fiction much more likely to come through as a place of exile" (*Survival*, p. 121). And yet, as Howard Temperley notes, "if Turner's theories work

for the United States, there is no logical reason why they should not work for Canada," since "the Loyalist settlements would seem to meet Turner's requirements more precisely than many of the communities about which he and his disciples actually did write" ("Frontierism, Capital, and the American Loyalists in Canada," *Journal of American Studies*, 13 [1979]:8). It amounts to a sweeping testament to the power of rhetoric in shaping perception and experience.

24. Frye, "Conclusion," p. 324; Douglas Le Pan, "A Country Without a Mythology," in *The Book of Canadian Poetry*, ed. A. J. M. Smith (Chicago, 1957, 3d. ed.); Barbara Novak, "American Landscape: The Nationalist Garden and the Holy Book," *Art in America* 60 (1972): 50, 52; Richard Slotkin, *Regeneration Through Violence* (Middletown, 1973), pp. 272–73; Cotton Mather, *Magnalia Christi Americana* (1702), ed. T. Robbins (Hartford, 1853), I, 33; Herman Melville, *White-Jacket*, ed. H. Hayford, H. Parker, and G. T. Tanselle (Evanston, 1970), p. 151.

25. Lyman Beecher, *A Reformation of Morals* (Andover, Mass., 1814), p. 9; Charles G. Finney, *Lectures on Revivals of Religion* (1835), ed. W. G. McLoughlin (Cambridge, Mass., 1960), pp. 87, 120; William G. McLoughlin, Introduction to *The American Evangelicals*, ed. W. G. McLoughlin (Gloucester, Mass., 1976), p. 1; Francis Wayland, *The Duties of an American Citizen* (Boston, 1825), p. 19; Albert Barnes, *The Gospel Necessary to Our Country* (Washington, 1832), p. 22; William Sprague, *Lectures on Revivals* (New York, 1833), p. 212; Mark Hopkins, cited in Emerson Davis, *The Half-Century* (Boston, 1851), p. xvi; William C. Conant, *Narratives of Conversions and Revivals* (Boston, 1858), p. 29.

26. Perry Miller, *Life of the Mind*, pp. 22, 47–48, 11; Lawrence J. Friedman, *Inventors of the Promised Land* (New York, 1975), pp. 286–87 (quoting Finney and the Oberlinites); George M. Frederickson, "A Founding Family," *New York Review of Books*, 9 November 1978, p. 40 (commenting on Lyman Beecher); Timothy L. Smith, "Righteousness and Hope: Christian Holiness and the Millennial Vision in America, 1800–1900," *American Quarterly* 31(1979): 21–23, 44 (citing Nathaniel Ward Taylor, the evangelical Calvinists, and the "perfectionists").

27. Philip Schaff, *America* (1854), ed. Perry Miller (Cambridge, Mass. 1961), pp. 4, 15–16, 18, 20–24. Compare Paul Tillich's account of how, "in spite of [his] permanent contacts with the Old World, the New World grasped [him] with its irresistible power of assimilation" (*Theology*, ed. R. W. Bretall and C. W. Kegley [New York, 1961], p. 60).

28. As William A. Clebsch notes, in "Christian Interpretations of the Civil War," *Church History* 30(1961), pp. 219–22: "destiny itself was the ultimate issue [of the war] . . . and Schaff counted it a 'priceless privilege to be able to view near at hand . . . such a passage of the world's history. . . . In God's characteristic way . . . the evil of war was made the hour [when] . . . the true national vocation was regenerated.' " For the representative character of this view, see James H. Morehead, *American Apocalypse* (New Haven, 1978).

29. On the links between abolitionism and middle-class ideology, see Peter F. Walker, *Moral Choices* (Baton Rouge, La., 1978) and Aileen S. Kraditor, *Means and Ends in American Abolitionism* (New York, 1972). The gradualist view is well represented in Hawthorne's comments on the antislavery militants bent on "severing into distracted fragments that common country which Providence brought into one nation, through a continued miracle of almost two hundred years, from the first settlement of the American wilderness until the Revolution" (*Life of Franklin Pierce*, in *Works*, ed. G. P. Lathrop [Boston, 1887], XVII, 165–66). On Lincoln and Douglas, see George B. Forgie, *Patricide in the House Divided* (New York, 1979), and Edmund Wilson's comments on Douglas's speeches (concerning "that great mission, that destiny which Providence has marked out for us") in *Patriotic Gore* (New York, 1962), pp. xxii–xxiii. McLoughlin notes that "the Southern Evangelicals could not resist the strong patriotic nationalism and optimism which interpreted the war as the ultimate sanctification in blood of the divine mission of the United States" (Introduction to *American Evangelists*, p. 21), and James P. Maddex, Jr., amplifies this view in "Proslavery Millennial-

ism: Social Eschatology in Antebellum Southern Calvinism," *American Quarterly* 31(1979): 46–62. As Thomas V. Peterson observes in *Ham and Japheth* (London, 1978), "the Southerners inherited the belief from the Puritans that America was God's beacon of light to the world," and they used it between 1830 and 1860 to "validate" their "racial ethos," whereas, for their part, the abolitionists "claimed that the Southern order represented neither the civil nor the religious ideals of the American nation" (pp. 95, 92).

30. John Higham, "Hanging Together: Divergent Unities in American History," *Journal of American History* 61(1974): 10–18. Cf. Raimondo Luraghi, "The Civil War and the Modernization of American Society: Social Structure and Industrial Revolution in the Old South Before and During the War," *Civil War History* 18(1972):213–42, and Eric Foner, "The Causes of the Civil War: Recent Interpretations and New Directions," *Civil War History* 20(1974):197–214.

31. Alan Trachtenberg, *The Incorporation of America*, forthcoming from Hill and Wang (New York, 1981); Frye, *Bush Garden*, p. 104; Victor Turner, "Liminal to Liminoid, in Play, Flow, and Ritual: An Essay in Comparative Symbology," *Rice University Studies*, 40(1974):86. The development I speak of here is discussed from a somewhat different perspective by Raymond Williams. In *Culture and Society, 1780–1950* (New York, 1958), Williams traces the emergence and growth of a concept of culture that refers not to the integrated wholeness of a society, but, on the contrary, to a private wholeness, a spiritual and moral integrity embodied in certain privileged individuals, derived from the broad inheritance of the best of past civilizations, and often directly opposed to the values of modernization. "Culture" in this sense provided the grounds for dissent through the Romantic and Victorian periods. It emboldened "a certain number of *aliens*," in Matthew Arnold's words, to struggle against "the common tide of men's thoughts in a wealthy and industrial community," and inspired them to assert in its place "a general *humane* spirit," a "love of human perfection" that was grounded in one's "best self" as distinct from one's social identity, whether national, political, or economic (*Culture and Anarchy*, ed. I. Gregor [New York, 1969], pp. 169–76, et passim). The classic American writers never perceived art or culture in quite this sense. Rather, they tended to associate the "best self" with a mythic American self, the "humane spirit" with the American "spirit of place," "human perfection" with the "true American Way," and culture itself with the mission of American democracy. None of them adopted the Romantic-Antinomian stand of Byron or Baudelaire against "the common tide." None of them envisioned, with Schiller, an "aesthetic state" beyond and apart from national ideals. And none of them challenged the political and economic *premises* of capitalism. As John Higham observes, "Even the troubled response to technology of an occasional Nathaniel Hawthorne or Herman Melville pales in comparison to the outrage of a Thomas Carlyle or a John Ruskin," and he attributes this, accurately I think, to the American "ideological cast of mind" ("Hanging Together," pp. 19–20). The most incisive and far-ranging analysis of American literature from this perspective is Myra Jehlen, "The New World Epic: The Novel and the Middle-Class in America," *Salmagundi* 36(1977):49–68.

32. Ralph Waldo Emerson, *Journals and Miscellaneous Notebooks*, ed. W. H. Gilman (Cambridge, Mass., 1960–77), II, 3, 90, 114; *Works*, ed. E. W. Emerson (Boston, 1903–4), XI, 537–38; VIII, 233–34; I, 127 (see also II, 218; III, 71–72; XI, 205, 397).

33. Emerson, *Works*, I, 156; VI, 105–6, 90, 93, 97; idem, quoted in John Cawelti, *Apostles of the Self-Made Man* (Chicago, 1965) pp. 88–89, and in F. O. Matthiessen, *American Renaissance* (New York, 1941), p. 4; idem *Works*, XI, 529; *The Correspondence of Emerson and Carlyle*, ed. J. Slater (New York, 1964), pp. 37–38, 48, 52; Emerson, quoted in John C. Gerber, "Emerson and the Political Economists," *New England Quarterly* 22 (1949):345; Emerson, *Works*, IX, 199 and XI, 541 (see also *Journals*, IX, 340, and X, 228; idem. *Works*, VI, 85, and X, 248). Matthiessen felt that it was "staggeringly innocent" on Emerson's part to "commit himself to such remarks" (*American Renaissance*, p. 4.). If so, it was the same staggering innocence that allowed multitudes of Americans to believe that the

principles of their culture were the laws of God, reason, and nature. As the *Schenectady Reflector* reported, following a lecture by Emerson in December 1852: "Those who went to hear Transcendentalism came away astonished to find that they had understood, admired, and most heartily approved" (quoted in Joel Porte, *Representative Man* [New York, 1979], p. 85; see also Porte's brilliant analyses in this book of *English Traits* and "Wealth").

34. William Charvat, *The Profession of Authorship in America* (Columbus, Ohio, 1968), pp. 61–65; Emerson, quoted in Matthiessen, *American Renaissance*, p. 77; Emerson, *Journals*, VII, 431; Jesse Bier, "Weberism, Franklin, and the Transcendental Style," *New England Quarterly* 43(1970):179–92. In this regard, one index to Thoreau's outlook (symbolic and idealistic as well as political and economic) is his review of J. E. Etzler's tract on the utopian prospects of technology, *Paradise to be Regained* (1833), where Thoreau condemns Etzler not—as many European Romantics and Victorians would have done—because of his faith in the limitless advantages of laissez-faire industrialism, but, on the contrary, for his neglect of the laissez-faire notion that before "we may enjoy our success together" we "must first succeed alone" *(Writings* [Boston, 1906], IV, 299). In this belief, Thoreau and Whitman may be compared with many evangelicals of their time (see William G. McLoughlin, "Pietism and the American Character," *American Quarterly* 17 [1965]:170). Whitman's attacks on "wage slavery" and "mere materialism" resemble those of the Southern free enterprise advocates (see Marmor, "Anti-Industrialization," pp. 387–91). Thoreau's praise of the "spare, simple" life—based on "improvement of mind and character: a life of independence disciplined by virtue"—invites comparison with the libertarian democrats described by Marvin Myers in *The Jacksonian Persuasion* (Stanford, 1957; the quotations above come from p. 184). See further David Noble, *Historians Against History* (Minneapolis, 1965), p. 111; John F. Lynen, *The Design of the Present* (New Haven, 1969), p. 193; Herbert F. Smith, "Thoreau Among the Classical Economists," *Emerson Society Quarterly* 23(1977):120 ff.; and John P. Diggins, "Thoreau, Marx, and the 'Riddles' of Alienation," *Social Research* 39(1978):571–97.

35. Donnelly, quoted in Michael Fellman, *The Unbounded Frame* (New York, 1973), pp. 124–25, 135–36, 142; Bellamy, quoted in Kenneth M. Roemer, *The Obsolete Necessity* (Kent, Ohio, 1976), p. 3; Walt Whitman, "American Futurity," in *Gathering of the Forces*, ed. C. Rogers and J. Black (New York, 1920), I, 27–28, and *Democratic Vistas* in *Collected Poetry and Selected Prose*, ed. J. E. Miller, Jr. (Boston, 1959), p. 496. Cf. Curtis Dahl, "The American School of Catastrophe," *American Quarterly* 11(1959):380–90, David DeLeon, *The American Anarchist* (Baltimore, 1978); Taylor Stoehr, *Nay-Saying in Concord* (Hamden, Conn., 1979); and Robert Bellah, *The Broken Covenant* (New York, 1975).

36. Melville, *White-Jacket*, p. 151, and *Clarel*, ed. W. Bezanson (New York, 1960), p. 70 (see also Bezanson's discussion [Introduction, p. cvi] of "the social myth which [Melville] had often criticized but which had nourished his life and art"); Emerson, *Journals*, III, 14, and *Works*, XI, 544 and VIII, 142–43 (see also VII, 399, 417 and XI, 383–87).

37. Emerson, *Works*, XI, 530 (from "The Fortune of the Republic," one of the major instances of the rhetoric of American consensus).

38. Dorothy Ross, "The Liberal Tradition Revisited and the Republican Tradition Addressed," in *New Directions in American Intellectual History*, ed. J. Higham and P. K. Conkin (Baltimore, 1979), pp. 116, 131 (see also her essay on "Socialism and American Liberalism: Academic Social Thought in the 1860s," *Perspectives in American History* 11 [1977–78]:7–79); Rush Welter, "The Idea of Progress," *Journal of the History of Ideas* 16 (1955), 414–15, Trachtenberg, *Incorporation of America* (the references to labor leaders, Howells, and Douglass come from this study, with permission of the author); Edmund S. Morgan, "Conflict and Consensus in the American Revolution," in *Essays on the American Revolution*, ed. S. G. Kurtz and J. H. Hutson (New York, 1973), pp. 289–90; Aileen Kraditor, "American Historians on their Radical Heritage," *Past & Present* 56(1972): 140–41; Paul Sniderman, *A Question of Loyalty*, forthcoming from University of California Press (Berkeley,

1981); Warren Weaver, Jr., "Citizens Party Born in Unorthodox Way," *The New York Times*, 13 April 1980, p. 15. Sniderman's research involves interviews with a large group of "alienated" members of the Berkeley community. He reports that to the question " 'how close does it ["the American form of government"] come to fitting your idea of what the best possible form of government should be?' . . . there seems to be little alternative to America. . . . What they most often call for is not a transformation of the system . . . but rather a modification of a *specific government policy* . . . even if they are politically embittered . . . [Thus] the choice we thought we had to make—whether there are a great many alienated or hardly any—is a false choice. . . . The idea of another promised land, one that might surpass the promise of America itself, has never taken hold. . . . Even in the years of bitter discord which this study records [the late 1960s], in an area of the country where nearly every form of political disillusion and rejection wins a substantial measure of symbolic support . . . the idea of America remains the idea of promise." (Quoted by permission of the author.)

39. Margaret Atwood, *The Journals of Susanna Moodie* (Toronto, 1970), pp. 12–13; Roland Barthes, *Mythologies*, trans. A. Lavers (London, 1972), p. 110. Atwood's lines are of course a poetic rendition of Moodie's outlook, as presented in *Roughing It in the Bush* (New York, 1852). See also David Thompson, *Travels in Western North America, 1784–1812*, ed. V. G. Hopwood (Toronto, 1971).

3

Fiction and the American Ideology: The Genesis of Howells' Early Realism

Henry Nash Smith

In a book published under the title *Democracy and the Novel*,[1] I discussed the uneasy relationship between major American writers of the nineteenth century and the large popular audience that came into existence with the industrial revolution and the spread of free public education. Here I should like to develop further one of the topics touched on in that book, the work of William Dean Howells. For almost fifty years, down to his death in 1920, Howells was associated in the eyes of the reading public with the doctrine of "realism" that he advocated in season and out. As a residue of this chapter in our literary history, Howells' *The Rise of Silas Lapham* continued until quite recently to appear on high school reading lists, although even before the First World War the inevitable pendulum swing of taste had begun to generate a rejection of realism by advanced-guard writers, and in 1930, when Sinclair Lewis denounced Howells in his Nobel Prize acceptance speech, he was voicing an attitude that was already a cliché among intellectuals.[2]

I think I am fully aware of Howells' limitations as a writer; in fact some of the things I shall have to say about him later may seem excessively severe. But his work has great historical interest because it provides access to the attitudes that were dominant in American society during several decades before and after the turn of the twentieth century; the technical difficulties with which Howells struggled were faced by a whole generation of writers. In *Democracy and the Novel* I dealt at some length with these problems as they appear in *A Modern Instance* (1882), the novel that he regarded as his "strongest."[3] Now I should like to extend the historical inquiry backward in time by looking at a book by Howells published ten years earlier (in 1873) during what might be called the prenatal phase of his development of the realistic method.

Howells had tried his hand at novel writing while he was still in his teens, first with a Dickensian story that began to appear serially in an Ohio newspaper but collapsed in mid-course, and again in his twenties, with a novel of village life that has not survived: we know only that it was rejected by several publishers in London and New York.[4] These failures and the success of Howells' two books of essays about Italy during the 1860s suggested a different tack. In 1871 he wrote his father (with whom he discussed all his literary plans) that he had in mind a book based on a summer trip he and his wife had taken down the St. Lawrence River. He said the new work would differ from standard travel books in having "the form of fiction so far as the characters are concerned," but apparently it was not to be exactly a novel. He continued: "If I succeed in this—and I believe I shall—I see clear before me a path in literature which no one else has tried, and which I believe I can make most distinctly and entirely my own." Later he declared, "The thing is quite a new species of fiction," being not at all "dependent on plot," but relying on "the interest of character . . . and some notable places."[5]

The book that carries out this experimental program, entitled *Their Wedding Journey*, appeared serially in the *Atlantic Monthly* in 1872. In it Howells scrupulously avoids such melodramatic features as suspense, "big" scenes, and exalted language, relying instead on his powers of observation in describing "notable places," on deftness of style, and on humor. But his self-confidence was not misplaced: no less a critic than Henry Adams, writing for the *North American Review*, found in *Their Wedding Journey* an "extreme and almost photographic truth to nature, and remarkable delicacy and lightness of touch."[6] It is true that Howells does not avoid fictional convention altogether, for Basil and Isabel March, the pair of newlyweds (closely resembling the writer and his wife) whose journey provides the book's only structure, enact to some extent the role ordinarily assigned in novels to the two lovers. But most of the time Howells' handling of the Marches avoids the beaten track of sentimental practice, and he often has them converse about topics that would never find a place in the usual fictional courtship. For example, he introduces a discussion of the technical problems he faced in writing the book, assigning to Isabel the role of a partisan of established aesthetic doctrine and causing Basil to deliver little lectures for her benefit in which he expounds the new ideas that Howells was incubating.

We Americans, Basil tells Isabel, "shall never have a poetry of our own til . . . we make the ideal embrace and include the real. . . ."[7] The notion of the "ideal," although difficult to define, was thoroughly familiar. The meaning of "the real," on the other hand, was elusive. Adams implied a definition in his remark that Howells had undertaken "the idealization of the commonplace." This could be taken as a description of the effect Whitman had achieved in *Leaves of Grass*, for example in the following lines from one of the magnificent catalogues in "Song of Myself":

> . . . the mechanic's wife with her babe at her nipple interceding
>   for every person born,
> Three scythes at harvest whizzing in a row from three lusty
>   angels with shirts bagg'd out at their waists,
> The snag-tooth'd hostler with red hair redeeming sins past
>   and to come,
> Selling all he possesses, traveling on foot to fee lawyers
>   for his brother and sit by him while he is tried for forgery . . .[8]

Here the intercession of the Madonna in behalf of sinners is somehow represented in the love of the workman's wife for her child; the hostler establishes the possibility of the redemption of sins because simply as a human being he is capable of every virtue; and reapers in the harvest field are as full an embodiment of the angelic nature as has ever existed.

But how could such ideas be applied to fiction? The standard sentimental novel had striven to depict the ideal by choosing characters of high social status and exquisite sensibilities, by focusing on a love story, and by excluding everything "low." This formula, however, was evidently worn out. The task of the new generation of writers was to discover a new way of revealing ideal values in the novelist's materials. When Howells wrote *Their Wedding Journey*, he had solved only half the problem. Although he had found in the narrative of travel a tolerable framework for a long prose narrative, he had not found a satisfactory way to elevate it above the level of observed fact. I shall examine a few passages from the book in order to illustrate the various ways in which Howells tried to carry out the program set forth by Basil.

What is most striking about these early fumblings is the extraordinary effort required to reach the ultimate goal. Howells' procedure is instructive becase it reveals clearly what factors entered into the solution he would eventually find. That solution was nothing less than his highly individualized conception of realism—which can be recognized as the ultimate development of Basil's formula of a synthesis of the ideal and the real. The reality was of course the novelist's inevitable subject matter— the society to which Howells was exposed in his own daily life in Cambridge and New York. What was original in his theory was the notion of the ideal that he considered to be latent in that commonplace material. This was simply the spirit of democracy, which was for him identical with equality.

There can be little doubt that Howells was led to this discovery by his experience as a child in postfrontier Ohio and then by the exalted spirit of nationalism generated by the Civil War. Despite the fact that he had spent the war years as American consul in Venice, or perhaps because he felt guilty for having been spared military service,[9] he shared in the fullest degree the fervor expressed in such utterances as the sermon preached by an otherwise unknown clergyman in Troy, New York, during the bleak year of 1864. God, declared this speaker, " has been striking, and trying to make us strike at elements unfavorable to the growth of a pure democracy," which he declared to be "the consummation of human civilization."[10] Howells was convinced that the War had been a holy crusade for the basic American principles of freedom and equality. He would later assert that in America, "the race has gained a height never reached before," and that the reunited nation radiated both "the light of democracy" and "the light of equality."[11]

Howells' emotional commitment to this belief was so strong that it biased his perception of the society around him. I think one must recognize that he was the victim of an ideology in the sense of "a system of meanings and values [which] is the expression or projection of a particular class interest."[12] Although Howells himself did not stand to profit directly from the control of the national economy by the corrupt Republican party, he identified the interest of the nation and indeed of the entire human race with a middle class in the society of the victorious North to which he belonged and which provided the dominant element of that party.[13] The ideological nature of his thinking is remarkably clear; again and again he speaks as if this middle class, statistically speaking a small minority of the population even of that section, embraced virtually the whole of the nation.[14] He thought of these people as living in a style devoid of elegance but notably comfortable. Collectively they constituted "the large, cheerful average of health and success and happy life."[15]

Economic historians tell an entirely different story. A recent study based on census returns concludes that in 1850 the top 1 percent of adult males in the United States held 30 percent of the real estate owned by all adult males, and the top 2 percent held 40 percent of the total. Furthermore, the pattern of distribution of wealth among freemen in 1850, 1860, and 1870 showed "remarkable stability." The author continues, "This inequality was surprisingly great; on the one hand, a few had large amounts of wealth, counterbalanced by the many who were essentially property-less. . . ."[16]

Howells was firmly convinced that the primary obstacle to truthful representation in fiction was the persistence of outworn literary conventions. Looking back a hundred years later, however, we can see that the most serious distortion of his vision was caused by his uncritical acceptance of the standard American ideology. In all good faith he took it for granted that his own social class (represented for example by Basil and Isabel March) made up the bulk of the American people. To depict this class in fiction, he thought, was to democratize the novel.[17] Moreover, he believed that the "honest" portrayal of such characters would necessarily reveal moral principles or laws operating in society.[18] Thus although Howells recognized that realism as a literary mode had originated in

Europe, and praised many continental European writers for their achievements in it—Turgenev, Dostoevsky, Tolstoy, Valdés, in certain moods
even Flaubert and Zola—he believed the American novelist had a great
advantage over his transatlantic rivals because in this country the writer
need do nothing more than tell the truth about society in order to illustrate
the ideal of democracy and equality. After Howells' conception reached
its full development he tended to repudiate even the great Victorian
novelists on the ground that English fiction and criticism expressed "class
interests," grew out of "class education," and admitted "only class claims
to the finer regard and respect of readers," whereas the American novel
was characteristically in "sympathy with race interests"—that is, the interests of all mankind. He claimed for "the American novelist" the "inherent, if not instinctive perception of equality: equality running through
motive, passion, principle, incident, character, and commanding with the
same force his interest in the meanest and the noblest, through the mere
virtue of their humanity."[19]

In following the development of Howells' theory of realism I have
moved chronologically far beyond the date of composition of *Their Wedding Journey*. Let me now return to that work and consider some passages from it within the conceptual framework I have established. The
debates between Isabel and Basil March show that Howells had not yet
clearly defined the relation between ideal and real in his own mind. In
the first passage I shall quote, the oversimplified dyadic contrast tends to
force Isabel into an indiscriminate partisanship for the ideal that is not far
from mere snobbishness, whereas Basil is forced into defending folklore
and vernacular humor simply because they embody a characteristic American reality. But he is not fully convinced that an ideal value is immanent
in these elements of popular culture, with the result that his defense is
rather lame, and he soon abandons it.

The Marches are viewing the Genesee Falls near Rochester from a high
bluff. Basil points out to his bride

> the table-rock in the middle of the fall, from which Sam Patch had
> made his fatal leap; but Isabel refused to admit that tragical figure to
> the honors of her emotions. "I don't care for him!" she said fiercely.
> "Patch! What a name to be linked in our thoughts with this superb
> cataract" (p. 68).

Basil has previously explained to Isabel that Sam Patch "invented the
saying, 'Some things can be done as well as others,' and proved it by
jumping over Niagara Falls twice," but when he attempted "the leap of
the Genesee Falls," he was killed (p. 66). The name in fact had great
resonance in the masculine world of barbershops and popular theaters. In
addition to Patch's significance as stunt man and exemplar of the "Go

Ahead" spirit of the mid-nineteenth century, he represented native American humor. Although he had been an actual person, his position in popular culture resembled that of the fictitious Mose, the Bowery B'hoy, protagonist of Ned Buntline's novel *The Mysteries and Miseries of New York* (1848) and of several plays starring Francis S. Chanfrau in the 1850s. Similarly, the actor Danforth Marble, noted for his rendering of Down East dialect, played the role of Patch in two comedies that were popular in the 1840s. The flavor of these plays can be inferred from the fact that Marble was also celebrated for his representation of the folklore Yankee, Brother Jonathan, ancestor of Uncle Sam.[20] In mentioning Patch, Basil means to remind Isabel that they have spent much time along the way exchanging reminiscences of European travel, taking it for granted that the United States is in comparison a cultural desert. And he speaks for Howells the apprentice writer in finding serious implications in Isabel's scorn for the name of Sam Patch.

> "Well, Isabel [Basil replies], I think you are very unjust. It is as good a name as Leander, to my thinking, and it was immortalized in support of a great idea—the feasibility of all things; while Leander's has come down to us as that of the weak victim of a passion" (p. 68).

I must interrupt Basil here to supply a gloss. Patch's remark that "Some things can be done as well as others" is strikingly similar in spirit to the observation of the Stranger in Angel's Camp concerning Jim Smiley's celebrated jumping frog, Daniel Webster: "I don't see no p'ints about that frog that's better'n any other frog." In other words, Howells has arrived at a point in his narrative where he has an opportunity to exploit the kind of native American humor that Mark Twain would show to be so rich a vein of literary ore. Howells can be forgiven for not recognizing his opportunity, since Mark Twain himself would need another decade of experiment before he could make an *Adventures of Huckleberry Finn* out of such material.

What Howells does is to modulate rather awkwardly toward a quite different subject. He has Basil notice that he and Isabel are standing outside a German beer hall. Though Basil's tone is jocose, Howells uses him as a mouthpiece to make a serious point:

> "The Germans are braver than we, and in them you find facts and dreams continually blended and confronted. Here is a fortunate illustration. The people we met coming out of this pavilion were lovers, and they had been here sentimentalizing on this superb cataract, as you call it, with which my heroic Patch is not worthy to be named. No doubt they had been quoting Uhland or some other of their romantic poets, perhaps singing some of their tender Ger-

man love-songs, the tenderest, unearthliest love-songs of the world.
At the same time they did not disdain the matter-of-fact corporeity
in which their sentiment was enshrined; they fed it heartily and
abundantly with the banquet whose relics we see here."

On a table before them stood a pair of beer-glasses, in the bot-
toms of which lurked scarce the foam of the generous liquor lately
brimming them; some shreds of sausage, some rinds of Swiss cheese,
bits of cold ham, crusts of bread, and the ashes of a pipe (p. 69).

Howells' difficulty in defining the contrast between the ideal and the
real is shown by the images he chooses to represent commonplace experience in the two passages I have quoted: first Sam Patch, redolent of
vernacular humor and the popular theater, and then an empty beer glass,
scraps of cheese and sausage, the ashes from a pipe. The emblems of the
ideal are a waterfall seen by moonlight and German love-songs. In yet
another passage exploiting the same contrast Howells comes nearer representing an actual synthesis of outer and inner worlds, although the
result still falls short of revealing the immanence of the ideal realm in the
actual: the significant transaction takes place entirely in the mind of the
observer. Sitting alone at daybreak on the deck of a Hudson River steam-
er, Basil observes "a fisherman drawing his nets, and bending from his
boat, there near Albany, N.Y., in the picturesque immortal attitudes of
Raphael's Galilean fisherman" (p. 49). In producing the association with
Raphael's painting, Basil is linking ordinary American life with an image
that belongs to the ideal realm on four counts: it relates to the remote
past; it is European (and therefore exotic); it concerns one of the fine arts;
and it alludes to the New Testament. Yet the total effect of the passage is
to isolate Basil in his function as registering consciousness from the commonplace average of humanity. An observer who is reminded of Raphael
by a Hudson River fisherman is obviously cultivated; he has traveled
abroad and has stored his mind with memories of the paintings of old
Masters. The unnecessary initials "N.Y.," suggesting the address of a
business letter, convey a mild astonishment that so prosaic a place can
have any relation to so exalted an image. And there is a further overtone
in the Biblical allusion: not only does the physical posture of the fisherman recall a certain painting, but also the scriptural story sanctifies the
humble labors of daily life everywhere—a suggestion certainly intended
by Raphael. But the difference between Howells' effort to make the ideal
include the real and the true consummation of the synthesis becomes
obvious if we place this passage beside Whitman's references to the "me-
chanic's wife with her babe at her nipple interceding for every person
born" and "the snag-tooth'd hostler with red hair redeeming sins past and
to come."

Having entered upon Basil's reverie, Howells makes a rather arbitrary transition to the recollection of a collision with another vessel during the previous night in which a sailor was badly scalded. The link, by way of heat, is awkward:

> . . . and now a flush mounted the pale face of the east, and through the dewy coolness of the dawn there came, more to the sight than to any other sense, a vague menace of heat. But as yet the air was deliciously fresh and sweet, and Basil bathed in his weariness in it, thinking with a certain luxurious compassion of the scalded man . . . (pp. 49–50).

Although the phrase "luxurious compassion" places Basil for a moment at an ironic distance from the narrative voice, Howells abandons this perspective at once and develops Basil's reverie quite seriously. The language grows correspondingly abstract and conventional:

> He bade his soul remember that, in the security of sleep, Death had passed them both [i.e., Isabel and himself] so close that his presence might well have chilled their dreams. . . . But . . . sense and spirit alike put aside the burden that he would have laid upon them; his revery reflected with delicious caprice the looks, the tones, the movements that he loved, and bore him far away from the sad images that he had invited to mirror themselves in it (p. 50).

In contrast with the linkage between the fisherman on the Hudson and Raphael's painting, which at least places an ideal image beside the commonplace scene, the allusions here to Basil's soul, to Death as an allegorical entity, and to a carefully bowdlerized lover's reverie drop all connection with actual experience and thus surrender all claim to novelty in narrative technique. Basil's feeling for Isabel is particularly conventional; it has only a remote basis in conceivable psychological fact. Thus the passage does not make "the ideal embrace and include the real" because it captures almost no reality.

A more important shortcoming of this way of linking the two realms of experience, from the standpoint of Howells' ultimate goal, is that there is little if any democracy about it. Basil feels no human tie with the fisherman; he might be an eighteenth-century aristocrat noting an example of the picturesque. In Howells' own terminology, the ideal coloring here is merely aesthetic; it has no moral or political significance. Many years later, when Basil and Isabel March would appear once again as protagonists of his most ambitious novel, *A Hazard of New Fortunes* (1889), the narrative voice would make this distinction. The husband and wife, a dozen years older than the newlyweds who figure in *Their Wedding Journey*, are shocked by their first exposure to the slums of the lower east side of Manhattan. The narrative voice comments:

> The time had been when the Marches would have taken a purely aesthetic view of the facts as they glimpsed them in this street of tenement-houses; when they would have contented themselves with saying that it was as picturesque as a street in Naples and Florence, and with wondering why nobody came to paint it.[21]

The moral sense of the couple is now engaged, but we are not appreciably nearer the discovery of an ideal value in the spectacle of poverty: the pity and moral outrage are in Basil's and Isabel's minds. That Howells was aware of this distinction is evident from the fact that he introduces into this novel two characters who undertake some action—admittedly rather vague—in behalf of the wretched people of the slums: the German emigré radical Lindau and the young Christian socialist Conrad Dryfoos. Yet having introduced these men, the novelist does not know what to do with them, and resorts to the expedient of having them killed as a consequence of street fighting between striking horsecar workers and the police. No significant relation is set up between Howells' surrogates in the story, the Marches, and these characters who are seriously committed to the ideal of democracy.

In order to illustrate Howells' long but on the whole unsuccessful struggle to find a way of affirming the democratic ideal in fiction, let me consider another passage from *Their Wedding Journey*. Leaving their steamboat at Albany, the Marches take a train for Buffalo and Niagara Falls. At the outset the first-person narrator intrudes for some two pages to describe his own response to a landscape that he loves "for its mild beauty and tranquil picturesqueness." As these epithets suggest, he is elaborately literary. While the animistic train "strives furiously onward," he fancies himself loitering and sauntering "up and down the landscape," pausing for a cup of buttermilk served him by "old Dutch ladies . . . with decent caps upon their gray hair," or "some red-cheeked, comely young girl, out of Washington Irving's pages, with no cap on her golden braids . . ." (p. 53). Or again, he says: "I walk unmolested through the farmer's tall grass . . . and learn . . . that his family has owned that farm ever since the days of the Patroon; which I dare say is not true" (p. 54). (The skepticism must represent a hint of self-consciousness in a writer who suspects that this mood of nostalgia is too fragile for post–Civil War America.) After a few more fantasies, the narrator turns the responsibility for producing associations over to the "wedding-journeyers." But they in turn are treated with apologetic irony. "They cast an absurd poetry over the landscape," he says; "they invited themselves to be reminded of passages of European travel by it; and they placed villas and castles and palaces upon all the eligible building-sites." When this amusement palls, Basil "patriotically tried to reconstruct the Dutch and Indian past of the Mohawk Valley. . . ." But his effort is frustrated by Isabel's absolute ignorance of American history (a subject that is less essential to general cultivation than is European history) (p. 54).

Wearied by their failure to "extract any sentiment from the scenes without," Basil and Isabel turn instead to look about them for amusement within the railway car. The narrator approves of the decision on ideological grounds: it is merely "an ordinary carful of human beings" and "perhaps the more worthy to be studied on that account." For "the sincere observer of man will not desire to look upon his heroic or occasional phases, but will seek him in his habitual moods of vacancy and tiresomeness." Howells probably believed he was turning here from an outmoded sentimental exercise in the ideal (extracting sentiment from the landscape) to a more profound undertaking, that in fact of the realistic novelist. For this reason, the narrator's comment is worth quoting at greater length. Man in his vacant and tedious phases, he goes on to say, is

> very precious; and I never perceive him to be so much a man and a brother as when I feel the pressure of his vast, natural, unaffected dulness. Then I am able to enter confidently into his life and inhabit there, to think his shallow and feeble thoughts, to be moved by his dumb, stupid desires, to be dimly illumined by his stinted inspirations, to share his foolish prejudices, to practise his obtuse selfishness (p. 55).

Howells presumably thinks that the superciliousness of this comment is offset by the narrator's declaration that he himself enters into the dullness and stupidity of common humanity. This, one supposes, would represent the democracy that is expressed in realism. Thus the Marches take an important step in the right direction by turning their attention to the interior of the railway car and observing their fellow passengers. But the tone seems patronizing nevertheless. Basil and Isabel, we are told, "had deliberately rejected the notion of a drawing-room car as affording a less varied prospect of humanity, and as being less in the spirit of ordinary American travel" (pp. 52–53). Now they "were very willing to be entertained." "They delighted" in some of the passengers, "they were interested in" others, they "found diversion" in yet others. The Marches invent elaborate and sympathetic biographies for several characters, but Isabel is outraged by the indecent behavior of "tender couples" who "reclined upon each other's shoulders and slept," and she is disgusted by having to overhear a detailed account of a case of typhoid fever. Presently she is punished for her censoriousness by falling asleep herself with her head on Basil's shoulder (pp. 55–58). He consoles her for her embarrassment with an amused irony that would often serve Howells in future novels as a device for ending scenes that seemed on the point of placing his protagonists in awkward situations.

Thus the implied challenge to Isabel's right to sit in judgment—which threatened to raise questions about class feeling and perspectives—has been turned into a stock joke about the inconsequence of women. Yet the issue is a real one. What is the basis for Basil's and Isabel's assumed superiority to their fellow passengers? Their status is a residue from conventional fiction that Howells has not looked at closely enough. They occupy a position equivalent to that of the genteel hero and heroine in the traditional narrative structure. Even though the narrator occasionally backs away from them with ironic comments showing that he judges them in turn, they share with him the innate sensibilities and acquired cultivation which in this fictive world confer on a character the capacity for transcendence. That is to say, both the Marches and the narrator have access to the mental processes of the people they observe and can evaluate them by reference to absolute moral and esthetic principles, whereas the other characters remain sealed within their limited horizons. The Marches and the narrator are free because they are in contact with the ideal; the other characters are not free. The ideal is still made to embrace the real only within the consciousness of privileged observers, the implied author or his surrogates.

What, in fact, has Howells accomplished in *Their Wedding Journey* toward creating a new species of fiction? In cutting himself loose from plot as conventionally conceived he has eliminated the standard devices of the sensation novel: mysteries, ghosts, gothic wickedness, disguises, long-lost heirs, physical combat, and so on. In choosing the Marches as hero and heroine he has avoided such absurdities as perfect lovers and superhuman renunciations as well as fiends in human form. He has made a perceptible effort to get rid of the stylized motivations and melodramatic moral contrasts of popular fiction. But he has not completely freed himself from outworn fictional conventions. Although using a husband and wife—even a recently married pair—as the lovers is mildly innovative, what tangible plot the story has is after all still centered on the relation of a man and a woman; and this relation, like the characters of the two protagonists, retains important vestiges of ideality: they are very genteel lovers. The Marches' status is not technically aristocratic, but it is functionally so: they consider themselves and the author considers them to be equal or superior in intellect, taste, and cultivation to anyone they encounter.

The systematic blindness, or perhaps one should say "tunnel vision," that prevented Howells from recognizing the contradiction between his doctrine of equality and his failure to recognize the existence of a hierarchy of classes in American society based on differences in wealth and cultivation is the characteristic effect of any ideology that is firmly held by the observer and reinforced by being generally accepted throughout his own social class. Howells cherished an almost subliminal belief that the settlement of North America by English-speaking colonists had set in motion a providentially ordered historical scheme which would lead, indeed was already leading, toward a millennial consummation. For him, the United States had a meaning not available to empirical observation: it was destined to bring freedom and democracy to the world, and he was convinced that the facts of American society, as contrasted with those of European societies, demonstrated the operation of the process. I think this ideologically determined belief proved to be an insurmountable obstacle to Howells' full development as a novelist. The social reality of urban industrial America refused to yield the ideal truth and beauty that his theory of realism claimed would be revealed by an honest examination of it. Yet he was unable to conceive of any other fresh and interesting approach to the material.

By way of a coda to this discussion of the effect of the American ideology on Howells' work, I should point out that the decision of his friend Henry James to live in Europe showed James to be free of such a bias. This fact lends a particular interest to James's interpretation of realism. For a couple of years in the late 1860s, before James decided to stay in Europe, the two young men had both been residents of Cambridge, and had taken long walks together during which they canvassed the problems they both faced as apprentice writers of fiction. They must have talked about realism, for some of James's first stories, much in the spirit of Hawthorne, deal with artists (usually painters) who are either accepting or rejecting the new mode. But whereas Howells was developing an almost religious devotion to scrupulous representation of commonplace facts in art, James took a very detached attitude toward the issue. If anything, he tends to defend his own version of idealism, conceived as an indefinable nuance of meaning and implication beyond the reach of explicit statement. In "The Story of a Masterpiece" (1868), a painter executes a portrait of a beautiful young woman that is superbly accurate but along with the triumph of technique conveys to her fiancé an imaginative insight into "a certain vague moral dinginess" in her.[22] The implication is that truth in art transcends mere accuracy of denotation.

James's "Madonna of the Future" (1873) is less subtle perhaps but even more teasingly ambiguous in its handling of the theme of idealism versus realism. An American artist has lived in poverty in Florence for many years while he devoted himself to plans and studies for painting "a madonna who was to be a résumé of all the other Madonnas of the Italian school." The woman he expects to use as his model, a woman he idealizes in the sense of worshiping her beauty without having a carnal relation with her, is revealed to a Jamesian tourist-narrator as a thoroughly ordinary person now well advanced into middle age, with no education and quite mundane tastes. She seems to be the mistress of an Italian artist who makes a good living by modeling in clay "peculiarly cynical and vulgar" statuettes, each consisting of "a cat and a monkey, fantastically draped, in some preposterously sentimental conjunction," which "illustrated chiefly the different phases of what, in delicate terms, may be called gallantry and coquetry."[23] This story is evidently a commentary on the contrast between the impulse to idealize the actual, and the counterimpulse to degrade it into grotesque ugliness. But exactly what is James saying? The intrusion of a comic perspective complicates the rather shopworn antithesis of idealism and realism in art, for James seems to be mocking both attitudes, and indeed the story might be taken as a suggestion that the polar contrast is a crude oversimplification.

During the 1880s critics regularly bracketed James with Howells as a leading realist, and it is true that in *The Bostonians* and *The Princess Casamassima* (both published in 1886) James deliberately experimented with something like Zola's dense specification of detail in urban settings. But eventually the striking differences between James and Howells came to be recognized. These differences can be summed up by saying that Howells' determination to reveal moral principles immanent in society led him to avoid extensive probing of mental states and processes—what he called analysis—while James became more and more preoccupied with precisely this material. In the novels of James's so-called major phase— *The Wings of the Dove* (1902), *The Ambassadors* (1903), and *The Golden Bowl* (1904)—the outer world hardly exists.

The cumulative result of James' technical innovations was that questions of epistemology became the underlying themes of all his later work. He was thus in tune with the general trend of modernism and could become a major influence on the next generation of novelists. Howells, on the other hand, although steadily productive during the last decades of his long career (he lived until 1920), seemed confined to the treadmill of his own formulas, with only an occasional touch of freshness in matter or technique.

NOTES

1. Henry Nash Smith, *Democracy and the Novel: Popular Resistance to Classic American Writers* (New York, 1978).

2. Lewis' denunciation of Howells makes use of three British images within a few lines: Howells "had the code of a pious old maid whose greatest delight was to have tea at the vicarage," he sought "to guide America into becoming a pale edition of an English cathedral town," and he is to be contrasted with "surly and authentic fellows—Whitman and Melville, then Dreiser and James Huneker and Mencken—who insisted that our land had something more than tea-table gentility." "The American Fear of Literature," in *The Man from Main Street*, eds. Harry E. Maule and Melville B. Caine (London, 1954), pp. 3–19.

3. "Mr. Howells His Own Critic," *Literary News* (New York, n.s.) 18(October 1897), p. 313.

4. Olov W. Fryckstedt, *In Quest of America: A Study of Howells' Early Development as a Novelist,* (Upsala, 1958), pp. 67–68; Mildred Howells, *Life in Letters of William Dean Howells,* 2 vols., (Garden City, N.Y., 1928), 1:125.

5. Howells, *Life in Letters,* 1:162.

6. Henry Adams, *North American Review,* 114(April 1872):444.

7. William Dean Howells, *Their Wedding Journey,* ed. John K. Reeves, (Bloomington, Ind., 1968), p. 68. Page references to this edition will be included within parentheses in the text.

8. Walt Whitman, *Leaves of Grass,* Comprehensive Reader's Edition, eds. Harold W. Blodgett and Sculley Bradley (New York, 1965), p. 75.

9. Howard Munford, "The Genesis and Early Development of the Basic Attitudes of William Dean Howells" (Ph.D. diss., Harvard University, 1951), pp. 234, 288.

10. The Reverend Marvin R. Vincent, of the First Presbyterian Church of Troy, quoted in Ernest Tuveson, *Redeemer Nation: The Idea of America's Millennial Role* (Chicago, 1968), p. 203.

11. William Dean Howells, *Criticism and Fiction and Other Essays,* eds. Clara M. Kirk and Rudolf Kirk (New York, 1959), pp. 85, 369.

12. Raymond Williams, *Marxism and Literature* (London, 1977), p. 108. There is a fuller discussion in Ben Halpern, " 'Myth' and 'Ideology' in Modern Usage," *History and Theory* 1 (1961):129–49.

13. Howells, for example, was greatly distressed by the fact that his friend Mark Twain joined the Mugwump desertion from the Republican Party in 1884. George M. Frederickson, *The Inner Civil War: Northern Intellectuals and the Crisis of the Union* (New York, 1965), p. 194.

14. This conception of the American people is at least as old as Thomas Jefferson's *Notes on the State of Virginia* (1784), and is prominent in Timothy Dwight's *Greenfield Hill* (1794) (quotations in Tuveson, *Redeemer Nation,* pp. 109–10). It is one of Whitman's favorite themes ("the native-born middle-class population of quite all the United States,—the average of farmers and merchants everywhere,—the real, though latent and silent bulk of America, city or country, presents a magnificent mass of material, never before equalled on earth . . .," quoted from *North American Review,* 1881, in *The Native Muse. Theories of American Literature,* ed. Richard Ruland, 2 vols., [New York, 1972–76], 1:426–27).

Arthur Boardman has shown by an analysis of all Howells' thirty-two novels that he identified himself with a social stratum situated in a well-defined hierarchy, beneath a very small upper class that he looked up to with admiration only slightly tinged with resentment and moral criticism, but distinctly above a lower class or classes which he felt to be inferior in cultivation and probably in morals to himself and his associates ("Social Point of View in the Novels of William Dean Howells," *American Literature* 39 [1967]:42–59). Boardman comments, "The attitudes shown [in most of his novels] have the effect of contradicting the egalitarian theme Howells expressed in the novels protesting great social injustice" (p. 42).

15. Howells, *Criticism and Fiction,* p. 66.

16. Lee Soltow, *Men and Wealth in the United States, 1850–1870,* (New Haven, 1975), pp. 93, 183.

17. Howells maintained that the novelist should write stories "of our own life." He declared that "We [Americans] are really a mixture of the plebeian ingredients of the whole world; but that is not bad; our vulgarity consists in trying to ignore 'the worth of the vulgar,' in believing that the superfine is better" (*Criticism and Fiction,* p. 41). Also: "Democracy in literature . . . wishes to know and to tell the truth" (ibid., p. 87).

18. "We must ask ourselves before we ask anything else, Is it true?—true to the motives, the impulses, the principles that shape the lives of actual men and women? This trust, which necessarily includes the highest morality and the highest artistry—this truth given, the book cannot be wicked and cannot be weak . . . if the book is true to what men and women know of one another's souls it will be true enough, and it will be great and beautiful" (*Criticism and Fiction,* p. 49).

19. William Dean Howells, *Harper's Monthly* 81(July 1890), p. 318.

20. *Dictionary of American Biography*, s.v. "Sam Patch" and "Danforth Marble."

21. William Dean Howells, *A Hazard of New Fortunes* (New York, 1890), p. 21.

22. Leon Edel, ed., *The Complete Tales of Henry James*, 12 vols., (Philadelphia, 1960–64), 1:292.

23. Ibid., 3:44.

4

Cultural Revisions in the Twenties:
Brooklyn Bridge as "Usable Past"

Alan Trachtenberg

Hart Crane's *The Bridge* (1930) has its origins in the twenties. As much autobiography as "myth of America," the poem belongs not only to the decade's syncopated tempos and aesthetic entrancements, but as well to its deep changes and conflicts. The poet's own life in these years of encroaching mechanization, standardization, and consumer capitalism, is the historical ground of the poem, a ground too rarely allowed more than passing notice in criticism. It is characteristic of our criticism that it knows less about history than it does about literary forms and influences, and knowing less about the ground of art, it inevitably knows less about the ideas that inform works of art, and the intrinsic powers that reside within them. We know that the twenties brought a renascence into American art, a flourishing of energies that had been launched in the previous decade. We know too little, however, of how those energies confronted new social and cultural formations, how they were shaped by struggles of artists to realize visions antithetical to their times, especially to the be-havioristic model which in these years established itself in the media, in advertising, and in popular and academic social thought.[1]

The twenties witnessed a flowering of literary and artistic experiment, an assimilation of European modernism, of Surrealism and Dada, and the achievement of a new speech in the poetry of Pound, Eliot, Frost, Stevens, and Williams. Crane himself breathed deeply in this atmosphere of aesthetic excitement, of jostling manifestoes and doctrines, and *The Bridge* might be read, as Frederick Hoffman shows, as a typical document of experimentation.[2] But we need also a way of reading the poem, and understanding the aesthetic production of the period in general, as embodying a resistance to what Crane and other artists perceived as the ultimate menace of modern bourgeois society: its assault on the realm of autonomy, on the very sources of art. For the first time in American life, at least in such coherent form, art began to appear as a separate realm: not merely a vehicle for criticism, but an alternative way of life.

The implicit ambition of modernist art in the twenties was to open a space for itself (as for the daily life of artists and a new intelligentsia in Bohemian colonies) within the larger culture, a culture in which older patterns of gentility and puritan moralism were adapting themselves to new social demands of consumership and technological change. Crane's poem has yet another emphasis, an additional ambition: to alter the larger culture itself, to revise its sense of itself, its dominant values, and especially its idea of its history. As a revisionary epic, *The Bridge* shares a common project with works of criticism and cultural history by Waldo Frank, Van Wyck Brooks, Lewis Mumford, Paul Rosenfield, and especially William Carlos Williams—the project of creating a "usable past."[3] Crane's is the epic statement of this concerted effort, at the heart of which lay (even in the more conventional historical writings of Lewis Mumford) a vision of an aesthetic self, a poetic sensibility, as the true mediator of a true cultural history. How else are we to understand the epic scale of *The Bridge* except as the effort of the poet to discover *himself* in all of American history, from Columbus's voyage to the western settlement, from the building of Brooklyn Bridge to invention of the airplane? To discover himself as the redemptive poetic consciousness of the history as a whole, as a totality. Revision of history becomes a mode of self-discovery and self-possession. The poem, like Williams' project to "re-name the things seen" in *In The American Grain* (1925), is a deliberate act of such revision, a rethinking and recasting of the past into a future represented by the poet's present.

The Bridge strives for transcendence, for a conversion of the everyday into the spiritual, of modern American into a symbol of a new consciousness. Or, in terms the great Dutch historian Johan Huizinga used in his account of the way of life he found in American in 1926, to transform the "transitive culture" of "This, Here, and Soon," into a "transcendental culture."[4] Crane's method of transcendence is the Romantic fusion of self and world, the planting of the self at the center of his world. His nameless narrator is a Crispin, searching to become "the intelligence of his soil,/ The sovereign ghost." Crane performed his quest without Stevens' muted comedy of the voyaging imagination, and his poem now seems less reflective upon the dilemmas of the artist in an inhospitable environment (Stevens' comedian learns eventually that "his soil is man's intelligence./ That's better.") than a pained reflection of them. The poem insists upon the sovereignty of art, and although its confidence suffers often against appalling evidence of murderous engines, rigid buildings, and the mental prison of billboards and airwaves, it never pauses to question its own aesthetic ideology. Where Stevens investigates and redefines the imagination's ground in reality, Crane defends and asserts the primacy of a Romantic relation to the world as the premise of his "usable past." His stance is defensive without secondary defenses: his singer either floats or sinks, and his world either glows in the radiance of art or dies in the "muffled slaughter of a day in birth."

The Bridge belongs to the twenties also by virtue of what Huizinga might call a "higher naivete": its hope for a purely aesthetic transformation of a world already remade, reconstituted by industrial and corporate capitalism into mechanized space and time. The poem concedes a fully technologized and rationalized world (only fleeting visions of Indian voluptuousness, of "ancient men . . . hobo-trekkers," and of resolute but defeated artists like Melville and Dickinson, evoke historical alternatives to the "elevators [that] drop us from our day"), and its ringing optimism in the final section (only momentarily qualified by the final question: "Is it Cathay . . .?) seems willed, more programmatic than earned by the cumulative energies of the poem. The hopefulness of the opening prayer ("lend a myth to God")—which has nothing in common with the "transitive" optimism of Overstreet and the hucksters of the age—is charged with aesthetic power precisely because it encloses an anxiety that continues to live irrepressibly throughout the poem. Thus the poem's naivete is "higher," a higher mode of aspiration than the surrender to environment and to machine in the name of adjustment, maturity, and progress everywhere urged in the larger culture.

Crane's defense of art is a defense of an idea of culture, an alternative culture of aesthetic modes of experience. The entire poem, and his entire "usable past" project, rests upon the "naive" belief that such forms might appropriate the machine and subordinate its mechanicalness to human spirituality. His machines are not forms of exploitation or stolen labor power, but modes of experience, capable of aesthetic redemption. Crane's symbol of such a possibility, symbol and pledge of its historical imminence, is of course, Brooklyn Bridge: the paradigmatic structure of an older urban modernity, itself a fusion of science and love, technology and art. The choice of this bridge was not arbitrary; other artists chose it as well in the same years as an arch emblem of modernity.[5] Crane's bridge, like the poem, belongs to the decade. The coincidence of what I am calling re-visions of Brooklyn Bridge in these years, and what lay behind that coincidence, is the phenomenon of cultural revision I will explore here. My own method will be a reconstruction of consciousness: an attempt to recover the subjective features of the bridge's remarkable hold upon the imagination in the twenties. My purpose is to begin to uncover motives and intentions invested in the revisionary project Crane shared with other aspiring form makers in the twenties: to see if and how their efforts at making a "usable past" suggest a useful lesson for us.

"TO BE, GREAT BRIDGE, IN VISION BOUND OF THEE"

Imagine yourself midway. How you arrive is of no account. Here the looming form takes command, governs every neural response. This visual and kinetic surrender begins what we can call the classic moment of Brooklyn Bridge: the classic moment in the imagination of the bridge. The self is obliterated to a bare eye bound in space. Everything else falls away. Mere walking ceases, and crossing begins: the bridge sweeps the body into the modulated measures of an upward passage, and sweeps the eye into new harmonies of motion and sound. Midway, above, alone. Joseph Stella recounts:

> Many nights I stood on the bridge—and in the middle alone—lost—a defenceless prey to the surrounding swarming darkness—crushed by the mountainous black impenetrability of the skyscrapers—here and there lights resembling suspended falls of astral bodies or fantastic splendors of remote rites—shaken by the underground tumult of trains in perpetual motion, like the blood in the arteries—at times, ringing as alarm in a tempest, the shrill sulphurous voice of the trolley wires—now and then strange moanings of appeal from tug boats, guessed more than seen, through the infernal recesses below—I felt deeply moved, as if on the threshold of a new religion or in the presence of a new DIVINITY.[6]

Alone with the bridge: and walking, the city man's customary slice through dense space, ceases, and *crossing*, the act of piety, devotion, belief, begins. The bridge is now a threshold to a new realm, "as though a god were issue of the strings." "And midway on that structure," writes Hart Crane in his first composed lines, later canceled, toward *The Bridge:* "And midway on that structure I would stand/ One moment, not as diver, but with arms/ That open to project a disk's resilience/ Winding the sun and planets in its face."[7] The classic moment achieves its classic form in the opening stanza of the final poem of *The Bridge:*

> Through the bound cables strands, the arching path
> Upward, veering with light, the flight of strings—
> Taut miles of shuttling moonlight syncopate
> The whispered rush, telepathy of wires.
> Up the index of night, granite and steel—
> Transparent meshes—fleckless the gleaming staves—
> Sibylline voices flicker, waveringly stream
> As though a god were issue of the strings . . .[8]

But surely Crane and Stella and their coreligionists of the bridge in the twenties were not the first to walk across the structure—only the first to single out that experience and build another structure upon it: the first to *imagine* the bridge in this way: or to make a walk across the bridge an intensified moment in their imagination of what it was like to be alive in America in their day. Others had walked before. Why now does the walk seem a momentous crossing? Why, say, from 1917 to 1930 does the classic moment dominate the imagination of the bridge, as it appears, at least, in painting, photographs, fiction, criticism and poetry?

Let us first understand more precisely the meaning of the classic moment—its historical meaning, its place in the history and in the celebration of the history of Brooklyn Bridge. A usual way of speaking is to say that Crane and Stella and others are part of the history of the bridge: their celebrations additional data in a list of celebrations, reaching from at least the Opening Ceremonies and surrounding hoopla to what promises to come at the hundredth anniversary. We might also say that this history, engaging as it does both an object and responses to it (or a fact and symbolic interpretations of it), belongs to another, broader history: a phase or chapter in the history of the coming of the modern, of the big industrial city, of new styles and new materials of building—and of making artworks. In the usual way of speaking, the classic moment takes its place as another item to be classified, another response to the bridge and to what it manifestly represents: the stage of urban modernity in the history of American life.

Further: taken as a response to a significance-laden object, the classic moment might be classified as one among many indices to what we call culture: meaning, in normal usage, an interior realm where personal need meets exterior value, combining into a shared picture of the world. We might then study the classic moment and other individual responses to the bridge, along with the bridge itself, to piece together a picture of culture: the object of our scholarship, perhaps our admiration and nostalgia.

But there is a flaw in this way of speaking and of thinking. As Emerson might say, it leaves history *outside* of me. Culture is not merely the object of my attention, but *how* I attend to anything, the form and style of my attending, as well as the ingrained decision itself about what is worth attending to. What remains simply an object in my field of vision is not yet part of me, not yet culture: or, if I see something as existing only as an object-in-the world, and do not see that my own way of seeing affects my perception of the object, then I am not yet aware of how deeply cultural a creature I am.

The classic moment is a moment of profound subjectivity, even of privacy. Yet it is profoundly cultural—all the more cultural, all the more profound to the extent that it subjectivizes the bridge itself—that it re-sees or revises the bridge. Through its power of communication the classic moment has revised the bridge for us: not so much into a specific revision, a specific image, but into an unforgettable lesson that *any* seeing of the bridge, through personal experience or historical document, is a re-seeing, a revision that constitutes and reveals our own cultural being. Does the bridge as a thing have a history apart from a chronicle of *physical* revision? Any thing is historical only in the role it plays in the life, the total life, of the people it serves. Thus the classic moment is a paradigm of the making of the bridge into a historical object. Granted, this seems to insist upon a paradox, for what is the classic moment of lonely suspension upon the form of the bridge but a severing of ties, a breaking of connections with history? The paradox dissolves, however, when we recognize, as I hope we shall, that the severance is only apparent, a precondition thought necessary by a surprising number of people in the same period for a re-connection with history. Typified by the walk that becomes a crossing, the classic moment is an imaginative history: a discovery that the making of a history is radically subjective, yet (another function of bridging) capable of being shared. To study the classic moment is to study the making of Brooklyn Bridge into history and into culture. It is not another datum we are after, but the most essential fact of Brooklyn Bridge: its role as an event, a symbolic act, in the imagination.

"SOME SPLINTERED GARLAND FOR THE SEER."

"Beyond any other aspect of New York," wrote Lewis Mumford in *Sticks and Stones* (1924), "the Brooklyn Bridge has been a source of joy and inspiration to the artist." The appeal lay in the visual elegance of the structure: "the strong lines of the bridge," as Mumford writes, "and the beautiful curve described by its suspended cables," and especially the steel work and "the architectural beauty of its patterns." Brooklyn Bridge was among those "great bridges" that surpassed the more "grotesque and barbarous" features of the first age of industrial building and survived as "enduring monuments." "To this day they communicate a feeling of dignity, stability, and unwavering poise."[9]

Dignity, stability, and poise describe well the feeling one has in the paintings of the bridge by Jonas Lie, by Twachtman and Childe Hassam and Bellows and Joseph Pennell—and are not at odds with, but by themselves inadequate to describe the effects of the much different painterly intentions of John Marin, Albert Gleizes, and Joseph Stella. At the time Mumford wrote, a change was already in process in the representation of the bridge in painting—a change measured by the eruption into American painting of modernist styles such as cubism, fauvism, and futurism, but also indicative of a change in the kind of appreciation artists felt for the bridge. We might, of course, consider the change in appreciation and feeling as effects of the changed notion of what a painting is and how its framed composition relates to an ostensible subject in the world, but that would be to assign to style or mode the power of causing changes in feeling. Feeling and style more likely arise from a common source, and the new styles might also be taken as "answerable" to a new set of feelings and circumstances. Did futurism by itself instigate the revised vision of the bridge in works by Marin and Stella, or did it provide elements of a vocabulary that answered to the revised relation of artist to bridge?

A full cultural history would have to take into account the subtle interplay of forces that intersect and become palpable in any single expression. Here we are looking for the origins or the ground of a changed relation to the bridge I am calling the classic moment: the moment on the bridge when *walking* crosses over to *crossing*. In 1954 Mumford comments in a new preface to *Sticks and Stones* on the fact that he and Hart Crane were at work on their respective treatments of the bridge at the same time: "Our common appreciation of this great work of art became part of a wider movement, which owes so much to the polarizing effect of *The Seven Arts* and *The New Republic*, the working toward the creation of a 'usable past' for our country."[10] Common to the appreciation of the "wider movement" as well as of Crane and Mumford (and we include Mumford's own long-unknown but recently restored and published play of 1925–27, *The Builders of the Bridge*) was some variant of the classic moment, the momentous walk and the eye-crossing at midway. Mumford's reference to "usable past" suggests a focus to bring that moment into relation with a common cultural project of the period.

Consider the innocent walk. To cross the bridge on foot, on the elevated promenade, is to know the bridge from the inside: to discover that it has an inside, or a siding of crossing cables and stays which construct the illusion of an enclosure. For the first thirty years or so the bridge was predominantly a walkway: walking across the bridge was the common way of using it. Walking across, getting to and fro, from home to work and back, was a way of marking a precious transition. Rarely were you alone. The bridge, like a boulevard, provided company. There are written records of the innocent pleasure of this promenade, but we no longer read them; they lie buried in old reportage and letters to the editor of the nineties and the turn of the century. But photographs made for stereoscopic parlor viewing tell of the charm of a walk on the bridge, on the civic parade ground in the sky.

This is an older vision of Brooklyn Bridge, before vehicular traffic surpassed the volume of pedestrian traffic in 1916. An older bridge, and its place in the imagination shows it whole, complete, a unitary thing: a bridge between two places, the separate roadways (for walkers and for riders) together serving the multiple needs of city life. The bridge would meet the "interests of the community as well as of the Bridge Company," Roebling explained in his master plan of 1869: a roadway for vehicles and an elevated boardwalk to "allow people of leisure, and old and young invalids, to promenade over the Bridge on fine days, in order to enjoy the beautiful views and the pure air." And in the older vision the towers, "its most conspicuous features," still serve, as Roebling promised, "as land-marks to the adjoining cities . . . entitled to be ranked as national monu-ments."[12] They stood high above the city, as yet without the defiant challenge of skyscrapers. And thus the older bridge appealed to the eye—an older eye, too, we might say, which saw the world itself as whole, com-pact, reliable, in a manner much like Roebling's own confident vision. The dominant vision before, say, 1912 was lateral and iconic: a public bridge seen from some clear and impersonal perspective everyone would recognize.

Walking the bridge then must have seemed in its very commonness not especially worthy of remarkable comment. The midway vision, the eye-crossing along mystic strings, had not yet emerged, as true as it might have been to the feelings of midnight crossers, divers, lovers, and other bedlamites. Still thinking of it as contemporary, not a survival of the past (as it appeared to Mumford and his generation) but an immediate fore-runner, virtually a breeder of new bridges, new constructions, writers of the Progressive period appropriated the bridge in its monumentality. For Ernest Poole in *The Harbor* (1915) it is the "Great Bridge," whose "sweep-ing arch . . . seemed high as the clouds." The novel sets the hopes represented by harbor and bridge, hopes "of the power of mind over matter, and of the mighty speeding up of a world civilization and peace, a successful world, strong, broad, tolerant," against the realities of class conflict and social unrest.[13] The sweeping bridge remains an emblem of hope. As it does in an obscure but intriguing verse drama published in 1913 by the avant-garde house of Mitchell Kennerley. The play, *The Bridge*, by one Dorothy Landers Beall, is also torn by conflict, between rich and poor, workers and owners, and projects a union of the selfless engineer and the passionate settlement-house worker as a solution to the rifts of the age. Brooklyn Bridge here is "Long Bridge," the sovereign spirit of bridges as such, and it inspires the young engineer to persist in his struggle with the elements, and with labor agitators and crooked businessmen, to raise a new bridge alongside the old. The doubts and anguish of his beloved Hilda give way when she hears "The Spirit of the Bridge" explain:

> Do you not see grave bridges, free suspensions,
> All woven, builded, swinging in the sunlight
> Over the bitter streams of old neglect,

>   Like a glad-going company of workers
>   Linking the separate and the little-souled,
>   The great, the tiny, the unfortunate.

The play concludes with a shining reconciliation between the engineer
and his workers, to the tune of Hilda's bright song: "Quick, O Bridge—
rise surely—/ Bridges—world-Bridges, span like sympathy,/ Till there are
left no bitter gulfs to pass![14]

From an icon of public reconciliation to a private event of mystical
eye-crossing: this passage, which occurred between 1912 and 1915, marks
a rupture between the old bridge and the new, a rupture at least in the
kind of joy and inspiration the bridge offered to artists. As we know, the
whole cultural past of America itself took on a new and oppressive look
to a growing number of young Americans in the same years, the years of
the Armory Show (1913), of Van Wyck Brooks' *America's Coming of Age*
(1915), and of *The Seven Arts* (1917–18). One of the modes of the new
look of things, the new look *at* the world, was deconstructive: the old
integrity of vision, of seeing, begins to dissolve. Marin's swift expressions
of visible urban energy in his views of the bridge of 1912 and 1913 are
symptoms as well as acute modernist achievements. "I see great forces at
work," Marin wrote in the exhibition catalogue to his 1913 show at "291":

>   great movements; the large buildings and the small buildings; the
>   warring of the great and small; influences of one mass on another
>   greater or smaller mass. Feelings are aroused which give me the
>   desire to express the reaction of these "pull forces," those influences
>   which play with one another; great masses pulling smaller masses,
>   each subject in some degree to the other's power. . . . And so I try
>   to express graphically what a great city is doing.[15]

A new idea of the modern itself appears here, in Marin's revisions of the
bridge and in his words: a nervous tropism toward the abstract yet concretely emotional structures lurking within the changing city and bursting
the seams of conventional realism: the mode not only of earlier representations of the bridge, but correspondingly of the actual making of the
original bridge itself.

An impulse to revise, to remake, arose in these years in literary and
artistic circles in New York: an impulse that found one coherent expression in a new attention to the American cultural heritage. Sensing a
creative anarchy in the American scene—"the sudden unbottling of elements that have had not opportunity to develop freely in the open"—Van
Wyck Brooks in 1918 deplored "the lack of any sense of inherited resources" to fertilize and tutor the energies of the young. What passed for
culture—the genteel collocations of the chiefly European "best that had

been thought and said," and the severely bowdlerized and domesticated version of American literature—had discredited itself, largely by its blatant subservience to the powers of business and industry in this period of heightened conflict. As a result, Brooks wrote, "the present is a void, and the American writer floats in that void because the past that survives in the common mind of the present is a past without living value. But is this the only possible past? If we need another past so badly, is it inconceivable that we might discover one, that we might even invent one?"[16] Brooks' call for the invention of a "usable past," a past that would answer the question, "What is important for us?", led to the breaking of new ground in literary study and, especially in the work of Lewis Mumford in the 1920s, in the study of the tangible past in architecture and building. It was under the aegis of this impulse to invent, to remake, to discover and forge alternatives to the lame and pallid and defunct culture of their fathers that Brooklyn Bridge appeared in the 1920s as a survival, a *historic* monument, a link with valuable cultural forces of the past. Crane's use of the bridge as in part a scaffolding for a reconstruction of the cultural past, a retelling of American history, falls properly under the heading of Brooks' "usable past." Part of the attention to Brooklyn Bridge in the period derives from this collective project of discovery, invention, and reconstruction.

But describing it in this way, as invention and revision, we make the project seem too calculating, too programmatic; we miss its urgency and inner sense of need. To look at Brooklyn Bridge and to see it as a monument of industrial heroism and creativity is one thing; to walk across the bridge and take possession of it in a radically subjective way, the way of the classic moment, is another. Is there a continuity of need between the two ways?

Consider in Waldo Frank's novel of 1917, *The Unwelcome Man*, the first instance in literature of the classic moment:

> Before him swept the bridge. He felt that every cable of the web-like maze was vibrant with stress and strain. With these things he was alone. Yet he felt no insecurity, such as the crowds inspired. Beyond, through the net-work of steel, huddled Brooklyn. And below his very feet, tumbled together as if some giant had tipped the city eastward and sent all the houses pell-mell toward the down-tilted corner, lay the wharves and slums of Manhattan. It seemed to Quincy that he was being caught upon a monstrous swing and swept with its pulsed lilt above the grovelling life of the metropolis. Suddenly, the fancy flashed upon him that from his perch of shivering steel the power should indeed come to poise and judge the swarm above which he rocked. The bridge that reeled beyond him seemed

> an arbiter. It bound the city. It must know the city's soul since it was
> so close to the city's breath. In its throbbing cables there must be a
> message. In its lacings and filigrees of steel, there must be subtle
> words! . . .[17]

What are the novel elements here? The hero is alone on the bridge, in a
solitude more consoling than the isolation of the city crowds. The bridge
permits him to enact his true condition: alone, separate from the shabby
and groveling city, poised above, prepared for an access of power lost to
him on the streets, in the crowds. The bridge is an arbiter; it stands
above; it binds; it judges. And it has a message, a word, which the hero
almost hears.

But he rejects the bridge's demanding message, and in the passage that
follows he descends the bridge's "unattainable pathway," moves in a
panic through the narrow streets, in an effort to "escape the omnipresent
Bridge." "Crowds jostled him; cars clashed; machines were braying, shut-
tling. The taste of New York was bitter on his lips." "Under the Bridge
itself he went—looming above him like a curse." Frank made clear the
cause of his hero's malaise: he could not face the need to struggle for
personal liberation, to find a perspective in which to reconcile the ugliness of the manifest city with the beauty of its wholeness and its potential-
ity. The bridge offers such a perspective: not merely as a physical platform
but as a message, a word.

Frank described his hero as a victim of "the culture of industrialism,"
and Brooks saw the novel as proof of John Stuart Mill's prediction that
industrialism would lead to "an appalling deficiency of human prefer-
ences." In the same year Brooks published an essay in *The Seven Arts*
called "The Culture of Industrialism," an essay which, like Frank's novel,
sheds light on the inner needs of the quest for a "usable past." "The world
over," he wrote, "the industrial process has devitalized men and produced a poor quality of human nature." Industrialism has ruptured the
fabric of life; it has cut off sources of nourishment from traditional culture,
and has demeaned the orthodox "high" culture by turning it over to "the
prig and the aesthete." In Europe at least some vestige of the traditional
culture remains, and "a long line of great rebels"—Nietzsche, Renan,
Morris, Rodin, Marx, Mill—have kept it alive by reacting "violently"
against the "desiccating influences" of industrialism. "They have made it
impossible for men to forget the degradation of society and the poverty of
their lives and built a bridge between the greatness of the few in the past
and the greatness of the man, perhaps, in the future."[18] While here in
America, "our disbelief in experience, our habitual repression of the
creative instinct with its consequent overstimulation of the possessive
instinct, has made it impossible for us to take advantage of the treasure
our own life has yielded." "The real work of criticism in this country,"

Brooks continues, is "to begin *low*," to find and accept "our own lowest common denominator." Then, he concludes in another image suggesting a bridge, a joining of forces around a vital center:

> As soon as the foundations of our life have been reconstructed and made solid on the basis of our own experience, all these extraneous, ill-regulated forces will rally about their newly found center; they will fit in, each where it belongs, contributing to the essential architecture of our life. Then, and only then, shall we cease to be a blind, selfish, disorderly people; we shall become a luminous people, dwelling in the light and sharing our light.[19]

"O THOU STEELED COGNIZANCE"

And Crane, in the final walk, the crossing-into-light that concludes *The Bridge:*

> And on, obliquely up bright carrier bars
> New octaves trestle the twin monoliths
> Beyond whose frosted capes the moon bequeaths
> Two worlds of sleep (O arching strands of song!)—
> Onward and up the crystal-flooded aisle
> White tempest nets file upward, upward ring
> With silver terraces the humming spars,
> The loft of vision, palladium helm of stars.

The concluding poem, Crane had written to his patron, Otto Kahn, in 1926, would be "a sweeping dithyramb in which the Bridge becomes the symbol of consciousness spanning time and space."[20] And a year later, ten years after Brooks' call for a new structure of experience, a "newly found center," again to Otto Kahn, regarding the kind of "history" the poem will be: "What I am after is an assimilation of this experience [American history], a more organic panorama, showing the continuous and living evidence of the past in the inmost vital substance of the present."[21] What he is after is "usable past," an act of *bridging* past and present in a more vital connection than orthodox histories provide.

The coincidence of the figure or trope of bridging in Crane and Brooks is not remarkable: it is a common rhetorical figure for transcendence through connection. Crane's writings, his poetry and prose, are rife with such crossings. But the coincidence of *need*, the sense of inner division that needs healing, especially a division, a breach that feels both personal and cultural at once: so personal and so cultural that the solution to the problem of "America" appears as the form of the solution to the problem of *being:* this is worth remarking as a deep feature of the age, or of the life of its estranged and unhappy artists and intellectuals. Especially for Crane, a personal divided consciousness—the "curse of sundered parentage"—became the scene for a symbolic action, a bridging, of cultural consequence. The poem would perform his "essential architecture" doubly or trebly: it would reconnect the American present to the American past in a new, "vital" way; it would reconnect the poet to his personal experience; and it would, by the fusion of these two goals, build a bridge between the poet and his people: between poetry as such and "America." And this theory of multiple connection descends into Crane's poetics, into the very performance and "synergies" of his poetic language.

Among the meanings of Crane's bridge, then, is the rhetorical trope of "bridging," the *act* of crossing over. A bridge crosses and unites; it mediates, like the priestly function in the word *pontiff:* mediates between here and there, now and to come. In this function alone, apart from its concreteness as Brooklyn Bridge, the bridge provides fusion, transcendence, healing. It promises connection: simultaneously to earth, here-and-now, and to a realm beyond, a connection that transforms the here-and-now itself into a meaningful pattern of details. In its immediacy as *at once* bound and unbound, it promises new power of experience.

"History and fact, location, etc.," Crane wrote to Gorham Munson in 1923, "all have to be transfigured into abstract form that would almost function independently of its subject matter."[22] Transfiguration is a phase of the bridging act, and the achievement of the "abstract form"—the form of bridge—is its culmination, for now the transcending act can perform its ultimate work: making it possible to see and to experience each discrete detail of "history and fact" as connected to all others, as constituting one totality, which can be named Bridge, and which in its oneness can be named also as One, Thou steeled Cognizance, Deity's glittering Pledge: As though a god were issue of the strings. . . .

But the bridge is also Brooklyn Bridge, a shuttle between two mundane places, an instrument, as Crane put it in a famous despairing letter to Waldo Frank in 1926, of "shorter hours, quicker lunches, behaviorism and toothpicks."[23] Can such a bridge, a crude servant of capitalism, also serve the bridging function, the crossing over that the poet needs? Crane stalled in the making of his poem when this question occurred to him. And the completed poem, with its final apparent apotheosis of the bridge, has troubled many readers as embodying an aesthetic flaw: a confusion of the real bridge, in its multiplicity of function, with the imaginary bridge of transcendence. Does it matter, it is asked, that the bridge of the poem is Brooklyn Bridge? Are we not concerned after all with the revisionary powers and practices of the imagination, not with the bridge of granite and steel, but the bridge of metaphor: not with Roebling's bridge but with Hart's?

The question turns on whether Hart's bridge is a symbol, or a symbolic act: a thing or an event. Consider the striking coincidence between Crane's bridge and Stella's. Some scholars have asked whether Stella's canvases, the *Brooklyn Bridge* of 1917–18 and the bridge panel of *New York Interpreted*, of 1922 might not have influenced Crane. Certainly Crane himself was taken with the coincidence of "sentiments" when he wrote to Stella in 1929, and he thought to include one of the paintings (exactly which one remains unclear) as frontispiece to the Black Sun edition of *The Bridge*. The plan collapsed, apparently for technical reasons, and the poem appeared in 1930 with three tactfully placed photographs by Crane's friend Walker Evans.

The question whether the painter's vision has priority to the poet's must now take into account the contribution of the photographer to the poem. Is the poet's bridge a symbol in the sense of an icon, a physical "shrine," as Stella described his first painting, a symbolic "meeting point of all forces arising in a superb assertion of their powers, in APOTHEOSIS?" It is noteworthy that John Marin considered Stella's painting excessively formalistic: having no more relation with the actual bridge "than if he had put up some street cables and things in his studio—painted a rather beautiful thing and called it the 'Bridge.' "[24] Marin misses the *experience* of the bridge, precisely what he himself attempted to capture and convey in his *The Red Sun, Brooklyn Bridge*, of 1922. Stella's paintings, in fact, in their stylization project an idea of bridge linked only by iconic association to the specific Brooklyn Bridge. Partly he calls up associations with popular imagery of the bridge. Although the compositions are dynamic, the geometric formality of the icon freezes the bridge into a static image of towers, arches, and cables. The action of the paintings is not so much *crossing* as *recognizing*, and in the recognition, enhancing the actual bridge with heroic energies, *raising* the bridge above the common experience of it. We look *up* to Stella's bridge, as a figurative projection and elevation of the familiar bridge.

Crane, too, in his program for the poem, speaks of the bridge as a "climax," a "symbol of our constructive future, our unique identity, in which is included also our scientific hopes and achievements of the future." Much of the worry critics have displayed toward the poem comes from taking this early (1923) statement too literally. In fact the bridge does not appear anywhere in the poem as a symbol of this sort, a sign which stands for the abstraction "America." Apart from the transfiguration of details of the bridge (through Crane's "logic of metaphor") into elements of the poem's governing "abstract form"—the curve becomes a "curveship," for example, and the span of steel a "cognizance,"—the bridge always appears in its aspect as Brooklyn Bridge: a shuttle for traffic ("Again the traffic lights that skim thy swift/ Unfractioned idiom . . ."), a parapet for bedlamites, a pier under which the poet waits in the bridge's shadow, a walkway ("I started walking home across the Bridge") from which the poet has a vision of clipper ships—and on which he walks his final walk and crossing into a vision of Oneness that *may* be "Cathay." And Evans' photographs reinforce and elaborate the implications of this literalness of Brooklyn Bridge in the poem.

At the time Evans lived near Crane on Brooklyn Heights, and also knew the bridge as a walker. Presumably at Crane's behest or encouragement, tacit or otherwise, Evans took along a hand camera on one or two of his strolls, and although he published only three of the images in the Black Sun edition, and another (very close to the first Black Sun image) as frontispiece to the first American edition (Boni & Livright, 1930), the entire group (at least those images that survive) make up an ensemble with a consistent inner conception. First, they represent an original photographic representation of the bridge, breaking decisively from the lateral or heroic or iconic views of earlier serious photographers like Coburn or the clichés of commercial views. The view from beneath, of the dark underside of the bridge's floor pinned against the sky, was entirely novel, with no predecessors at all in the popular or naive iconology of the bridge. But the originality of the group lies not only in composition. The bridge here is viewed freshly, in a series of images, as the experience of a specific eye; the vision of each print is the vision of all: a visual possession of the bridge as someone's—a walker's—palpable experience.

The three images accompanying the poem suggest a remarkable coincidence of vision. The first, which faces the opening lines of "Proem," shows the bridge from underneath; the second, dead midway during the poem, faces the lines in "Cutty Sark" in which the poet, walking home across the bridge, envisions a fleet of sailing ships: the exquisite framing of coal barges and tugboat in the photograph works as counterpoint to the poet's fantasy: grounding it in the literal (though aesthetically transformed) experience recorded in the photograph. The final image faces the concluding lines of "Atlantis," where the poet crosses and asks of the transfigured towers and cables and meshwork, "Is it Cathay?" The swinging antiphonal whispers of the last line awaken the lines of the photograph, and together, words and image, ground the question in the living, kinetic experience of crossing the bridge. The poem is then framed by two images *of* the bridge, and punctuated at mid-point by an image *from* the bridge. We begin and conclude with Brooklyn Bridge: beginning low, under its piers, and concluding high, eye-crossing amidst the pattern of cables, tower, and stays on the walkway.[25]

The photographs achieve what Stella's paintings would not: they mediate, or connect, or *bridge* the poem to the real bridge. They keep before us shifting images of that bridge as the poet's object in the poem—as what he is aware of. Moreover, taken as rhetoric, far more understatedly than Stella's images do, they connect the reader's experience of a real bridge, a specific bridge, with the bridge and the bridging of the poem. They assist the communciation of the poem—and reveal what kind of communication Crane wished the poem to achieve.

> And Thee, across the harbor, silver-paced
> As though the sun took step of thee, yet left
> Some motion ever unspent in thy stride,—
> Implicitly thy freedom staying thee!

Here, in the opening view of the bridge, it lies across the harbor, an object of the poet's vision. It is external to him, yet focuses his attention. As an object in "Proem" it reveals itself as possessing a place, a set of connections and relations: to the city, the cinema, office buildings, Wall Street, traffic. Yet it looms above just as it remains connected, and bespeaks a pledge, a promise, that its "curveship" might "lend a myth to God." The curveship and the promise were already prefigured in the "inviolate curve" of the seagull's wings in stanza 1 (but they flicker and are gone), and especially in the progress of the sun crossing the diagonal stays seeming to *take step* of the bridge, to climb its ascending cables. The motion of sun, free yet restrained by the form of the bridge—bound yet unbound—prefigures the poet's own walk in the concluding section of the poem.

The motion, the walk, the crossing into a visionary vision: these compel the recognition that the bridge is not merely an object, but also a subject, a Thee. Possessed by the kinetic eye and thus transfigured into a personal event, animated by the poet's eye-crossing, it performs the act of bestowing upon the poet what he most urgently needs: the kind of centrality that will make his recovery of experience—personal and historical experience—possible. The pledge of the bridge is not simply (or not at all) to yield *itself* to the properly devout poet: it promises, in short, a "usable past," and in the fullest, deepest, life-giving sense of the word, it promises "culture."

Simultaneously springing from a ground and joining, the bridge as symbolic act is the very act of culture itself, as Crane and his colleagues understood the term: culture not as a set of objects but culture as an ongoing process of mergings, makings, and crossings toward a totality. The bridge offers what Crane in his programmatic statement of 1924–25, "General Aims and Theories," called "an absolute experience, an experience that will engross the total faculties of the spectator." Such totalizing endows the spectator with centrality: he is the focal point, the organizing center of his own experience. Nothing is superfluous, nothing is missing: "Our imagination is unable to suggest a further detail consistent with the design of the aesthetic whole."

"And I have been able to give freedom and life which was acknowledged in the ecstasy of walking hand in hand across the most beautiful bridge of the world," Crane wrote in 1924, about crossing the bridge with a lover, "the cables enclosing us and pulling us upward in such a dance as I have never walked and never can walk with another."[26]

> As soon as the foundations of our life have been reconstructed and made solid on the basis of our own experience, all these extraneous, ill-regulated forces will rally about their newly found center; they will fit in, each where it belongs, contributing to the essential architecture of our life. Then, and only then, shall we cease to be a blind, selfish, disorderly people; we shall become a luminous people, dwelling in the light and sharing our light.

The evangelical, apocalyptic accents of Brooks' bridging vision come to a fruition in Crane's poem. The poem is not "about" Brooklyn Bridge. It translates the bridge into culture, into the simultaneous possession of world and self the vision of which served Crane and his fellow artists as their high alternative to American "normalcy." The vision still lives in the poem, even if the anticipated luminosity (or even the hope of it) has long since dimmed in the culture: lives not only as a vestige of what historians have called the first decade of our own times, but perhaps also as an inducement. As excessive, exaggerated, and, in their own way, blind to the real possibilities of their everyday culture as Crane and others may have been, they were the first in our era to understand that re-vision in the light of a universal idea (their "America") was the central condition for a living culture. Insofar as we concern ourselves not only with their vision but with what they failed to see, their enterprise might yet succeed as our own "usable past."

NOTES

1. These terms are prominent in Johan Huizinga's observations, in *America: A Dutch Historian's Vision, from Afar and Near* (New York, 1972). I have also profited a great deal from the discussion of technological and economic changes in the 1920s in Martin J. Sklar, "On the Proletarian Revolution and the End of Political-Economic Society," *Radical America* 3, no. 3 (May-June 1969):1–41.

2. Frederick Hoffman, *The Twenties* (New York, 1955), pp. 163–239.

3. See Lewis Mumford, "Prelude to the Present," in *Interpretations and Forecasts, 1922–1972* (New York, 1973), pp. 110–21. Also, Alan Trachtenberg, ed., *Critics of Culture* (New York, 1976).

4. Huizinga, *America*, p. 283.

5. Alan Trachtenberg, *Brooklyn Bridge: Fact and Symbol* (New York, 1965), surveys much of the relevant material.

6. Quoted in Irma Jaffe, *Joseph Stella* (New York, 1970), p. 58.

7. Quoted in Brom Weber, *Hart Crane* (New York, 1948), p. 425.

8. Brom Weber, ed., *The Complete Poems and Selected Letters and Prose of Hart Crane* (New York, 1966), p. 114.

9. Lewis Mumford, *Sticks and Stones* (New York, 1924), pp. 115–16.

10. Ibid.

11. Quoted in Trachtenberg, *Brooklyn Bridge*, p. 74.

12. Ibid., p. 79.

13. Ernest Poole, *The Harbor* (New York, 1915), p. 193.

14. Dorothy Landers Beall, *The Bridge and Other Poems* (New York, 1913), pp. 13–131.

15. Quoted in Sheldon Reich, *John Marin: A Stylistic Analysis and Catalogue Raisonné* (University of Arizona Press, 1970), pp. 54–55.

16. Clair Sprague, ed., *Van Wyck Brooks: The Early Years* (New York, 1968), p. 223.

17. Waldo Frank, *The Unwelcome Man* (New York, 1917), pp. 167–69.

18. Sprague, ed., *Van Wyck Brooks*, p. 199.

19. Ibid., p. 202.

20. Brom Weber, ed., *The Letters of Hart Crane* (New York, 1952), p. 241.

21. Ibid., p. 305.

22. Ibid., p. 124.

23. Ibid., p. 261.

24. Reich, *John Marin*, p. 148.

25. For an interesting discussion of the function of the Evans photographs, see Gordon K. Grigsby, "Photographs in the First Edition of *The Bridge*," *Texas Studies in Language and Literature* 4(1962):4–11. A more general, and suggestive, essay on the appeal of photography to Crane, is F. Richard Thomas, "Hart Crane, Alfred Stieglitz, and Camera Photography," *Centennial Review*, 1977, pp. 294–309.

26. Weber, ed., *Letters*, p. 181.

Some Varieties of Howells' Religious Experience

George Arms

In 1875, the year of Henry Ward Beecher's adultery trial, Howells jestingly complained to an associate in the *Atlantic Monthly* office that someone was extracting the part of the New York *Tribune* which reported that titillating event. He went on, "and so I know nothing about the Beecher. I cannot remain ignorant of this great moral spectacle, and edit the Atlantic properly."[1] Here perhaps we have a clue to a cause of Howells' interest in religion that has been too much neglected and is of utmost importance. As novelist and editor, Howells regarded religion as central in the American experience of his time. That he also felt religion personally and constantly is true, but in the several excellent studies of Howells' use of religion in his literature and life, it seems to me that a committed but objective curiosity, not unlike that of William James in his *Varieties of Religious Experience*, has been overlooked.

Of these studies, to which I am much indebted in this essay, that of Hannah Graham Belcher in 1943 comes first. Nine years later Arnold B. Fox made a somewhat wider exploration with greater emphasis on what he regarded as the troubled agnosticism of "Howells as a Religious Critic." Frequently Edwin H. Cady in his two-volume biography (1956, 1958) made extensive comment on Howells' religious views. A year after the second volume, Clara and Rudolf Kirk produced the most specific and detailed essay on a significant religious connection, "Howells and the Church of the Carpenter." Then after a decade Edward Wagenknecht in *William Dean Howells: The Friendly Eye* (1969) wrote an extended survey, emphasizing the nonskeptical aspects; and in the same year in *The Darkened Sky* John T. Frederick devoted one of his six chapters to Howells, again surveying widely but with greater concern for the belief in immortality.[2] As I have said, these studies are excellent, yet all neglect the impetus I have suggested, and several (without quite saying so) suggest the exasperation with Howells voiced by the elder Henry James to Emerson: "Oh you man without a handle!"[3]

Born the son of Swedenborgian parents in 1837, even at Martins Ferry, Ohio, Howells achieved chronological and ideational connection with both Emerson and James. The date was a year after *Nature*, much indebted to Swedenborg, appeared, and the same year James left Princeton Seminary after a series of spiritual disappointments that were to lead him to Swedenborg. For several reasons this was a good start for an author whose religious views present a panorama of American religious thought in the nineteenth and early twentieth century—a panorama that leaves out a few main objects, yet on the whole gives as full a sweep of the theological landscape as is possible for one person.[4] Certainly the more than thirty novels show a constant intermingling of literature and religion. "What do you think of my preaching yesterday in the church here?" Howells wrote his wife in 1909 from Kittery Point. "Their 'supply' didn't come and the crowd got round and pleaded with me so to speak or read, that I raced over to the Barnbury [his study], got the Trav. from Alturia, and gave 'em a good dose of socialism."[5]

This was Howells' only appearance in the pulpit, and it would seem to place him at a distance from the heavenly arcana of Emanuel Swedenborg, with their mystical sense of man's redemption through efforts that are his own yet must be passive through infusion by godhead, and with their detailed revelation of life after death. Certainly it is a good distance from the beliefs of the father, who had conducted a magazine in defense of Swedenborgianism and written two pamphlets about it. Yet the acceptance of dogma was regarded by the son as subject to the father's nature:

> It was easy for him, whose being was in some sort a dream of Love and good will, to conceive all tangible and visible creation as an adumbration of spiritual reality; to accept revelation as the mask of interior meanings; to regard the soul as its own keeper, and the sovereign chooser of heaven or hell, but always master of the greatest happiness possible to it. To his essential meekness and unselfishness it was natural that he should think of himself as nothing in himself, and only something from moment to moment through influx from the Lord.[6]

Yet as the son later wrote: "The question of salvation was far below that of the annexation of Texas, or the ensuing war against Mexico, in his regard. . . ."[7]

By this time Howells' own Swedenborgianism had even lower priority. Terms and concepts that he picked up from regular Sunday readings from Swedenborg he used frequently, though more in his correspondence than in his published writing. To Swedenborgian literary men he was drawn: Hjalmar Boyesen, Howard Pyle, Henry James the son, and Henry James the father. Admiring the father as he did, he was forced to remark of one of his works that James had written *The Secret of Swedenborg* and kept it; but in his *Atlantic* review—one of the few reviews Howells did there on religious works—he paid tribute to it, emphasizing particularly the equality of men before divine love and the superiority of love to law.[8] Indeed the moral tone—love, goodwill, self-mastery, unselfishness—and not the creed were Howells' heritage from his own father's religion. Still, Howells persisted in his reading of Swedenborg, as in 1868 after the death of his mother ("I long to have the spiritual world described over and over again and ever so minutely"), and in 1871–72 when he and his wife suspended their theological readings since "the subject had grown a little too exciting." On that occasion he announced his disappointment that Swedenborg "makes a certain belief the condition of entering the kingdom of heaven," while from his father he had inferred that the test was to do "right from a love of doing right."[9] All the same, he remained a younger intimate of Henry James, Sr., and could see the fun of James's remarking on another Swedenborgian's book on *Animals in Heaven* that James wished the author "was among them."[10] Finally, as associated with a small but influential sect, Howells learned tolerance of much religious belief, a tolerance encouraged directly by his father, who further allowed his children to attend the established churches of the community.[11]

"It seems to me," Howells wrote again of his father, "that I can render him intelligible by saying that while my very religious-minded grandfather expected and humbly if fervently hoped to reach a heaven beyond this world by means of prayers and hymns and revivals and conversions, my not less religious-minded father lived for a heaven on earth in his beloved and loving home: a heaven of poetry and humor, and good-will and right thinking." The paternal grandfather was a Methodist, and the Deans (the mother's family) were Methodists too. But of this denomination Howells recorded that "I cannot suppose that there was much common ground between [my mother's family] and my grandfather's family except in their common Methodism."[12] Probably the word "common" looked two ways: for this is a part of the theological panorama that our author does not present, ignoring mostly except for occasional witticisms the larger evangelical groups. As an editor he felt the indiscriminate pressure of all sorts of protestants when he rejected Mark Twain's "Some Learned Fables for Good Old Boys and Girls" for the *Atlantic*: ". . . a little fable like yours wouldn't leave a single Presbyterian, Baptist, Unitarian, Episcopalian, Methodist or Millerite *paying* subscriber. . . . Send your fable to some truly pious concern like Scribner or Harper, and they'll extract it into all the hymn-books. But it would ruin *us*."[13] However, in one of his several bouts of churchgoing, Howells reported of a

Methodist chapel meeting that he "heard more bad grammar and good religious feeling than I supposed to exist in Cambridge."[14]

The grandfather had been a Quaker before his conversion to Methodism, a choice that he apparently made at the division in the late 1820s that produced the Hicksite and orthodox branches. Even though the grandfather became a Methodist and the father a Swedenborgian, the influence of the Friends seems to have remained in the family. The eschewing of a formal creed, the strictness of a moral code, the witness of the Inner Light, and the humanitarian impulses are all so thoroughly ingrained in Howells that their early presence is strongly suggested.

Elements of Swedenborg and George Fox are also historically present in New England Transcendentalism; and for this religion, as we may rightly call it, they prepared Howells both when as a boy he met it in the Western Reserve region and as an adult during his Cambridge residence. True, he reached New England after the flowering of both its literature and idealism; yet at least toward the aftermath of Transcendentalism, his Swedenborgian and Quaker background brought him close. Thus Belcher in her examination of Howells' religious opinions has spoken of his optimistic intuitionalism, his assumption of a benevolent God, of a purposeful universe, of the moral law, and of the infinite capacities of man.[15] Add to this self-reliance, which, with all his personal uncertainties, Howells at least liked to think he had, and you have the standard repertoire of transcendental belief in its romantic mode. As with the Transcendentalists, too, Howells showed an impatience with official Unitarianism ("the pale Unitarian worship" he once wrote):[16] and though of the later generation he was able to escape the soft blandishments of such later developments as Christian Science—"the illiterate twaddle of Mrs. Eddy's book" he remarked in his memoir of Mark Twain.[17] But the challenge of the Social Gospel he accepted, when it developed in the 1880s and 1890s, associating himself closely with such latter-day transcendental reformers as Thomas Wentworth Higginson and Edward Everett Hale.[18]

With this background Howells became a religious Marxist, if not quite Christian Socialist, in the late 1880s, though the impact of Tolstoi directly prepared him for his period of radical economics. As Howells said later, reading Tolstoi had been for him a revelation "somewhat comparable to the old-fashioned religious experience of people converted at revivals."[19] The analogy is borne out by his famous chapter on Tolstoi in *My Literary Passions:* "As much as one merely human being can help another I believe that [Tolstoi] has helped me, he has not influenced me in aesthetics only, but in ethics, too, so that I can never again see life in the way I saw it before I knew him."[20] Speaking of Tolstoi's living as a peasant, Howells raised his voice in exclamation points beyond his usual manner to show how difficult was the acceptance of the kind of life that he felt we should follow:

In that case, how many of us who have great possessions must go
away exceedingly sorrowful! Come, star-eyed Political Economy!
come Sociology, heavenly nymph! . . . Save us, sweet Evolution!
Help, O Nebular Hypothesis! Art, Civilization, Literature, Culture!
is there no escape from our brothers but in becoming more and
more truly their brothers?[21]

From the Swedenborgians, the Quakers, the Transcendentalists, perhaps even the Methodists, Howells had seen glimpses of a life which
would regard the moral code of Christ as a sufficient guide. But Tolstoi
first gave him a full emotional sense of it: "Tolstoy gave me heart to hope
that the world may yet be made over in the image of Him who died for
it. . . ."[22] Along with this deep recognition of the force of Tolstoi ("Tolstoi
tells us simply to live as Christ bade us. . . . There's no more of it, but
Heaven knows that's enough, and hard enough"),[23] there are particulars
all reinforcing earlier religious ideals: the renunciation of self (cf. the
Swedenborgian vastation), abhorrence of violence (cf. Quaker pacifism),
God-given equality (cf. Transcendentalism's brotherhood within the over-
soul). Thus, though Tolstoi only reinforced what Howells had already
recognized, through a power approaching that of religious conversion he
revitalized those ideals. From Tolstoi, Howells went on to a full or partial
acceptance of the religious Marxism of Laurence Gronlund. Actively he
was brought to a defense of the Chicago anarchists, the support of labor in
the strikes of the late 1880s and early 1890s, and opposition at the turn of
the century to America's imperialistic ventures. In literature many of his
novels from 1887 to 1894 became examinations of the social and economic
scene. Though Tolstoi did not bring Howells to the cobbler's bench,
there was even a moment when "Elinor and I both no longer care for the
world's life, and would like to be settled somewhere very humbly and
simply, where we could be socially identified with the principles of progress and sympathy for the struggling mass."[24]

Ironically, in this period of religious reform, Howells was most bitter
toward organized Christianity, even when he came closest to an acceptance of Christ as more than an ethical teacher. Though he favored the
platform of the Christian Socialists he would not join them, for they "have
loaded up with the creed of the church, the very terms of which revolt
me."[25] The typical church he scorned because of its strict class lines and
its satisfaction with the status quo. In *A Traveler from Altruria* the minister is forced to confess to his own shame that there is not a single laborer
in his congregation, and in the same novel it is suggested that if America
had a national church there would be some sort of affirmation of economic
conditions in the creed.[26] Reviewing Richard T. Ely's *Social Aspects of
Christianity* a few years earlier, Howells had concurred in the indictment
of the church for its attitude toward the working class.[27]

As Tolstoi attached a mystical though not theological import to the crucifixion, Howells would also have seemed to. One of the best known passages on the subject occurs late in *A Hazard of New Fortunes*, when March and his wife discuss the death in a strike of the Christ-like Conrad. First, Mrs. March "in an exultation" makes her comment, "he suffered for the sins of others." To this March gives somewhat grudging assent, but within the next page he repeats her phrase and goes on, "Isabel, we can't throw aside that old doctrine of the Atonement yet," and in his theological enthusiasm expands even more upon his wife's view. Yet the passage ends with such easy banter that only naive readers can accept it as an implied or open statement by the author.[28]

Whatever view one takes of this passage, it is well to remember that it was written soon after the death of Howells' oldest daughter in 1889, an event that brought home poignantly the problem of personal immortality. It remained with him in a series of poems that were published in the intervening years, and was then resolved in the religion of the citizens of his ideal commonwealth. The visitor from Altruria says:

> When one dies, we grieve, but not as those without hope. . . . the presence of the risen Christ in our daily lives is our assurance that no one ceases to be, and that we shall see our dead again. I cannot explain this to you; I can only affirm it.

Thus the religion of Altruria is distinctively Christian, with an implicit recognition of the atonement and resurrection, a position which Howells himself recognized through his interest in Tolstoi's attempt to realize again the early Christian church in its communistic stage. Still, the Altrurians practice a nondogmatic Christianity. As the Altrurian explains: "We have several forms of ritual, but no form of creed, and our religious differences may be said to be aesthetic and temperamental rather than theologic and essential."[29]

Just after Howells made his closest approach to Christianity he also showed some concern with spiritualism. Evidently he followed the proceedings of the Society for Psychical Research with some closeness, though perhaps he was most aware of the Society through the intermediary writings of William James.[30] We have at any rate two collections of short stories that touch upon this, *Questionable Shapes* (1903) and *Between the Dark and the Daylight* (1907). Though spiritualism is in a wide sense their subject, the approach tends to be psychological, and indeed a good many of the stories are presented through a psychologist named Wanhope.[31] Abnormal phases of consciousness, personification, telepathy, and dream transference are rather more the considerations than communication with the dead. But this latter phase is present in a few of the stories and elsewhere. In a review of Oliver Lodge's *Raymond Lodge* (1917) we find the principal complaint not that of an unbeliever but of a Swedenborgian:

There is, in fact, nothing in the things reported from Raymond
which may not be paralleled and amplified a thousand-fold from the
Memorabilia of Swedenborg. . . . If the reader chooses to dwell in
these wonders, he may, but if he chooses he may learn all their
meaning and the piety they embody and typify, in terms of such
dignity as shall make the gibberish of the ordinary "control" of the
ordinary medium seem an affront to the human intelligence.[32]

So acceptable to Swedenborgians was the review that from its magazine
appearance until the middle 1930s it was reprinted as a pamphlet and
circulated by the New-Church Book Rooms.

Yet to receive a balanced picture of Howells and spiritualism, we should
remember that his early novel *The Undiscovered Country* partly deals
with the impostures of the movement,[33] and should recall the whimsical
skepticism when he describes the people of the Western Reserve: "A
belief in the saving efficacy of spirit phenomena still exists among them,
but not, I fancy, at all in the former measure, when nearly every household had its medium, and the tables that tipped outnumbered the tables
that did not tip."[34] Such a comment also prepares us for another phase of
Howells' religion, skeptical agnosticism,[35] which in spite of the various
faiths I have ascribed to him is the most constant element in his religious
experience. His father's Swedenborgianism had not kept him and his son
from reading together Strauss's *Life of Jesus* in the early Ohio days, and
the two had seemingly agreed upon its rational examination of Christianity.[36] We also recall the shocked surprise Howells expressed to his
father on rereading Swedenborg in 1872. Whatever the extent of Howells'
misunderstanding, it is clear that from his youth Howells had been a
disbeliever in any religion other than at most a vague deism. As Fox has
said, "The young people of Jefferson were largely unreligious, often irreverent, and the existence of God and the immortality of the soul were
openly denied." Or again, "His old skepticism died hard—if, indeed, it
ever died."[37]

Again and again Howells expressed a blackness of despair approaching
that voiced by Mark Twain in the latter years of his life. Still, from
nineteenth-century scientific materialism Howells had emerged as a reader
of his friend John Fiske, whose *Idea of God As Affected by Modern
Knowledge* and other books he had reviewed: "[Fiske] evolved from the
agnosticism of the whole contemporary thinking world a deistic belief,
and established our civilization in the comfort of a credence unknown
outside of his following."[38] But by and large, as we have seen and shall
see, Howells kept the discomfort of doubt.

The discomfort and comfort often appear simultaneously, as in a sentence of a letter to Howard Pyle just after he announced that he believed
in nothing: "I do not always feel sure that I shall live again, but when I

wake at night the room seems dense with spirits."[39] At a memorial meeting Henry Van Dyke pointed in much the same direction: "He did not lose the will to believe, though sometimes he had to fall back on sheer moral loyalty to defend it. He was an inveterate questioner, a temperamental skeptic in the old Greek sense of the word, which means an inquirer, a searcher. But underneath all he was a mystic, unwilling to surrender realities invisible and eternal, or to 'Deny the things past finding out.' "[40]

Van Dyke's use of the phrase "the will to believe" recalls the title of William James's book, to which Howells referred upon one occasion in a short story.[41] Curiously Howells did not review *The Varieties of Religious Experience*, though he makes general reference to it in his "Editor's Easy Chair" paper in June 1903, two months after the short story appeared in *Harper's Monthly*: "We read eagerly whatever Mr. William James writes upon his favorite themes because it similarly abounds in the substance of things hoped for, the evidence of things not seen."[42] James's position in that book—"So I seem doubtless to my audience to be blowing hot and cold, explaining away Christianity, yet defending the more general basis from which I say it proceeds"[43]—appears one congenial with Howells' own attitudes. The only book by William James that he did review was *The Principles of Psychology*, in which he sensed the incipient pragmatism in James at that stage: "The fascination of the quest forever remains, and it is this fascination that Professor James permits his reader to share."[44] And in another letter to Pyle written at the time he was reading *Psychology* for his review, he commented more directly on the religious side: "James is one of the few scientific men who do not seem to snub one's poor humble hopes of a hereafter." Still, after his wife's death in 1910 he acknowledged James's letter of condolence by concluding: "I wish I could believe in a meeting with her, but she believed in none, and how can I?" James might have replied with the instinctive pragmatism that Howells himself had displayed in writing Mark Twain on the death of Susy in 1896: "You are parted from her a little longer, and that's all, and the joint life will go on when you meet on the old terms, but with the horror and pain gone forever. This is the easiest and the most reasonable thing to believe, and it is not to be refused because it is so old and simple."[45]

Did Howells then have a "handle"? Yes, if I am right in proposing that he displays an attitude close to that of James in his *Varieties*—a fascination with religious experience, at times a commitment to "over-beliefs" ("absolutely indispensable," as James called them), and a wariness concerning both belief and agnosticism.[46] It is the fascination and wariness I would stress. When Howells heard that the Unitarian Higginson was building a house in Cambridge between those of a Roman Catholic priest and a professor at the Episcopal Theological School, he asked, "What religion will you be of, with that 'environment'?"[47] Perhaps he answered the question more than twenty years later in his description of the church of a Unitarian minister (who as much as anyone solves the family's problems) in *The Kentons* as "that pied flock, where every shade and dapple of doubt, from heterodox Jew to agnostic Christian, foregathered, as it had been said, in the misgiving of a blessed immortality."[48] At his best, Howells does what he praised in Ibsen, resisting "the conventional acceptations by which men live on easy terms with themselves."[49]

Though I do not think that such an emphasis will make a revolutionary difference in our criticism of Howells' novels with religious dimensions, it may cause some shifts in shadings. For example, the sermon on complicity at the end of *The Minister's Charge* has generally seemed to me over-emphasized as the author's own commentary on the action of the novel and on the more generalized human situation.[50] It is true that it has close parallels with Howells' introduction to *Sebastopol*, that to Tolstoi more than anyone else Howells made a commitment, and that the concept of complicity pervades Howells' fiction.[51] But within the novel the sermon is suggested by the journalist Evans as a newspaper feature and undergoes a subtle transformation when delivered by Sewell.[52] The undercutting at the end by Bromfield Corey and Mrs. Sewell has its point, and whether Miss Vane weeps for the aesthetics or the ethics I'm not sure. Their comments have been so much neglected that I repeat them here. COREY: "I didn't know that they had translated it Barker [the name of the minister's charge] in the revised version." MISS VANE: "Do you think I threw away my chance?" MRS. SEWELL: "Well, David, I hope you haven't preached away all your truth and righteousness."

A second example may emerge from the many interpretations of *The Leatherwood God*, some of which approach the novel in terms of Jamesian pragmatism, most notably that of William McMurray.[53] All, I believe, are subject to some revision in view of Eugene H. Pattison's intensive studies of the manuscript revisions and the historical source.[54]

My own interest, stimulated by Pattison's work, arises from Howells' overt connection of the novel with William James. On 15 August 1913 he wrote to James's son that he was reading the book by his father and would be at fault if he did not find the meaning and moral of his own novel (then incomplete) in its commonsense psychology.[55] Because it was the most recent of William James's three posthumous books and because it uses the phrase "common sense" twenty-four times, almost certainly the volume James's son gave Howells was the fascinating *Essays in Radical Empiricism*, a work regarded by many philosophers as James's most important and influential. Unless we discover a marked copy by Howells, it will be hard to guess which passages affected him most.[56] I would locate them generally in the essay on "The World of Pure Experience" and tentatively select this one as getting close to the essence of *The Leatherwood God:*

There is no other *nature*, no other whatness than this absence of break and this sense of continuity in that most intimate of all conjunctive relations, the passing of one experience into another when they belong to the same self. . . . Practically to experience one's personal continuum in this living way is to know the originals of the ideas of continuity and of sameness, to know what the words stand for concretely, to own all that they can ever mean.

But others may have their own choices and they may well be better. Many would agree that in defining radical empiricism as "essentially a mosaic philosophy, a philosophy of plural facts," James would have appealed to Howells both with his old voice and his new one.[57]

NOTES

1. George Arms, et al. eds., *W. D. Howells: Selected Letters* (Boston, 1979), 2:96. Hereafter cited as *Selected Letters*.

2. Hannah Graham Belcher (Blackstock), "Howells's Opinions on the Religious Conflicts of His Age As Exhibited in Magazine Articles," *American Literature* 15(November 1943): 262–78; Arnold B. Fox, "Howells as a Religious Critic," *New England Quarterly* 25(June 1952):199–216; Edwin H. Cady, *The Road to Realism* (Syracuse, 1956) and *The Realist at War* (Syracuse, 1958); Clara Kirk and Rudolf Kirk, "Howells and the Church of the Carpenter," *New England Quarterly* 32(June 1959):185–206; Edward Wagenknecht, *William Dean Howells: The Friendly Eye* (New York, 1969), pp. 235–59; John T. Frederick, *The Darkened Sky* (Notre Dame, Ind., 1969), pp. 177–228.

3. Ralph B. Perry, *The Thought and Character of William James* (Boston, 1935), 1:51.

4. Notably Howells neglected the Catholic and Jewish traditions, though see Frederick, *Darkened Sky*, pp. 189–90, et passim, on the former and Kermit Vanderbilt, *The Achievement of William Dean Howells* (Princeton, 1968), pp. 116–26, 188–89, et passim, and George Monteiro, *New England Quarterly* 50(September 1977):515–16, on the latter.

5. Mildred Howells, ed., *Life in Letters of William Dean Howells* (New York, 1928), 2:266. Since her text has been regularized, when available, photocopies of manuscript letters are used. Hereafter cited as *Life in Letters*.

6. William Dean Howells, "Introduction" to William C. Howells, *Recollections of Life in Ohio* (Cincinnati, 1895), p. vi.

7. William Dean Howells, *Years of My Youth*, ed. David J. Nordloh (1916; CEAA ed. Bloomington, Ind., 1975), p. 19.

8. Cady, *The Road to Realism*, p. 150; *Atlantic* 24(December 1869):762–63.

9. *Selected Letters*, 1:304, 390.

10. *Selected Letters*, 2:88. See also Kenneth S. Lynn, *William Dean Howells: An American Life* (New York, 1971), pp. 188–89, for a delightful account of the whole relationship.

11. Howells, *Years of My Youth*, p. 22.

12. Ibid., pp. 84, 14.

13. *Selected Letters*, 2:69.

14. Quoted in Wagenknecht, *William Dean Howells*, p. 241.

15. Belcher, "Howells's Opinions on the Religious Conflicts of His Age," p. 265.

16. William Dean Howells, *The Lady of the Aroostook* (Boston, 1879), p. 93.

17. William Dean Howells, *My Mark Twain* (1916) in *Literary Friends and Acquaintance*, eds. David F. Hiatt and Edwin H. Cady (CEAA ed. Bloomington, Ind., 1968), p. 310.

18. Kirk and Kirk, "Howells and the Church of the Carpenter," pp. 188–91.

19. William Dean Howells, *North American Review* (December 1908), reprinted in *W. D. Howells as Critic*, ed. Edwin H. Cady (London, 1973), p. 461. On the whole subject see Louis J. Budd, "William Dean Howells' Debt to Tolstoy," *American Slavic and East European Review* 9(December 1950):292–301.

20. William Dean Howells, *My Literary Passions* (New York, 1895), p. 250.

21. William Dean Howells, *Harper's Monthly*, 75(July 1887):316.

22. Howells, *My Literary Passions*, p. 251.

23. Quoted by Budd, "William Dean Howells' Debt to Tolstoy," p. 295.

24. *Life in Letters*, 1:404.

25. Ibid., 2:3.

26. William Dean Howells, *A Traveler from Altruria* (1894) in *The Altrurian Romances*, eds. Clara and Rudolf Kirk et al. (CEAA ed. Bloomington, Ind., 1968), pp. 126, 64.

27. William Dean Howells, *Harper's Monthly* 80(February 1890):484–85.

28. William Dean Howells, *A Hazard of New Fortunes* (1890), ed. Everett Carter et al. (CEAA ed. Bloomington, Ind., 1976), pp. 451–52.

29. Howells, *The Altrurian Romances*, pp. 170–71, 169.

30. Charles L. Crow, "Howells and William James: 'A Case of Metaphantasmia' Solved," *American Quarterly* 27(May 1975):169–77.

31. See notably John W. Crowley, "Howells' *Questionable Shapes:* From Psychologism to Psychic Romance," *Emerson Society Quarterly* 21(1975):169–78, and Crowley and Crow, "Psychic and Psychological Themes in Howells' 'A Sleep and a Forgetting,'" *Emerson Society Quarterly* 23(1977):41–51. For a more general and earlier treatment, see Arnold B. Fox, "Spiritualism and the 'Supernatural' in William Dean Howells," *Journal of the American Society for Psychical Research* 53(October 1959):121–30.

32. William Dean Howells, *Immortality and Sir Oliver Lodge* (n d), pp. 2, 4.

33. But only *partly*. See the comprehensive treatment of the novel by Vanderbilt, with its convincing conclusion that the work is "a national study of religious, psychological, and social dislocation" (*Achievement of William Dean Howells*, p. 47).

34. William Dean Howells, *Impressions and Experiences* (New York, 1896), p. 21.

35. My term is consciously redundant, recognizing the objection of Wagenknecht to "agnostic" as a label (*William Dean Howells: The Friendly Eye*, p. 244).

36. Cady, *The Road to Realism*, p. 150.

37. Fox, "Howells as a Religious Critic," pp. 201, 204.

38. William Dean Howells, *Harper's Monthly* 140(January 1920):279.

39. *Life in Letters*, 2:10.

40. *Public Meeting of the American Academy . . . in Honor of William Dean Howells* (New York, 1922), pp. 67–68. Though Van Dyke had his sentimentalities, Sydney E. Ahlstrom reminds us in *A Religious History of the American People* (New Haven, 1972), p. 815, that his becoming a professor of English at Princeton saved him from heresy proceedings by the Presbyterian church.

41. William Dean Howells, "Though One Rose from the Dead," *Questionable Shapes* (New York, 1903), p. 159.

42. Reprinted in *W. D. Howells as Critic*, p. 423. On 28 September 1902 (MS at Harvard) James asked Howells whether he had received *Varieties*. Howells replied (7 October, *Life in Letters*, 2:161–62) that he had not but "I am wanting to read it." No further correspondence on the book is extant.

43. Henry James, ed., *The Letters of William James* (Boston, 1920), 2:150, James's self-characterization comes close to a major thrust of a remarkable story by Howells, best analyzed by John W. Crowley, "Howells' Minister in a Maze: 'A Difficult Case,'" *Colby Library Quarterly*, 13(December 1977):278–83. Though "A Difficult Case" appeared two years before *Varieties*, probably Howells had read *The Will to Believe* by the time he wrote it.

44. William Dean Howells, *Harper's Monthly*, July 1891, reprinted in W. D. *Howells as Critic*, ed. Cady, p. 198.

45. *Life in Letters*, 2:14, 285, 72.

46. For explorations of Howells' relation to James and Peirce, see William McMurray, *The Literary Realism of William Dean Howells* (Carbondale, Ill., 1967) and James E. Woodard, "Pragmatism and Pragmaticism in James and Howells," *Dissertation Abstracts International* 31(1970):408A (New Mexico).

47. *Selected Letters*, 2:253.

48. George C. Carrington, Jr., et al. eds., *The Kentons* (CEAA ed. Bloomington, Ind. 1971), p. 126.

49. William Dean Howells, *North American Review*, July 1906, reprinted in W. D. *Howells as Critic*, ed. Cady, p. 435.

50. George N. Bennett, *William Dean Howells: The Development of a Novelist* (Norman, Okla., 1959), pp. 169–70, makes a convincing comparison between the sermon and Howells' introduction to *Sebastopol* (New York, 1887). More recently Howard M. Munford, "Introduction," *The Minister's Charge* (1887; CEAA ed. Bloomington, Ind., 1978), pp. xv–xvi, has added critical and historical detail.

51. Munford lists the three treatments of complicity by the Kirks, Fox, and McMurray. Of these I prefer McMurray for its less restricted view.

52. William Dean Howells, *The Minister's Charge*, pp. 176–85, 340–42. I am less sure than Bennett. *William Dean Howells*, p. 169, and Munford, "Introduction," p. xvi, of Howells' tone in calling the sermon "a complete philosophy of life." In treating *The Son of Royal Langbrith*, which has another minister as a moral expositor, Bennett makes what appears to be a more pluralistic approach—"the novel is not prescriptive." But in fairness to Bennett, he views the two novels as quite different, in that there are several expositors in *Langbrith* in addition to the minister. See *The Realism of William Dean Howells* (Nashville, Tenn., 1973), pp. 206, 210.

53. McMurray, *The Literary Realism of William Dean Howells*, pp. 111–21.

54. Eugene H. Pattison, "Introduction," *The Leatherwood God* (1916; CEAA ed. Bloomington, Ind., 1976); and "From History to Realism. Howells Composes *The Leatherwood God*," *Old Northwest* 4(September 1978):195–218.

55. MS at Harvard. In May 1913 Howells had read enough of the book to T. S. Perry for him to pronounce it "the broadest and strongest thing I've done." See Pattison, "Introduction," p. xviii. The implication of the 15 August letter is that Howells also read the still incomplete novel to both the Jameses, uncle and nephew.

56. McMurray, *The Literary Realism of William Dean Howells*, pp. 121, 139, is the only critic to cite the letter. At the time I had urged that the book was *Memories and Studies* (New York, 1911) edited by the younger Henry James. Though it is "good" William James, containing such essays as those on Emerson, the moral equivalent of war, and the Ph.D. octopus, it lacks the excitement of the other work. More to the point, it uses the phrase "common sense" only twice. For several reasons I have discarded *Some Problems in Philosophy* (1911) as a probability; in it "common sense" appears nine times, mostly with disapproval. *On Some of Life's Ideals* (1912) is a reprint.

57. William James, *Essays in Radical Empiricism*, ed. Ralph B. Perry (New York, 1912), pp. 50, 42. On two occasions James pairs "common sense" with radical empiricism (pp. 148, 200), but he uses the label both with disapproval (5 times) and approval (6 times). Mostly he regards "common sense" as a stage toward radical empiricism (8 times) or makes a neutral use of the phrase (3 times).

The American Quest for Religious Certainty, 1880–1915

Ferenc Szasz

In 1907, Charles E. Jefferson, popular pastor of New York City's Broadway Tabernacle, gave a series of sermons on what he termed the "Fundamentals," proclaiming the "undoubted fact" that "we are living in an age that is full of confusion."[1] Jefferson placed his finger squarely on one of the obvious realities of his day: most aspects of turn-of-the-century American life teemed with uncertainty.

At the heart of this "age of confusion," however, lay the ferment that characterized the world of American religious thought. *Fin de siècle* citizens watched in bewilderment as a new variety of religious expressions emerged. These included self-proclaimed Christs, new prophets, new sects, communal experiments, heresies, and the introduction of Eastern faiths. For many, whirl had become king, having displaced Zeus.

A number of contemporary accounts attest to this religious turmoil.[2] Journalist Ray Stannard Baker, for example, recalled the era of Jacob Coxey's march to Washington in 1893–94, which he covered, as filled with the marvels of faith healing, hypnotism, mind cure, and spiritualism. He entitled his later study of American religious life *The Spiritual Unrest* (1910).[3] In 1913, George T. Bushnell of Pacific Grove University charted the number of movements as follows: "organized philanthropy, social service, laymen's missionary movements, Sunday school reform, psychical research, spiritualism, Christian Science, New Thought, theosophy, gifts of tongues, psychical therapeutics—their number is without end."[4] Some observers saw this as a sign of irreligion, but Charles M. Stuart, president of Garret Biblical Institute in Evanston, disagreed. "The immense number of religions and quasi-religious cults is indicative not of an irreligious but of a religious age," he said, "bewildered and vagrant if you will, but seriously and positively religious."[5] This confusion became so much a part of everyday life that in 1910 the Equitable Life Insurance Company could run an advertisement stating, "Old-fashioned life insurance—like old-fashioned religion—is what is needed today in this age of 'isms' in theology and fads and schemes in life insurance."[6]

Contemporary scholars were fascinated by this phenomenon. Philosopher William James noted that it was obvious that a wave of religious activity, analogous in some respects to the spread of early Christianity, Buddhism, and Islam, was passing over American life. He could not have improved on the title of his classic work, *The Varieties of Religious Experience* (1902). Religious statistician H. C. Carroll could find no other nation in the world to match the variety of faiths available in *fin de siècle* America.[7] Writing in 1932, Gaius Glenn Atkins suggested that one would have to return to the first three hundred years of Christendom to find a similar creative period in religion such as America had undergone since 1880.[8] The English jibe that America was a "vast commonwealth of sects," and the French sneer that America had "thirty-six religions but only two sauces" was never so true as in the years flanking the end of the nineteenth century.[9] One would have to return to antebellum Boston, where, as Emerson said, every man carried the plan for a new community in his waistcoat pocket, or to college campuses in the late 1960s to find a comparable period of popular religious ferment.

Why such activity at this time is a question easier posed than answered. Psychohistory to the contrary, the world of the prophet and his intimate contact with God has proven a difficult region for historians to enter. In general, however, one can say that new prophets and new sects tend to rise and/or succeed whenever the existing religious frameworks do not provide sufficient flexibility to transmit their message. Certainly this was true for the rise of Quakers, Baptists, and Methodists in colonial times; it was also true at the turn of the nineteenth century.

Although contemporaries were never certain that one of the new movements (Christian Scientists being the most likely) might not sweep over the nation, eventually these fears proved groundless. None of the sects matched the triumph of the nineteenth-century Baptists or Methodists.

In fact, the successes of these movements were as varied as the movements themselves. Many have completely disappeared. The utopian communities have vanished and one looks in vain today for the followers of Francis Schlatter, devotees of the Oahspe Bible, or adherents of the Church Triumphant. Others, such as the experiments begun at Shadyside, Washington, or Zion, Illinois, have changed beyond recognition. Today Shadyside is just another small town in the Yakima Valley and Zion is just another suburb of Chicago. Still others, such as the Spiritualists, both branches of the Bahais, and the Theosophists, are secure from collapse; but they have given up hopes of ever having a mass following. The fortunate few—Christian Scientists, Seventh-Day Adventists, the Salvation Army, Unity Church, Jehovah's Witnesses, and the Church of the Nazarene have all traveled the familiar road from sect to denomination.[10]

In general one may say that the Protestant denominations were the ones most affected by this turmoil. Papal Encyclicals halted the spread of Modernism in the Catholic Church and Reform Judaism still remained small in numbers. As far as can be determined, most of the newer sects directed their appeal primarily to dissatisfied Protestants. Perhaps one way to examine the rise and success of the new groups is to classify them as (1) those which moved beyond the traditional Christian framework regarding reason, and (2) those which moved beyond the traditional Christian framework regarding faith.

American Protestantism has always been strongest when it held faith and reason in a creative tension. The various denominations—say, Congregationalists, Unitarians, and Episcopalians on one hand as opposed to Baptists, Methodists, and Adventists on the other—have offered considerable latitude in their emphasis on faith and/or reason. Still, the merging of the two was deemed essential for proper perspective. In the period under discussion, however, the balance between faith and reason began to become unsettled.

The late nineteenth century had great confidence in the power of reason. Given this outlook, one might have expected considerable expansion from those Protestant denominations which already had strong tendencies in that direction. Yet for the Congregationalists and Unitarians, the most likely candidates, no such expansion seems to have occurred.[11]

Instead, people who placed increased stress on the rational faculties of the mind often moved beyond traditional Congregationalism and Unitarianism. One early split came in 1867 when a group of dissatisfied Unitarians set up the Free Religious Association. This organization was based in the large eastern cities, but in spite of able leadership from Francis E. Abbott, O. B. Frothingham, and Felix Adler, its influence never extended very far.

Felix Adler's Society for Ethical Culture proved a more lasting testimony to the power of reason. Brilliant son of the rabbi of New York's Temple Emanu-El, Adler was only twenty-five when he began his new society in 1876. Frankly admitting that a wave of skepticism was passing over the country, the Ethical Culturists tried to build up the moral life of those whom the churches had ceased to influence. Revising the dominant opinion that morality was a corollary of religion, Ethical Culturists argued that when people became morally regenerate, they were then more open to spiritual truths. The organization boasted of having no creed, prayers, or music. It laid its stress directly on ethics and social righteousness. In 1894 Felix Adler defined their message: "that the good life is possible to all without the previous acceptance of any creed, irrespective of religious opinion or philosophic theory; that the way of righteousness is open and can be entered directly without a previous detour through the land of faith or philosophy."[12]

Similar rationalist organizations arose simultaneously, but they tended to be smaller, more ephemeral, and, oftentimes, more militant in their outlook. In 1883 a "gentleman" advertised in the New York *Herald* for others "who, while they do not recognize the existence of the Deity, desire to make some organized effort for the establishment of a rational system of worship." Interested parties were to write "Reformation." In Waco, Texas, J. D. Shaws began a short-lived Religious and Benevolent Association which held "Sunday discussions" instead of sermons. A Miss Bartlett headed a "People's Church" in Kalamazoo, Michigan. With no creed or regulations, its stated object was to make people happy in this world. Freethinker Robert G. Ingersoll attended one of Bartlett's services and spoke well of it.[13]

Rather loud support for the rationalist outlook came from two iconoclastic editors with national circulation: William Cowper Brann and Elbert Hubbard. In February 1895, Brann began his paper, *The Iconoclast*, in Waco, Texas. It soon achieved such notoriety that circulation soared to 100,000 a year. Born the son of a midwestern Presbyterian minister, Brann escaped formal schooling but gained his considerable knowledge through prodigious reading. All this he turned into shotgun attacks on pretense, intolerance, hypocrisy, and religious sentimentality in general, and Baylor University and the Southern Baptists in particular.

While Brann insisted that he was not against Christianity or the churches, the burden of his message spoke otherwise. He seldom missed an opportunity to denounce the Salvation Army, foreign missionaries, or clergymen. He loudly defended Robert G. Ingersoll and free thought and delighted in having *The Iconoclast* labeled an atheist sheet. Here are some examples of his rhetoric: "The Baptists of today would crush liberty of conscience and freedom of speech." "The average pulpiteer is a party who persistently stinks for attention. Like the skunk, he compels even the nobility to notice him."[14] Not surprisingly, he was shot and killed in 1898. But, and this is surprising, he had support from several liberal clergymen in his area, and he was given an Episcopal funeral.

Brann's northern counterpart, who turned out to be much more important in the long run, was Elbert Hubbard. He is remembered now, if at all, for his little pamphlet *A Message to Garcia*. Cut from the same piece of cloth, Hubbard was also raised in a deeply religious middlewestern atmosphere. His education, too, came entirely through reading. In June 1895, four months after Brann began his *The Iconoclast*, Hubbard founded *The Philistine* in East Aurora, New York, subtitling it "a periodical of protest." His long and successful career gave *The Philistine* and his numerous other publications wide circulation. They spread doubt about conventional religion wherever they landed.

A man of many facets, Hubbard should not, perhaps, be seen solely as a spreader of popular doubt. But for much of his career—until 1910 or so—he played the role of national lay philosopher, asking (and answering) the big questions of existence. Where religion was concerned, the answers he gave were resoundingly gray. He wrote a rationalist commentary on the *Song of Songs* and the book of *Job*, and he borrowed heavily from Ernest Renan for his rationalist biography of Jesus entitled *The Man of Sorrows*. Removing all supernatural references from Scripture, he published *An American Bible*, which was described as "a book without mystery, myth, miracle or metaphysics—a common sense book for red-blooded people who do their own thinking."[15]

Although Hubbard is frequently dismissed by historians as appealing chiefly to the sentimental, his influence can hardly be overestimated. Being the nation's foremost popular philosopher is not an easy task, yet he remained in the public eye steadily for over twenty years until he and his wife went down with the Lusitania on 7 May 1915.[16]

Neither Brann nor Hubbard was exactly a freethinker, for both believed in an amorphous spiritual power greater than humanity. But they were much against the prevailing Christian orthodoxy, and their attacks often hit the churches at their weakest points. Even farther to the left in their use of reason were the American freethinkers, who also began to appear prominently in the magazines and newspapers of the late Gilded Age. While freethinkers had played a part in American life ever since the Revolution—for some reason they were usually blacksmiths or doctors—they seldom had lasting influence. Dwight D. Eisenhower once recalled that during his boyhood in Kansas, every little town had its village freethinker and its village Democrat. In the late nineteenth century, however, they began to organize. In 1873 the periodical *The Freethinker* first appeared and in 1873, 1874, and 1875, Englishman Charles Bradlaugh, infamous president of the National Society of Secularists, came over for popular lecture tours. In 1876 the American Secular Union was formed. National conventions were held periodically, and by 1915 there were few large cities without some type of organized freethinkers' society.[17]

Most of the national publicity that free thought received, however, came from the activities of Robert G. Ingersoll. From the middle 1870s until his death, "Royal Bob," with his trinity of "reason, observation, and science," played the role of national infidel with style and verve. Through his Chautauqua appearances—one of his managers called him the "best card in America"—and his collected speeches (*What Is Religion? Why I Am An Agnostic, About the Holy Bible, The Mistakes of Moses,* and others) he served as America's ideal enemy. Humorist Josh Billings once remarked that he wouldn't give five cents to hear Bob Ingersoll on the mistakes of Moses, but that he would give $500 to hear Moses on the mistakes of Bob Ingersoll. Historian Martin Marty has suggested that had Ingersoll not existed as the ideal enemy of conventional society, America would have had to invent him.[18]

The social impact of Gilded Age free thought is hard to assess. Few people actually joined freethinking societies, for joining them meant, in effect, a binding commitment to attack religion. In spite of claims to the contrary, they never numbered over a few thousand. Instead, the writings of Ingersoll and others helped break down the hold which conventional religion had on ordinary people. This, in turn, sent people on different searches in different directions.

The angst of ordinary churchgoers, the public hand-wringing of the clergy, the jibes of Brann and Hubbard, and the thrusts and defiance of Ingersoll all fed into a mood of disbelief that characterized much of the late nineteenth and early twentieth century. All the nation's religious leaders noticed it. Rabbi Gustave Gottheil of New York's Temple Emanu-El declared his generation was living in "a material, skeptical age."[19] The Bishop's Address to the General Conference of the Methodist Episcopal Church in 1888 called attention to the "subtle and ever-varying forms of skepticism rife in our times." Henry Van Dyke entitled his popular Yale lectures on preaching *The Gospel for an Age of Doubt* (1896). This phrase remained current in religious circles for over twenty years.[20]

Usually this mood of doubt was labeled simply "agnosticism." By the 1890s this term had assumed a life of its own. From recent college graduates to fearful ministers, it was glibly bandied about on all sides. "Agnosticism" was often associated with the English writers Thomas Huxley and Herbert Spencer, for they were among the first to popularize it. They and other adherents insisted that agnosticism was not denial—the thundering "No"—but simply doubt: the gray "I do not know."[21]

Regardless of definition, however, the idea was very much in the news during these years. The *New York Times* termed agnosticism "a temper of mind."[22] Contemporary citizens, it noted, moved between the world they lived in and the living God they half believed in.[23] Few religious leaders could be convinced that agnosticism was not atheism in a new disguise. Many saw it as the chief opposition to late-nineteenth-century Christianity. The traditional foes of Christianity—atheism, Deism, Gnosticism, and so forth—were often subsumed under this new phrase.[24] "The agnostic fever is even now far more prevalent than the typhoid," warned W. P. Marwick in 1886, "and much more fatal in its results."[25]

While many pushed reason beyond the bounds of traditional Christianity, so, too, did many search in other directions for faith. A surprising number of prophets, communal sects, Asiatic faiths, and splits from existing denominations appeared during the turn-of-the-century years.

In late 1890, the *New York Times* marveled at the number of false Christs who had recently emerged. The number was, indeed, amazing. In 1888, a man named Patterson, who resided in Soddy, a town in eastern Tennessee, claimed that his assistant, A. J. Brown, was the second coming of Christ. They attracted large crowds as Brown went around forgiving sins and healing diseases. The sheriff of Chattanooga eventually drove both of them out of the area. Similar excitement developed in 1889–90 among the black community along the Savannah River in Georgia and South Carolina. There a whole series of men emerged, each proclaiming himself the Christ. The most prominent of these was a man named Bell who traversed the area urging all who would be saved to follow him. Hundreds of blacks heeded his advice. They left their sawmills and cotton fields to set up a "temple" where they assumed the name "Wilderness Worshipers." Bell was soon arrested, but on his release he spoke to even larger crowds. According to his prediction, the world was to end on 16 August 1890. At that time, all white men would turn black and all black men white. Any who wished to purchase wings for the occasion could do so from him alone. Eventually, Bell was committed to an asylum but his successors, who also claimed to be divine, prolonged the excitement for over a year afterward.[26]

About the same time, the Reverend George T. Schweinfurth of Rockford, Illinois, proclaimed himself divine. He alleged that he was the spiritual heir of the late Dora Beekman, who, in 1874, had declared herself the immortal reincarnation of Jesus. Other local evangelists in Indiana, Missouri, and Illinois initiated similar extravagances with wild prophecies, visions, and trances. In western Missouri in 1888, a man named Silas Wilcox formed a band of "Samaritans." These people preached that drinking blood was a major means of curing diseases. This led to the bleeding of children. A woman in Oak Ridge Park, Illinois, proclaimed that she could change water into wine. A Mrs. Woodworth attracted many followers by predicting that a tidal wave would crush Oakland, California. In 1895 Benjamin Purnell announced that he was the Seventh Messenger appointed to fulfill the prophecy of old. Later he proclaimed himself "the younger brother of Christ." After 1903 he and his followers retired to Benton Harbor, Michigan, where he founded a religious colony, the House of David, later famed for its baseball teams.[27]

Perhaps the most fascinating of these *fin de siècle* prophets was Francis Schlatter, the "Western Messiah," who astounded New Mexico and Colorado with his divine healing during 1895. Schlatter's memoirs—only four copies of which are still extant—offer a fascinating key to his thought, which was extremely radical. Conversant with the New Thought writings, not only did he provide personal healing (if people would only have faith), he also predicted the imminent destruction of America because of the injustices he saw all about him. Remembering his own days as a workingman, he bitterly attacked the "Plutocracy" as "the blood-sucking parasites on the common people." When the time came, he predicted, all would be avenged. There was little hope for Americans unless they established the Kingdom of God immediately.[28]

The antebellum period is usually seen as the high tide for experiments in communal living arrangements, but the *fin de siècle* years were almost as prolific. Numerous leaders were able to gather their followers into communes. Historian Robert Fogarty has counted thirty-six communal experiments which began in the 1890s and twenty-two others originating between 1910 and 1919.[29] In 1910, H. C. Carroll discovered thirty-seven with a total membership of over 4,000 people. Over fourteen states hosted such experiments, with several in Georgia, Alabama, Washington, New Mexico, and California.[30] The Faithist Community outside of present-day Las Cruces, New Mexico (based on the Oahspe Bible) and the healing community of Zion, Illinois (founded by John Alexander Dowie), were probably the two most famous of these experiments.[31]

Such activities were so common that the editor of *The Chautauquan* said he had begun to expect a number of "freak" movements of salvation each year. When 1901 arrived, he was pleasantly surprised when none occurred.[32]

Some of the other movements of faith, however, proved more lasting— the Seventh-Day Adventists, Jehovah's Witnesses, New Thought, and Christian Science. Here the prophets were able to institutionalize their messages and to offer major contributions to the American religious tradition.

In the late 1830s New York farmer William Miller began preaching that the world would end in 1843–44. The Seventh-Day Adventists, officially formed in 1860, were the largest group to base their ideas on Miller's teachings. They remained small during their early years—perhaps only 20,000 or so. But from the 1880s on, they began to increase in numbers and their teachings began to spread across the country.

This expansion was due to the writings of Ellen G. White, especially her *The Great Controversy* (originally published in 1888) and to the numerous food reforms which emerged from their world-famous Battle Creek Health Sanitarium in Michigan. Wheat flakes, corn flakes, grape nuts, coffee substitutes, and peanut butter are only a few of the health foods introduced there.

Although Ellen G. White was never as widely known as Mary Baker Eddy, when White died in 1915, at the age of eighty-seven, she had firmly established herself as one of the founders of a major religious sect.

The Loma Linda College in California, begun in 1910, soon made the mission worldwide.[33]

The name Jehovah's Witnesses was not assumed until 1931, but the organization was founded in the early 1870s by "Pastor" Charles Taze Russell, ex-haberdasher, of Allegheny, Pennsylvania. Initially, his followers were termed the International Bible Students Association, Russellites, or Millennial Dawnists; from the beginning they were the most militant of the Adventist sects. Russell claimed himself the Seventh Messenger of the Church, declared that the Parousia had already occurred, and announced that the world was now in the millennium. Christ returned to the "upper air" in 1874, and in 1875 all apostles and "the little flock" who had died were raised to meet him. They also were floating about in the air. Russell predicted that the consummation of all things would occur in 1914, and the outbreak of World War I that year lent his prophecies special credence. Before long, the Witnesses were distributing their *Watchtower* tracts in every state of the Union. As Jehovah's sole witnesses, they were most eager to spread their message.[34]

While some have traced the origins of spiritualism back to Immanuel Swedenborg and the seventeenth century, modern spiritualism really dates from the "demonstrations" of Margaretta and Catherine Fox of Hydesville, New York (near Rochester) in 1847–48. From there it spread to the East Coast and, aided by the writings of Andrew Jackson Davis, achieved considerable influence during the Civil War years. Spiritualism influenced such diverse people as Robert Owen, Robert Dale Owen, Abraham Lincoln (who allowed seances to be held in the White House to humor his wife), William Cullen Bryant, George Ripley, George Bancroft, and Mark Hanna. In 1870 Lester Frank Ward predicted that spiritualism would eventually become America's prevailing faith.[35]

Attractive to all types of quacks and to a large number of ex-actors, spiritualism grew steadily in the post–Civil War years. Then, on 21 October 1888, perhaps the most dramatic incident occurred—in a movement filled with drama—when Margaretta Fox Kane, with sister Kate sitting nearby, confessed to a packed crowd that she and her sister had only been cracking their toe joints to simulate contact with the spirit world. Oddly enough, this confession only stunned spiritualism; it did not kill it. In fact, the "confession" gave the movement even more publicity. When Margaretta retracted her words the following year, she was reaccepted into medium circles. Kate, too, continued to hold occasional seances for years afterward.

By the 1890s, spiritualism had become a familiar, albeit still somewhat peripheral, part of American life. It had found its way into the pages of B. O. Flower's *Arena*, and the literature of William Dean Howells, Henry James, and Mark Twain, though not always favorably.[36] It found more positive support from novelist Sir Arthur Conan Doyle and scientist Alfred

R. Wallace, one of the early theorists of evolution. In fact, Alfred R. Wallace broke from Darwin's naturalistic view of the evolutionary process largely because he felt that spiritualism could be scientifically proven.[37]

Spiritualism grew steadily—in the late 1890s it claimed several million followers—but the seance proved a difficult item on which to base an organized religion. "Spiritualism, in short," said the Chicago *Chronicle* in 1899, "is an unorganized body of people who agree upon one proposition and disagree concerning pretty nearly everything else in theology, ethics, and revelation."[38] This is still true today.

Few contemporary observers could divorce themselves from an emotional reaction of either support or contempt for the movement to see it for what it was: an unorthodox response to the problem of increasing religious doubt. Spiritualism was a search for tangible proof of a faith beyond faith itself. For many people it took the place of organized religion or fused with the old beliefs. Spiritualism purported to harmonize religion and science. It claimed that a person could believe in an afterlife without fear; the seance showed that the afterlife could be proven "scientifically." Few other churches could promise so much.

Of more lasting impact than the spiritualists were the numerous sects grouped under what we now call New Thought, although contemporaries often termed it Mind Cure. Rejecting ideas of sin and guilt, New Thought grew largely out of the American experience and drew heavily on such varied sources as Ralph Waldo Emerson, the Transcendentalists, Andrew Jackson Davis, P. P. Quimby, and Warren F. Evans. Basically, New Thought stressed the Quaker idea of the "Christ consciousness," or the still small voice within. Since it, too, considered itself scientific, New Thought also tried to bridge the gap between science and religion. Many of its adherents also became involved in healing. In the East, the movement emerged as Christian Science; in the West as Divine Science or the Unity Church of Practical Christianity.

At first, adherents of New Thought ideas had no plans to found separate denominations; only gradually did they emerge as distinct entities. The Divine Science Church, which had its beginnings in the middle 1880s, claimed several founders. Malinda E. Cramer, who supplied the name "Divine Science," was one of the more important. After years of suffering, Cramer had moved to California where she suddenly found herself miraculously cured. This occurred when she intuitively realized that she could be healed only by and through the Omnipresent Spirit. In 1885 she began to teach the results of her thinking and soon made this her life's mission.

In the early 1880s, the three Brooks sisters of Pueblo, Colorado— Althea Brooks Small, Fannie Brooks James, and Nona Lovell Brooks— began to study similar metaphysical subjects. Malinda Cramer moved to Denver in 1887 and soon began working with them. In 1898, Nona Brooks was ordained by Mrs. Cramer, and the next year the Divine Science Church was formally organized. Nona Brooks became Denver's first woman minister, serving her church for thirty years. When Mrs. Cramer died in 1907, Denver became the center of the western branch of the New Thought movement.[39] The last major New Thought group to emerge in the West was the Church of Religious Science, founded in the second decade of the new century by Ernest Holmes. All of these groups stressed the realization or consciousness of God's presence as the main healing force. Healing came from an awareness that God works through each person. "God is everywhere," the Brooks sisters told their pupils, "therefore God is here. God is health. Health is everywhere. Therefore health is here."[40]

In addition to Divine Science, New Thought groups came in many other forms. Some tended toward a non-Christian eclecticism, recognizing a divine inspiration in all religions. Others tried to interpret the Bible both metaphysically and metaphorically, and still considered themselves Christian. Eventually many of the sects joined to form a loose union in the National New Thought Alliance.

The largest offshoot of the New Thought movement, and one of the few groups to consider itself definitely Christian, was the Unity Church of Practical Christianity. It was founded in Kansas City, Missouri, in 1889 by Myrtle and Charles Fillmore, after Mrs. Fillmore's miraculous recovery from illness. Thoroughly conversant with Buddhism, Brahminism, Theosophy, Rosicrucianism, as well as all sects of Christianity—they confessed to having taken over forty courses in metaphysical subjects—the Fillmores moved gradually from the middle 1880s to what would eventually become Unity.

Except, perhaps, for their belief in reincarnation, Ralph Waldo Emerson and the early Quakers would have felt comfortable with most of the Fillmores' ideas. In his nine books and countless articles and speeches, Charles Fillmore endeavored to show that science and religion were but two approaches to the same truth. Modern scientists were only using a different set of terms to describe the same truths proclaimed by Jesus when He spoke of the Kingdom of Heaven and the power of faith and prayer. Once Charles Fillmore said that Unity could be defined simply as "Christian mysticism practically applied to everyday living."[41]

Probably the most important of the New Thought movements—although they denied the connection—were the Christian Scientists. The origins of this faith are still shrouded in mystery. While most historians feel that P. P. Quimby, eccentric New England healer, provided many of the formative ideas, Christian Scientists trace their founding solely to the thoughts of Mary Baker Eddy, one of the most remarkable women of the nineteenth century.

Long troubled by anguish and ill health, Mrs. Eddy published the first edition of her *Science and Health* (later frequently revised) in 1875 and four years later founded the Church of Christ, Scientist. She taught that evil in general and physical illness in particular could be overcome through prayer and a deeper understanding of God. In the 1880s, the movement grew slowly, for there were many similar forms of competition. In fact, wrote a California follower in 1886, "Institutes of Metaphysical Science have been started [here] which include the teaching of mind-cure, animal magnetism, mesmerism, spiritualism, clairvoyance, and mediumship; while we, as Christian Scientists, are denounced for having our jacket on too straight."[42]

Gradually, however, Mary Baker Eddy distinguished Christian Science from its rivals, and while many of them began to fade, the Scientists continued to grow. By the early 1890s, they claimed about nine thousand adherents. The Mother Church in Boston was founded in 1892, and the *Christian Science Monitor* dates from 1908. By the middle 1890s, moreover, Christian Scientists had clearly entered the American religious mainstream. In 1901, the *Atlantic Monthly* named Mrs. Eddy as the most popular author of the day. When *Outlook* reporter Ernest H. Abbott made his religious tour of the nation that same year, he was astounded to find Christian Science reading rooms in every city he visited. At her death nine years later, Mary Baker Eddy's faith had become a secure part of American life.[43]

The variety of sects reflected the diversity of the New Thought prophets. While most of the sects remained small, as a whole the movement was very important. William James was most impressed with it and considered the rise of New Thought as significant for American life as the Reformation had been for its day. In 1950, Sidney E. Mead estimated that between fifteen and twenty million Americans had been influenced by its teachings. One need only pick up the works of the Reverend Norman Vincent Peale, Bishop Fulton J. Sheen, or Rabbi Joshua L. Liebman to see the extent (largely unnoticed) to which it has influenced modern Christianity and Judaism.[44] By the first decade of the twentieth century, then, New Thought had assumed a distinct place among the American faiths. It touched numerous denominations and formed a specific body of thought, related to, yet separate and distinct from, orthodox Christianity.[45]

From 1887 through 1889, the *North American Review* ran a series of articles on the theme of religious pluralism, entitled "Why I Am a (Quaker, Heathen, Moslem, Spiritualist, Free Religionist, and so on)." A few years later the Parliament of Religions, held in conjunction with the Chicago World's Fair of 1893, gave a major impetus to this idea of the diversity of faiths. Here Americans first became acquainted with Theosophy, the Baha'i Movement, Hinduism, and Islam.

The darling of the fair, by all accounts, was Theosophy, founded by another of the nineteenth century's store of remarkable women, Madam

Helena P. Blavatsky. The first Theosophical Society in America emerged in New York in 1875. Bearing resemblances to the ideas of Emerson, Transcendentalism, and Spiritualism, the movement grew slowly until 1890 when it claimed thirty-eight chartered branches and several publications, *The Path*, edited by W. Q. Judge, being the most important. Yet it was not until 1893 that the nation really became aware of Blavatsky's ideas. Events surrounding the World's Fair gave them wide publicity.

Madam Blavatsky taught the existence of spiritual beings, the Mahatmas, who lived in the Himalayas, and who sent psychic messages to those who believed. She also felt that she had been entrusted by them to reveal "The Path" to the world. Although Theosophists did engage in some social activities, such as setting up a labor exchange and safe, cheap lodging houses for women, their main goal was more ethereal: "to form a nucleus of a Universal Brotherhood of Humanity without distinction of race, creed, and color"; to promote the study of Eastern literature, religion, and science, and to "investigate unexplained laws of nature and the physical powers latent in man."[46]

Although the movement was heaped with obloquy, even its enemies regarded Madame Blavatsky with awe. Journalist W. T. Stead praised her for restoring mystery and spiritual values to a generation obsessed with the material and mechanical.[47] She died in 1891, but her ideas continued to grow under her successor, Annie Besant. In 1916 the organization claimed several thousand adherents in the United States alone and boasted a thriving Theosophist commune in Point Loma, California.[48]

Most Americans knew virtually nothing about the Baha'i faith until the 1893 Parliament. Founded in 1844 by a rich Persian, Baha' u' llah, Bahais advocated the oneness of mankind and the union of all religions into one universal religion. With the publicity provided by the parliament, however, interest in the movement began to widen considerably.

Numerous Oriental faiths also gained popularity from the World's Fair. After it was over, several Hindu priests remained in the United States to tour the country giving lectures·on their religion. Their reception was often disappointing, however, for the Christian clergy warned their flocks not to attend. Swami Vivekeanda, perhaps the most famous of these itinerants, remained in the United States for several years afterward. In 1894 he founded the Vedanta Society in New York. Another branch of the society emerged in California shortly after 1900.[49] "As a result," groaned Upton Sinclair, "we have here in America a plague of Eastern cults, with 'swamis' using soft yellow robes and soft brown eyes to win the souls of idle society ladies."[50]

In 1899 the Japanese Buddhists began missionary work in America, and it was not long before the first Buddhist temple was erected in San Francisco. Another appeared shortly afterward in Sacramento and a third in Chicago.

The doctrines of Mohammed were first introduced to the American public by Alexander Russell Webb, a New Englander who had converted to Islam while heading the United States consulate at Manila. In the fall of 1893, Webb helped establish small branches of the Moslem Brotherhood in Brooklyn, Manhattan, Philadelphia, and Washington. In the fall of the previous year he had visited India, where he advocated the conversion of America to Islam. Able to convince several wealthy Indians to help finance this operation, Webb returned to the states to set up headquarters on the Hudson River. Although he published a monthly paper, *The Moslem World and the Voice of Islam,* his successes were nil. The Nawab of Basoda, a ruling prince of India, left America in disgust when he could find no concrete results from his extensive financial contributions. In spite of claims to the contrary, there is no evidence that Webb convinced any Americans to accept the Islamic faith. The rise of mosques in America had to await later Arab immigration.[51]

In addition to the introduction of Eastern faiths, the existing Protestant denominations were themselves not immune to change. Not all of the new sects were imported from abroad, for several were formed by splits from the existing churches. These splinterings were often created by differences which were sometimes theological, sometimes social, but most often a combination of the two. Social class distinctions were very clear at the turn of the century, and by 1900 the major Protestant denominations had become largely institutions of the middle class.[52] Consequently, between 1890 and 1910 over fifty splinter groups emerged in protest against this situation. The most important of these were probably the numerous holiness groups (several of which combined in 1907–8 to form the Church of the Nazarene) and the Pentecostals. The British Salvation Army—a familiar sight on most American city streets by 1895—was one of the few groups that addressed itself primarily to the social question of the Gilded Age.

Churchgoers of the time were amazed by this panorama. Methodists and Baptists looked with envy on the 200–300 percent membership gains claimed by Spiritualists and Christian Scientists, remembering fondly their earlier, more halcyon years. Moreover, as far as can be determined (the Salvation Army excepted), the new sects drew their followers not so much from the unchurched as from members of existing churches. Spiritualists initially drew from the Presbyterians. Christian Scientists drew chiefly from Spiritualists in their early days, but it was not long before they were raiding other denominations for members, chiefly Congregationalists and Methodists. The dean of the Moody Bible Institute claimed that the departure of so many church members to the Christian Scientists was a major tragedy of the time. John Dowie's converts for Zion, Illinois, seem to have been largely Baptists, Presbyterians, and Methodists.[53] As a result, these sects soon came under severe condemnation from the established denominations.

Contemporaries found themselves bewildered by this religious ferment but from a later perspective the picture becomes a little clearer. With new immigrants, new knowledge, new technology, and new social class divisions, it was obvious that the established churches were not meeting the religious needs of the American people. Where they failed, the sects moved in to fill the gaps. This occurred primarily in the following: the expanding areas of knowledge and reason (all rationalist groups) in those of deep, personal communion with God (New Thought, Christian Science, Holiness, Pentecostals), social action (Salvation Army, Holiness, Communes, Volunteers of America), healing (Francis Schlatter, Christian Science, New Thought, Unity, John A. Dowie), the awareness of comparative religion and the messages of other faiths (Bahais, Theosophy), and the blending of science and religion (Spiritualism, Theosophy, New Thought).

The "long search" for religious certainty was in full force during the tumultuous years 1880–1915. It introduced a variety of new faiths, many of which were very different from the familiar Judaism or Christianity, in any of their varied forms. During these years the spectrum of the American religious experience widened steadily; a genuine religious pluralism was in the making.

NOTES

1. Charles Edward Jefferson, *Fundamentals* (New York, 1907), pp. 11–12.

2. John R. Commons, *Myself* (New York, 1934), p. 53; Edward Roundthaler, *The Memorabilia of Fifty Years, 1877–1927* (Raleigh, 1928), p. 291; Lord Bryce as cited by William Prall in "Socialism," *Papers and Speeches of the Church Congress* [Washington, 1891] (New York, 1892), p. 61.

3. Ray S. Baker, *The Spiritual Unrest* (New York, 1910); *American Chronicle* (New York, 1945) is his autobiography.

4. George T. Bushnell, "The Place of Religion in Modern Life," *American Journal of Theology* 17(October 1913):530.

5. Charles M. Stuart, "Foreword," in Paul Little, ed., *The Pacific Northwest Pulpit* (New York, 1915), p. 10.

6. Quoted in Daniel Pope, "The Development of National Advertising, 1865–1920" (Ph.D. diss., Columbia University, 1973), p. 167.

7. William James, *The Varieties of Religious Experience* (New York, 1902); H. C. Carroll, *The Religious Forces of the United States* (New York, 1912), pp. xiv–xvi.

8. Gaius G. Atkins, *Religion in Our Times* (New York, 1932), p. 63.

9. Paul A. Carter, *The Spiritual Crisis of the Gilded Age* (Dekalb, Ill., 1971) is an excellent study of this period. It stops around 1895.

10. For a superb survey of America's religious life see Sydney E. Ahlstrom, *A Religious History of the American People* (New Haven, 1972).

11. David B. Parke, *The Epic of Unitarianism* (Boston, 1957), p. xi; Earl M. Wilbur, *The First Century of the Liberal Movement in American Religion* (Boston, 1916), pamphlet in the archives of Andover-Newton Theological Seminary, Newton Centre, Mass.

12. Felix Adler *What Do We Stand For?* (Philadelphia, 1894), p. 3, pamphlet Andover-

Newton. Howard B. Radest, *Toward Common Ground: The Story of the Ethical Societies in the United States* (New York, 1969).

13. Robert G. Ingersoll, *New York Times*, 24 January 1883; Charles Carver, *Brann and the Iconoclast* (Austin, 1957), pp. 38–39; The Rochester *Herald*, 25 February 1896, in *Sixty-Five Press Interviews with Robert G. Ingersoll* (Girard, Kans., n.d.), p. 141.

14. W. C. Brann, "The Iconoclast and the Clergy," and "If Our Country Were Catholic," in *The Complete Works of Brann the Iconoclast*, (New York, 1919), 5:119, 279.

15. Elbert Hubbard II, ed., *The Philosophy of Elbert Hubbard* (New York, 1930); Elbert Hubbard, *A Thousand and One Epigrams* (New York, 1973), p. 184; Freeman Champney, *Art and Glory: The Story of Elbert Hubbard* (New York, 1968), p. 113.

16. Charles F. Hamilton, *As Bees in Honey Drown: Elbert Hubbard and the Roycrofters* (London, 1973), is a good biography.

17. Stow Persons, *Free Religion: An American Faith* (New Haven, 1947) and Sidney Warren, *American Freethought, 1860–1914* (New York, 1943) are two excellent studies.

18. Eva Ingersoll Wakefield, ed., *The Life and Letters of Robert Green Ingersoll* (London, 1952), pp. 72–76; Cf. J. M. Peebles, "Ingersollism or Christianity: Which?" (Hammonton, N. J., 1882), pamphlet at the Stowe-Day Library, Hartford, Conn.; Martin Marty, *The Infidel* (Cleveland, 1967); C. H. Cramer, *Royal Bob: The Life of Robert G. Ingersoll* (Indianapolis, 1952), is the best biography.

19. Gustave Gottheil, *New York Times*, 23 January 1887.

20. *Journal of the General Conference*, 1888, p. 40, cited in Emory S. Bucke, ed., *The Century of American Methodism*, (Nashville, 1964), 2:595; Henry Van Dyke, *The Gospel for the Age of Doubt* (New York, 1896); Herbert Swan Wilkinson, "The Gospel for an Age of Doubt," in Paul Little, ed., *The Pacific Northwest Pulpit* (New York, 1915).

21. *New York Times*, 25 March 1889; Lyman Abbott, "A Word with Professor Huxley," *North American Review* 149(July 1889):157; Robert G. Ingersoll, "Professor Huxley and Agnosticism," *North American Review* 148(April 1889):403–5.

22. *New York Times*, 24 February 1889.

23. Even though the *Times* was not the national newspaper it is today, it did provide a thorough coverage of the world of the churches and the changes in religion.

24. Edwin Mims, "The Religious Tone of Victorian Literature," *Methodist Quarterly Review* 61(July 1912):456.

25. W. P. Marwick, "Overcoming: A Sermon," February 7, 1886, pamphlet in the Methodist Archives, Lake Junaluska, N. C.

26. *New York Times*, 30 November 1800.

27. Vance Randolph, *Americans Who Thought They Were God* (Girard, Kans., 1943), pp. 11–13.

28. *The Life of the Harp in the Hand of the Harper* (Denver, 1897), pp. 147, 153, 154, 167, 176. I have treated him more fully in "Francis Schlatter: The Healer of the Southwest," *New Mexico Historical Review* 54(1979):89–104.

29. Robert S. Fogarty, "American Communes, 1885–1914," *Journal of American Studies* 9(August 1975):145–62.

30. Charles Pierce LeWarne, *Utopias on Puget Sound, 1885–1915* (Seattle, 1975); Robert V. Hine, *California's Utopian Colonies* (San Marino, Calif., 1953); Paul Kagan, *New World Utopias* (New York, 1975).

31. Daniel Nathan Simundson, "John Ballou Newbrough and the Oahspe Bible" (Ph.D. diss., University of New Mexico, 1972) is the best study of Shalam. "God raised up John Alexander Dowie for a specific work," noted a biographer, "which was to reintroduce Divine healing to the church." Gordon Lindsay, *The Life of John Alexander Dowie* (n.p., 1951), p. ix; John A. Dowie, "Do You Know God's Way of Healing" and "He Is Just the Same Today," *A Voice from Zion* 4(January 1900):12–13.

32. *The Chautauquan* 32(January 1901):362.

33. The essays in Edwin S. Gaustad, ed., *The Rise of Adventism: Religion and Society in Mid-Nineteenth-Century America* (New York, 1974) are informative as is P. Gerard Damsteegt, *Foundations of the Seventh-day Adventist Message and Mission* (Grand Rapids, Mich., 1977), especially Chapter 5; Ronald L. Numbers, *Prophetess of Health: A Story of Ellen G. White* (New York, 1976), pp. ix, 199. See also Hardee B. Powell, *The Original Has This Signature—W. K. Kellogg (Englewood Cliffs, N. J., 1956), pp. 85–113.*

34. Elmer T. Clark, *The Small Sects in America* (Rev. ed. Nashville, 1949), pp. 45–47; cf. Royston Pike, *Jehovah's Witnesses* (New York, 1954); Morley Cole, *Jehovah's Witnesses* (New York, 1955).

35. R. Laurence Moore, "Spiritualism," in Gausted, ed., *The Rise of Adventism*, pp. 79–103; Robert W. Delp, "Andrew Jackson Davis: Prophet of American Spiritualism," *Journal of American History* 54(June 1967):43–56; cf. Emma Hardinge, *Modern American Spiritualism* (New York, 1870).

36. Howard Kerr, *Mediums, and Spirit-Rappers, and Roaring Radicals: Spiritualism in American Literature, 1850–1900* (Urbana, Ill., 1972), pp. 173, 188.

37. Malcolm Jay Kottler, "Alfred Russel Wallace, The Origin of Man and Spiritualism," *Isis* 65(June 1974):145–92.

38. *Chicago Chronicle* as reported in *Public Opinion* 26(March 1899):275.

39. Virginia Culver, "Divine Science Origins Traced," *Denver Post*, 19 August 1972: cf. A Whitney Griswold, "New Thought: A Cult of Success," *American Journal of Sociology* 40(November 1934):309–18.

40. Culver, "Divine Science Origins Traced."

41. James Millet Freeman, *The Household of Faith: The Story of Unity* (Lee's Summit, Mo., 1951), p. 188.

42. Quoted in Stephen Gottschalk, *The Emergence of Christian Science in American Religious Life* (Berkeley, 1973), p. 115. Cf. J. Stillson Judah, *The History and Philosophy of the Metaphysical Movements in America* (Philadelphia, 1967), pp. 242–43.

43. Eugene Wood, "What the Public Wants to Read," *Atlantic Monthly*, October 1901, p. 569. The foremost historian of Christian Science is Robert Peel. See his *Mary Baker Eddy: The Years of Discovery, 1821–1875* (New York, 1966); *Mary Baker Eddy: The Years of Trial, 1876–1891* (New York, 1971); *Mary Baker Eddy: The Years of Authority* (New York, 1977).

44. Cf. Sidney Mead's review of Charles S. Braden, *These Also Believe* and Elmer Clark, *The Small Sects in America, Journal of Religion* 30(April 1950):142–44; Joshua L. Liebman, *Peace of Mind* (New York, 1946); Fulton J. Sheen, *Peace of Soul* (New York, 1949); Norman V. Peale, *The Power of Positive Thinking* (New York, 1952).

45. Judah, *Metaphysical Movements in America*, p. 273.

46. Carroll, *Religious Forces*, pp. 353–54; E. T. Hargrove, "The Progress of Theosophy in the United States," *North American Review* 162(January–June 1896):698–704.

47. William T. Stead, "Two Views of Madame Blavatsky," *American Review of Reviews* 3(January–July 1891):613–14.

48. *Christian Century* 27(March 1911):297; Madame Blavatsky, "Recent Progress in Theosophy," *North American Review* 151(July–December 1890):177–78. Exposés were in New York *Sun*, 1 June 1890 and 20 July 1890; *New York Times*, 8 June 1893.

49. *Current Literature* 32(March 1902):291.

50. Upton Sinclair, *The Profits of Religion* (Pasadena, 1918), p. 255.

51. *New York Times*, 1 December 1895; 6 August 1893.

52. Gregory H. Singleton, " 'Mere Middle-Class Institutions': Urban Protestantism in Nineteenth-Century America," *Journal of Social History* 6(Summer 1973):489–504.

53. Gottschalk, *Emergence of Christian Science*, pp. xv, xxi, 143, 199; John A. Dowie, "The Life of the Ram's Horn," *A Voice from Zion* 4(March 1900):8–9.

7

The New Covenant: The Jews and the Myth of America

Sam B. Girgus

For Europeans America began in the imagination. The New World was, as Howard Mumford Jones documents, a "strange new world" where "the Earthly Paradise, Arcadia, or the Golden Age was practicable and could actually be found."[1] Thus not only before the settling of New England but even before the accounts of Columbus, there was a "myth of America." Of course, the term "myth" has been the subject of considerable controversy among scholars in diverse disciplines for many years. The controversy concerning the uses and meaning of myth carries over when applied to the study of American culture and character. One generation of scholars such as Henry Nash Smith, Leo Marx, R. W. B. Lewis, and Leslie Fiedler has been followed by another including John Cawelti, Ann Douglas, Richard Slotkin, and Annette Kolodny, each of whom places a different focus and understanding on the meaning of myth and its application to America.[2] A provocative new study of the myth of America has been rendered by Sacvan Bercovitch, who approaches the myth through the rhetoric of the Puritan jeremiad. Bercovitch follows Perry Miller in seeing the jeremiad as a political sermon which became a public ritual. In the performance of the jeremiad the community perpetually renewed itself by grieving over its failure to live up to its heavenly inspired mission and by proclaiming again its allegiance and devotion to that mission. Bercovitch, however, also sees this ritualistic rhetoric of mission and conscience as providing the cohesion for the formation of an "ideological consensus." The jeremiad and the ideology of consensus give America the sense of being one culture and one people with a shared history and a common destiny. As Bercovitch says, "The ritual of the jeremiad bespeaks an ideological consensus—in moral, religious, economic, social, and intellectual matters—unmatched in any other modern culture. And the power of consensus is nowhere more evident than in the symbolic meaning that the jeremiads infused into the term America. . . . Of all symbols of identity, only *America* has united nationality and universality, civic and spiritual selfhood, secular and redemptive history, the country's past and paradise to be, in a single synthetic ideal. The symbol of America is the triumphant issue of early New England rhetoric and a long-ripened ritual of socialization."[3] In this view, therefore, the Puritans had the most pervasive and lasting impact upon the myth of America. John Winthrop's vision in 1630 aboard the *Arbella* "that wee shall be as a Citty upon a Hill, the eies of all people are uppon us" initiated a rhetorical tradition whose influence can be found throughout American literature and thought.[4] Images and symbols of a "chosen people" in a New Zion and a new Promised Land have helped to define our national character in terms of a national mission ever since.

It was this sense of the myth of America as a new "promised land" that attracted millions of Jews from both Germany and Eastern Europe to America during the nineteenth and twentieth centuries. It also was this sense of the myth and symbol of America that helped turn Jewish writers and thinkers into New Puritans of American consciousness by stirring them to carry forward the tradition of the moral psychology of the jeremiad. Of course all Jewish writers and thinkers did not perceive America through the same set of beliefs, values, and theories about politics, art, religion, and culture. Many, however, were united in that their vision of America was determined to a considerable extent by their understanding of the myth and symbol of America. For several generations of writers the myth grasped the center of Jewish consciousness in the same way that the Statue of Liberty dominates the view of New York harbor. They contributed to the life of the myth not only by focusing their attention upon it, but also by viewing it critically and analytically in a way that helped to adapt it to history. Thus, they modified and changed much of the rhetoric and the ideology of the myth. They also helped to devise a new narrative structure of the myth that dramatized the elements of cultural change and the transition from a rural nation dominated by a Protestant establishment to a nation of cities and new immigrants. As Allen Guttmann indicates, the millions of Jews who followed the original Puritans to America tended to "complicate the metaphor that made America the Promised Land."[5]

Even for confirmed critics and devoted dissidents the subject of the special mission and destiny of America along with the place of the Jew in that mission became a central concern for many Jewish writers. Accordingly, this concern for the myth touched upon most other aspects of the Jewish experience in America including the contribution of Jews to American literature, thought, and culture; the question of assimilation and identity; changes within Judaism and the Jewish community; the

heroism and sacrifice involved in overcoming the anxiety, dangers, and
hardships of the immigration experience; the tradition of Jewish radical
and revolutionary thought; the impact of Jews upon America's urban
history; the brief emergence in New York of a dynamic Yiddish culture;
the meaning for American culture as a whole of both ideological anti-
semitism and social discrimination; the Jewish experience as a model for
modern democratic culture and ethnic and cultural pluralism.

The importance of the myth of America to the Jewish experience
becomes clearer when we survey the extent to which the myth pervades
the whole body of writing and thinking of Jews from widely diverse
disciplines, professions, and areas of interest. The Puritans, of course, were
limited primarily to the sermon for articulating the rhetoric and ideology
of the American experience. Not so for Jewish writers, who utilized a
number of modes of expression and communication to deal with the
complex set of relationships involving Jews, the myth of America, and the
American experience. For Jews the novel has been one of the most important vehicles for dramatizing these relationships. Jewish novelists from
Abraham Cahan, Henry Roth, and Waldo Frank to Nathanael West,
Bernard Malamud, Philip Roth, Joseph Heller, Norman Mailer, and Saul
Bellow all have been concerned with using their fiction for probing and
illuminating the meaning of America and the Jewish relationship to America. In fact, many of them have assumed a modern-day prophetic function
which requires them to deal with the myths that relate Americans to their
culture. Waldo Frank provides a self-conscious example of this mythic
impulse in the Jewish writer. In *Our America* he writes, "America was a
conception to be created: in the painful labor of disclosing America to you
by word and symbol, I understood how close this need lay to my heart,
how I was in a casual way rehearsing in my talks with you the solemn role
of all my generation. America is a turmoiled giant who cannot speak."[6]

However, the mythic impulse also was central to a broad spectrum of
Jewish intellectuals, critics, political philosophers, public figures, and
leaders who worked and wrote outside the novelistic mode. These writers
and thinkers held views that cover the range of modern political ideologies and philosophical positions. Thus, figures who helped to situate the
Jew at the center of the myth of America include Oscar Straus, ambassa-
dor to Turkey and the secretary of commerce and labor under Theodore
Roosevelt, who forcefully argued that the Puritan spirit of freedom had its
roots in their identification with the Hebrews of the Old Testament; Louis
Marshall, the head of the American Jewish Committee and a fighter for
Jewish and black civil rights; Louis Brandeis, the influential labor attorney, liberal reformer, Zionist and Supreme Court justice; Horace Kallen,
the philosopher of pragmatism and cultural pluralism. The myth and
symbol of America also was important to the consciousness of Jewish
intellectuals and critics who have been at the center of the literary and

intellectual life of America for several decades. This group includes people of widely diverse political opinions and backgrounds. There are some leftist and radical literary figures but most are disaffected former radicals of the "Partisansky Review" and traditional liberals such as Lionel Trilling, Alfred Kazin, Paul Goodman, Harold Rosenberg, Isaac Rosenfeld, Robert Warshow, Clement Greenberg, Leslie Fiedler, Daniel Aaron, Leonard Kriegel. In addition, a new group labeled "neoconservative" includes Daniel Bell, Nathan Glazer, Norman Podhoretz, and Irving Kristol.

In the works of these writers, intellectuals, and public figures the myth of America becomes a complicated matter. However, three basic ways of dealing with the myth of America and the Jewish relationship to the myth emerge in their writings. The first involves a basic espousal of the myth as an ideal and vision of America. The second way of expressing the myth is in terms of antimyth which constitutes an attack on the culture because of the failure to live up to the myth. In this form the reality of failure serves as a means to strive for the ideal. Thus, alienation from the myth becomes an expression of a greater affirmation of it. The third way of dealing with the myth, however, involves a deeper form of alienation through ideological disavowal and psychological rejection of the myth of America. Sometimes these different attitudes toward the myth and different ways of expressing it operate together in the same work. In other writers, however, we get clear-cut models of these different forms of the myth of America. For example, in her autobiographical writings Mary Antin offers one of the strongest expressions of the myth of America as an ideal and vision. She speaks of her "healing ointment—my faith in America" and writes, "No! it is not I that belong to the past, but the past that belongs to me. America is the youngest of the nations, and inherits all that went before in history. And I am the youngest of America's children, and into my hands is given all her priceless heritage, to the last white star espied through the telescope, to the last great thought of the philosopher. Mine is the whole majestic past, and mine is the shining future."[7]

Such enthusiastic idealism invites a counterstatement. The idealism of the myth creates its own negation or antimyth in the interests of achieving a truer form of the mythic vision. As in the long tradition of the American jeremiad including works by Paine, Thoreau, Emerson, Whitman, Howells, the Jameses, Fitzgerald, and others, myth and antimyth operate together in the Jewish mind. In our own time, one of the most provocative examples of this use of the antimyth can be found in an often quoted section from Normal Mailer's *Armies of the Night:*

> Let the bugle blow. The death of America rides in on the smog. America—the land where a new kind of man was born from the idea that God was present in every man not only as compassion but as power, and so the country belonged to the people; for the will of the

people—if the locks of their life could be given the art to turn—was then the will of God. . . . Brood on that country who expresses our will. She is America, once a beauty of magnificence unparalleled, now a beauty with a leprous skin. She is heavy with child—no one knows if legitimate—and languishes in a dungeon whose walls are never seen. Now the first contractions of her fearsome labor begin—it will go on: no doctor exists to tell the hour. It is only known that false labor is not likely on her now, no, she will probably give birth, and to what?—the most fearsome totalitarianism the world has ever known? or can she, poor giant, tormented lovely girl, deliver a babe of a new world brave and tender, artful and wild? Rush to the locks. God writhes in his bonds. Rush to the locks. Deliver us from our curse. For we must end on the road to that mystery where courage, death, and the dream of love give promise of sleep.[8]

Mailer's attack, of course, constitutes an affirmation of the dream and ideal. In fact, as someone who so strongly espoused radical and alternative causes, his ultimate faith in and hope for the dream provides an important example of the power of the myth of America. His own version of the myth indicates how difficult it has been throughout our history to find viable and meaningful alternatives to the myth. Of course, there were many Jews who resisted with varying degrees of success any accommodation to the symbol of America. One example of orthodox resistance is Rabbi Jacob Joseph of Vilna, who was brought to New York's Lower East Side in 1887 to be chief rabbi; the results were marked with failure, frustration and pathos. Other Jews nourished hopes for maintaining a culture of Yiddish in America or fervently espoused Zionist proposals that did not become a popular movement until after the holocaust. In his classic study of the Jewish Lower East Side at the turn of the century, Hutchins Hapgood saw this culture of resistance to America as presenting Protestant America with an important example of an alternative way to live. "What we need at the present time more than anything else," he wrote in *The Spirit of the Ghetto*, "is a spiritual unity such as, perhaps, will only be the distant result of our present special activities. We need something similar to the spirit underlying the national and religious unity of the orthodox Jewish culture."[9]

However, the world of Yiddish writers and socialists Hapgood describes did not last. Most Jews assimilated into the mainstream. About a decade after the appearance of Hapgood's book, writers in *The New Republic* and *The Nation* saw the style and interests of the Yiddish writers as something of an oddity and deviation from the dominant trend. Similarly, the rigid Socialistic programs of other Jewish immigrants from Russia also declined in popularity and political significance after the First World War. As Arthur Liebman demonstrates in his new study of American Jews and radicalism, the Jewish left in America always functioned as an important minority voice within the larger Jewish community. This view runs contrary to the popular belief that the majority of Jews held leftist views and were active in radical politics. In fact, their interest in the myth and symbol of America led most Jewish writers and thinkers to sympathize with the political ideology that constitutes the counterpart to and foundation of the myth. This ideology involves the belief in the individualistic values of liberal democracy and in the importance of maintaining free institutions. Thus, the growing interest today of Jewish writers and thinkers in neoconservatism, or, as Podhoretz prefers to call it, centrist liberalism, has roots that go far back into the Jewish experience in America. In fact, Podhoretz's recent book, *Breaking Ranks: A Political Memoir*, reads like a celebration of the myth and the ideology that sustains it: "I was speaking that day as an American in defense of America, in defense of the liberal democratic system under which the country lived, and in defense of its rights and its duty to ensure the survival of that system against all who wished to discredit or destroy it. The fact that I as an individual, and the ethnic group of which I was a member, had experienced the blessings of the liberal democratic system in such abundance certainly inclined me to speak in its defense."[10] Thus, the myth of America and its attendant ideology help to provide for Podhoretz the unity and framework for a series of beliefs and positions involving equality, ethnicity, authority, race, and achievement in America.

Other Jewish writers also adopted a perspective that gave central concern to the national consensus. They dealt consciously with the myth of America. The fate of those who operated outside the myth is interesting. Such writers are in the tradition of what Bercovitch calls the anti-jeremiad in which the disappearance of the myth becomes equivalent to turning off the sun in the cosmos. "When they abandoned their faith in America," Bercovitch writes, "they had no other recourse. . . . In this country both the jeremiad and the anti-jeremiad foreclosed alternatives: the one by absorbing the hopes of mankind into the meaning of America, the other by reading into America the futility and fraud of hope itself."[11] Michael Gold serves as an example of a writer in the anti-jeremiad tradition. He rejected the myth of America but ultimately failed to produce a meaningful alternative because of his inability to mediate between his bitterness over America and his adherence to Communism. However, there is an important irony involved in other such writers who rejected the myth. Some of these writers found a perfect way to express their sense of futility and exhaustion by helping to create the new "plastic" culture of Hollywood. Samuel Ornitz, who expressed his desperate concern about the deterioration of Jewish life in a corrupt America in two brilliant and largely ignored books, wrote more than a dozen screenplays for relatively minor Hollywood movies. He was a member of the Hollywood Ten, the group of writers who were blacklisted from the film industry because of their left-wing backgrounds. Besides working with Nathanael West on several films, Ornitz also collaborated with Budd Schulberg. Both Schulberg and Ben Hecht, who also succeeded in Hollywood, in some ways are similar to Ornitz in their alienation and rejection of both the American myth and Jewish life in America. As with Ornitz, such alienation results, for both Schulberg and Hecht, in a form of nihilism and cynicism. For example, Schulberg's screenplay for *On the Waterfront* anticipates and signals the demoralization in the fifties and sixties of the liberal creed before the cultural and political problems of modern America. The hard-nosed realism of the film's script and cinematography masks a nihilistic sense of hopelessness about urban life, the fate of democracy, the morality of our institutions, and the character and fiber of the American people. Also, in Schulberg's popular novel *What Makes Sammy Run?* he perverts Jewish characters and the Jewish experience into a series of stereotypes and conventions that meet the expectations of the audience and say a great deal, therefore, about the author's self-image. Similarly, Ben Hecht in his novel *A Jew in Love* evidences profound Jewish self-hatred and contempt. Even Ludwig Lewisohn's novels and works espousing the rejection of a culturally bland America are dominated by characters who seem like projections of mass-culture images of Jews. They relate to equally unbelievable gentiles in a fictional world in which Lewisohn unsuccessfully attempts to create new cultural myths based upon Jewish defensiveness and Christian ignorance and insensitivity. The attraction of these writers to Hollywood and their proclivity to project in their work popular culture images and stereotypes of Jews and Jewish values and beliefs serve as an indication of their cultural isolation and alienation. Service to mass culture becomes a substitute for a sense of meaningful national culture and Jewish culture.

The writers of the anti-jeremiad generally were involved in a double rejection of American and Jewish culture which freed them from the basic challenge facing those writers working in the tradition of the myth of America. This challenge was to relate the myth of America to the context and conditions of modern America. According to at least one school of thought such an effort involves a contradiction within the very nature of mythology. Thus, Richard Slotkin maintains that throughout American history there has persisted an attempt "to fabricate" an American mythology based upon an "essentially artifical and typically American" idea of the meaning of myth. "True myths," he argues, "are generated on a sub-literary level by the historical experience of a people and thus constitute part of that inner reality which the work of the artist draws on, illuminates and explains." Slotkin further extends his criticism of the artificial myth makers to scholars. "Even scholarly critics who address themselves to the problem of the 'myth of America' have a marked tendency to engage in the manufacture of the myth they pretend to analyze in an attempt to reshape the character of their people or to justify some preconceived or inherited notion of American uniqueness. Such critics are themselves a part of this national phenomenon of myth-consciousness, this continual preoccupation with the necessity of defining or creating a national identity, a character for us to live in the world."[12]

Nevertheless, Slotkin goes on to accept Philip Wheelwright's theory of myth based on "stages of development in the evolution of myth-arti-facts"—the primary, romantic, and consummatory. It is in the third stage that Jewish writers of the past hundred years fall. Slotkin maintains that the "consummatory myth-maker" operates in a mode distinctly different from that of his predecessors. Slotkin writes,

> First, he is aware of and capable of articulating the need for myth *as myth*—that is, as a construction of symbols and values, derived from real and imaginary experience and ordered by the imagination according to the deepest needs of the psyche. In addition, he has the benefit of historical knowledge and can look back over a span of time in which myths have developed and decayed, have shaped and been shaped by human and national history. Given this double awareness, the consummatory myth-maker has a degree of critical distance from his material and his works which does not exist for the mystic of the primary myth or the conventional imitator of romantic myth.

The Jewish writers in this study, therefore, are performing a function consistent with the nature of myth "in highly sophisticated cultures, such as that of modern Europe and the West."[13] Moreover, in working with the unique "construction of symbols and values" known as the myth of America, they also are operating in an ongoing historical tradition and cultural process that sees the meaning of America in terms of continual redemption, renewal, and revolution. In his analysis of this cultural tra-dition Bercovitch summarizes it succinctly in his description of one of Emerson's essays as "a summons to continuing revolution that joins New England's errand, the Great Awakening, the War of Independence, and the Civil War, through the typology of America's mission."[14] Jewish writ-ers in America extended this process by dealing with the myth of America during a time of shattering change and turmoil characterized by such factors as urbanization, industrialization, and immigration itself. They thereby were reinventing American identity in a manner that gave major significance to the concomitant reinvention of Jewish identity in America.

Accordingly, within the context of the rhetoric and ideology of America as the symbol of redemption, renewal, and revolution, the most influen-tial Jewish writers of the past century constructed a narrative structure for the myth of America composed of symbols and metaphors relevant to the conditions of the modern American experience. The elements in this narrative structure are worth examining, especially insofar as they contrast with the traditional frontier version of the myth as derived primarily from the archetypal figures of Daniel Boone and James Fenimore Cooper's Natty Bumppo. The most outstanding element of change may be the most obvious: the hero of the piece is Jewish and as such stands for an aspect of the modern condition, modern consciousness or the modern sensibility. As in so many other matters, Abraham Cahan was a pioneer in this invention of a new American hero. In his first novel, *Yekl: A Tale of the New York Ghetto*, the hero simply represents the new immigrant. Later, however, in his masterpiece, *The Rise of David Levinsky*, Cahan develops a far more complex figure that anticipates many of the literary and cultural themes of the following decades. The influence of William Dean Howells was significant in the recognition of the importance to American literature and American culture of Cahan's work as an example of the new school of realism. Cahan was in effect beginning a tradition of the Jewish novel that came to dominate a large part of the American literary scene.

Another major element in the new narrative involves the importance of the urban landscape. The city is depicted in ambivalent terms bringing together opposing images and values. The city in the myth is an urban wilderness of violence, danger, and corruption but it also can be a place of opportunity for the aggressive, ambitious, and intelligent. The classic picture of the city as a jungle environment can perhaps be found in Henry Roth's *Call It Sleep*, in which the young David Schearl suffers all the pains and agonies of growing up on the New York streets. Even in that novel, however, Roth clearly has in mind a vision of the city as a place that ultimately could allow and nurture the formation of a Whitmanesque American character composed of the individualities of various representative Americans. Such conflicting images about the city appear throughout this literature in Nathanael West's visions of the city, Mailer's numerous essays, stories, and novels about New York, and Bellow's novels about the individual in the city from Augie March to Artur Sammler and Von Humboldt Fleisher.

The radical change in the landscape of this modern myth of America from the myth of the frontier leads to another important change. We go from a nineteenth-century idea of lateral mobility across frontiers to a new emphasis on upward mobility so that success and all the problems and ambiguities related to it become a major theme in the new narrative. Appearing first and in some ways in its most influential expression in *The Rise of David Levinsky*, the theme of success remains a pervasive idea up until the most recent works of Norman Podhoretz, Philip Roth, and Joseph Heller. A parallel and related theme is the concern for moral elevation in a competitive and brutal world. It dominates David Schearl's quest for both freedom and some kind of moral certainty, and plagues David Levinsky, who feels guilty throughout the novel because of his rejection of his past. The moral theme represents an important current in West, Mailer, Malamud, Roth, Heller, and Bellow.

Often this problem of moral elevation in a morally ambiguous and complicated age is compounded by another theme of assimilation or the confrontation with America—a theme Allen Guttmann sees as basic for understanding the Jewish experience in America. In this theme the hero questions his identity and the purpose of his life in a confrontation with the moral environment of a predominantly gentile America with which he deals on a daily basis. One expects this theme to be crucial in early writings but in fact it has achieved considerable intensity in some of the most recent Jewish literature such as Heller's *Good as Gold* and the novels and short stories of Philip Roth. Moreover, this confrontation leads to another basic theme of alienation and the confrontation with the self in which a hero such as Herzog, Bruce Gold, Levin in Malamud's *A New Life*, or David Kepesh in Roth's *The Professor of Desire* must deal with existential questions of anxiety, doubt, and identity in the attempt to find a place and a home.

The shikse or "gentile love goddess" theme is deeply involved in the development and resolution of all these themes. In the love goddess theme we find in Jewish writers the continuation on a psychological and metaphorical level of the symbol of America as a woman. Even in David Schearl we see this theme in his subconscious associations with the Statue of Liberty. Leslie Fiedler identifies and deprecates a counterpart to the shikse in the form of the image of the Jewish writer "as the exponent of the instinctual life, as the lover." Although such an idea, as Fiedler sees it, runs counter to the Jewish tradition, "it is in the role of passionate lover," he writes, "that the American-Jewish novelist sees himself at the moment of his entry into American literature; and the community with which he seeks to unite himself he sees as the *shikse*."[16]

Finally, this narrative form places a new emphasis upon the ideas of creativity and mind, by which I mean the use of language, metaphor, and mind as subjects in themselves. This accounts partially for the crucial role of education in the narrative as well as in the ideology of the myth. In fact, one critic sees Jewish-American novels primarily as "education novels."[17] Education as part of the overall theme of mind and creativity not only allows for upward mobility but also provides the individual with a means to perceive and therefore attempt to achieve the freedom of artistic and intellectual superiority, which in turn relates to moral elevation. Thus, we get in modern Jewish-American literature a self-conscious myth in which the main figures frequently are themselves involved intellectually and emotionally in the process of myth making or of understanding the myths, symbols, and values of their time.

Significantly, we find that this body of fiction and literature produced by Jewish writers and critics exists within the self-contained and ever-expanding universe of American rhetoric and thereby constitutes a continuation of the tradition of the jeremiad in American literature and culture. These writers from Cahan, Henry Roth, and West to our modern "jeremiahs"—Roth, Mailer, Heller, Malamud, Bellow—helped to effect a new covenant perpetuating the centrality of the myth of America for a new population and a new cultural environment. Thus, they follow in the path of earlier American "jeremiahs." As Bercovitch says, "What distinguishes the American writer—and the American Jeremiah from the late seventeenth century on—is his *refusal* to abandon the national covenant."[18] The commitment of Jewish writers and thinkers to this tradition of the myth and the national covenant grew out of and reflected the interest of the overall Jewish culture in achieving a secure place within the national consensus. While some established leaders of the dominant Protestant culture like Howells, Twain, and Hapgood encouraged Jewish participation in the cultural process of renewing the myth, others saw in the Jews as a people a challenge to their own class and cultural hegemony. In this sense, the antisemitism of such figures as Henry Adams and Frederick Jackson Turner provides a negative form of documentation of Jewish interest in the myth and symbol of America. Thus, Henry Adams wrote about himself: "His world was dead. Not a Polish Jew fresh from Warsaw or Cracow—not a furtive Yacoob or Ysaac still reeking of the Ghetto, snarling a weird Yiddish to the officers of the customs—but had a keener instinct, an intenser energy, and a freer hand than he—American of Americans with Heaven knew how many Puritans and Patriots behind him, and an education that had cost a civil war."[19] In his reaction to the Jews, as E. Digby Baltzell indicates, Adams not only "increasingly blamed the Jews for all he disliked about his age," but revealed something deep within himself. "The Adams family," Baltzell says, "had always taken a leading part in the destiny of America, and Henry's anti-semitism was indeed a kind of self-hate born of his abhorrence of the path now taken by 'His America.' In fact, the more one contemplates the mind of Henry Adams, the more one sees it as a symbol *par excellence* of the powerless brahmin who is finally forced to embrace the idea of caste after losing faith in aristocracy."[20]

Frederick Jackson Turner had somewhat similar feelings and problems. Daniel Aaron quotes Turner's description in 1887 of his discomfort upon being lost in the Jewish ghetto of Boston. "I was in Jewry," he wrote, "the street consecrated to 'old clothers,' pawnbrokers, and similar followers of Abraham." He describes the streets as "filled with big Jew men—long bearded and carrying a staff as you see in a picture,—and with Jew youths and maidens—some of the latter pretty—as you sometimes see a lilly in the green muddy slime." He notes further, with relief, that he finally was able to extricate himself "after much elbowing" from "this mass of oriental

noise and squalor." More than three decades later the descendants of
many of those Jews were crowding into Harvard, and Turner expressed his
concern about the ultimate issue of reconciling "New English ideals of
liberalism" with the fear of the growing influence and power of the immigrants. He confessed, "I don't like the prospects of Harvard a New Jerusalem and Boston already a new Cork. Bad old world and the times out of
joint."[21]

Turner's point of view may be based in part upon his understanding
of the frontier as the source of America's strength. He developed and
took for granted the thesis that the greatest qualities of American character derived from the frontier experience. In his famous address before
the American Historical Association in Chicago in 1893, Turner further
suggested that with the frontier closed, American culture would be
forced to endure a distressing change. Clearly, the immigrants arriving in
America indicated the wave of the future that seemed to Turner to counter the heart of what he considered to be most American. Ironically, the
very qualities of national character that Turner calls the "traits of the
frontier" could be cited with validity to describe the character of new
immigrants. Thus, Turner attributes to the frontier character "that coarse-
ness and strength combined with acuteness and acquisitiveness; that practical, inventive turn of mind, quick to find expedients; that masterful grasp
of material things, lacking in the artistic but powerful to effect great ends;
that restless, nervous energy; that dominant individualism, working for
good and for evil, and withal that buoyancy and exuberance which comes
with freedom." To modern immigrants America still seemed to offer
what Turner thought was possible only from the conditions of an open
frontier—"a new field of opportunity, a gate of escape from the bondage
of the past; and freshness, and confidence, and scorn of older society,
impatience of its restraints and its ideas, and indifference to its lessons."[22]
In a way these immigrants did more than challenge Turner's sense of
America. Even more galling for a historian, in effect they proved his thesis
to be part of a larger myth rather than an analytical fact.

Accordingly, to be meaningful and useful to Jewish immigrants the
myth of America could not be relegated exclusively to the myth of regeneration on the frontier. In the modern immigrant experience the frontier was closed, but the belief in America as a "promised land" and as an
idea remained. At the same time, the myth of the frontier and the West
with its suggestion of freedom and renewal could titillate and captivate
the imagination of Jews as much as gentiles. For example, Alfred Kazin
reports his lasting disappointment with his father for failing to remain in
the West where he could have settled permanently on a homestead. Kazin
writes, "*Omaha* was the most beautiful word I had ever heard, *homestead*
almost as beautiful; but I could never forgive him for not having accepted
that homestead."[23] However, while many Jews dreamed about finding
their freedom and acceptance in the West, the actual experience often

proved quite different from their expectations. For such Jews the encounter with the West inspired reactions that included irony and sometimes suspicion and fear.

One of the most interesting autobiographical accounts of the West as a place for rebirth as an American can be found in Marcus Ravage's *An American in the Making*. In the book Ravage seems to become a confirmed adherent to the myth of the regeneration and rebirth of the individual in the West. Beneath the surface of his affirmation, however, one senses làyers of doubt and insecurity about the permanence and reality of his transmogrification into a "real American." Ravage's account describes the typical immigrant's journey from Rumania to New York. After years of labor, education, and struggle he decides to go to college in what he and his friends consider to be a portion of the wild West—the University of Missouri. "I was going," he writes, "to the land of the 'real Americans.' "[24] He spends a bitterly long and frustrating first year feeling like an alien and outsider among his college mates. With some justification he decides that "unpalatable as the truth was, there was no evading the patent fact that if I was not taken in among the Missourians the fault was with me and not with them." By the end of the autobiography, Ravage has become convinced that "the loneliness I had endured, the snubbing, the ridicule, the inner struggles—all the dreariness and the sadness of my life in exile" had been worthwhile when compared with the "idealized vision of the clean manhood, the large human dignity, the wholesome, bracing atmosphere" that had opened itself to him in the West. He comes to feel that his manhood and freedom depend upon his completion of the break with the East that would enable him to continue the process of Americanization in the West. His new sense of alienation from his past becomes distressingly apparent during a return visit to New York when he feels uncomfortable among his old friends. Changed by his vision of the real America, he hears old radical arguments in New York that now seem based on a misunderstanding of the true nature of the American system. "I listened to it all with an alien ear," he writes. "Soon I caught myself defending the enemy out there. What did these folks know of Americans, anyhow?" Finally, he makes an emotional appeal to his best friend to follow him to Missouri to find her salvation as an American. " 'Save yourself, my dear,' " he says, " 'Run as fast as you can. You will find a bigger and freer world than this. Promise me that you will follow me to the West this fall. You will thank me for it. Those big, genuine people out in Missouri are the salt of the earth. Whatever they may think about the problem of universal brotherhood, they have already solved it for their next-door neighbors. There is no need of the social revolution in Missouri; they have a generous slice of the kingdom of heaven.' "[24]

While Ravage admits to the likelihood of exaggeration on his part, his statement and feelings about the West indicate a deeper level of insecurity and defensiveness. He seems caught in a classic bind. Wanting to

escape a minority culture in order to achieve dominant culture acceptance, he also feels an equally powerful need to defend and justify his own
culture. The ambiguity and conflict in Ravage's position lead him in his
autobiography to see in the West, and in Missouri especially, qualities
that not only were superhuman but super-American as well.

In other works by Jews about the encounter with the West the same set
of conflicts and ambiguities occur and lead to a process of irony and
demythologization. Thus, David Levinsky, like Ravage, equates "the real
America" with the West. "The road," Cahan writes, "was a great school of
business and life to me. . . . I saw much of the United States. Every time
I returned home I felt as though, in comparison with the places I had just
visited, New York was not an American city at all, and as though my last
trip had greatly added to the 'real American' quality in me." In contrast to
Ravage, however, Cahan views this feeling with irony because he under-
stands about the guilt and insecurity involved in this process of self-
transformation. This real America turns out to be one of manners and
gestures which will never give Levinsky any sense of peace or place.
Rather than a new sense of self, Levinsky only finds himself caught in a
drive toward conformity. He grows embarrassed by "my Talmudic gestic-
ulations, a habit that worried me like a physical defect. It was so distressingly un-American."[25] For other Jewish writers as well, the myth of the
West became filled with irony. Perhaps it achieves its most bitter treatment in West's *The Day of the Locust* in which the West in the form of
California becomes the exact opposite of the place for renewal. California,
the end of the road where Americans go to die, is a burial ground rather
than a garden.

A more explicit treatment of the encounter of the city Jew with the
myth of the West can be found in Bernard Malamud's *A New Life*. As the
title suggests, the novel is literally about the myth. The hero, Sy Levin, a
former drunkard, moves from New York to a small college in the Pacific
Northwest in a modern version of the traditional frontier pursuit for "a
new life." "One always hopes," he says, "that a new place will inspire
change—in one's life."[26] Moreover, he has bought the myth that such a
change can occur most readily in the West, which theoretically has been
the scene of regeneration for millions of Americans. "My God, the West,
Levin thought," writes Malamud. "He imagined the pioneers in covered
wagons entering this valley for the first time, and found it a moving
thought. Although he had lived little in nature Levin had always loved it,
and the sense of having done the right thing in leaving New York was
renewed in him. He shuddered at his good fortune" (p. 8). His gratitude
for being part of this experience in the West is both naive and honest.
"He was himself a stranger in the West but that didn't matter," Levin
intimates to his students. "By some miracle of movement and change,
standing before them as their English instructor by virtue of his appointment, Levin welcomed them from wherever they came: the Northwest

states, California, and a few from beyond the Rockies, a thrilling representation to a man who had in all his life never been west of Jersey City" (p. 85). His naiveté allows him to believe that he approaches a successful metamorphosis. Malamud writes that "in his heart he thanked them, sensing he had created their welcome of him. They represented the America he had so often heard of, the fabulous friendly West" (p. 85).

Of course, Levin must come to realize that there is no "new life" in a myth that takes him outside his essential self. He is the classic schlemiel-schlimazel figure in Jewish writing and humor who cannot escape his past. Malamud writes, "His escape to the West had thus far come to nothing, space corrupted by time, the past-contaminated self. . . . A white-eyed hound bayed at him from the window—his classic fear, failure after grimy years to master himself. He lay in silence, solitude and darkness. More than once he experienced crawling self-hatred. It left him frightened because he thought he had outdistanced it by three thousand miles. The future as new life was no longer predictable. That caused the floor to move under his bed" (p. 155).

Malamud intends in the novel for Levin to succeed through failure by seeing through himself and the society around him. In the reverse of the usual interpretation of David Levinsky's career, Sy Levin fails in the professional world in order to rise in a moral and ethical sphere. By finally accepting this failure he transcends and overcomes the false values of the new world in which he wanted so desperately to succeed. It is this aspect of the novel that so annoys Leslie Fiedler. In a typically brilliant and compelling article about the novel Fiedler complains that the book fails to fulfill its potential of "becoming the first real Jewish anti-Western." Fiedler maintains that Malamud either "out of lack of nerve or excess of ambition" attempts to turn Levin into "a heroic defender of the Liberal Tradition, which is to say an insufferable prig like Stephen Dedalus rather than an unloved, loveable victim like Leopold Bloom."[27]

It seems to me, however, that Levin's strength ultimately derives not from false heroics or brave deeds that are inconsistent with his character, but from the very elements that constitute and govern his sense of self. In other words, a major force behind his qualities as a schlemiel-victim figure is the intensity of his beliefs and his unswerving sincerity. He is a victim and schlemiel because he cares. In this sense, he accepts responsibility for his character. Those around him, like the Missourians who so intrigued Ravage, would be more than happy to have him act like one of them. Levin's charm, however, is a product of his inability to go along with the group in spite of his desire to be part of it. He finds that he cannot do the easy thing. In one of his conversations with a colleague Levin reveals these aspects of himself.

"The way the world is now,"Levin said, "I sometimes feel I'm engaged in a great irrelevancy, teaching people how to write who don't

know what to write. I can give them subjects but not subject matter.
I worry I'm not teaching how to keep civilization from destroying
itself." The instructor laughed embarrassedly. "Imagine that, Buck-
et, I know it sounds ridiculous, pretentious. I'm not particularly
gifted—ordinary if the truth be told—with a not very talented intellect, and how much good would I do, if any? Still, I have the
strongest urge to say they must understand what humanism means
or they won't know when freedom no longer exists. And that they
must either be the best—masters of ideas and of themselves—or
choose the best to lead them; in either case democracy wins. I have
the strongest compulsion to be involved with such thoughts in the
classroom, if you know what I mean" (p. 109).

In one sense, this speech sounds like Malamud's voice in almost a How-
ellsian form of address to the audience announcing moral priorities and
principles. Clearly, however, it also is designed for comic effect, portraying
Sy Levin for sophisticated readers as a kind of Miss Lonelyhearts of the
humanities and academic freedom. At the same time, the speech opens
an important window to Levin's consciousness and adds depth to his
qualities as a character. The result is not an epic clash between Sy
Levin, the Matthew Arnold of Cascadia, and the forces of darkness and
evil in the form of the corrupt and cowardly department administration.
Rather, we get a realistic encounter between a born loser, a defender of
lost causes who fumbles his way to a self-determined defeat that leaves
him carrying the moral baggage for others. Certainly, any sense of victory
or triumph for Levin comes along with enough ambiguity, irony, and loss
to maintain consistency with the central qualities of his character. True,
he leaves with the woman, but the value of this victory remains questionable. The problem of her dubious physical, emotional, and intellectual
endowments is furthered by the fact that Levin also served, at least
initially, as something of a surrogate lover for her. Furthermore, any
moral victory he achieves goes unrecognized while his slight impact on
improving the department meets a deep silence from his colleagues. He
leaves as a failure again but seems able to face his new problems and his
"new life."
    While Sy Levin functions as a realistic modern hero in the manner of
the victim and the schlemiel figure, the novel itself belongs to the tradition of the American jeremiad. Through the character of a lonely "pariah"
figure, who is not that much unlike classic American loners and noncon-
formists, Malamud attacks and criticizes his society and culture for failing
to live up to its ideal vision of itself. Moreover, he does this by debunking
one myth of America, the myth of regeneration in the West, while revivi-
fying a modern version of America as an idea consistent with the rhetoric
of the jeremiad. Clearly, Malamud sees Levin as a fragile guardian of the

values and ideals of the myth of America, just as Yakov Bok in *The Fixer* must tragically assume the burden of being Jewish in a way that makes him appear like the archetypal victim and hero both. In addition, in *A New Life*, Malamud leaves intact the narrative structure of the myth of America as it has emerged out of the Jewish urban experience. The one important variation involves the Northwest setting for the novel, but in this case Malamud in effect simply has moved the city novel in the form of Sy Levin's consciousness into the country. The *shikse* in the novel ties many of these themes together by indicating that she had literally "called" Levin in the mythic sense to perform his mission in the Northwest because of his Jewish looks. Through her involvement in the selection process for the job, she was instrumental in hiring Levin. She says, "Your picture reminded me of a Jewish boy I knew in college who was very kind to me during a trying time in my life." " 'So I was chosen,' Levin said" (p. 231).

In the light of the rhetorical aspects of this novel it is significant that the hero of Malamud's recent novel *Dubin's Lives* has studied and written biographies of some of America's most important nineteenth-century jeremiahs—Lincoln, Thoreau, Whitman, Twain. It is also interesting that *The Tenants*, another Malamud novel written after *A New Life*, concerns a conflict between a Jewish writer and a black writer. In their competition and hostility they live what they write so that fantasy, fiction, and reality all intermingle. The novel suggests that the outcome of their struggle will help determine who will write the future story of America. "No Jew can treat me like a man—male or female," the black writer says to the Jew. "You think you are the Chosen People. Well, you are wrong on that. *We* are the Chosen People from as of now on. You gonna find that out soon enough, you gonna lose your fuckn pride."[28] The novel ends with no false resolution of the conflict or bright promise for the future. It does, however, perform the vital function of dramatizing the central challenge facing the myth of America today. Can the myth work as a means of consensus and unity for blacks and other minorities?

In 1883, a Jewish poet, Emma Lazarus, who saw herself as a disciple of Ralph Waldo Emerson, metaphorically extended the myth of America to new immigrants through her poem "The New Colossus," which transformed the meaning of the Statue of Liberty into a symbol of asylum. More recently some black leaders also saw the destiny of blacks in terms of joining the myth of American destiny and national consensus. As Bercovitch has noted, Martin Luther King, Jr., attacked segregation "as a violation of the American dream."[29] Similar rhetoric has been adopted by Jesse Jackson and by leaders of other ethnic and minority groups such as César Chávez, the Mexican-American leader of the migrant farm workers of the Southwest.

At the same time, the question of the viability of the myth in our own day remains. Strident voices that emerged out of the radical rhetoric of the sixties, such as Vine Deloria, Stokely Carmichael, Angela Davis, and Kate Millett, call for a kind of separatism reminiscent of the anti-jeremiad tradition. Such speakers fear, among other things, destruction through absorption into the national consensus. Moreover, some of our best students of American pluralism and consensus question whether any meaningful consensus can exist today. Thus, John Higham believes that contemporary concerns with power and status among ethnic groups have superseded the earlier quest for "an inclusive community" that makes pluralism possible. "Apparently," Higham writes, "a decent multiethnic society must rest on a unifying ideology, faith, or myth. One of our tasks today is to learn how to revitalize a common faith amid multiplying claims for status and power."[30]

The response of Jews to this "task" and challenge is interesting. For one thing, for some Jews the myth of America itself may serve as a conservative influence. The so-called new conservatism of some Jewish intellectuals perhaps can be explained not just as an abandonment of earlier radical or liberal ideologies but as a natural outgrowth of those values associated with their original allegiance to the myth of America.[31] Unfortunately, such conservative positions may cast some Jews in the role once played by Adams and Turner. A failure to incorporate new people and groups into the myth and national consensus can lead to the kind of caste system and cultural isolationism that at one time assured the political impotence and eventual downfall of the established Protestants who were so afraid that the New Jerusalem of America would become a home for too many Jews.

NOTES

1. Howard Mumford Jones, *O Strange New World: American Culture, The Formative Years* (New York, 1968), p. 33.

2. See Henry Nash Smith, *Virgin Land: The American West as Symbol and Myth* (Cambridge, 1950); Leo Marx, *The Machine in the Garden: Technology and the Pastoral Ideal in America* (London, 1964); R. W. B. Lewis, *The American Adam: Innocence, Tragedy, and Tradition in the Nineteenth Century* (Chicago, 1955); Leslie Fiedler, *Love and Death in the American Novel*, rev. ed. (New York, 1966); John Cawelti, *Adventure, Mystery, and Romance: Formula Stories as Art and Popular Culture* (Chicago, 1976); Ann Douglas, *The Feminization of American Culture* (New York, 1978); Richard Slotkin, *Regeneration Through Violence: The Mythology of the American Frontier, 1600–1860* (Middletown, Conn., 1973); Annette Kolodny, *The Lay of the Land: Metaphor as Experience and History in American Life and Letters* (Chapel Hill, 1975).

3. Sacvan Bercovitch, *The American Jeremiad* (Madison, Wis., 1978), p. 176.

4. John Winthrop, "A Model of Christian Charity," in *Puritan Political Ideas, 1558–1794*, ed. Edmund S. Morgan (Indianapolis, 1965), p. 93.

5. Allen Guttmann, *The Jewish Writer in America: Assimiliation and the Crisis of Identity* (New York, 1971), p. 16. Of course, an enormous amount of scholarship has dealt with the Jewish experience in America. For recent bibliographies with works of interest to both the scholar and the general reader see Max I. Dimont, *The Jews in America: The Roots, History,*

and Destiny of American Jews (New York, 1978), pp. 263–76; Stanley Feldstein, *The Land That I Show You: Three Centuries of Jewish Life in America* (New York, 1978), pp. 462–83; Irving Howe, *World of Our Fathers* (New York, 1976), pp. 685–93; Moses Rischin, *The Promised City: New York's Jews, 1870–1914* (Cambridge, 1977), pp. 275–82.

6. Waldo Frank, *Our America* (New York, 1919), p. 4.

7. Mary Antin, *The Promised Land* (1912; reprint ed., Boston, 1969), pp. 197, 364.

8. Norman Mailer, *The Armies of the Night: History as a Novel, The Novel as History* (New York, 1968), p. 288.

9. Hutchins Hapgood, *The Spirit of the Ghetto: Studies of the Jewish Quarter of New York* (1902; reprint ed., New York, 1976), p. 37.

10. Norman Podhoretz, *Breaking Ranks: A Political Memoir* (New York, 1979), pp. 349–50. See also Arthur Liebman, *Jews and the Left* (New York, 1979); A. A. Roback, "Yiddish Books and Their Readers," *The Nation* 107(October 1918):408–12 and "Jews as Radicals," *The New Republic* 15(June 1918):209.

11. Bercovitch, *The American Jeremiad*, p. 191.

12. Slotkin, *Regeneration Through Violence*, pp. 3, 4.

13. Ibid., pp. 12, 13.

14. Bercovitch, *The American Jeremiad*, p. 201.

15. See Rudolf Kirk and Clara M. Kirk, "Abraham Cahan and William Dean Howells: The Story of a Friendship," *American Jewish Historical Quarterly* 52(1962):27–57.

16. Leslie A. Fiedler, "Genesis: The American-Jewish Novel Through the Twenties," *Midstream* 4(Summer 1958):28. For the first part see Fiedler, "The Breakthrough: The American Jewish Novelist and the Fictional Image of the Jew," *Midstream* 4(Winter 1958): 15–35.

17. See Bernard Sherman, *The Invention of the Jew: Jewish-American Education Novels (1916–1964)* (New York, 1969).

18. Bercovitch, *The American Jeremiad*, p. 181.

19. Henry Adams, *The Education of Henry Adams* (1918; reprint ed., Boston, 1961), p. 238.

20. E. Digby Baltzell, *The Protestant Establishment: Aristocracy and Caste in America* (New York, 1964), pp. 92, 93.

21. Quoted in Daniel Aaron, "Some Reflections on Communism and the Jewish Writer," in *The Ghetto and Beyond: Essays on Jewish Life in America*, ed. Peter I. Rose (New York, 1060), pp. 260, 17n, 21n.

22. Frederick Jackson Turner, "The Significance of the Frontier in American History," in *Frontier and Section: Selected Essays of Frederick Jackson Turner*, ed. Ray Allen Billington (Englewood Cliffs, N. J., 1961), pp. 61, 62.

23. Alfred Kazin, *A Walker in the City* (New York, 1951), p. 60.

24. M. E. Ravage, *An American In the Making: The Life Story of an Immigrant* (New York, 1917), pp. 196, 234, 263, 264.

25. Abraham Cahan, *The Rise of David Levinsky* (1917; reprint ed., 1969), pp. 325, 327.

26. Bernard Malamud, *A New Life* (New York, 1963), p. 20. All subsequent references to this book will be to this edition and will be quoted parenthetically in the text.

27. Leslie A. Fiedler, "Malamud's Travesty Western," *Novel* 10(Spring 1977):218. For a brilliant study of the schlemiel figure in literature, including a discussion of the works of Malamud, see Ruth R. Wisse, *The Schlemiel as Modern Hero* (Chicago & London: University of Chicago Press, 1971). See also Hannah Arendt, *The Jew as Pariah: Jewish Identity and Politics in the Modern Age*, ed. Ron H. Feldman (New York: Grove Press, 1978).

28. Bernard Malamud, *The Tenants* (New York, 1972), p. 206.

29. Bercovitch, *The American Jeremiad*, p. 11.

30. John Higham, *Send These to Me: Jews and Other Immigrants in Urban America* (New York, 1975), p. 230.

31. See Peter Steinfels, *The Neoconservatives: The Men Who Are Changing American Politics* (New York, 1979).

8

The "Limitless" Freedom of Myth: Paul Laurence Dunbar's *The Sport of the Gods* and the Criticism of Afro-American Literature*

Houston A. Baker, Jr.

In "Myth and Symbol,"[1] Victor Turner observes:

> Myths and liminal rites are not to be treated as models for secular behavior. Nor, on the other hand, are they to be regarded as cautionary tales, as negative models which should not be followed. Rather are they felt to be high or deep mysteries which put the initiand temporarily into close rapport with the primary or primordial generative powers of the cosmos, the acts of which transcend rather than transgress the norms of human secular society. In myth is a limitless freedom, a symbolic freedom of action which is denied to the norm-bound incumbent of a status in a social structure.

Under the terms suggested by this observation, myth—narratives explaining the origin and nature of the world by reference to the acts and intentions of supernatural beings—is to be distinguished from history. While myth draws our attention to the divine origins of things, the prag-

*An earlier version of this essay, *"The Sport of the Gods* as a Literary Work of Art," was presented as part of Morgan State University's Dunbar Commemoration in 1978. The research and writing of the earlier version were supported by the Center for Advanced Study in the Behavioral Sciences and the National Endowment for the Humanities. A John Simon Guggenheim Memorial Foundation Fellowship made possible the revised and expanded essay that appears here.

matic constraints of history direct our concern to discrete sets of human circumstances that mark determinate events. However, it is the "symbolic freedom" of myth that distinguishes it most sharply from a historical universe of discourse, for the boundaries of a historical universe are coextensive with communicative ends. Literary criticism, for example, comprises a historical domain. To achieve the status of "accepted and learned" critic, a person must transmit readily comprehensible messages to a historical audience, that is, an audience implicitly defined as possessing determinate needs, habits, customs, and the like. The role of recommending or commending works of literary art is thus historically situated. It relies for social efficacy on the "ordinary language" and historical grounding of a human community.

The myth, by contrast, and its various performances, are unbounded by such historical considerations. They find their conditions of existence in an a-historical, symbolic universe of discourse. Denoting myths as "transitional phenomena," as occurrences lying between two distinct social statuses, Turner continues:

> What the initiand seeks through rite and myth is not a moral *exemplum* so much as the power to transcend the limits of his previous status, although he knows he must accept the normative restraints of his new status. Liminality [a transitional or marginal state] is pure potency, where anything can happen, where immoderacy is normal, even normative, and where the elements of culture and society are released from their customary configurations and recombined in bizarre and terrifying imagery. (p. 577)

It is, finally, this inversion through imagery, this countermanding of social norms by symbolic means that governs the mythic universe of discourse. I would argue that a similar form of symbolic freedom characterizes the literary universe of discourse. And mythic and literary acts thus defined are different orders of phenomena from normative, historical acts of criticism.

The distinctions drawn here between the historical and other domains are intended to offer a statement of propositions designed to clarify a long-standing difficulty in the criticism of Afro-American literature. This difficulty consists in the propensity of literary critics to take Afro-American works of verbal art exclusively as historical acts of language. Given the foregoing stipulations on criticism's historical orientation, such an approach to Afro-American texts hardly seems anomalous. When it is pursued in isolation, however, this socio-historical critical approach can be inhibiting. For it generally ignores, or minimizes, the creative symbolic potency of Afro-American literary works of art. By invoking the example of Paul Laurence Dunbar and his novel *The Sport of the Gods*, I want to suggest in the discussion that follows that the analysis of works of Afro-American literature in terms of their "symbolic freedom" can dramatically (and profitably) alter our perspectives on such works.

My fundamental assumption is that though the mythic-literary and the historical domains are distinguishable, they are not mutually exclusive. A Venn diagram, for example, would represent them as overlapping circles whose area of intersection contains the historically grounded critic as mediator—as an agent summoning and interpreting for a human audience the symbolic force of literary or mythic narratives. Such a state of affairs, however, is contingent upon what might be called a "clarity of expectations." The *sine qua non* for the kind of prospect I have in mind is an expectation on the part of the critic that a novel like *The Sport of the Gods* is capable of generating a symbolic, mythic, or distinctively literary force that is irreducible to simple historical explanations. In order to arrive at this position, one must postulate, I think, the type of heuristic distinctions that appear above, and then strive to make the interpretive intersection a position that promises new meanings.

What I intend to suggest with the foregoing qualification is that the criticism of Afro-American literature at the present time may be thought of as a liminal enterprise. Today's critic is perforce bound to engage the terms of an old historical criticism in order to demonstrate its sharp limitations. He is, moreover, compelled to look to a contemporary and historically determinate universe of literary critical discourse for methods of analysis and for an audience. At the same time, however, he has the possibility of moving beyond the inadequacies of a past historical criticism by engaging Afro-American literary texts in their symbolic potency. In a sense that will be defined and explored in the concluding section of this discussion, he possesses a "limitless" freedom akin to the authorial prerogatives of the creator of *The Sport of the Gods*.

II

Like the eighteenth-century black American poet Phillis Wheatley, Paul Laurence Dunbar's life and works have normally been taken by critics as documentary evidence in what might be termed an ongoing historico-critical discourse. This discourse, which has the effect of a "state of the race" address, sees the Afro-American literary work of art as a covariant sign of what it considers historical, racial "progress." The fundamental notion generated by this correlation is the idea that a critic of Afro-American literature will discover ever more sophisticated works of art as he follows the historical path of black Americans from slavery to freedom. A further entailment is that the critic should expect to read in the black literary works of any given historical moment a report on the "state of the race" at that moment.

The logic of this historico-critical approach to Afro-American literature automatically curtails the attention granted to writers such as Wheatley and Dunbar by its implicit claim that twentieth-century works of black literature are more "advanced" and, hence, more worthy of attention than earlier productions. It also assumes that Afro-American literary texts, in their supposed historical reflexivity, directly mirror the social, political, and psychological conditions prevailing in Afro-American culture at any given time. Critical pronouncements on Wheatley and Dunbar governed by this prospect have, at their best, been useful descriptions and summaries.[2] At their worst, they have left a legacy of half-truths and tendentious clichés.[3]

Situated at some distance from the heroic couplets of Wheatley, critics who have produced such misleading judgments have usually begun with the assertion that the Boston poet's creations do not merit serious critical investigation because there was no articulate black literary tradition (presumably, one with which the critic sympathizes) and little social, political, and psychological freedom among black Americans during her era. Similar assumptions have marked critical evaluations of Dunbar, i.e., during the nadir of race relations in turn-of-the-century America, one such assumption might be summarized, and unaided by the sophisticated literary influences and opportunities enjoyed by his successors, Dunbar could not have produced literary works that deserve the serious attention of today's scholars. When the historico-critical analysts have considered it worthwhile to attempt an in-depth look at the writings of either Dunbar or Wheatley, they have almost always ended by detailing the "historical information" they think such works communicate—the messages they are supposed to convey about the context of their emergence.

The reasons for the endurance of the historico-critical discourse just described are manifold. But it seems to me that the grammar holding it intact includes two principal elements—the awesome history of American slavery and the blatant racism of American society. The force of these aspects of American life has been so quintessential in shaping Afro-American life and culture in the United States that critics of black literary texts are led to the position that acts of historical interpetation and acts of literary criticism are coterminous. The effects and meanings of a novel like *The Sport of the Gods* become, in this view, determinate, historical phenomena rounding out the critic's peculiar reading of history. And any facet of the work that appears to lie beyond this interpretive framework is ignored or minimized by the critic in his attempt to explain the novel in terms of a bedrock historicity. In sum, one might say that critics of Afro-American literature have not only felt the weight of a specific history on their shoulders, they have also been driven by a compulsive urge to conflate their unique interpretations of this history with their analyses of literary works of art, achieving thereby what they consider an adequate and unequivocal mechanism of critical explanation. The import of this observation becomes clearer in view of actual historico-critical estimates that have touched Dunbar's novel.

A critic like Robert Bone, for example, is clearly governed by an *a priori* interpretive stance on Afro-American history when he asserts the following of *The Sport of the Gods:*

> . . . at the height of the post-Reconstruction repression, with the Great Migration already under way, Dunbar was urging Negroes to stay in the South, where they could provide a disciplined labor force for the new plantation economy. His only fear was that the stream of young Negro life would continue to flow Northward, a sacrifice to "false ideals and unreal ambitions."[4]

Between the 1880s and the second decade of the twentieth century, more than two million black Americans left the south and migrated to the northern and western states of America. Since there were at least two geographical regions of black life in America when *The Sport of the Gods* was published, and since both regions are represented in the novel, Bone concludes that not only must he take an interpretive stance on this historic demographic shift among black Americans, but that he must also force the black author's novel into the service of his interpretation. His interpretive design sweeps all before it, implying in its course that the most vital meanings of *The Sport of the Gods* can be referred to a historical dichotomy between northern and southern, industrial and agrarian modes of black life in America. The historical bias of another critic, Kenny Jackson Williams,[5] is not so obvious as Bone's. She locates her interpretive intentions in the terminology of a critical debate that has exhausted much of the twentieth century in its attempt to determine whether Afro-American writers are, have been, or should be "protest" writers.[6] She concludes that Dunbar's novel proves that he was, indeed, a protest writer since *The Sport of the Gods* is, in her view, a critique of the "evil influences" the city exerts on black life. We are, of course, back at square one. Williams' discussion goes no farther than the historical dichotomy noted by Bone. A third variation on the historico-critical method—which obviously presents itself in myriad guises—situates its argument in an ideological context. Addison Gayle, Jr., argues that Dunbar merely imitated "the old Plantation Tradition"[7] in creating *The Sport of the Gods*. The ideological context that gives force to his argument is one which insists that Afro-American authors should create "positive" images and symbols of black life in order to promote the social "progress" of Afro-America. Gayle assures us that Dunbar was unable to contribute to this endeavor because he failed to transcend the negative stereotypes cast by the white authors of his day. And then by a deduction implicit in his underlying interpretive

design, Gayle asserts that *The Sport of the Gods* documents the fact that
black American migrants to the North were destined for tragedy in the
cities since they, like the author of the novel, would be helpless without
white support and influence. We are again returned to a narrow preoccupation with the historical context in which *The Sport of the Gods* emerged.
For Gayle seems bent on answering the question: "Was Dunbar's authorial
response to a determinate set of historical circumstances in accord with
my interpretation of Afro-American history?"

When T. S. Eliot wrote of the "cunning passages" and "contrived corri-
dors" of history perhaps he had in mind the difficulty human beings face
in avoiding the allure of seemingly adequate historical explanations. Certainly, the critics just discussed are so moved by an impulse to unravel the
"supple confusions" of history that they yoke Dunbar's novel to their
implicit interpretive accounts. Their expectations of *The Sport of the Gods*,
that is to say, are conditioned at a generative level by their assumption
that such a text is a historical document that communicates historical
information about the context of its creation. The irony of these expectations
lies in the fact that the allure of historical explanation comes first, prompting
false expectations and resulting in literary critical accounts that seem to
justify the impulse for historical explanation. What we have, therefore, is
self-fulfilling prophecy, the solacing embrace of a tautological circle. A
remark from Wittgenstein's lectures on aesthetics succinctly describes
the type of cognitive activity at work among those who take *The Sport of
the Gods* and other Afro-American literary texts as narratives continuous
with a historico-critical universe of discourse.

Discussing Freud's theory of dreams—particularly the notion that all
dreams are reducible to psychosexual explanation—Wittgenstein says:

> The attraction of certain kinds of explanation is overwhelming. At a
> given time the attraction of a certain kind of explanation is greater
> than you can conceive. In particular, explanation of the kind "This is
> really only this." There is a strong tendency to say: "We can't get
> round the fact that this dream is really such and such." . . . If
> someone says: "Why do you say it is really this? Obviously it is not
> this at all," it is in fact even difficult to see it as something else.[8]

Rephrased in terms of the present discussion, the remark suggests that
the claim that Afro-American literary texts are "really only" historical
documents whose meanings are ultimately referable to a determinate set
of human circumstances has an overwhelming explanatory charm. Further, Wittgenstein's observation alerts us to the fact that it is extremely
difficult—given this "charm"—for critics to see such texts in any other
way. Our perceptions are a function of hypotheses or theories that we find
comforting. The only way that we can come to perceive that an object, an

event, a process—or a novel—is not what we had at first taken it to be, therefore, is by assuming a different hypothetical or theoretical orientation. A critical orientation that looks not to history, but to the "limitless" freedom of the mythic and literary domains offers such a prospect where *The Sport of the Gods* is concerned. Under the aspect of a symbolic or representational universe of discourse, the novel can be seen to possess semantic resources that are difficult (if not impossible) to comprehend from a historico-critical perspective.

III

Mythic and literary acts of language are not intended or designed for communicative ends. That is, rather than informational or communicative utterances that assure a harmonious normalcy in human cultures, they are radically contingent language events whose various readings or performances occasion inversive symbolic modes of cognition and other non-quotidian human responses. Considered in these terms, *The Sport of the Gods* must be taken as a phenomenon different in kind from the communicative, historical document. The novel's conditions of existence are found not in the determinate circumstances of an historical moment, but in what Jonathan Culler calls "the institution of literature."[9] What is implied by Culler's phrase, however, is not the familiar disjunction between "literature" and "life." For an "institution" is, finally, a conventional or systematic behavioral pattern that is valued by a human community. To distinguish literature as an institution is to focus on the systematic linguistic behavior conventionally entailed among human beings by a particular kind of discourse. The justification for concentrating on language lies in the fact that the medium for literary works of art is language and in the fact that the linguistic behaviors associated with literary discourse are, in my view, different from those surrounding the speech of everyday contexts. The manner in which performative[10] speech acts function in ordinary discourse offers a case in point.

When I say, "I promise that I will come to the party" to a friend, I have performed a specific action on a specific historical occasion. My utterance is historically determinate. When the party takes place my friend expects my attendance. When, however, a character in a novel, or the speaker of a poem or play, says, "A distant relative of mine once had a great grief. I have never recovered from it," we do not assume that an historical action has been *performed*, nor do we go in search of a death certificate or a report of an actual disaster. We assume that the fictive or dramatic speaker's remarks (those of Sadness, a character in *The Sport of the Gods*, in this instance) offer a *representation* of the act of speaking and that the utterance, like the unfortunate relative, is historically indeterminate.[11]

In *The Theory of Literary Criticism*,[12] John Ellis provides a broad

description of what might be termed the audience expectations that surround literary language, or acts of literature:

> When . . . we treat a piece of language as literature, we characteris-
> tically do something quite surprising: we no longer accept any in-
> formation offered as something to act upon, nor do we act on its
> exhortations and imperatives. We do not generally concern our-
> selves with whether what it says is true or false, or regard it as
> relevant to any specific practical purpose. In sum, we no longer
> respond to it as part of the immediate context we live in and as
> something to use in our normal way as a means of controlling that
> context; nor do we concern ourselves with the immediate context
> from which it emerged, and so [we] are not taking it up to learn, in
> our normal way, something about that actual everday context.

Ellis' observation sets literary texts apart from both the historical moment
of their emergence and from the utilitarian, communicative goals of everyday language. It suggests, therefore, a *sui generis* institutional status for
a work like Dunbar's *The Sport of the Gods*, a status that augurs well for
the analytical potential of a criticism that seeks the nonhistorical, mythic,
or distinctively literary force of the narrative. Such a critical orientation
would immediately direct attention, I think, to the novel's title.

The title of Dunbar's work finds its reference not in the historically
documented betrayals and confusions of American Reconstruction, but in
the domain of literature. The blinded and deceived Gloucester remarks in
King Lear, "As flies to wanton boys are we to the Gods; / They kill us for
their sport." The origin and nature of the world, this utterance implies,
are functions of capricious supernaturals. The mythic universe of discourse
is thus invoked as an explanation of man's failings: Man is nothing special; he is a toy in the ludic world of the gods. While the title of Dunbar's
novel alone suggests its association with Gloucester's mythic view of human
events, the narrator's concluding line suggests an even more direct parallel with the Shakespearean character's remark:

> It was not a happy life [that of the black servant Berry Hamilton and
> his wife, who have returned to the South], but it was all that was left
> to them, and they took it up without complaint, for they knew they
> were powerless against some Will infinitely stronger than their own.[13]

An apotheosized "Will" that is "infinitely stronger" than human powers
can only find its being in the world of myth.

The "limitless" freedom of myth and its efficacy as a causal explanation
in human affairs, however, exist in the works of both the Renaissance
dramatist and the Afro-American novelist as ironic postulates. There may
well be powerful, invisible beings in the wings, but the reader of *King*

Lear is aware that the sufferings and deaths of the play have more to do
with distinctively human shortcomings than with the ludic wielding of
authority by immortals. That Gloucester, whose incredible folly is matched
only by that of his aged counterpart Lear, is the character who summons
"the sport of the Gods" as an explanation reinforces a reader's decision to
concentrate on human agents and actions in understanding Shakespeare's
drama. Similarly, having followed the controlling voice of the narrator
from the first to the concluding line of *The Sport of the Gods*, a reader
knows there is little need to summon incomprehensible supernatural
powers to explain the human affairs represented in the novel. For the
characters of Dunbar's work are, finally, the victims of their own, individual modes of processing reality. Their failings are the paradoxical results
of their peculiarly human ability (and inclination) to form theories of
knowledge. The narrator's recourse to what seems a mythic dimension (an
invincible "Will"), therefore, like Gloucester's evocation of the Gods in
Lear, not only stands in ironic contrast to the novel's representations of a
mundane reality, but also suggests an authorial awareness on Dunbar's
part that is crucial to a full understanding of his narrative.

The *Sport of the Gods* is the story of a theft. During a social gathering
in honor of Maurice Oakley's younger half-brother Francis, the latter
reports that a substantial sum of money loaned to him by Maurice and
intended for his artistic education has disappeared. Oakley's black servant, Berry Hamilton, is accused of the theft and convicted by the grand
jury. When Berry is sentenced to ten years at hard labor, his wife Fannie
and his two children, Joe and Kit, are forced to relocate in New York. Joe
becomes involved with a Broadway chorus girl and, finally, murders her.
Kit, meanwhile, rises to celebrity as a Broadway chorus girl. Fannie
Hamilton enters an ill-fated marriage with a "race horse man" named
Gibson. Oakley's world, in the interim, is shattered by a letter from
Francis. The half-brother, and *soi-disant* artist, confesses in the letter to
having gambled away the money loaned by Maurice. In the name of
"Southern honor" and to protect the good name of his family, he has
reported his loss as a theft. Prompted by the same motives, Oakley refuses to share his brother Frank's confession with the world. He becomes
an obsessed man, carrying the letter inside his shirt, clutching what he
calls his "secret" to his bosom. It is Skaggs, a man described as a "monu-
mental liar," who goes South, wrests the secret from Oakley's bosom, and
obtains Berry Hamilton's release. The black servant and his wife are
reunited and return to their former cottage on the Oakley estate. Maurice's
wife, Leslie, has reopened the cottage for them. The husband is now
completely insane. His wild shrieks serve as sound effects for the novel's
concluding tableau: the black couple sits alone, forlornly holding hands,
listening to the cries of a white madman.

It is tempting, in view of this summary, to label Dunbar's narrative a

minor romance of the South, to salvage what one can of historical import
and move on. I have already suggested, though, that such an approach
forecloses the possibility of an adequate account of the novel as a literary
work of art. The act of theft, which is central to the story, for example,
cannot be comprehended in its textual implications unless one appre-
hends the narrative's implied view of human understanding. *The Sport of
the Gods* is essentially a discourse, I think, on the fallibility of human
habits of thought. Maurice Oakley offers a case in point.

Considering himself a shrewd businessman beyond the reach of sentimentality, Oakley takes what he considers an analytical position on his
servant's alleged theft. He says: "I shall not condemn any one until I have
proof positive of his guilt or such clear circumstantial evidence that my
reason is satisfied" (p. 25). Only the flimsiest "circumstantial evidence"—
the fact that Hamilton has more than the amount of the reported theft in a
savings account and the fact that he has access to the half-brother's bed-
room—is available. Yet, it is sufficient to satisfy the master of his servant's
guilt. Indeed, Oakley's vaunted empiricism and proclaimed analytical
bent are no more than linguistic masks. They are verbal shows that conceal a sentimental and prejudiced ("No servant is beyond suspicion," he
says [p. 25]) fantast. Having received Frank's confession letter from Paris
later in the text, he sits and weaves elaborate fantasies of his brother's
abilities:

> First, now, it might be a notice that Frank had received the badge of
> the Legion of Honour. No, no, that was too big, and he laughed
> aloud at his own folly, wondering the next minute, with half shame,
> why he laughed, for did he, after all, believe anything was too big
> for that brother of his? Well, let him begin, anyway, away down.
> Let him say, for instance, that the letter told of the completion and
> sale of a great picture. . . . His dreams were taking the shape of
> reality in his mind, and he was believing all that he wanted to
> believe (pp. 183–85).

When such sentimental musings are shattered by the actual contents of
the letter, Oakley has no way of processing reality. His mental operations
are at an end. Bereft of his governing fancy, he goes mad, weeping "like a
child whose last toy has been broken" (p. 194).

The black servant who suffers the consequences of Oakley's weak intellect is a man falsely accused. The text, however, does not grant him the
status of a noble victim where human understanding is concerned. Instead, the narrative implies that Berry Hamilton has been as driven by a
misleading abstract idealism as his master has been controlled by a groundless fantasy. Berry has conducted his life in accordance with an ideal of
frugal, convivial Christian respectability that he takes as the moving force

of the white world occupied by his employer. He feels that by conducting his life in harmony with this ideal, he will transcend the limits that mark the black life of his own community. He has set his goals and established his "fictional finalisms,"[14] however, without considering the nearly mindless state of Maurice Oakley and his class. For in the servant's world view, the white world of the masters represents "quality." "It's de p'opah thing," he says, "fu' a man what waits on quality to have quality mannahs an' to waih quality clothes" (pp. 4–5). The paradoxical results of the servant's idealism achieve apt representation when he is sentenced to ten years of hard prison labor as a function of his life of industrious thrift. The bank account signaling adherence to his ideal is the evidence that condemns him in the eyes of the world.

The very existence of the "theft" that disrupts the Oakley estate is, thus, contingent upon a fragile psychological economy. A prejudicial fantasy and an infirm idealism offer its conditions of possibility. And Oakley's mode of processing experience is so prevalent among his fellow white townspeople and so forceful as a mode of explanation that no one is able to see that the servant is not "really" a thief. The town concurs that Hamilton could not have accumulated thirteen hundred dollars by honest means despite the fact that he

> had no rent to pay and no board to pay. His clothes came from his master, and Kitty and Fannie looked to their mistress for the larger number of their supplies. . . . Fannie herself made fifteen dollars a month, and . . . for two years Joe had been supporting himself (p. 57).

The narrator interjects that these aspects of Hamilton's situation did not "come up" in discussions of the alleged theft. And he later reflects on the inability of a clear and balanced empiricism to prevail against the epistemological sets of the master's and the servant's worlds:

> In vain the lawyer whom he [Berry] had secured showed that the evidence against him proved nothing. In vain he produced proof of the slow accumulation of what the man had. In vain he pleaded the man's former good name. The judge and the jury saw otherwise. Berry was convicted (p. 61–62).

The black townspeople respond in the manner of their white overlords. There is an immediate audit of the books Berry has kept as treasurer of his lodge, the Tribe of Benjamin. And the black A.M.E. church promptly expels him from membership. Finally, the servant's response to events surrounding him is not unlike Oakley's response to his brother's letter. "The shock," we are told by the narrator, "had been too sudden for him, and it was as if his reason had been for the time unseated" (p. 58).

In the fictional world that *The Sport of the Gods* establishes with the representation of a theft, men and women are undone by their limited and limiting modes of perception. They are incapable of seeing any object, person, or event steadily and whole because their cognitive strategies always mandate a partial view. At its most absurd level of representation this human inadequacy is captured by the denizens of the Continental Hotel. Horace Talbot, Beachfield Davis, and Colonel Saunders gather at the "Continental" (a devastatingly ironic label of sophistication in view of their discourse) to drink and to discuss the topics of their own and of southern days past. The adequacy of their means of apprehending the world reveals itself in their reflections on black Americans. Talbot advances what he calls his "theory" with the claim that blacks are irrepressible children who are unprepared for a "higher civilization." They have been mistakenly liberated from their bondage, says Talbot, by well-intentioned northerners. "Why gentlemen," he intones, "I foresee the day when these people themselves shall come to us Southerners of their own accord and ask to be re-enslaved until such time as they shall be fit for freedom" (p. 57). Beachfield Davis, by contrast, suggests that blacks suffer a condition of "total depravity." His evidence for the claim is the fact that one of his servants once used Davis' finely bred hound dog for possum hunting. Finally, Colonel Saunders' epistemological mettle is revealed when he retracts even his speculative remark that Berry Hamilton may be innocent. The three characters who occupy the Continental stand as parodic representations of "choice spirits of the old régime" (p. 220). They are men who take pride in a manner of ordering experience that blinds them to their own patent absurdity. Even Oakley, who is one of their number, refers to them as "a lot of muddle-pated fools" (p. 187).

The black counterparts of such unknowing whites are found in New York's Banner Club, a northern parallel to the Continental Hotel. Pretense, self-deception, masking, and indolence are the norm at the Banner Club. It is here that Berry's son Joe meets Hattie Sterling (who is anything but "sterling"). The chorus girl's fast-disappearing physical beauty is sufficiently masked to attract the young man's idolatry:

> . . . nothing could keep her from being glorious in his eyes,—not even the grease-paint which adhered in unneat patches to her face, nor her taste for whiskey in its unreformed state. He gazed at her in ecstasy . . . (p. 125).

Joe has been primed for this ecstatic response to a cosmetic beauty by his experiences among the "quality" young whites of the South:

> Down home he had shaved the wild young bucks of the town, and while doing it drunk in eagerly their unguarded narrations of their

> gay exploits. So he had started out with false ideals as to what was
> fine and manly. He was afflicted by a sort of moral and mental
> astigmatism that made him see everything wrong (p. 100).

Like his father, Joe is undone, in part, by his adoption of what he feels is a
suitable white standard of conduct. When he finally realizes how his naive
enthusiasm and sense of triumph in gaining Hattie's attention have played
him false, he becomes what the text describes as a "Frankenstein." Manipulated and shaped by misleading ideals, the young Hamilton is driven
to murder. His state when he is apprehended by the law is characterized
as follows:

> . . . there was no spirit or feeling left in him. He moved mechanically
> as if without sense or volition. The first impression he gave was that
> of a man over-acting insanity (p. 210).

When the boy's mode of understanding the world is destroyed, he is left a
prey to madness.

Kitty and Fannie Hamilton fare little better than Joe in their choice of
constructs for ordering experience. The girl's reaction to her first view of
the New York stage is described as one of enchantment:

> The airily dressed women seemed to her like creatures from fairy-
> land. It is strange how the glare of the footlights succeeds in deceiv-
> ing so many people who are able to see through other delusions.
> The cheap dresses on the street had not fooled Kitty for an instant,
> but take the same cheese-cloth, put a little water starch into it, and
> put it on the stage, and she could only see chiffon (p. 102).

Her mode of understanding life is fixed in this narrative moment. Her
vision and sympathies hardly extend beyond her own theatrical world
when the novel draws toward its climax with Joe's act of murder.

The unfortunate ends to which the characters come in *The Sport of
the Gods* are the logical results of their misguided modes of understanding the world. The narrator of the novel, however, does not situate this
human failing in a single geographical setting, nor does he suggest that it
is solely the function of an unalterable and determinate set of historical
events. Men and women in the city are as prone to misapprehensions of
experience as are those in the country. The events of an implied historical
progression (the "old days") may have left a legacy of inexact ideas and
fragile ideals, but all of human life is not helplessly shackled by these false
constructs. There is release from erroneous habits of thought in a domain
that transcends the ordinary course of affairs. This redeeming area of
human action is signaled by the first line of the novel, which introduces
the implicit subject of the narrative.

> Fiction has said so much in regret of the old days when there were plantations and overseers and masters and slaves, that it was good to come upon such a household as Berry Hamilton's, if for no other reason than that it afforded a relief from the monotony of tiresome iteration (p. 1).

From the outset, we are thus alerted that the text which follows is a "fiction" whose implied goal is to avoid the "monotony" of a traditional pattern of narration. This oft-repeated narrative pattern has been called the "Plantation Tradition."[15]

By inference, I suggest that the narrative strategy of *The Sport of the Gods* moves from its announced subject of "fiction" to an implicit *reductio ad absurdum* of the Plantation Tradition. The desire of Oakley and his confreres to see their mode of life raised to acclaim by an idealizing art conditions the pallid and deceptive romanticism of the southern artist. This reciprocal relationship is ultimately responsible for the true theft of the novel. Berry Hamilton's liberty and rightful earnings are the genuine items of theft. Their appropriation by southern justice is a function of the distorting modes of perception that both condition and gain support from the fictions of the Plantation Tradition.

The "surplus value" accumulated by the servant is seen by the South as a theft. Basing its conviction of the servant's guilt on the prevailing stereotypes of an idealizing fiction, the town is incapable of perceiving the genuine theft. Oakley offers a parodic illustration of this conditioned myopia when he says:

> . . . as soon as a negro like Hamilton learns the value of money and begins to earn it, at the same time he begins to covet some easy and rapid way of securing it. The old negro knew nothing of the value of money. When he stole, he stole hams and bacon and chickens. These were his immediate necessities and things he valued (p. 26).

The implication here, of course, is that the black American who honestly assumes values lying beyond a subsistence level of existence—that lie beyond the status prescribed for blacks as happy servitors—is "unthinkable." The art in which Oakley and his class place their entire faith supports such staunch ignorance. In a sense that constitutes a striking indictment of the southern businessman and his art, the black servant is the hapless victim of a fiction. When he leaves prison, the extent of the theft perpetrated against him is captured as follows:

> All the higher part of him he had left behind, dropping it off day after day through the wearisome years. He had put behind him the Berry Hamilton that laughed and joked and sang and believed, for even his faith had become only a numb fancy (p. 243).

As integral to the narrative strategy of *The Sport of the Gods* as the work's representation of the implications of a Plantation Tradition is the novel's implicit critique of black American popular art in the North. On the day the Hamiltons arrive in New York, their landlady suggests an evening out to them. "Why, yes," says one of the occupants of the rooming house, "what's the matter with tomorrer night? There's a good coon show in town. Out o'sight. Let's all go" (p. 94). In *Black Magic: A Pictorial History of Black Entertainers in America*,[16] Langston Hughes and Milton Meltzer write:

> Slowly [at the turn of the twentieth century] the tradition of minstrel exaggerations began to give way to a non-blackface pattern in Negro musicals which incorporated large choruses of pretty girls. At first, however, these shows were not termed musicals. They were called "coon shows" in contrast to the minstrels and Tom shows.

While Hughes and Meltzer consider such shows the "groundwork for public acceptance of Negro women and of the Negro male on the stage in other than burlesque fashion,"[17] the narrator of *The Sport of the Gods* characterizes them as theatricals combining "tawdry music and inane words" (p. 102). Their audiences are described as "swaggering, sporty young negroes" (p. 100) who move about the theatre as though they were the "owners" of the shows. Later in the text, Kitty is represented as dropping "the simple old songs she knew to practise the detestable coon ditties which the stage demanded" (p. 130). The coon show, finally, comes to stand in the narrative as the emblematic and ordering mode of perception for northern blacks.

At their first show, the Hamilton family capitulates to the vision of life that the coon show represents. Kitty gives way to the enchantment noted earlier. Her brother Joe is not only impressed by the pomp and swagger of the black audience, but also by the appearance of the women of the chorus:

> His soul was floating on a sea of sense. He had eyes and ears and thoughts only for the stage. His nerves tingled and his hands twitched. Only to know one of those radiant creatures, to have her speak to him, smile at him. If ever a man was intoxicated, Joe was (pp. 102–3).

Mrs. Hamilton at first has reservations, but these give way before the vigor of the performance:

> At first she was surprised at the enthusiasm over just such dancing as she could see any day from the loafers on the street corners down

home, and then, like a good, sensible, humble woman, she came around to the idea that it was she who had always been wrong in putting too low a value on really worthy things. So she laughed and applauded with the rest, all the while trying to quiet something that was tugging at her away down in her heart (pp. 105–06).

The force of the coon show as a symbol of northern black life is reflected not only by the narrative careers of Joe and Kitty (a lover of a chorus girl and a chorus girl respectively), but also by the remarks of those who "sermonise" on the plight of Joe and other young blacks who migrate to New York. Such sermonizers, the narrator tells us,

> wanted to preach to these people that good agriculture is better than bad art,—that it was better and nobler for them to sing to God across the Southern fields than to dance for rowdies in the Northern halls (p. 213).

All of northern black life, *The Sport of the Gods* implies, is a stage—the province of a gaudy coon show. And the lives guided by this "tawdry" means of processing experience stand in contrast to those that are governed by what the text refers to as the "old teachings and old customs" (p. 152) of black southern life. The irony of this contrast, however, is that the "customs" and "teaching" associated with singing to God "across the Southern fields" have provided no security for the lives of the Hamiltons, nor have they in any sense enabled them to withstand the allure of a northern coon show. Even more ironic, of course, is the fact that the coon-show representations that win them over are not radically different from the representations of the Plantation Tradition. The opening scene of the show they attend is one of jovial, energetic black picnickers on holiday, singing their contentment to the world. The turn-of-the-century black theatrical, then, is hardly an art—a means of understanding life—that can redeem the theft perpetrated by plantation fiction. What is needed for this task, *The Sport of the Gods* makes clear, is a new "idea," a new theory that will produce a dramatically different reading of life. Skaggs, the yellow journalist of the novel, is the character who arrives at such an idea.

Hearing Joe drunkenly speak of a theft, Skaggs "was all alert. He scented a story" (p. 204). When his first hypothesis that Joe is himself the thief fails, he says to an inhabitant of the Banner Club who taunts him, "I confess I am disappointed, but I've got an idea, just the same." His "idea" is that he can uncover the genuine theft and set matters right in print. It is this construct that he slowly nurtures:

> . . . that idea had stayed with him. . . . He thought and dreamed of it until he had made a working theory. Then one day, with a boldness

that he seldom assumed when in the sacred Presence [of his editor
of the New York *Universe*], he walked into the office and laid his
plans before the editor (p. 218).

What Skaggs' theory amounts to is a speculative ordering of unaccus-
tomed propositions, and the editor calls it "a rattle-brained, harum-
scarum thing" (p. 219). Yet the editor is alert to the universe of discourse
that the reporter is invoking, for he adds, "Yes, it [the theory] looks
plausible, but so does all fiction" (p. 219). Earlier, the narrator has commented that Skaggs is one with a penchant for the "bizarre" (p. 118). He is
also described as a person whose "saving quality . . . was that he calmly
believed his own lies while he was telling them, so no one was hurt, for
the deceiver was as much a victim as the deceived" (p. 122). The reporter,
in fact, begins his relationship with Joe by telling the boy an elaborate lie
about his white boyhood on a southern plantation. By the end of *The
Sport of the Gods*, however, he has ferreted out the crime perpetrated by
the Plantation Tradition and its artist. Skaggs' narrative progress, therefore, involves the introduction of a new and revealing perspective into the
universe of fictive discourse. I think he both represents (as a "monumen-
tal liar") and inhabits (given the text's strategies on the subject of "fiction")
this universe of discourse in the world of *The Sport of the Gods*.

IV

"Well, you see, Mr. Skaggs, none are so dull
as the people who think they think."

The final sentence of *The Sport of the Gods*, as I have previously
mentioned, invokes an unseen "Will" before which human beings are
powerless. I suggested earlier that this invocation signals a certain authorial
awareness on Dunbar's part. I want to hypothesize now that given the
framework of the text in which it appears, the narrator's concluding line
implies that the causal explanations and theories that human beings em-
ploy to organize experience are generally only half-truths, or worse, pal-
pably distorted frames of reference. When such modal epistemologies are
overthrown by "shocking," "bizarre," or "unthinkable" events, men give
way to the impotence of madness. Every man is, thus, under the narrator's implicit terms, his own Lear.

Art's role in this drama of human fallibility can be that of an abettor,
ceaselessly confirming and reiterating the partial view. On the other
hand, a properly oriented "fiction" growing out of an idea or theory that
looks beyond traditional modes of understanding can open the way for a
just conceptualization of the world. After such a fiction has been complet-

ed, however, men may still feel powerless. For the fresh propositions and persuasive, symbolic reorderings of life represented by such a fiction may so alter the customary ways of perceiving experience that the old norms of society are completely destroyed. In the fictive world of *The Sport of the Gods*, Skaggs' fiction has just this effect. It undercuts, disrupts, indeed destroys, both the stale monotony of the Plantation Tradition and the gay triviality of the northern coon show. Since these artisitc constructs are but extensions of the false or partial epistemologies of Maurice and Leslie Oakley, Berry and Fannie Hamilton, and of most of the other characters in the novel, human beings are logically represented as "powerless" after Skaggs' story had done its work. "After such knowledge, what forgiveness?"

The "Will" referred to in the narrative's final tableau, therefore, is, in my view, the force that generates a new mode of fictive discourse. The author of *The Sport of the Gods*, however, seems patently aware that the text's representation of the redemptive potential of fiction is, in itself, but one proposition in a fiction. His narrator self-consciously announces "fiction" as a subject of the narrative in the opening line of the novel. What I am suggesting is that Dunbar knew there was no such thing in the world of actual human events as a "limitless" freedom—mythic or otherwise. He knew that his own novel would not have the kind of immediate effect on the context in which it emerged as Skaggs' story has on the novel's fictive world of southern governors and northern readers. The black author realized, in short, that actual fictions operate within the "institution of literature" and are, like myths, marked by certain constraints. Turner notes:

> . . . this boundlessness [of the mythic performance] is restricted . . . by the knowledge that this is a unique situation and by a definition of the situation which states that the rites and myths must be told in a prescribed order and in a symbolic rather than a literal form. The very symbol that expresses at the same time restrains; through mimesis there is an acting out—rather than the acting—of an impulse that is biologically motivated but socially and morally reprehended.[18]

The Sport of the Gods, viewed in terms of this observation, is Dunbar's symbolic "acting out," as it were, of the effects on American life and letters of a supreme, revelatory fiction that will enable human beings to see life steadily and whole, that will enable them to break free from both their "artistic" and "ordinary" modes of structuring experience. The novel, thus, explores the proposition that a literary tradition governed by plantation and coon-show images of Afro-Americans can be altered through an ironic, symbolic, fictive manipulation of these images and of the tradition in which they have played a formative part.

NOTES

1. *International Encyclopedia of the Social Sciences* (New York, 1968), 10:576–82. The quotation that follows is found on p. 577.

2. For example, Margaretta Matilda Odell, *Memoir and Poems of Phillis Wheatley* (Boston, 1835), or Benjamin Brawley, *Paul Laurence Dunbar, Poet of His people* (Chapel Hill, 1936).

3. One of the more notable recent examples of the tendentious cliché is Amiri Baraka's condemnation of Wheatley in his essay "The Myth of a 'Negro Literature,' " *Home: Social Essays* (New York, 1966), p. 106. Baraka [at the time of the essay, LeRoi Jones] writes: "Phyllis Wheatley and her pleasant imitations of 18th century English poetry are far and, finally, ludicrous departures from the huge black voices that splintered southern nights with their *hollers, chants, arwhoolies*, and *ballits.*" Since Wheatley was hundreds of miles removed from the scene of the forms Baraka champions, it seems understandable that she would not have imitated them. The condemnation is, thus, gratuitous, tendentious, in the service of a particular ideological, historical interpetation. Wheatley criticism abounds in such critical acts. A reading of M. A. Richmond's *Bid The Vassal Soar* (Washington, D.C., 1974), makes this clear.

4. Robert Bone, *The Negro Novel in America* (New Haven, 1965), p. 42.

5. Kenny Jackson Williams, "The Masking of the Novelist," in *A Singer in the Dawn, Reinterpretations of Paul Laurence Dunbar*, ed. Jay Martin (New York, 1975), p. 195.

6. One of the most notable essays in this debate is James Baldwin's "Everybody's Protest Novel," which appears in the collection *Notes of a Native Son* (Boston, 1955), pp. 13–23. For an update of the issues involved in the debate, one might turn to Hoyt Fuller's essay, "The New Black Literature: Protest or Affirmation," which appears in *The Black Aesthetic*, ed. Addison Gayle, Jr., (New York, 1971), pp. 346–369.

7. Addison Gayle, Jr., "Literature as Catharsis: The Novels of Paul Laurence Dunbar," in *A Singer in the Dawn*, p. 149. Gayle brings forth essentially the same argument in his study of the Afro-American novel entitled *The Way of the New World*, (Garden City, N.Y., 1975).

8. *L. Wittgenstein: Lectures and Conversations on Aesthetics, Psychology and Religious Belief* ed. Cyril Barrett (Berkeley and Los Angeles, 1967), p. 24.

9. Jonathan Culler, *Structuralist Poetics* (Ithaca, 1975), p. 116.

10. In *How To Do Things With Words*, ed. J. O. Urmson and Marina Sbisa (Cambridge, Mass., 1975), the volume containing the William James Lectures delivered at Harvard by J. L. Austin, we find the following definition of a "performative": "One of our examples was, for instance, the utterance 'I do' (take this woman to be my lawful wedded wife), as uttered in the course of a marriage ceremony. Here we should say that in saying these words we are *doing* something—namely, marrying, rather than *reporting* something, namely *that* we are marrying. And the act of marrying, like, say, the act of betting, is at least *preferably* (though still not *accurately*) to be described as saying *certain words*, rather than as performing a different, inward and spiritual, action of which these words are merely the outward and audible sign." The characterization appears on pp. 12–13. For a discussion of speech acts in ordinary language, one can also turn to John R. Searle's *Speech Acts: An Essay in the Philosophy of Language*, (Cambridge, 1969).

11. I am indebted for this insight to Barbara Herrnstein Smith's "Poetry as Fiction," which appears in *New Directions in Literary History* ed. Ralph Cohen (Baltimore, 1974), pp. 165–87. Professor Smith explores the insight at greater length in her recent work, *On The Margins of Discourse: The Relation of Literature to Language* (Chicago, 1978).

12. John Ellis, *The Theory of Literary Criticism* (Berkeley, Los Angeles, London, 1974), p. 43.

13. Paul Laurence Dunbar, *The Sport of the Gods* (New York, 1969), p. 255. All citations from the novel in my text come from this Arno Press edition and are, subsequently, noted by page numbers in parentheses.

14. The notion captured by this phrase is that human beings are motivated in their present actions by their expectations of the future. For a further discussion of the notion in the history of psychology, one can consult C. S. Hall and Gardner Lindzey's *Theories of Personality* (New York, 1978), pp. 160–61.

15. For a useful discussion of the Plantation Tradition in American letters, one can consult Jean Fagan Yellin's *The Intricate Knot: Black Figures in American Literature, 1776–1863,* (New York, 1972). For a brief and provocative analysis of this tradition, one can turn to Addison Gayle's essay, "Cultural Hegemony: The Southern White Writer and American Letters," *Amistad I* (New York, 1970), pp. 1–24.

16. Langston Hughes and Milton Meltzer, *Black Magic: A Pictorial History of Black Entertainers in America* (New York, 1967), pp. 47–48.

17. Ibid., p. 48.

18. Turner, "Myth and Symbol," p. 577.

9

American Values and Organized Crime: Suckers and Wiseguys

Peter A. Lupsha

Eliot's statements about time in the opening of *Four Quartets* are also statements about culture. Our symbols of self all contain our collective past in our individual present. And indeed, our individual and collective future is but a hall of mirrors reflecting past on present as we go forward. Culture brands our behavior so that most sensitive observers are both looking in and acting at the same time. Our cultural images of what we ought to be often define what we are and become. We are trained to think in stereotypes, standardized images that hide individual uniqueness.

To create a unique self is a difficult task, a luxury few have the wit or leisure even to attempt. Most of us are thus content to be molded by a role as defined by culture.[1] This process, however, is a subtle one. Patterns are drawn not only from sense data and technological reality, but also from a desire to be, as well as an understanding of what has worked in the past. Thus we are not only cultural creations at best, caricatures at worst; we are ongoing representations of myth as repeated and delimited by our society over time.

When we ask "What's American about American crime?" the answer is flashed for all of us (Americans) to see. If we say "violent urban street crime," a host of modern American cultural images appears. A different set appears if we say "Jesse James," and a third set if we say "organized crime." This paper concentrates on the third set of images. Organized crime provides a panoply of American images containing all of the relativity of Eliot, while bearing the unique imprint of our American culture.

The taproots of American culture are those Lockeian values embodied in the writings, declarations, and documents of the Founding Fathers and their interpreters. These values are based in beliefs in individualism, property, or "materialism," competition, and freedom of action, or inde-

144

pendence. From the interplay of these values come our perceptions of opportunity, democratic procedural equality, substantive equality, material success, acquisitiveness, and a belief in right vested in the individual rather than in the community.[2] As these values and ideas shape our political and economic system, so too, they shaped the development and evolution of organized crime in America.

Organized criminal groups have operated in the United States from its very beginnings.[3] Whenever there is an opportunity to enhance profit or create wealth, wherever there are imbalances in the market system or government has through its actions created scarcity and black markets, or wherever local culture and mores make for illicit actions or behaviors against which there are no universal taboos, enterprising individuals will take advantage of the opportunity, risking potential sanction in order to accrue windfall profits. Such fields of illicit action are limited only by culture, precedent, opportunity, and the swiftness and certainty of sanction. If large profits are easily available with relatively little risk, the potential for organized criminal entrepreneurship is enhanced. This point seems obvious enough, yet history and experience show that it has rarely been acted upon by designers of criminal justice systems, at least in the United States. The reason is not a failure of understanding; it is that such planning must operate within the cultural framework that allows the development of organized crime in the first place. Thus cultural and juridical treatment of symptoms, rather than causes, must be the rule; the opportunity for entrepreneurial and syndicated criminal enterprise remains.

America has always been a haven for the entrepreneurial endeavor of organized crime. John Hancock amassed his fortune financing smuggling operations that overcame the Crown's attempts at orderly regulation of West Indian commerce. Robert Morris and James Wilson, two of the important draftsmen of our Constitution, were, as a U.S. senator and associate justice of the Supreme Court respectively, involved with a number of prominent others in the famous Yazoo land fraud.

Land fraud and land speculation in America are older than our form of government. Such enterprise has been assisted, as Tocqueville noted, by the relative equality of condition in the United States, which "naturally urges men to embark on commercial and industrial pursuits, and . . . tends to increase and to distribute real property".[4] Americans have always been willing to opt for personal gain against the possibility of sanction and condemnation. The line between sharp practice and criminal act has always been a blurred one.

James Truslow Adams, of the illustrious Adams family, put it this way:

> Lawlessness has been and is one of the most distinctive American traits. . . . It is impossible to blame the situation on the "foreign-

ers." The overwhelming mass of them were law-abiding in their
own lands. If they become lawless here it must be largely due to
the American atmosphere and conditions. There seems to me to be
plenty of evidence to prove that the immigrants were made lawless
by America, rather than America made lawless by them. If the
general attitude towards law, if the laws themselves and their administration, were all as sound here as in the native lands of the
immigrants, those newcomers would give no more trouble here
than they did at home. This is not the case, and Americans themselves are, and most always have been, less law-abiding than the
more civilized European nations.[5]

In America *caveat emptor*, let the buyer beware, was a ruling principle
of commerce until this generation of consumers began to seek to restrain
it. Our values and predisposition for material gain have always made the
"Murphy game," "the pigeon drop," "three card Monte," and other ancient con games and swindles commonplace. P. T. Barnum's admonition
"There's a sucker born every minute" rings as true today as it did a
hundred years ago, as recent commodity and diamond investment swindles indicate. Indeed it is useful to examine the use and operation of the
concept of "sucker" in our history and thought. This concept is an ingrained part of our nation, one of the most American things about American crime. It states, in part, that an avaricious individual, or just a naive
and easily deceived one, is fair game for those who are sharper, quicker
witted, or more worldly. All, in America, are at liberty to be suckers or
swindlers.

As there are suckers, so there are "sharpies." Americans have always
been willing to engage in sharp, often illegal, practice if the opportunity
presents itself. We are told that the political epitaph of Boss Plunkett of
Tammany Hall was, "I seen my opportunities, and I took 'em!"—an epitaph that is often seen not as a motto of avaricious behavior, or a violation
of public role and trust, but simply as an example of living off politics as
well as for it. In engaging in "white graft," Plunkett, Tweed, and other
political bosses were simply combining "good business" with politics.

Tycoons like Cornelius "Let the public be damned" Vanderbilt, Andrew
Carnegie, and John D. "The Lord gave me my money" Rockefeller,
whom Theodore Roosevelt referred to as the "malefactors of great wealth,"
were not dismayed by the political bosses as long as they were not losing
their share of what was there to be gained.[6] These captains of industry
and politics were models for the street-gang immigrant kids who were to
use the black market opportunity of Prohibition to accumulate capital and
form the organizational connections that created modern organized crime
in America.

Add to this the image of America as the land of opportunity, a land of milk and honey, where the streets were paved with gold. In such an early. paradise, where the good things of life were for the taking, one would seem a fool to work long hours for low pay and slow advancement. America was a land of opportunity; its values prevented swift or easy punishment of those who interpreted liberty as a license to steal. The arrival of Prohibition simply added the hypocrisy of law, and its corruption, to this ethic, and it gave a certain veneer of legitimacy to the entrepreneurship of the bootlegger and rising organized gangster. Flowing alongside this social, economic, and political flotsam in our cultural stream was our concept of the "sucker."

A second aspect to the sucker concept must be mentioned here. This is the notion that one is a sucker if one who is outside the dominant value system, or social strata, lives by the values of that dominant system. This aspect of the concept is important because, along with freedom of individual choice, it lies behind much of the development of organized crime in America. In 1930 Courtney Terret published a novel about organized crime entitled *Only Saps Work*.[7] In the same period the celluloid mobsters of Hollywood—Edward G. Robinson, James Cagney, Humphrey Bogart—echoed this theme, as did the real-life gangster Charlie "Lucky" Luciano.

> A "crumb," according to Luciano, was one "who works and saves, and lays his money aside; who indulges in no extravagance." Luciano wanted "money to spend, beautiful women to enjoy, silk underclothes and places to go in style.[8]

Luciano had no intention of being a "crumb" or "sucker" or of participating in the "grind" of ordinary existence any more than his associates did. Vincent Teresa, a nonmember associate of the Patriarca Italian-American La Cosa Nostra (LCN) organized crime family, more recently repeated this theme:

> I knew that the only way I could live in the style I liked was by being a thief. It was easier than working for a living. The money rolled in. Sometimes it went out faster than I could steal it, but I liked the life. I liked the excitement. There was kind of a thrill to everything I did.

A close study of Teresa's life suggests that these images of ease and excitement were mostly mythic, but there was more to it than that. Teresa continues:

> It's hard to explain, but there was a feeling of power being on the street with men that were always hustling, outfiguring the straights. It seemed that everyone I knew or grew up with was a thief of one kind or another. We were all living pretty good, spending high, dressing fine, hitting all the good spots. It was a helluva life.[10]

Now we have images of power, as well as excitement, in "conning" the modern version of the hard-working sucker. There is also the "high living" that Luciano referred to, as well as something else—the avoidance of a nine-to-five life at an ordinary job, the "grind." Teresa makes this explicit. He and an associate had opened a successful nightclub which Teresa wanted to burn down for the insurance money. His partner prevented him from doing so because the nightclub was making such a good profit. To Teresa, "The nightclub was making money, but it was strictly a grind, and who needs a grind when there is easy money to be made?"[11] Such statements by career professionals in syndicated crime tell us a lot, not only about crime in America but also about its roots in our cultural ideas about the "sucker."

Alongside the concept of the sucker, the willingness to engage in sharp practice, and visions of liberty and opportunity, stands the notion of material success. The organized criminal hungers for success while desperately seeking to avoid being a sucker. Wealth without work, however, is difficult to achieve. Thus the organized criminal seeks to place a veil of romance and myth over his activities to endow them with apparent ease and success so that he will not be thought of as society's fool.

The organized criminal must establish a code of conduct that permits success, or rationalizes success, without considering the successful criminal a "sucker." This is a paradox. If the "straight" world and work are the domain of suckers, then criminal actions—even failure, arrest, and imprisonment—must be endowed with ease, glamor, success, and correctness. This world view is accomplished in two ways, first, by the establishment of an internal personal code, a set of rules and ethics, which may seem perverse to the outside world, but which permits a sense of self-worth for the criminal, and second, by the establishment of an image of the outside world that considers suckers and straights as inherently corrupt, dishonest, and hypocritical. Paradoxically, this image suggests that the suckers lack the courage and grace to act on the insight that the world is a "con." They know that those with political and economic power get the good things of life, but because they are afraid, the suckers toil long and hard, accepting hardship, and deferring gratifications. Lucky Luciano summed it up like this:

> Everybody's got larceny in 'em, only most of 'em don't have the guts to do nothin' about it. That's the big difference between us and the guys who call themselves honest. We got the guts to do what they'd like to do only they're too scared to.[12]

This cynicism toward the outside world, plus a personal code of incorruptibility and loyalty to kin, peers, and criminal cohorts, permits the organized criminal to invert the mirror of reality and view his values as correct and society's as perverse.

"To be straight is to be a victim." So states a common La Cosa Nostra "borgata" expression. As Donald Cressey tells us about this code,

> A man who is committed to regular work and submission to duly constituted authority is a sucker. When one Cosa Nostra member intends to insult and cast aspersion on the competence of another, he is likely to say, sneeringly, "Why don't you go out and get a job?"[13]

To get a job requires education. During the first decade of this century, when young street hoodlums learned the habits and skills essential for success during Prohibition, education was just beginning to "emerge as an increasing important qualification for employment." But as Nelli notes:

> To slum area youngsters like Salvatore Lucania (Charlie Lucky Luciano), John Torrio, and Alphonse Caponi (Al Capone), excitement and economic opportunity seemed to be out in the streets rather than in the classroom. As soon as they reached the legal withdrawal age of fourteen, they left school.[14]

According to Luciano, he knew "that school had nothing to teach him," but in the streets he saw "some people had money, some people didn't."

> When I looked around the neighborhood, I found out that the kids wasn't the only crooks. We were surrounded by crooks, and plenty of them was guys who were supposed to be legit, like the landlords and storekeepers and the politicans and cops on the beat. All of them was stealing from somebody.[15]

Here is a glimmer of that world view of society as corrupt emerging in the child, a view that was reinforced by Luciano's experiences in the Brooklyn Truancy School and Hampton Farms Penitentiary.[16] It is this world view that sets the organized criminal apart from his fellow street-gang members.

Nelli notes:

> Unlike most of their contemporaries, who also belonged to street gangs and were involved in occasional mischief-making, the criminals-in-the-making had little or nothing to do with legitimate labor, which they believed was only for "suckers," men who worked long hours for low pay and lived in overcrowded tenements with their families.[17]

The picture painted here is rather different from the "queer ladder thesis" of crime as a method of upward mobility, which has been stressed by some sociologists.[18] Yes, some of these young immigrants chose careers in crime, but they did not act out of frustration, or any long struggle of being excluded from the political ladder, or because they were blocked from other avenues of career advancement. They turned to crime because they felt that the legitimate opportunity structures were for "suckers," and they were not going to be trapped in the nickel-and-dime world of ordinary work.

The young organized criminals of the Prohibition era saw themselves as the "wiseguys," a term still used in LCN circles to denote soldiers who appear to make an easy buck without working. These "wiseguys" could have economic mobility without ever climbing the status ladder. Their choice was an individual decision, reinforced by peers, experience, and a talent for violence. They were not more frustrated, nor more deprived (relatively or absolutely) than their classroom peers and fellow street-gang members who chose to be "straights" and suckers, following the legitimate socioeconomic ladder, narrow and crowded as it may have been.

To avoid becoming trapped as suckers in the grind of work and subservience to superiors, this alternative world view was created. As one was surrounded by crooks and hypocrites in the guise of legitimate businessmen and politicians, one could at least be honest with oneself, true to some personal code, and be an excellent thief. Luciano always said he needed nothing in writing because "his word was his bond." Luciano and the others had proved as street-gang kids that they had guts, courage, criminal skills, and a capacity for depersonalized violence, but they were also lucky. They arrived at adulthood just as the doors of criminal opportunity swung wide with Prohibition.

At the time of enactment of the legislation Lucky Luciano was twenty, Vito Genovese nineteen, Carlo Gambino seventeen, Al Capone eighteen, Thomas Lucchese eighteen, Joseph Profaci twenty, and Frank Costello twenty-six. By the time Prohibition went into effect, 16 January 1920, other street-gang teen-agers were coming of age to make themselves a name in organized crime: Meyer Lansky, seventeen, Pete Licavoli, sixteen, Jerry Catena, seventeen, Joe Adonis, seventeen, and Albert Anastasia, fifteen. By March 1933, when the legislation repealing Prohibition was enacted, these teen-agers had grown to manhood and had capital, organizational skills, and influence. Thus the serendipity of Prohibition provided opportunity, capital, and organization to routinize organized crime. Prohibition and personal choice, not career blockage or frustration with the legitimate mobility paths, moved these small-time hoodlums into leadership positions in organized crime.

Another aspect of our cultural system reinforces and further legitimizes and justifies the perverse world view of the organized criminal. This is the relationship between politics and the public, particularly the political party nominating and financing system that maintained the urban political machine.

As Ianni has succinctly put it,

> The corrupt political structures of the major American cities and organized crime have always enjoyed a symbiotic relationship in which success in one is dependent on the right connections in the other.[19]

To understand how this symbiosis raises the organized criminal to a superior personal status above politicians, one must recognize that the corruptor always feels superior to the corruptee. The politician who accepts "favors" and in return provides protection to the illegal enterprises of organized crime not only gives a living witness to the criminal's world view but also confirms for the organized criminal, in violating his oath of office, that a criminal's code is superior to society's.

In a Chicago *Tribune* interview in 1927 Al Capone put it this way:

> There is one thing that is worse than a crook and that's a crooked man in a big political job. A man who pretends he's enforcing the law and is really making dough out of somebody breaking it—a self-respecting hoodlum doesn't have any use for that kind of fellow—he buys them like he'd buy any other article necessary for his trade, but he hates them in his heart.[20]

Here is one of America's leading organized criminals stating his moral code, indicating his superiority over crooked politicians and his belief in fundamental American values which he himself does not follow. Above all, clearly contained in this statement is a disdain for another's hypocrisy and a lack of recognition of his own.

With their own world view, their blinders, their moral code, organized criminals are of American society but only tangentially part of it. The organized criminal's concern is for wealth and the good things of life that wealth can provide. Many sociologists feel that respectability is really what the organized criminal is striving for. Bell, Ianni, and Tyler, all say this. These sociologists fail to realize that organized criminals are committed to their own moral code and world view and couldn't care less about respectability in mainstream terms. Respect and respectability in the larger society are unimportant because the organized criminal has rejected many if not most of the procedures on which mainstream values rest. Thus Daniel Bell is wrong when he implies that a desire for respectability led "the quondam racketeer" to provide "one of the major supports for a drive to win a political voice for Italians."[21]

Respectability was not what Costello, Lansky, and Luciano sought in political links to Al Smith, Franklin Roosevelt, Huey Long, Tammany leader James Hines, Mayor Jimmy Walker, and numerous judges and aldermen. They simply understood what Paul Kelly and Arnold Rothstein had understood before them, and what organized criminals understand today, that it helps to have friends in high places. Nelli notes that at the 1932 Democratic Party Convention Costello shared a suite with James Hines, a Smith supporter. Lucky Luciano shared one with Albert Marinelli, leader of the Second Assembly District in New York and a Roosevelt supporter. This arrangement was not based on some "quondam racketeer's" desire for respectability; it was business.

Nelli puts it this way:

> This sharing of quarters was of symbolic as well as practical significance for it demonstrated that criminal syndicate leaders from New York had achieved . . . power and influence equal to that of local party bosses.[22]

Bell himself notes that Tammany Hall had to turn to Costello and Luciano for support and funds, yet he overlooks the evidence in the court trial of James Hines, the resignation of Albert Marinelli, as well as Costello's movement of slot machines to Huey Long's Louisiana, calling them attempts at respectability when they were simply business trade-offs. Sounding the same note, Bell states:

> The early Italian gangsters were hoodlums—rough and unlettered and young (Al Capone was only twenty-nine at the height of his power). Those who survived learned to adapt. By now they are men of middle age or older. They learned to dress conservatively. Their homes are in respectable suburbs. They send their children to good schools and have sought to avoid publicity.[23]

Of course organized criminals buy homes in respectable suburbs and send their children to good schools. Such actions are common to anyone of affluence in our society, criminal or college professor. That they dress conservatively and avoid publicity likewise tells us nothing about either respectability or having left organized crime. Such comments focus on the trappings and appearance of a noncriminal life-style; they show nothing of the substance.

The organized criminal operates by a different standard of values from that of the ordinary citizen seeking upward mobility and status within some dominant community. He seeks respect within his *borgata*, his "family," and not in that larger community which he mocks. Thus sociologists who point to the following as signs of mob desire for respectability can only be thought naive.

> Many of the top "crime" figures long ago had forsworn violence, and even their income, in large part, was derived from legitimate investments . . . or from such quasi-legitimate but socially acceptable sources as gambling casinos.[24]

The use of business "fronts" as laundries to wash illegally gained wealth and to create a basis for taxable income has been well documented.[25] The use of gambling casinos to skim millions of dollars in cash and as fronts for acts of corruption and blackmail is also well documented and is a common reason for organized crime's interest and hidden ownership in such enterprises.[26] Surely these facts suggest goals other than respectability.

What is American about American crime? Obviously, it is our values, their openness and pragmatism, our beliefs in competition, material success, individual action, freedom, and liberty. The openness of our values permits their reversal, which can be a very good and creative force, enhancing adaptability and change. As we have seen, it can also be a rather perverse one. Our values and the needs of our popular political institutions permit the creation of alternative ethical codes, and thus our values can be turned upside down.

Lucky Luciano, without fully being conscious of it, neatly captured both the possibilities and the paradox.

> I had Masseria and Maranzano knocked off to get to the top. What I did was illegal; I broke the law. [Franklin] Roosevelt had us and other guys like Hines and Walker sent to the can or squashed. What he did was legal. But the pattern was exactly the same; we was both shitass doublecrossers, no matter how you look at it. Now, I don't say we elected Roosevelt, but we gave him a pretty good push. . . . I never knew that a guy who was gonna be President would stick a knife in your back when you wasn't looking. I never knew his word was no better than lots of rackets guys.[27]

Poor Luciano. He expected mainstream values to be different from his own chosen world view. In that, he failed to realize just how much a product of the American system he was.

NOTES

1. See Leslie A. White, *The Science of Culture* (New York, 1970).

2. Gary Wills would agree on the values, but disagree with their Lockeian roots. He gives Francis Hutcheson credit for influencing Jefferson's thought. The authors of the Constitution, and Jefferson was not among them, were more influenced by Locke. See Gary Wills, *Inventing America* (New York, 1978).

3. Common definitions of organized crime run the gamut from New York District Attorney Frank Hogan's—"Organized crime is two or more persons engaged in criminal activities"—to the more recent: Organized crime includes any group of individuals whose primary activity involves violating criminal laws to seek illegal profits and power by engaging in racketeering activities and, when appropriate, engaging in intricate financial manipulations. Whatever the definition, organized crime has been part of America since the first colonists realized how to take advantage of the Indians.

4. Alexis de Tocqueville, *Democracy in America*, vol. 2 (New York, 1967), p. 304.

5 James Truslow Adams, *Our Business Civilization* (New York, 1929), cited in Gus Tyler, *Organized Crime in America* (Ann Arbor, 1962), p. 44.

6. See Arthur Schlesinger, *Paths to the Present* (New York, 1949); Max Lerner, *America as a Civilization* (New York, 1957); Wayne Moquin, ed., *The American Way of Crime* (New York, 1976).

7. This is a futuristic novel in which organized crime has gained control of government and much of industry. Courtney Terret, *Only Saps Work* (New York, 1930). The view that only suckers work is less discussed today but a 1942 sociology textbook gives this view as a prime cause of organized crime. See the "Something for Nothing Philosophy" in Harry E. Barnes and Oreen M. Ruedi, *The American Way of Life* (New York, 1942, 1950), pp. 827–29.

8. Humbert Nelli, *The Business of Crime* (New York, 1976), p. 106.

9. Vincent Teresa, *My Life in the Mafia* (Greenwich, Conn., 1973), p. 73.

10. Ibid.

11. Ibid., p. 111.

12. Martin A. Gosch and Richard Hammer, *The Last Testament of Lucky Luciano* (Boston ,1975), p. 37. This work was developed from interviews with Luciano in Italy a few years before his death.

13. Donald R. Cressey, *Theft of the Nation* (New York, 1969), pp. 177–78.

14. Nelli, *The Business of Crime*, p. 105.

15. Gosch and Hammer, *The Last Testament of Lucky Luciano*, p. 8.

16. Ibid., p. 16.

17. Nelli, *The Business of Crime*, p. 195.

18. Tyler, *Organized Crime in America;* Daniel Bell, "Crime as an American Way of Life," in *The End of Ideology*, ed. Daniel Bell (New York, 1960), pp. 127–50; Francis A. J. Ianni, *Ethnic Succession in Organized Crime* (Washington D.C.: U.S. Government Printing Office, 1973); Idem, *A Family Business* (New York, 1972).

19. Francis A. J. Ianni, *The Black Mafia* (New York, 1974), p. 107.

20. Chicago *Tribune*, 6 December 1927; reprinted in *The American Way of Crime*, ed. Moquin, p. 69.

21. Bell, "Crime as an American Way of Life," p. 143.

22. Nelli, *The Business of Crime*, p. 195.

23. Bell "Crime as an American Way of Life," p. 147.

24. Ibid., p. 148.

25. See Melvin K. Bers, *The Penetration of Legitimate Business by Organized Crime* (Washington, D.C.: National Institute of Law Enforcement and Criminal Justice, 1970); Jonathan Kwitny, *Vicious Circles: The Mafia in the Marketplace* (New York, 1979); Annelise G. Anderson, *The Business of Organized Crime* (Stanford, Calif., 1979).

26. See Ed Reid and Ovid Demaris, *The Green Felt Jungle* (New York, 1963); Teresa, *My Life in the Mafia;* Gosch and Hammer, *The Last Testament of Lucky Luciano;* Hank Messick, *Lansky,* (New York, 1974). Also 1,098 pages of affidavits of electronic surveillance of the Kansas City, Nick Civella, LCN family, June 1979 (author's personal copy).

27. Gosch and Hammer, *The Last Testament of Lucky Luciano*, p. 167.

10

Frontier Families: Crisis in Ideology

Lillian Schlissel

As Americans we have held particular affection for certain images in our national history. Frontier images provide a case in point. Barn raisings, sewing bees, corn husking, harvesting—all these reinforce a vision of the frontier tradition. We see this period of our past as an uncomplicated time of indomitable individualism and egalitarian exchanges between men. The frontier family was stable and strong and healthy. The pioneer father was resourceful; children learned independence virtually at their mother's breasts. Such images have held powerful sway. But when we undertake to reconstruct the actual texture of the frontier family, to examine the reality of its day-to-day existence, the simplicity of forms becomes less secure, the object before our eyes begins to shimmer with uncertainty.

I want to suggest that life on the frontier west of the Mississippi was not a time of simplicity; simplicity is only the reflection of our own need to locate our past, our national "childhood" within the secure realm of nostalgia. The men and women who settled the western frontier—the historical frontier, not the mythical frontier—were caught willy-nilly between currents of a premodern agricultural society and a society of technology and modernism. Diaries, journals, and family papers tell of the tensions that surrounded ideological ambiguity.

The frontier west of the Mississippi between 1850 and 1880 existed at the confluence of powerful and complex forces. Railroads quickly crossed these regions. Newsprint and telegraphy brought cosmopolitan values and expectations. Cities like San Francisco, Denver, St. Joseph, and Kansas City sprang up virtually in advance of the frontier. The settlers of the West were farmers, but they were also town builders, planners, and speculators. The men and women who made the overland crossing, almost a quarter of a million of them between 1850 and 1860, were what we might call farmer-entrepreneurs. Factory workers and wage laborers of the eastern cities could rarely save enough money to make the transcontinental journey. Horace Greeley's injunction to "Go West" was never heard by the lads or lasses in mill towns. The "safety valve" for the working classes that Frederick Jackson Turner postulated rarely applied.[1] The overlanders who did make the migration had owned land before and journeyed because they intended to own land again. They brought experience in liquidating property, in buying and selling land. They knew how to handle cash. Outfitting for the Overland crossing could cost between $600 and $1,000.[2] Helen Marnie Stewart, who crossed the continent in 1853, estimated that she and her husband had spent an additional $75 for travel expenses and she advised those who might wish to follow to keep at least $150 in cash for the expense of crossing.[3] Amelia Stewart Knight recorded carefully the family's finances on the journey: $124.15 for tolls and bridges and feed for the cattle. Their own resources gone, her husband had to sell an ox and a sorrel mare in order to provide for their first winter in Oregon.[4] Ferries and bridge tolls along the overland route were generally $5 per wagon. Cattle and provisions had to be replaced along the way. Even Indians soon learned the rudiments of capitalistic enterprise, selling buffalo and fresh salmon, moccasins and horses for a handsome price and bartering what they could not sell. Mormons in Salt Lake City sold provisions. By 1850 the Platte River route was a commercial road.

The overlanders were moderately well educated, both men and women. Their diaries attest to their literacy and to a certain sophistication about the world around them. Victorian ideology was already well articulated in their attitudes. They were upwardly mobile. Had they not uprooted themselves to make the two-thousand-mile crossing in order to better their positions in life? The majority of these families had previously owned land; they now wanted more and better. They were Protestant, white, given to modernism and to a belief in social change. They were willing to work hard and to postpone today's pleasures for tomorrow's rewards. They were vigorous believers in self-improvement and independence. They did not turn from the industrial revolution: they were the advance guard of industrialism. They brought technology to the West as fast as it could be provided.

Particularly because Victorian values were already clearly defined through American middle-class life by 1850, a family's decision to make the overland journey could generate real dislocation for women.[5] Victorian society, after all, vested signal importance in the home. The so-called cult of domesticity located the transmission of values in the women's role in rearing her children and in designing the moral fabric of her household. The home was conceived to be an orderly and secure place where motherhood was exalted. But the frontier household was neither secure nor stable. High mortality rates affected each of the principals, and dissolution of households was a commonplace of frontier life. For those women who already understood their lives within the Victorian prescriptions, the overland journey could be a primary assault. The trail reduced them to the work of hired hands. Women drove the teams of oxen; they trudged behind the wagons in great clouds of dust, collecting the buffalo "chips" that were needed to cook the evening meals. They set rocks behind the wheels of the wagons being pushed up the steep sides of the mountains. The diaries of overland women yield to historians what demographic information cannot: the complexities of the emotional life, the points of stress and trouble. Miriam Davis, who settled with her husband and children in Kansas in 1855, wrote: "I have cooked so much out in the sun and smoke, that I hardly know who I am, and when I look into the little looking glass I ask, 'Can this be me? Put a blanket over my head and I would pass well for an Osage squaw.' "[6] Davis thus saw herself transformed into an Indian. The retrogression of the westward journey had become more than social; it was racial.

To ward against the assault on their sense of propriety, some emigrant women demanded that their daughters preserve Victorian attitudes and practices. The following is an excerpt from the diary of Adrietta Hixon, who made the overland crossing while she was still a girl.

> While traveling, mother was particular about Louvina and me wearing our sunbonnets and long mitts in order to protect our complexions, hair and hands. Much of the time I should like to have gone without that long bonnet poking out over my face, but mother pointed out to me some girls who did not wear bonnets and as I did not want to look as they did, I stuck to my bonnet finally growing used to it.[7]

Sarah Bixby-Smith also remembered the hated bonnets. "Those sunbonnets . . . were my chief pests. . . . I would [untie the strings and] double back the corners . . . making it into a sort of cocked hat with a bow on top, made from the hated strings, thus letting my poor scratched ears free of captivity."[8] Mollie Dorsey Sanford recalled that

> It had occurred to me how much easier I could get through the tangled underbrush if I were a man, and I slipped out into the back shed, and donned an old suit of Father's clothes. . . . It was very funny to all but Mother, who feared I [was] losing all the dignity I ever possessed. . . .[9]

An emigrant named Loren Hastings recorded his shock upon seeing how the frontier had changed the nature of women.

> This day met a returning Co. from Oregon. In the Co. was Man & his wife & family . . . The woman rode with one foot on [one] side of

her pony & the other foot on the other side. This is the greatest
curiosity I have ever seen yet.[10]

Many young women, though, were not acquiescent about Victorian
restrictions. Lydia Milner Waters wrote, "I . . . learned to drive an ox
team on the Platte [River] and my driving was admired by an officer and
his wife. . . . I heard them laughing at the thought of a woman driving
oxen."[11] Mary Ellen Todd confided to her diary that she had not only
learned to crack the whip while driving the team of oxen, but that she
experienced "a secret joy in being able to have a power that set things
going." But she felt "a sense of shame" because she was performing a
man's job![12] Edith Stanton Kitt, born on her parents' Arizona ranch,
learned to ride bareback, to handle a sixteen-gauge, single-barreled shotgun, to hunt deer, and to keep the cowboys company, but her mother
resented such distortions of a women's role, believing that both class and
gender were thereby compromised.[13]

Whether the issue was riding astride vs. wearing trousers, or driving
teams of cattle, women of the western frontier were caught between
emerging standards of Victorian propriety and the demands of daily life.
The frontier continually *extended* the work assigned to women at precisely the time in history when Victorian ideology *restricted* the spheres
of female endeavor. The farm wife was expected to dig cellars, to help
build cabins, to plow and plant in addition to performing the traditional
female jobs of sewing, cooking, churning, washing, and baking. "As there
was no other man . . . [Father] could get to help him," Mother had to fill
in as the hired hand.[14] To such women, "the domestic ideal was a goal
which women could direct their efforts, the promise of a day when their
lives would not be so hard, their tasks so numerous. Domesticity, with its
neat definition of woman's place, helped [frontier] women bear what they
hoped were temporary burdens and reestablished their sense of identity
and self-respect."[15] The Victorian ideology of feminine domesticity seemed
infinitely preferable to the frontier's blurring of work roles for women.

Some frontier women viewed the terrible hardness of their daily lives
with great bitterness. As the years went by and their own hopes faded,
their diaries and letters reveal in such women the birth of a fierce determination that their daughters would not be overtaken by the life of the
farm. These women drove themselves to grueling labor in order that their
daughters might leave. Lucinda Dalton, eldest daughter of a Mormon
family that arrived in Utah in the winter of 1857–58, remembered how
her mother worked far into the night in order that she be free to attend
school and to study.[16] Mary Ann Hafen, a Mormon wife, picked cotton on
shares in Utah and took her baby with her to the fields in order that her
older children might remain in school.[17] Teaching at mid-century was not
yet a woman's profession, and it took stamina and discipline for farm

women to see their daughters through their training period. In 1870, Jane Jasper wrote to her daughter who had been sent to a boarding school, "It is no use for me to be thinking and working my life out for you to have the chance for a education unless you have the sense to appreciate what is done for your future."[18]

What these and other diaries and letters suggest is that, for some of the women on the western frontier, a form of negative identification was born. Mothers who resented the frontier determined to remove their daughters from the fate that had overtaken them. Daughters, who saw their mothers turned into drudges swore to leave the farm. Sometimes, on the other hand, young girls gladly reached out for the new freedoms the frontier offered. They rode and hunted; they expanded their lives with an eager acceptance of new roles and new expectations. Quite simply, they saw the needs of the new land and they did what had to be done. As vehemently as their brothers, daughters of the West sought to be free of social and parental restrictions. But mothers, whose ideas of propriety had already been formed, found accommodation more difficult. Older women, who had invested the taboos of society with their own emotional intensity, were quick to chasten the "waywardness" of their daughters.

In the final analysis, the New Country and the New World were not really dissimilar. Both worlds existed in a state of tension between conflicting ideologies, in the crosscurrents between the reassertion of older models and the birth of new ones.

II

One of the ways in which families made special adaptation to the needs of the frontier was in the periodic absences of either of the marriage partners for extended lengths of time. Chester Warner, for example, left his family for over a year. He traveled from Illinois to California to sell a string of horses. He returned by sailing down the Pacific Coast from San Francisco to Panama, traveling by mule across the isthmus to the Atlantic, north by steamship to New York, and by railroad back to Illinois. The next spring, he made the same trip again, but this time he took his brother Alexander with him; both were absent for yet another year. During that time, Chester's wife maintained the farm and cared for the children. On her husband's return, she gave back to him an ongoing enterprise of family and homestead.[19] On the central plains, men often hired themselves out for wages, leaving wives to care for crops and animals for weeks and months at a time. During the heavy snows of the long winter months, women and children remained, alone, with the nearest neighbor miles away.

Sometimes it was the wife who left the household, moving into town for the winter in order that the children have their schooling. In Arizona,

Jane Fourr, who her neighbors described as a submissive woman, despite her husband's disapproval, left him every winter and moved to town.

> Every summer she and the older children worked hard on the ranch. In the fall—no matter what "Mister Fourr" said—they loaded a few necessities into wagons and drove to Tombstone, where Jane rented some empty house in which they half lived, half camped, during the school year. Old timers in Tombstone said that the Fourr children and their mother came to town in this fashion for fifteen years.[20]

Edith Stratton Kitt also remembered that "Mother would rent a house in town and we all would spend the winter there."[21] During such separations, each spouse was an autonomous agent of the marriage. The frontier recognized such periods of female hegemony; the wife was her husband's surrogate in all matters of conducting family business.

The routine transfer of responsibility and authority from husband to wife seems to have been a basic mechanism of frontier adaptation. There is no indication in any of the hundred or more diaries I have read that the family, when it was composed of only wife and children, was expected to seek shelter from kin or neighbor. Quite the contrary: the expectation was that it would function autonomously. There was a mater-of-fact acceptance that the wife would conduct the family business as well as the husband. Women, as heads of frontier households, hired the extra men, repaired the house, took charge of buying the staples and selling the crops, fed and cared for the children, tended to any accidents, and successfully managed the ordinary affairs of living. They functioned far beyond the Victorian prescriptions for women. Their journals and letters show that they were as knowledgeable about the farm enterprise as were their husbands, and as strongly determined to make it a success.

But just how frontier women learned to make these major transitions in role playing is not clear. Similarly unclear are the ways in which the frontier community supported and recognized the wife's hegemony. But these shifts do indicate that family life on the frontier was characterized by fluid forms and complex arrangements and rearrangements. Patriarchy was the socially prescribed order of the family, but the frontier demanded modifications that thrust women into managerial functions and self-sufficiency. With Victorian patriarchy, there evolved another ordering which might be called *maritarchy*, if by that term one can delineate a relationship in which either spouse functions, routinely, as full surrogate for the other. The nineteenth-century family, and particularly the frontier family, was, as Tamara Hareven has suggested, "often more complex, more diverse, and less orderly than the family is today."[22]

III

The Western frontier brought some women to life-styles completely at variance with Victorian models of domesticity. Dorothea Mitchell was a lumberwoman who dedicated her book, *Lady Lumberjack*, to "every woman reader who may be pondering her ability to compete in what was once a man's work.[23]

The Homestead Act of 1862 provided that a homesteader had to be the head of a family or twenty-one years of age. The law did not restrict homestead entries to men, and suddenly single women and widows realized that they too could claim 160 acres of land. Thousands of homesteaders in the later part of the nineteenth century were women. The research of Gene and Sheryl Patterson-Black in Douglas, Wyoming, spanning the years 1891, 1907, and 1908 revealed that "an average of 11.9% of the sample of homestead entrants were women. The percentage increased as the years passed . . . from 4.8% in Douglas in 1891 to 18.2% in Lamar, Wyoming, in 1907." In a preliminary sampling, Patterson-Black reports 37 percent of the men succeeded in making final claim to the land they homesteaded, while women succeeded 42.1 percent of the time.[24] Elinor Stewart homesteaded on the Green River in Wyoming. She wrote, "To me, homesteading is the solution of all poverty's problem . . . . Any woman who can stand her own company, can see the beauty of the sunset, loves growing things, and is willing to put in as much time at careful labor as she does over the washtub, will certainly succeed; will have independence, plenty to eat all the time, and a home of her own in the end."[25] Women who homesteaded independently were untroubled by Victorian prescriptions of womanly behavior. They were unconcerned about Victorian ideas that a woman needed a man's protection. These women homesteaders, with their sister ranchers and lumberjacks, took the adventure of the West and built new lives with courage and spirit. But they were, at least statistically, a minority, and the path they cut was never one that many western women chose to follow.

IV

Victorian prescriptions reemerged in the lives of western women, finally in two diverse forms. Daughters of households in the semiarid regions of Nevada and California became increasingly accustomed to spending part of the year in wage labor, usually in factory work in Kansas City, Wichita, Denver, or San Francisco, and in smaller cities as well. The women and girls who entered the factories of the West discovered, like their sisters in the East before them, that they were among the most poorly paid workers; they could barely subsist on the wages they received. Western women found that Victorian ideology, which exalted them in the home, did little to elevate them in the marketplace. The West replicated the disparity in wages between men and women that had been established in the East, even though the scarcity of labor might have been expected to raise the working women's lot. Western women workers discovered that Victorian standards measured not only their wages, but also their lives. In *Wage Working Women*, a survey issued by the U.S. Department of Labor in 1888, the census takers, themselves middle-class women, judged working women harshly, finding that girls who lived in boardinghouses did not regularly attend church, had no libraries, and no proper chaperones when receiving gentlemen callers. Rooming houses in Kansas City, in Denver, and in San Francisco were judged a "perilous freedom from all restraint" and citizens were urged to keep watch lest working women in western cities become fallen women—the spectre that all Victorian moralists feared.[26]

In the matter of family planning, the frontier soon came to share Victorian ideology: census data confirm that birth rates fell as rapidly in the West as in the East. Recent monographs indicate that abortion during the first months of pregnancies was not uncommon in the nineteenth century. Although the traditional model of the pioneer family—the family with five or more children to share the work of settling the new land—was real, and continued to serve as a strong family model, nevertheless Elizabeth's Hampsten's recent work suggests that even rural women were beginning to share rudimentary information about methods of birth control. In 1885, Rose Williams and Allettie Mosher exchanged letters between Ohio and North Dakota, Rose advising "You want to know of a sure prevenative, Well plague take it, the best way is for you to sleep in one bed and your man in another. . . ." But Rose also had information of a more practical sort. "Well now there is the thing . . . I do not know whether you can get them out there. They are called Pessairres or female prevenative if you don't want to ask for a 'pisser' just ask for a female prevenative . . . They cost one dollar when Sis got hers it was before any of us went to Dak[ota]. The directions are with it. . . ."[27]

The women who made the overland crossing were just one generation too early for such information, but they were not without interest in it. Rose's suggestion about abstinence probably had widespread efficacy on the frontier; the birth rate did indeed curve downward. It is also likely that the decision to limit the size of families was one agreed to by husbands as well as by wives. Having journeyed two thousand miles and staked their lives and their fortunes on the expectation of improving their economic situation, men as well as women were determined to find their way toward middle-class status. If limiting the size of the family was the model of middle-class Victorian life, then family limitation was an imperative of the frontier as well as of the town.

In summary, then, I have tried to suggest that Victorian standards were prevalent in society as it emerged on the western frontier. It was the preferred ideology of the developing middle class. Victorian configurations, born of a middle-class urban culture, however, were often ill-suited to frontier life, and the decision to impose such standards often generated tension and conflict for women, far more so than for men. Because society's taboos and rituals most often inhere in the behavior of its women, major shifts in social values reverberate in the lives of women. The frontier, with its pull toward self-reliance and autonomy, with its constant blurring of gender roles and periods of wifely hegemony, bore women away from Victorian patterns of life and of family organization. Some women embraced the expanded freedom of unstructured social situations and liberalized legal codes to homestead land as single women and to obtain the franchise. They roped steers, mined, and ran hotels, mills, newspapers, and drygoods stores. Some women were gamblers and sharpshooters.

But the question of how to be a lady on the frontier was filled with uncertainty. Western women were sometimes frozen into attitudes of indecision, caught between different perceptions of their proper function and role. Miriam Davis, standing alone on the Kansas horizon, uncertain whether she dare get on a horse astride, when there was only the growing wheat to see her, bespeaks a generation of women torn between the actual needs of life on the frontier and the prescriptions of the Victorian ideology. Many frontier women believed that the pioneer experience had lowered them into work fit only for Indians and hired hands; they felt themselves torn rudely out of their homes, out of the domestic sphere, to labor in the fields. Such women held fiercely to an ideology of domesticity, even when, in a sod hut with dirt floors, it proved beyond their grasp. Western women who were forced to spend at least part of their years in factories in St. Louis, Iowa City, and Denver already knew the disdain of their middle-class sisters who considered wage labor demeaning for "proper" ladies. The same townswomen disdained the farm women who, at a county fair in Nebraska in the 1860s "would have nail-driving contests, the one who drove the most nails the quickest would win the prize."[28] The conflict expressed in the family papers and in the diaries of western women is the historian's clue to the development of class ideology and to the emergence of sex roles in a new society.

If a certain hardy independence grew out of the frontier experience of women, it was soon cut off from nurture by attitudes that spoke for Victorian propriety, domesticity, and restriction. The photographs of pioneer women that survive tell us, eloquently, of the struggles of the frontier woman to be all things to herself and to her family. One haunting photograph shows a mother and daughter in Colorado, in boots as thick as any man's, in their barnyard in early spring when the snows are still on the ground, feeding their stock, and both wearing white aprons.[29] The effort to maintain those white aprons in all that mud must have been the labor of Sisyphus!

The image of the Victorian household and of the Victorian family would sweep all variant models before it. Women of the West would enforce upon their cirumstances, and upon themselves, the standards of the emerging society. Victorian configurations would come to replace variations which might have led to broader scope for western women. When Victorian standards conflicted with frontier forms, women chose the more limited options. Western women, for the most part, strove to restore the stability of their old homes and to limit rather than to expand their roles. But during their lifetimes, and during the duration of the frontier, the question of how to be a woman, of how to pattern a family was fraught with ambiguity. The frontier provided no time for arcadian simplicity.

NOTES

1. Carter Goodrich and Sol Davison, "The Wage-Earner in the Westward Movement," *Political Science Quarterly* 50(1935):161; and 51 (1936), 108.

2. See John Mack Faragher and Christine Stansell, "Women and Their Families on the Overland Trail to California and Oregon, 1842–67," *Feminist Studies* No. 2 (1975); John D. Unruh, "The Plains Across: The Overland Emigrants and the Trans-Mississippi West, 1840–1860," (Ph.D. diss., University of Kansas, 1975).

3. Helen Marnie Stewart Knight, "Diary, 1853," Lane County Pioneer Historical Society, Eugene, Oregon, 1961.

4. Amelia Stewart Knight, "Diary, 1853," *Transactions of the Oregon Pioneer Association.* 46th Annual Reunion, 1918.

5. Lillian Schlissel, "Women's Diaries on the Western Frontier," *American Studies* 18(Summer 1975):87–100.

6. Miriam Colt Davis, *Went West to Kansas* (New York, 1862), p. 53.

7. Adrietta Appelgate Hixon, *On to Oregon! A True Story of a Young Girl's Journey into the West*, ed. Waldo Taylor (New York Public Library Pamphlet, 1947), p. 12.

8. Sarah Bixby-Smith, "Adobe Days," quoted in *Let Them Speak for Themselves: Women in the American West, 1849–1900*, ed. Christiane Fischer (New York, 1977), p. 250.

9. Mollie Dorsey Sanford, *Journal in Nebraska and Colorado Territories, 1857–1866* (Lincoln, Nebraska, 1947), p. 53.

10. John D. Unruh, "The Plains Across," p. 188.

11. Lydia Milner Waters, "A Trip Across the Plains in 1855," *Quarterly of the Society of California Pioneers* 6(June 1929):78.

12. Mary Ellen Todd, quoted in "Women and their Families," p. 157.

13. Edith Stratton Kitt, "Pioneering in Arizona," in *Let Them Speak for Themselves*, p. 290.

14. Julie Roy Jeffrey, *Frontier Women* (New York, 1979), p. 43.

15. Jeffrey, *Frontier Women*, p. 52.

16. Diary of Lucinda Dalton, 1876, Bancroft Library, University of California, Berkeley.

17. Mary Ann Hafen, "Memoirs of a Handcart Pioneer," in *Let Them Speak for Themselves*, p. 106.

18. Manuscript letters of Jane Jasper to her daughter, 2 October and 20 November 1870, Huntington Library, San Marino, California.

19. Diary of Mary Eliza Warner, 1864, Bancroft Library, University of California, Berkeley.

20. Christiane Fischer, "A Profile of Women in Arizona in Frontier Days," *Journal of the West* 16(July 1977):45.

21. Kitt, in *Let Them Speak for Themselves*, p. 295.

22. Tamara Hareven, "Family Time and Historical Time," *Daedalus* 106 (Spring 1977):57–70.

23. Dorothea Mitchell, *Lady Lumberjack* (Vancouver, 1967).

24. Sheryl and Gene Patterson-Black, "From Pack Trains to Publishing," in *Western Women* (Crawford, Nebraska, 1978), p. 6.

25. Elinore Pruitt Stewart, *Letters of a Woman Homesteader* (Lincoln, Nebraska, 1961), pp. 215–16.

26. Fourth Annual Report of the Commissioner of Labor, *Working Women in Large Cities*, U.S. Department of Labor, 1888, pp. 64, 69.

27. Rose Williams to Allettie Mosher, September 27, 1885, quoted in *To All Inquiring Friends, Letters, Diaries and Essays in North Dakota*, ed. Elizabeth Hampsten, Dept. of English, Univ. of North Dakota (Grand Forks, 1979), p. 122.

28. Mary J. Doom, W.P.A. Pioneer Interviews, Nebraska folder, uncatalogued manuscripts, National Archives, Washington, D.C.

29. Annette Baxter, *To Be a Woman in America*, 1850–1930 (New York, 1978), pp. 68–69.

11

Rawhide Heroines: The Evolution of the Cowgirl and the Myth of America

Shelley Armitage

Woman's place in the myth of America may be measured by a simple story. Two Indians are sitting on a fence. One is a big Indian, the other, a little Indian. The little Indian is the big Indian's son, but the big Indian is not the little Indian's father. How can this be? David Potter, who relates the riddle, solves it with this explanation: the big Indian obviously is the little Indian's mother, but we may initially fail to see this since social conditioning often makes us conceive of relationships from a masculine perspective.[1] Potter's story has particular import when we examine the myth of America specifically as the Western or frontier myth in which the qualities of heroism are traditionally masculine ones. Rugged individualism, bravery, nobility, and a love of the wilderness are noted by historians such as Frederick Jackson Turner and writers from Cooper on as traits indigenous to the frontier experience. Turner sees these qualities as part of the national character and evoked by the frontier's challenge to the *civilizing instinct;* yet woman, typically the civilizer, is not typically thought to exhibit them. Our imaginative writers, unlike the historians, view the frontier as *an escape from civilization* and thus seldom treat women heroically. Heroes, like Natty Bumppo, are not the apostles of progress but the antisocial, misanthropic refugees from civilization who bemoan the desecration of the wilderness and wish to defend it from settlement. It follows that such heroes, as William Humphrey observes, avoid the trappings of civilization by avoiding marriage:

> . . . if we are to judge by our imaginative literature, we are, beneath all the slogans extolling the democratic social organization and the virtues of family life, a nation of secret bachelors, hermits of the

166

woods and the plains. In books about such figures there is no place for any heroine.[2]

If heroines have not emerged from western history and literature, however, a predominant stereotype has—an image perpetuated by writers and historians as appropriate to woman's role in the Western myth. Emerson Hough describes her thus:

> She is the chief figure of the American West, the figure of all the ages. This major figure is not the long-haired, fringed legging man riding a raw-boned pony, but the gaunt and sad-faced woman sitting on the front seat of the wagon . . . her face hidden in the same ragged sunbonnet which had crossed the Appalachians and the Missouri long before. There was America. . . . There was the seed of America's wealth. There was the great romance of all America—the woman in the sunbonnet; and not, after all, the hero with the rifle across his saddle horn.[3]

This image of the sunbonnet woman is popular for a number of reasons. On a psychological level, her implied status as mother satisfies the needs of our writers to reconcile their attitudes about women. Leslie Fiedler says, "Women represent at once the ruined and redeeming virgin-bride dreamed by Sentimentalism, and the forgiving mother, necessary to sustain an imaginary American commonwealth of boy-children. . . . Both marriage and passion impugn the image of woman as mother and mean the abandonment of childhood."[4] The passivity of this creature on the wagon seat further compliments predominant nineteenth-century beliefs about women's natures and their roles. Emerson noted that civilization was the power of "good" women. Such a woman remained in the home and did all that was necessary to maintain that home, even to following her husband overland from friends, family, culture, and precious possessions. Any penchant for the wilderness, therefore, was regarded as evil on a woman's part; certainly in literature "white women who refuse to restrict their behavior to what society intends for them find the wilderness a natural habitat for forbidden sexuality, and for them, separation from the male, and solitary wandering in the wilderness are considered equivalent to the fall."[5] Thus, Hough's description of the pioneer woman as "gaunt" and "sad-faced" is appropriate to her expected sacrificial role. She was the "seed of America's wealth" in part because she perpetuated its seed. Men who had subdued the wilderness for its great riches were interested in establishing a "line." Material exploitation and sexual exploitation were closely aligned. This sunbonnet woman is therefore "the great romance of all America" because "she stoically transcended a situation she never would have freely chosen."[6] Long-suffering, pure, persevering, this pioneer woman reaches mythic proportions in her celebration in statues, histories, and literature across the country because she became the symbolic repository of values revered by men but often personally ignored for their own materialistic ventures on the frontier.

The sunbonnet woman thus seldom reaches the status of a true heroine. Unlike the dynamic heroines of European literature, Jane Eyre or Anna Karenina, for instance her compliance to tedious tasks has none of the heroic cut of her male counterparts in the West—the trappers, miners, cowboys, or soldiers. Characters like Beret Hansa in Rolvaag's *Giants of the Earth* (1926) or Dorothy Scarborough's crazed character in *The Wind* (1925) are not memorable but predictable. Such a woman most often serves as a plot motivator for the more dramatic activities of the hero, making Huck Finn "light out for the territory" or Daniel Boone move West one more time. For the most part, western writers have been content to follow the example of what Judith Fryer notes is a pattern of our major writers:

> Significantly, the women in the novels of Hawthorne, Melville, Oliver Wendell Holmes, Harold Frederic, Henry James, and William Dean Howells are not women at all, but images of women. They are reflections of the prevailing images of women in the nineteenth century, and like the predominantly male creators of utopian schemes, their male creators perceive with cultural blinders the women in the New World Gardens of their imaginations. [7]

Yet the real frontier offered a unique situation for altering these images. Recent historians such as Gerda Lerner suggest the sunbonnet stereotype is far too limiting, for pioneer women often had to be independent and frontier men and women were interdependent. [8] Current efforts to reconstruct history from diaries, letters, and newspapers indicate that historians such as William Sprague and Francis Parkman had not only a narrow but sometimes an erroneous view of women's attitudes, status, roles, and occupations on the frontier. Moreover, one frontier not only necessitated unique behavior by women, but engaged the popular imagination sufficiently to inspire the emergence of perhaps the only true American heroine. That frontier was the cattle frontier, and the "new woman" was the "cowgirl"— the rustler, wrangler, outlaw, or ranch woman whose occupation depended on her mastery of the horse. In real life, she had to exercise the masculine traits revered by historians such as Turner and by western writers. She attracted no attention from major American writers—perhaps because her character was particularly antithetical to their image of the American woman—but her character as it evolves in popular culture from the dime novel to films comes close to resolving the dilemma of the woman in American fiction as Fiedler and others see it. [9] She was neither mother nor virgin-bride. At times she was a full-fledged partner of the hero; at times she was the hero herself.

The particular manner in which the cattle frontier effected a heroic role for women may be attributed to its distinct nature. Unlike the other moving frontiers in which progress depended on settlement, the cattle frontier thrived on its own uncivilized expanses. In such a vast country as even the smaller ranches of New Mexico, Arizona, Texas, Montana, Wyoming, and other states encompassed, a rancher's wife was part of a self-sufficient unit and often had to take a nontraditional view of the home, division of labor, the land, and even the law. Thus Mrs. Charlie Hart of New Mexico was the only hand her husband had and when the first baby came, she placed him in a tomato box in front of the pommel of her saddle and took him with her to ride fence.[10] At least eight women are known to have gone up the trail with their husbands, and one, Lizzie Williams, drove her own herd up the Chisholm Trail from 1879 to 1889, even though she was married.[11] When the husband of Mrs. William Mannix was struck with polio, the care of thirteen children and their ranch fell to Mrs. Mannix. She drove a stage for fifteen years to supplement the family's income while she ran the ranch.[12] Mrs. Cassie Redwine of the Texas Panhandle was left with a ranch after her husband's death; when cattle rustlers began terrorizing the upper Red and Canadian rivers, she lost five hundred head of cattle and decided to take the law into her own hands. She and her cowboys captured a few of the rustlers in their camp, changed into their clothes, and ambushed the remainder of the gang when they rode into camp. Mrs. Redwine shot the leader herself when he rode into camp, and the next day the rest were hanged.[13] Thus, the isolation of ranch life not only demanded an adjustment in the traditional roles of women, but fostered a new independence as well. Though most women married into ranching or were second-generation ranch women, a few women bought their own spread and herd. In the 1880s Fanny Seabride of Chicago went to Texas as a governess, learned to ride and do ranch work, became a bounty hunter, and after bagging "531 coyotes, forty-nine lobos, thirty-nine wildcats, two bear cubs, and a Mexican leopard," established her own ranch with her $1,261 of bounty money.[14]

The results of this new independence were attitudinal as well as occupational. Alice Marriott in her book, *Hell on Horses and Women,* says: "Never once . . . did I hear a woman acknowledge the truth of the statement that 'The cow business is . . . hell on horses and women.' . . . I have come to the conclusion that that oft-quoted statement originated with a man and, manlike, they said the words and attributed them to women, without asking women how they really felt."[15] Agnes Smedley identifies herself positively with the land which women supposedly fear and abhor: "The deserts were indeed gray and sinister wastes . . . but . . . lay there, calling to you to come on and on. . . . The Arizona desert came closer to my spirit than has any place I have ever known."[16] The main reason for Smedley's lyricism is that of other cowgirls: she rode a horse almost everywhere she went and says "it was a land where women were strong."[17] The two go together, for as J. Frank Dobie explains in *The Mustangs:* No man by taking thought can add to his stature, but by taking a horse he can."[18] The same was true of women, perhaps even more so, since the horse not only added status for women but was an equalizer. Unlike other frontier women who were practically prisoners of their homes, cowgirls were mobile, and therefore not only could master ranch chores and be full partners to their husbands, but also could achieve a new identity. Folklorist Joyce Roach observes: "If you spend all your days in a field, behind a plow, looking at the rump of a horse, trying hard not to step in something, it affects your attitude. But if you get on that horse, ride him, then the world's a completely different place."[19] With the mastery of a horse often came a new mode of dress. Skirts gave way to split skirts or pants. Women learned to shoot guns and carried them both for protection when out on the range and for shooting coyotes and other threats to cattle. An example of this altered identity due to necessity, occupation, dress, and habit is Mrs. E. J. Guerin who was widowed at age fifteen and worked as a river pilot, a miner, a bartender, and a rancher:

> I would say from the fact of my being so long thrown among strangers and all along accustomed to depend on myself, I had attained a strength of character, a firmness, and self-reliance, that amounted to almost masculine force. In addition to this, I was impetuous, self-willed—traits induced by the peculiarities of my surroundings, and whose existence will account for much of my subsequent career.[20]

Though certainly not all ranch women rode the range, carried a gun, and assisted with branding and wrangling, even the more traditional wives like Mrs. Charles Goodnight found their roles expanded from those usually expected. Mrs. Goodnight's nearest neighbor in the Texas Panhandle was 200 miles away and she was doctor, nurse, homemaker, and spiritual adviser to innumerable cowboys, hunters, trappers, and traders. She also ministered to orphaned baby buffalo.[21] On the other end of the spectrum was Sally Skull, a hard-nosed business woman on the southern border of Texas who was a horse trader and freight wagon driver across the Mexican border during the Civil War. She had a reputation as a sharpshooter, landed in Mexican jails several times thanks to her bargaining, and was a veteran cardsharp and "cusser."[22] Some other women who had experience with guns and horses violated the law. Seventeen-year-old Annie McDoulet and sixteen-year-old Jennie Stevens—Cattle Annie and Little Britches—were delinquent teenagers who rode with the Doolin gang in 1894.[23] Thus, whether as partners of their husbands or widows, daughters, or independent women, to some degree these cowgirls shared

in the violence, various activities, and values of the range and, in proportion to the independence this life allowed, were able to shape their lives.

During the height of the cattle industry, the dime novel, which had
popularized western characters and action since 1860, transformed heroines from crinoline objects to active participants in the plots. First came
the use of Indian girls who could ride and shoot. Then writers disguised
women in men's clothing and explained their acts of violence and aggres-
sion in terms of revenge. But by 1878, in Edward L. Wheeler's *Bob
Woolf, the Border Ruffian; or the Girl Dead-Shot,* Hurricane Nell assumed
all the skills and functions of a Western hero. There may be several
explanations for this transition of the heroine's role, and each indicate that
real cowgirls could to some degree capture the popular imagination.

First, there were the requirements of Erastus Beadle, head of the firm
of Beadle and Adams, who had been to the frontier twice. Beadle recognized the impact of good storytelling that had dramatized the opening of
the Eastern states, the Revolutionary War, and the War of 1812, and he
expected his writers to achieve verisimilitude through adequate research
or, even better, first hand knowledge of the West. Thus, at least some of
his stable of writers—Joseph E. Badger, Prentiss Ingraham, Sam Hall,
Mayne Reid, and E. L. Wheeler—were not only familiar with the West
but had lived there. Certainly, they would have had opportunities to
observe real cowgirls, and several examples illustrate a direct connection
between real women and the characters in dime novels. For instance,
Rowdy Kate of *Apollo Bill, The Trail Tornado; or Rowdy Kate From
Right Bower* (1882) boasts in a typical Southwestern style: "I'm a regular
old double distilled typhoon, you bet." There was a Rowdy Kate in the
1870s who was a dance-hall girl, among other things, and possibly could
pass as a double-distilled typhoon.[24] In *The Jaguar Queen or, the Outlaws of the Sierra Madre* (1872), Katrina Hartstein goes about with seven
pet jaguars on a leash and is the leader of a gang. Anne Sokalski, who
accompanied her soldier-husband to his duty post in the mid-1860s, took
along her thirteen trained hunting dogs which she kept on a leash. She
wore a riding habit made of wolfskin and trimmed with wolf tails, topped
with a fur hat. She spent hours at target practice, was a deadly shot, and
could outride some of the cavalry.[25] The author of *The Jaguar Queen,*
Frederick Whittaker, who had served in the army, would have found
Anne inspiration for his character. Even Hurricane Nell has authentic
roots. Mountain Charley (Mrs. E. J. Guerin)joined miners at Pike's Peak
in 1859. She was dressed like, and passed for, a man.[26] In 1861, she
published her autobiography—ample time for the dime novel author to
have heard of her.

With the availability of real models—women, we must remember, who
were at home with horses, guns, and even violence—the addition of the
"Amazon" character in the dime novel was an effort to reconcile reality

with certain social predilections of an Eastern audience. Erastus Beadle's list of rules for writers ended with "We require unquestioned originality," but it began with "We prohibit all things offensive to good taste in expression and incident."[27] Though critics of the dime novel are quite right to note the disintegration of the novels due to overt sensationalism after about 1880, the development of two types of Amazon characters dramatized the cowgirl folk heroine and indicated a growth in the Western myth since Cooper. Dime novels, of course, were fashioned after Cooper's Leatherstocking adventures with a backwoods hero—comic, dialectal, unsuited for marriage—contrasted to his Eastern sidekick who, by virtue of his aristocractic breeding, always got the girl. As the writers refined the bifurcated plot—one part adventure, and one, love interest—into the activities of a single, cultivated protagonist, the two new heroines emerged. One, the "Sport," was usually a beautiful woman dressed in a mannish fashion, who performed manly feats with gun, whip, and knife, drank liquor straight, and swore expertly. She might save the hero from danger, but she almost never got his romantic attention. In this way, she replaced the noble backwoodsman, since she was strong, brave, capable of action. Moreover, since there was no love interest, she in no way threatened the hero with her strength; she was his equal, his friend. A classic example of the "Sport," and probably the most famous, is E. L. Wheeler's Calamity Jane. In *Deadwood Dick on Deck; or Calamity Jane, The Heroine of Whoop-Up*, she has a pretty, but hard face, wears buckskin pants, "met at the knee by fancifully beaded leggins," dainty slippers, a velvet vest, a velvet jacket, and a Spanish broad-brimmed hat "slouched upon one side of a regally beautiful head." Wearing one revolver on her waist and a rifle on her back, she rides a black pony fitted out Mexican style. When asked why she dresses like a man, she replies: "I don't allow ye ken beat men's togs much for handy locomotion and so forth, an' then, ye see, I'm as big a gun among men as any of 'em."[28] In *Deadwood Dick in Leadville; or A Strange Stroke for Liberty* (1881), she saves a man's life and calls ammunition "condensed death."

The "Pard" character, on the other hand, often won the hero. She was also masculine in her skills, but did not try to pass for a man like the rougher "Sport." Rather she was a partner to the hero, capable of doing what he did, sharing equally in danger and daring with occasional concessions to femininity. Probably she is one of the few egalitarian female creations. Two classic "Pards" ran in dime novel series from 1900 to the 1920s—Arietta Murdock, created by Cornelius Shea for *Wild West Weekly*, and Ned Taylor's Stella, the cowgirl heroine of *Rough Rider Weekly*. Arietta, displayed on about 80 percent of the *Wild West Weekly* covers, regularly rescued the hero by hurling dynamite, leaping chasms, shooting her gun, riding for the posse, and stealing guns or horses from outlaws. Like Arietta, Stella was a blonde, known in her native Texas as "Queen of the Range." She sidekicks with ex–Rough Rider Ted Stong and cuts a dashing figure in her white stetson, bolero jacket, white leggings, and red skirt, with her gun strapped to her hip. Thus, unlike the earlier pale heroines of Cooper's novels, these western women, whether friends or lovers, were strong, independent, brave, athletic, and full partners to the hero. Like their historic sisters, the ranch women, they fill a unique literary role.

An indication of this uniqueness, outside the fact that these heroines are fully "heroic" and share in the Western myth, is that they are called "Amazons." The use of this classical character for reference indicates the lack of any American literary predecessor. Unlike the dime novel hero, who has as his native reference the backwoodsman, the mythical forerunner of the cowgirl character is rooted in a legendary female culture where strength and athletic prowess were aspects of female heroism. The reference also indicates the difficulty of perpetuating a myth that runs so counter to nineteenth-century sensibilities about women. Perhaps only in popular culture, where myth making is intricately involved with entertainment, could such a heroine evolve. Nevertheless, in the pattern described by Richard Slotkin, the character of the cowgirl moves through the primary, romantic, and consummatory stages of myth development. That is, the character is identified in the repetition of formulas (as in the dime novel); the character is adapted to specific social and literary requirements by artists, thus obscuring the original meaning of the myth (as in the Wild West Shows, some literature, and films); and, finally, an attempt is made to recapture the real meaning of the myth by providing new visions (as in some recent novels and films). Moreover, as Slotkin points out, the effective use of myth depends on the development of traditional metaphors in the narrative that indicate change.[29] Crucial to this acculturation is the medium; in the case of the cowgirl character the narrative is told through literature, sport, and film.

Along with the dime novel, the evolution of the "Pard" or "Sport" characters continued in western literature dating from the turn of the century. Unlike the dime novels which emphasized action to the exclusion of character development, the evolution of the cowgirl in this Western popular literature establishes a workable metaphor for this character. As Slotkin notes, "The success of the myth in answering questions of human existence depends upon the creation of a distinct cultural tradition in the selection and use of metaphor.[30] Thus, the dime novel established the formula for the myth—action, dress, character type. Other writers adopted the formula but discarded the Amazon reference for an American metaphor: the natural woman.

In 1908, Lester Shepherd Parkman wrote a story in verse introducing this natural woman. *Nancy MacIntyre*, though strictly inferior poetry suitable perhaps for recitation, is about cowboy Billy, owner of eighty acres in Kansas and his love for Nancy, a cowgirl "Pard" who dresses in long skirt with a gun and cartridge belt. Nancy possesses all the attributes of a hero: she saves Billy from an ambush, stands off a posse in behalf of her father, and shoots Jim Johnson who steals Billy's eighty acres. But Billy admires her lack of artificiality:

> Now, those women that you read of
>   In these story picture books,
> They can't ride in roping distance
>   Of that girl in style and looks.
> They have waists more like an insect,
>   Corset shaped and double cinched,
> Feet just right to make a watch charm,
>   Small, of course, because they're pinched.
> This here Nancy's like God made her—
>   She don't wear no saddle girth,
> But she's supple as a willow
>   And the prettiest thing on earth.

Though Billy speaks in part of natural beauty, the poem connects scenes of the western landscape, and of her ability to deal with the harsh life of the prairie, with her authenticity.

Thus, like the pastoral hero, the natural woman as cowgirl is at one with nature. In the works of Eugene Manlove Rhodes, for instance, love of the land is connected to the heroine's capabilities. Eva Scales in "Maid Most Dear" (1930) says this about the desert country of New Mexico:

> "I've lived here all my life. Except for a few trips to Silver City and El Paso. I've never been out of these hills." Her head lifted, her eyes lingered on the long horizons, lovingly. "If it is any better outside, I'm willing to be cheated."

Eva is the brave and daring heroine of the story who shoots it out with a lynch mob in order to save Eddie and Skip, the heroes of the story. Other Rhodes stories reiterate the same idea. In "The Desire of the Moth" (1902), "Beyond the Desert" (1914), and "Bird in the Bush" (1917), the heroines derive their strength from nature.

Thus the "Pard's" ability to take full responsibility for her life depends on her capacity to enjoy harmony with man and nature. In the novels of Bertha "Muzzy" Sinclair, the cowgirl heroines often choose this harmonious relationship at the cost of approval by townspeople. Though Sinclair's novels often are humorous and avoid historical themes, she often juxtaposes the heroine's character, formed and sustained by the range land, against the expectations of society. In *Rim O' the World* (1919) Belle Lorrigan is a tough, athletic heroine. She races across the prairie in a buckboard pulled by two pinto ponies, Rosa and Subrosa. A sure shot, she teaches her three sons manners by plugging a hole in one boy's hat when he forgets to remove it. When the sheriff arrives to check the brands on some green hides, she threatens to put a bullet "about six inches above the knee," if he doesn't leave. He continues to talk and she determines to shoot his front tooth out. Needless to say, the women in town dislike Belle, but the author clearly illustrates that the "natural" woman maintains integrity by answering to the laws of the land, not the conscience of snooty town women.

The reconciliation of the strong woman with her role in the family further is handled by William Sydney Porter in his story "Hearts and Crosses" (1907). After Santa inherits a ranch from her father, she runs it so expertly that her husband leaves to become foreman of another ranch. When he orders a shipment of cattle from her, she sends a pure white steer with the brand—a cross in the center of a heart— which she and Webb had used before their marriage to denote a secret meeting. Webb returns to find he is father of a son, and he and Santa continue to share equally in the running of the ranch. Santa's acumen as a "Pard" is memorably described in the night scene when she ropes, ties, and brands the white steer single-handed.

The early literature of the cowgirl heroine, therefore, seized on the distinctive "active" behavior of the heroine—the skills necessary to survival and to heroism—and added to the one-dimensional dime novel authentic frontier situations. Character thus was a matter of independence, ingenuity, and physical skill fostered by the demands of the environment. The heroine typically coped with so-called female concerns—love, marriage, family, societal expectations—by exhibiting "masculine" traits. The metaphor of the "natural" women was a statement of her ability to cultivate these traits, yet still be a woman, and to achieve equal status with the hero or even be the center of the work herself. Other writers such as Owen Wister in *The Virginian* (1902) used this metaphor to test the fitness of Eastern values. In the westering of Molly Wingate, Wister indicates that her acquisition of the skills of the cowgirl favorably influence her character. But in the novels of Zane Grey, the cowgirl character changed and the metaphor of the natural woman was diverted to an earthiness that suggested sexuality rather than heroic dimension. In novels such as *Hash Knife Outfit* (1920), Grey, like Wister, tested the Eastern girl against the land or against western values, but, like his heroes, he essentially domesticated the heroines' love of independence and sense of freedom. The later novels of Luke Short, Max Brand, Nelson Nye, and Louis L'Amour continue this trend, returning to the pat stereotype of the woman as either "good" but inert, or active and assertive but sexual. Gone is the girl "Pard" who can coexist with the hero because of her androgynous abilities. The myth, therefore, is diverted from its original sources and content to a reflection of social or literary obligations—the second stage of mythogenesis Slotkin speaks of when the nature of reality is less important than the social requirements of the artist. Grey, for example, uses the Western myth to work out his own picadillos. John Cawelti notes:

> In a period where . . . traditional American values were under attack, Grey and other contemporary novelists . . . transformed the western formula into a vehicle for reaffirming a traditional view of American life. . . . In contrast to contemporary American society where women were increasingly challenging their traditional roles, the West of Grey . . . was, above all, a land where men were men and women were women. In novel after novel, Grey created strong, proud, and daring women and then made them realize their true role in life as the adoring lovers of still stronger, more virtuous, more heroic men.[31]

Another explanation for the loss of the original thrust of the cowgirl character was the historic or personal distance writers such as Grey had from the West. By contrast, many of the dime novelists and other writers such as Parkman, Sinclair, Rhodes, and O. Henry had either grown up in the West or spent time there. Their interest, though the works often were melodramatic, was in recording real Western characters and experiences. As an example, Joe B. Frantz and Julian Choate write of "Muzzy" Sinclair: "She had what so many cowboy writers lack, a real background of life among the bowlegged brethern. . . . She was reared in Montana where she rode the range and fraternized with men on horseback She did not try to pontificate about the epic role of the cowboy, and she had no pretense to history as such, but she was faithful to the Western historical milieu which she knew first hand."[32]

This same matter of historical distance affected the cowgirl's portrayal in another medium, the movies. Initially, the movies were affected by real cowgirls, women who had ridden in Wild West Shows and who originally were from ranches. Therefore, early silent films treated fairly authentically the cowgirl's skills and costume. Rodeo star Bertha Blanchett was an early stunt rider; Mildred Douglas and Dorothy Morrell did bit parts after the Miller Brothers' 101 Wild West Show folded in 1911 in Venice, California; Helen Gibson of the Miller Brothers' show played the heroine in the serial *The Hazards of Helen* (1914). Early celluloid cowgirls were cast in action-packed parts of the dime novel variety: in *Frontier Day in the Early West* (1910) a woman dresses like a man and rides her horse in a race; sisters in *Western Girls* also dress in cowboy clothes, capture stage robbers at gun point, and bring them to the sheriff; in *The Border Region* (1918) Blanch Bates rides wildly across the country and shoots a man during a struggle. Most of these parts were adjunct to that of the hero, however, and reminiscent of the popular events of the Wild West Show and rodeos. *Trail Dust* and parts of *North of 36* were filmed at the Miller Brothers' 101 Ranch. Occasionally, character development was attempted as in *The Prairie Pirate* with Ruth Delaney. Cornered after a valiant fight to escape a bandit and his gang, the heroine picks off the gang members, but, when the leader traps her in a cellar, she saves the last bullet for herself. During the 1930s just following the peak years of women's star performances in the rodeo, the cowgirl movie heroine was "more self-reliant, more athletic, and even sexier," but seldom the central figure of the film.[33] One exception was *The Singing Cowgirl*, starring Dorothy Page, where the heroine's role was more important than the hero's. By the 1940s and 1950s, the age-old dichotomy of the heroine as good girl or sexual temptress was the staple of Westerns; even the authenticity of dress, behavior, and riding and roping acumen was gone. The role of the "Pard" survived only in the Saturday afternoon kid show, played by the cowgirl who could rope, ride, and sing—Dale Evans. As in some western literature, film converted the cowgirl myth from its primary characteristics by using it as a means of perpetuating social expectations. The raw action of the early cowgirls was a necessary element for the visual media, but the metaphor of the natural woman or "Pard," as in the case of Grey's novels was lost. Moreover, the medium of expression was itself determining. Later actresses who had no notion of how to ride a horse, costume designers who glamorized female characters, and directors, such as John Ford, who depicted the West not as it was but as it should have been ignored the original character of the cowgirl.

Movies most conveniently illustrate probably the primary reason for the adaptation of the cowgirl's characteristics into other stereotypes of women. The delicate balance between hero and heroine seemingly precludes the heroine being too strong, capable, and independent. In *Giant*, for instance, Lutie, the hardened, outspoken, and capable ranchwoman, is killed off so that the true heroine, Virginia-born, can flourish. The dependency of the heroine is essential, if we trace the evolution of the Western. In fact, with few modern exceptions, the formula of the Western demands that the hero work within a masculine code that excludes, for the most part, civilization and women. Will Wright, in *Six Guns in Society*, names only three films in which the hero and heroine are partners, and one of these involves a child—Kim Darby in *True Grit*.[34] However, despite the lack of primary attention to cowgirls as central characters, films have managed to dramatize the various aspects of the cowgirl mystique. The early films characterized the cowgirl in terms of raw action. Later films, such as *The Big Country* (1958), coupled the realistic action of tending cattle and overseeing a ranch with attention to the heroine's thoughts, concerns, and motivations.

The final link in the evolution of the cowgirl—the Wild West Show and the rodeo—illustrate yet another manner in which the cowgirl heroine reached the public. These events are unique, for they may be said to be metaphors for the cowgirl without the context of narrative. As we have seen, the cowgirl was associated in various ways metaphorically in the changing Western of the dime novel, western literature, and film. But the Wild West Show and the rodeo centered on the *event* and, as such, allowed the cowgirl to function as part of the iconography of the old West. In fact, the name "cowgirl" was first applied to second-generation ranch women who demonstrated their skills at the Cheyenne Frontier Days in 1897 where the term appeared on the rodeo program. Personalities as well as gutsy performance of events made these early cowgirls popular. Teddy Roosevelt saw thirteen-year-old Lucille Mulhall perform in 1889 at a Cowboy Tournament at the Rough Riders' Reunion in Oklahoma City. As a child, Lucille had exhibited the daring that would make her a championship cowgirl. Her father told her she could have her own herd when she could brand her own cattle, and she went out and branded all the strays she could find—with her saddle cinch! After seeing her roping performance in Oklahoma City, Roosevelt told her she could ride in his inaugural parade if she could rope a wolf, and three hours later she returned from the range with the creature dragging behind. She was known during her career as a top roper, trick rider, and steer tier. An old cowhand reports:

> They had a big steer tying show, Zack Mulhall and his bunch at our fairgrounds, and his daughter, Lucille. She looked about eighteen and wore a divided skirt. First woman I'd ever seen that wasn't on a side saddle. And she was a fine steer tier. She could rope those steers, drag 'em down and tie 'em just like a man.[35]

Other famous cowgirls included Ruth Roach, Tad Lucas, and Florence Randolph, who, during the golden age of the rodeo in the 1920s, participated in all-male events such as bronc riding and bull dogging. These women were big drawing cards for the traveling shows and rodeos in different parts of the country. For example, one year at the Fort Worth rodeo Florence Randolph performed her trick riding on a grass mat in the lobby of a downtown hotel to publicize the local rodeo. Randolph was a great beauty and, as with the other rodeo cowgirls, the combination of her looks, her prowess on horseback, and her dashing costume cut a memorable figure in the public imagination. The rodeo today is a bland reminder of the remarkable feats of these earlier performers. Today women participate in their own events, primarily barrel racing, as trained athletes in a highly competitive business. Unlike their earlier sisters who at least suggested a historical affinity with the West, today's cowgirls, like the rodeo cowboy, are images of sports heroines rather than part of a metaphor of the western experience.

The athletic ability of the cowgirl, however, is her unique and sustaining attribute. From the deeds that distinguished her in real life throughout the physical escapades in the dime novel, western literature, the Wild West Show, rodeo, and film, her identity is grounded in physical capability. Studies show that athletically oriented people identify themselves with athletic traits associated with success—aggressiveness, tough-mindedness, dominance, self-confidence, and risk taking.[36] These traits, of course, are antithetical to those usually attributed to women. Hence, the cowgirl who can ride and rope and run her ranch as well as a man is able to carve out a portion of the Western myth for herself by means of her athletic bearing. Such talents not only put her on equal footing with the hero, but they allow her the very traits our writers attribute to the Western hero. Thus, if the behavior and attitudes of the hero are of interest because he exhibits these characteristics as a trapper or cowboy or soldier, the cowgirl also commands this interest. Indeed, one of the complaints of novelists such as Wallace Stegner is that women's lives on the frontier constituted a view "from the inside," that is, only from the home.[37] Such drama of dailiness has proved uninteresting to our novelists. No doubt the cowgirl had special appeal because she exhibited behavior thought to be unusual for women. She was, in fact, the "New Woman" of the frontier, and her popularity parallels new freedoms women were experiencing toward the end of the nineteenth century and during the 1920s. In this sense, however, her athletic inclinations presented as much of a problem as they did a unique status. Because she did contradict the typical female role, writers tended to refine her by centering her in melodrama or even making her exploits so sensational, they bordered on comedy. Audiences, no doubt, found this treatment of her entertaining and therefore acceptable. Later, of course, writers and film makers converted the qualities of the athletic heroine to sexual energy, so that she became the "dark" heroine.

But the athletic "Pard" offered an opportunity for writers to resolve their dilemma over the "masculine wilderness of the American novel," as Carolyn Heilbrun calls it.[38] Rather than pose a sexual threat to the hero by representing the marriage and civilization that inimitably followed association with a woman, the girl "Pard" functioned as a buddy would: she was friend, sidekick, and, if she became a wife, at least she could rescue the hero from a jam. If this cowgirl character was an "Amazon" she nevertheless was described by the dime novelists as a "honey-throated" Amazon; her androgyny made her a companion of the hero. The alternative —more prevalent in our literature—fits this description of Texas by J. B. Priestley in 1956:

> I am convinced that good talk cannot flourish where there is a wide gulf between the sexes, where the men are altogether too masculine, too hearty and bluff and booming, where the women are too feminine, at once both too arch and too anxious. Where men are

leavened by a feminine element, where women are not without some tempering by the masculine spirit, there is a chance of good talk. . . . But here was a society entirely dominated by the masculine principle. Why were so many of these women at once so arch and anxious? . . . Even here in these circles, where millionaires apparently indulged and spoilt them, they were haunted by a feeling of inferiority, resented but never properly examined and challenged. They lived in a world so contemptuous and destructive of real feminine values that they had to be heavily bribed to remain in it. All those shops, like the famous Neiman-Marcus store in Dallas, were part of the bribe. They were still girls in a mining camp. And to increase their bewilderment, perhaps their despair, they are told they are living in a matriarchy.[39]

Priestley not only gives good reason for a balance of male and female elements, but he fingers the reason for the dearth of heroines in western literature: heroic stature is conceived in purely masculine terms. Unlike the Greek goddesses and British, French, Russian, or Spanish women who assumed leading roles in mythology, literature, and history, American heroines are a pale lot—except for the cowgirl, whose evolution from the lives of real women on the frontier makes her embodiment of masculine and feminine traits unique.

NOTES

1. David Potter, "American Woman and the American Character," *Stetson University Bulletin* 17(January 1962):58.
2. William Humphrey, *Ah Wilderness: The Frontier in American Literature* (El Paso, 1977), p.15.
3. Emerson Hough, *The Passing of the Frontier* (New Haven, 1921), pp. 93–94.
4. Leslie A. Fiedler, "Evasion of Love," in *Theories of American Literature*, ed. Donald M. Kartiganer and Malcolm A. Griffith (New York, 1972), p. 246.
5. Dawn Lander, *Women and the Wilderness: Tabus in American Literature*, University of Michigan Papers in Women's Studies, 1976, no. 11, p. 66.
6. Ibid., p. 64.
7. Judith Fryer, *The Faces of Eve* (New York, 1976), p. 23.
8. Gerda Lerner, *The Woman in American History* (Berkeley and Los Angeles, 1972), p. 45.
9. Along with Fiedler's *Love and Death in the American Novel*, see Carolyn Heilbrun, "The Masculine Wilderness of the American Novel," *Saturday Review* 55(January 1972), Lander, *Women and the Wilderness*, and Fryer, *Faces of Eve*.
10. "From Cowboy to Owner and Operator of Vast Domain Marked Life of Charlie Hart," *Clovis News Journal*, 29 May 1938.
11. Emily Jones Shelton, "Lizzie E. Johnson: A Cattle Queen of Texas," *Southwest Historical Quarterly* 50(January 1947):351.
12. T. J. Tertula, "There Was No Christmas," *True West* 2(November–December 1963):20–21.

13. "Frontier Sketches," *The Denver Field and Farm*, 29 April 1911, p. 8.

14. "A Daring Western Woman," *Denver Times*, 7 February 1910.

15. Alice Marriott, *Hell on Horses and Women* (Norman, Okla., 1953), p. 10.

16. Agnes Smedley, *Daughter of Earth* (New York, 1935), p.56.

17. Ibid., p. 110.

18. J. Frank Dobie, *The Mustangs* (London, 1955), p. 32.

19. Interview with Joyce Roach, May 1978.

20. Mrs. E. J. Guerin, *Mountain Charley or The Adventures of Mrs. E. J. Guerin, Who Was Thirteen Years in Male Attire*, ed. Fred Mazzula and William Kostka (New York, 1971). pp. 13–14.

21. J. Evetts Haley, *Charles Goodnight, Cowman and Plainsman* (New York, 1936), p. 262.

22. Hobart Huson, *A History of Refugio County* (Austin, Tex., 1955), p. 203.

23. Evett Dumas Nix, *Oklahombres* (Norman, Okla., 1929), p. 147.

24. Henry Nash Smith, *Virgin Land* (New York, 1950), p 129.

25. Dee Brown, *The Gentle Tamers* (Lincoln, Neb., 1968), p.59.

26. See Guerin, *Mountain Charley*.

27. Albert Johannsen, *The House of Beadle and Adams*, (Norman, Okla., 1950), p. 204.

28. E. L. Wheeler, *Deadwood Dick on Deck: or, Calamity Jane, The Heroine of Whoop-up* (New York, 1899), p. 24.

29. Richard Slotkin, *Regeneration Through Violence: The Mythology of the American Frontier, 1600–1860* (Middletown, Conn., 1973), p. 12.

30. Ibid., p. 14.

31. John Cawelti, *Adventure, Mystery and Romance* (Chicago, 1976), p. 240.

32. Joe B. Frantz and Julian Earnest Choate, *The American Cowboy* (Norman, Okla., 1955), p. 175.

33. George Fenin and William Everson, *The Westerns: From Silents to Cinerama* (New York, 1962), p. 40.

34. See Will Wright, *Sixguns and Society* (New York, 1975).

35. Typed interview from a tape recording made by Mody Boatright, December 27, 1952.

36. I. Broverman, D. Broverman, F. Clarkson, P. Rosenkrantz, and S. Vogel, "Sex Role Stereotypes and Clinical Judgments of Mental Health," *Journal of Consulting and Clinical Psychology* 34(February 1970):5.

37. Wallace Stegner, "On the Writing of History," in *Western Writing*, ed. Gerald W. Halsam (Albuquerque, 1974), p. 26.

38. See Heilbrun, "The Masculine Wilderness of the American Novel."

39. Quoted ibid., p.44.

12

Pornography, Catastrophe, and Vengeance: Shifting Narrative Structures in a Changing American Culture

John Cawelti

History is full of watersheds. The unwary critic who points to his own times as an epoch of great transformation is all too likely to see his anticipated apocalypse turn into a minor tremor. This seems particularly true in the wake of the 1960s, when so many writers predicted an incipient cultural revolution that would green America, create a counterculture, and usher in a new postindustrial, postmodern society at the edge of history. The cultural revolutionary rhetoric of the 1960s rang hollow in the seemingly conservative 1970s. Perhaps all the tumult was a surface phenomenon tied to the agonies of a specific historical situation, the war in Vietnam. It did appear that when the war ended and things settled down a bit, many hippies cut their hair and began to worry about jobs and the energy crisis, while Americans in general seemed chiefly concerned about how they could continue to live their affluent suburban lives in an age of rising inflation and gasoline shortages. From this point of view, the changing attitudes and ideologies of the 1960s can be seen as only a temporary manifestation of the malaise caused by a particular situation and not a sign of long-term shifts in the popular consciousness.

However, before we accept the conclusion that the cultural turmoil of the 1960s was only a ripple in the even flow of the American mainstream, I would like to call attention to another kind of evidence that may signify the development of profound shifts in the popular consciousness. I refer to some recent and, I think, important changes in the basic patterns of narrative that characterize popular storytelling in the media of print, film, and television. Popular narrative and drama have traditionally been profoundly conservative; until recently, the basic patterns and genres domi-

182

nating this field have changed surprisingly little in the past one hundred years. We can point to a very long history for such popular fables as the success story, a product of the early nineteenth century, the romance, which originated in the late eighteenth century, the western, created by James Fenimore Cooper in the 1820s, the detective story, from the mid-nineteenth century, and the spy story from the early twentieth century. These genres have dominated popular formulaic fiction for nearly a century. They have, of course, undergone an evolution of their own, yet there is probably much more similarity than difference among the plots, characters, and themes in, say, *The Last of the Mohicans* (1826), *The Virginian* (1902), and *Shane* (1949). Similarly, most of the popular romances of Barbara Cartland are obvious imitations of Jane Austen's *Pride and Prejudice*, while the gothic romances of Victoria Holt and Phyllis Whitney show a definite if bastardly kinship to Charlotte Bronte's *Jane Eyre*. The early twentieth-century espionage entanglements of John Buchan's Richard Hannay are clearly reflected in the saga of Ian Fleming's James Bond, while the most recent Agatha Christie novels have all the major characteristics of Poe's C. Auguste Dupin stories.

But in the last decade the traditional patterns of popular storytelling have been deeply disrupted. One very important indication of this transformation is the emergence of new kinds of stories, and the eclipse of traditional genres. For example, there is the curious decline of the western, which once made up as much as one-fourth of the American movie output and which, in the late 1950s, dominated the television screen. Today, few westerns are in production, and long-lasting series like "Gunsmoke" and "Bonanza" have been canceled. The situation comedy plays, if anything, an even more important role, but most of the currently successful shows elaborate situations that undercut or explode the traditional affirmation of romantic love and family solidarity—for example "All in the Family," "Mary Hartman, Mary Hartman," "M.A.S.H.," "Mary Tyler Moore," and "The Bob Newhart Show." These programs have in common the comic exploitation of strains and inadequacies in the traditional institutions of marriage and the family.

Even more striking, I think, is what appears to be an upsurge in the production and popularity of the varied genres associated with science-fiction and fantasy on the one hand and pornography on the other. If we include in the former category those fantasies that verge on the occult as well as those that present themselves as futuristic extrapolations, we find that it includes a significant portion of the major film and television successes of recent years. *The Exorcist, The Omen*, and their many imitators are one sort of instance, while the startling retrospective popularity of "Star Trek" is another. Science fiction and fantasy, once the popular reading of a relatively small elite, are rapidly becoming a general popular interest. We can probably anticipate an increasing number of novels, films, and television programs dealing with this sort of material. Already it seems clear that the light reading of the current generation of students has shifted from the traditional formulas of crime and adventure to science fiction.

Pornography, long the underground playpen of a relatively small public, has become democratized and more generally acceptable. In the last decade, many neighborhood theaters, their audiences drawn off by television, have found economic viability in a program of porn. At the same time, pornographic magazines and books have become a major industry, its output purveyed through a large network of so-called adult bookstores that have sprung up all over the country.

These shifts in the major popular story formulas reflect, I believe, some significant shifts in popular mythology. The newer genres and the transformed versions of older genres are, in other words, based on different story patterns that embody an altered way of viewing and intepreting the world along with a different set of assumptions about the nature of society and the proper course of individual lives. In order to describe these shifts, I will first define what I take to be the primary story patterns, which are basic to the traditional repertory of popular genres. Then I will attempt to derive from the newer types of story a comparable set of patterns, those basic plots that seem to dominate the emergent genres and thus to constitute the emergent popular mythology.

Three primary myths have informed most popular narrative formulas during the last century. These can be called (1) the myth of proper sexuality; (2) the myth of effective individual action; and (3) the myth of racial temptation and conquest.

(1) The pattern of proper sexuality is seen in the kind of story in which the central characters go through various romantic trials and tribulations, but, if they adhere to the basic values of chastity before marriage and monogamous domesticity, are eventually brought to a happy and fulfilling marriage. Or, contrarily, if the protagonists transgress the rules of proper sexuality, they suffer and usually die. Proper sexuality implies not simply the avoidance of illicit sexual relations, but also the appropriate status and roles of the two sexes. In stories manifesting this pattern, women who are too aggressive and men who are not appropriately deferential to true femininity generally get into difficulty. Only when men and women achieve the right balance of roles and status with respect to each other are they conducted in to the eternal bliss of middle-class domesticity. This basic pattern was the predominant narrative emphasis of a large number of particular popular formulas such as the sentimental novel, various kinds of romance, the social melodramas, the soap opera, and many other popular types created primarily for women. But the same basic pattern can be found as a minor element in adventure stories like the western, in many detective stories, and in the situation comedy. This mythos was capable of

innumerable variations, but basically it presided over stories involving romances between men and women, which affirmed sexual differentiation and fulfillment in relation to the primary social institutions of monogamous marriage.

(2) The myth of effective individual action is embodied in stories which show that social and personal problems can be solved by a responsible and courageous individual operating largely without the support of larger groups or institutions. The stories that manifest this myth typically present a situation showing that the social institutions charged with solving problems are incapable of doing so, and then develop an individual hero who has the capacity to do something about the problem on his own. One important nineteenth-century formula embodying this myth was the Horatio Alger type of success story. In this story, the problem was poverty. At the beginning of the story, the protagonist was usually shown in relation to his family or to a custodial social institution like an orphanage. But the events of the story soon made it clear that neither family nor philanthropic organization could really help the protagonist rise from rags to riches. Only through his own individual efforts could the hero expect to solve the problem of poverty. The rest of the story showed how through exceptional diligence, attention to business, and occasional acts of personal courage, the poor individual could rise to a position of middle-class respectability, if not of great riches. Another very important form of this myth can be found in the popular western as it developed in the nineteenth-century dime novel and later in the film. Here the narrative focus was typically on a community beset by outlaws or by greedy and tyrannical railroad barons or ranchers who wanted to expropriate the community in order to seize its water rights, to prevent homesteaders from taking over the open range, or to take over the little people's land for a railroad right-of-way. Confronted with these aggressive threats, the townspeople were helpless and the official agencies of law enforcement corrupt or incompetent. Eventually, the cowboy hero who stood by himself outside the community and outside the law had to overcome the forces of lawlessness.

The detective story, particularly in its American hard-boiled form, embodies this myth of effective individual action. Indeed, the way in which both the western and the hard-boiled detective story draw on this myth makes them appear to be strongly related to each other.

However, though it embodies the myth of effective individual action, the hard-boiled detective story, at least in some of its chief manifestations, already shows some major ambiguities that do not appear in earlier versions of the myth of effective individual action. These ambiguities began to cluster around the hero's character and mission, and around the nature of his success. In one group of hard-boiled writers, those in the tradition of Mickey Spillane, the criminal antagonist is so vicious, so powerful, and so deeply embedded in the social structure that the heroic

individual must become as brutal, amoral, and bloodthirsty as his antago-
nists in order effectively to counter their power. In Spillane's stories the
hero begins as a courageous and isolated individual whose actions restore
order or bring new kinds of achievement that benefit a society with
problems. He is transformed into a vigilante avenger who generates a
brutal massacre in order to wipe out a few of the malign forces which have
almost totally subverted society. In the other group of hard-boiled writers, the more complex tradition of Dashiell Hammett, Raymond Chan-
dler, and Ross Macdonald, the hero's character remains relatively admirable,
but there is a good deal of ambiguity about the result of his mission. Though
the detective succeeds in exposing the criminal, he often regrets it and
shows a degree of sympathy and compassion for those who become criminals. In these stories, criminals become less figures of evil than embodi-
ments of society's own corruptions. Because of its tendency to undercut
the moral clarity of the hero's character and to raise questions about the
ultimate justice of his actions, the hard-boiled story may be viewed as a
kind of transitional form between the myth of effective individual action
and a newer mythology that has assumed increasing importance in popular formulas. Before developing that new mythology, however, we must
briefly describe the third primary myth of traditional American popular
culture: the myth of racial temptation and conquest.

(3) The myth of racial temptation and conquest is a basic story that
underlies an assortment of popular narrative formulas in the last century
and a half, including the western, the heroic spy story, the gothic romance, the monster story, much earlier science fiction, and the colonial
adventure. The immensely popular Tarzan series was in many ways the
epitome of this myth. The pattern embedded in these different formulas,
sometimes quite openly, sometimes rather indirectly, is a narrative situation in which a protagonist—usually a white man or woman—is confronted
with the danger of being destroyed, corrupted, or worse still, assimilated
into another culture or race. The protagonist overcomes the alien threat,
usually through a sequence of violent acts, and is restored to his own
people. Often as a consequence the alien being or race is itself conquered
or destroyed. The pattern of racial temptation, violence, and regeneration
has been brilliantly analyzed in the literature of the American West by
Richard Slotkin. As he points out, the western story and legend in the
eighteenth and nineteenth centuries almost always developed a confrontation between Christian whites and pagan Indians in which the Indian's
qualities of savagery and eroticism, though overtly portrayed as abhor-
rent, frequently showed signs of strong latent attraction for the white
protagonist. The earliest forms of western story—Indian captivity narratives and tales of battle between whites and Indians—were fairly straightforward portrayals of the overcoming of the threat of Indian subversion
by violent conquest. Later, as the actual threat of Indian power receded,

the conflict tended to become more symbolic. The emergence of the Leatherstocking figure who occupied the ambiguous middle ground between white and Indian cultures created new story formulas. Still later, outlaws began to play the role that had been earlier accorded to Indians in the mythical drama of the West. However, the nexus of conflict between ways of life, one representing the religious and moral order of white Christian civilization and the other an anarchic fantasy of lawless potency, violence, and unrestrained eroticism, continued to be a focal point of western action. Again and again, the hero or heroine had to pass through the threatening temptations of alien values in order to reestablish through violence the ordered restraint of Christian middle-class culture.

While the western was America's primary embodiment of the story of racial temptation and conquest, nineteenth- and twentieth-century Americans were also highly responsive to English versions of this myth in writers of colonial adventure like H. Rider Haggard, and in early spy stories like Sax Rohmer's Fu Manchu series. Here the alien race was represented by African or Oriental cultures. In addition to these explicit portrayals of racial conflict, symbolic forms proliferated with animals, monsters, or Martians playing the role of alien threat and temptation. Dracula, the Mummy, the Creature from the Black Lagoon, and King Kong all posed threats of violence, eroticism, and corruption, probably drawing much of their emotional force from the latent fears of racial temptation that were so powerful in English and American culture in the nineteenth and twentieth centuries. Tarzan was, of course, another version of the Leatherstocking hero. His power and potency derived from his position between white culture and the savage jungle, but his actions usually led to the salvation of representatives of white middle-class society. Dominating popular story formulas, the myth of racial temptation and conquest also fascinated many major writers who explored its ambiguities. Conrad's *Heart of Darkness* is perhaps the *locus classicus.*

The three myths I have described—proper sexuality, effective individual action, and racial temptation and conquest—were all, I think, expressions in story form of essential tensions in a white middle-class social order. Each of the myths addressed itself in its own way to some fundamental threat to middle-class cultural values—threats of unrestrained eroticism to the monogamous family, of crime and corruption to the values of individual enterprise and civic decency and order, of alien races and cultures to the whole complex of white, Christian moral and social ideals. Each myth portrayed a successful response to these threats by actions that were themselves symbolic of the central values of the middle-class order—the strength of the family; the totally fulfilling monogamous marriage; the efficacy of individual actions; and the power of white moral values to overcome the most dangerous alien threats. By confirming these values and resolving certain latent conflicts in middle-class culture, these myths became the mainstay of American popular film and fiction in the first half of the twentieth century. In commercial television, which is by all odds the most conservative of our mass media, these myths are still probably dominant.

However, when we look at those media which, like movies and the paperback novel, address themselves disproportionately to the younger elements of the population, we find a very different complex of story types emerging. Generic shifts, parodic and ironic transformations, and the increasing prevalence of new kinds of stories suggest the gradual emergence of a new pattern of popular myths. While it is too early to be absolutely certain about the character of these new patterns. I think we can discern at least the following three mythical shifts.

(1) The myth of proper sexuality is giving way to, or at least entering into, some kind of dialectic with a myth of erotic liberation and domination. Most pornography is a paradoxical combination of two primary themes: the freeing of erotic instincts from constraints, and the establishing of sexual and psychological domination by one person over others. As many myths seem to involve a yoking together of opposites and contraries, so the basic myth of pornography seems to center around the exploration of various ways in which erotic liberation and enslavement are inextricably linked to the extent that one cannot somehow be expressed without the other. Thus many pornographic stories are accounts of rape that supposedly leads to the erotic and emotional freeing of the victim. Other formulas portray a character in the process of freeing himself or herself from traditional sexual taboos in order to pursue new forms of erotic activity: bestiality, homosexuality, incest, pedophilia, sado-masochism, anal and oral eroticism. This quest for sexual freedom, however, seems invariably linked to themes of imprisonment and domination. One of the most successful pornographic films, *The Devil in Miss Jones*, linked Miss Jones's erotic liberation with death and eternal incarceration. The same paradox was developed in a different way in the highly successful French erotic novel *The Story of O*.

Most hard-core pornography is not as lucid as these two works about the ambiguous relationship of sexual liberation and enslavement. Indeed, as is the case with the general level of popular creation, the typical skin flick seems to conceal the inherent ambiguities and paradoxes of the myth it performs, but the presence of that myth is nonetheless evident in such features as the frequent presence of violence, the number of actions that are expressive of various forms of rape, and the strangely claustrophobic settings typical of low-budget porn. Far from a straightforward celebration of the joys of sex, pornography is an expression of profound emotional and cultural conflicts growing, I should think, out of the increasing ambiguity of sexual roles in modern Western society. The traditional myth of proper sexuality reflected a sense of the world in which sexual roles were relatively fixed; tensions and conflicts arose when individuals had to find their way into their appropriate sexual roles by becoming participants in an ordered family. Today, of course, the nature of proper sexual relations has itself become the problem, and the growing popularity of the myth of pornography is one attempt to work out a solution to this problem.

Thus far, pornography remains primarily a type of expression for men, and it is not surprising that most of its stories tend toward a resolution that involves masculine domination and feminine enslavement. However, in the last decade a literature of erotic liberation for women has also developed. This seems to consist of two main types: the feminine confessional novel that portrays a woman's quest for freedom from traditional sexual roles (French's *The Woman's Room*, Jong's *Fear of Flying*, Greene's *Blue Skies No Candy*) and the semipornographic historical romance in which a feminine protagonist undergoes a wide range of erotic adventures and enslavements before being finally united with her true love (e.g. the works of Rosemary Rogers, Kathleen Woodiwiss, and Jennifer Wilde). The latter type seems to imply that it is only through a series of sexual enslavements that a woman can become erotically free enough to enter into a totally fulfilling relationship with a man. In this way, the new-style historical romance seems to reinforce the basic myth of sexuality expressed in pornography: sexual liberation is inextricably connected with some form of enslavement. The woman's confessional novel typically has a different shape. These are usually stories about a woman's breaking out of a conventional marriage in search of personal freedom and fulfillment. But while the protagonist may achieve some success in a professional career and may find greater erotic fulfillment in temporary affairs than in her earlier marriage, she also discovers that men are simply not capable of a truly mutual relationship with a woman, that at some point the basic cultural assumption of male superiority will inevitably reassert itself and make a free sexual relationship impossible. The protagonists of these novels usually end up alienated from men and lonely.

The myth of erotic liberation and enslavement may be a transitional narrative pattern which mediates between traditional ideas about sexual roles and the newer ideals of sexual equality. By affirming the inescapable connection between sexual liberation and enslavement, this myth sets forth on the one hand a new possiblity of sexual freedom and openness while, on the other, it warns that there can be no permanent sexual satisfaction for a woman without accepting some kind of subordinate role. As sexual conflict and ambiguity become more intense in the years ahead, we can expect to see more of this mythology because, while it reaches out for a new vision of sexuality, it contains a built-in sense of the dangers and ambiguities inherent in this new vision. The myth of erotic liberation and enslavement thus attempts to resolve the conflicting values of sexual freedom and male dominance and has great power in a time of changing sexual patterns.

(2) The myth of racial temptation and conquest is giving way to a myth

of catastrophe. In the myth of racial temptation and conquest, the threat was typically posed by a group that, however tantalizing its values, was clearly inferior to Anglo-American bourgeois culture. Progressive evolution in effect guaranteed the ultimate conquest of the inferior race or group; the hero or heroine's confrontation with Indians, outlaws, or savage Africans was part of a mopping-up operation rather than a stand at Armageddon. In the myth of catastrophe, however, the threat derives either from the very technology of modern civilization (as in the various fantasies of nuclear holocaust and on a lesser scale in so-called disaster films like *The Towering Inferno*) or from nature (particularly from the sea as in *Jaws* or the many shipwreck sagas such as *The Poseidon Adventure*), or it represents a transcendant force so powerful that it threatens to transform the whole of human existence (a primary interest both in science fiction like *2001* and many episodes of "Star Trek," and in satanic possession fantasies like *The Exorcist* and *The Omen*). Because the danger is either an inescapable condition of life or a transcendant force, the catastrophe myth ends not in conquest but in the survival of a few or in a symbolic form of redemption.· Whether the catastrophe is a limited one, such as shipwreck or the destruction of a skyscraper, or a more cosmic one, such as nuclear holocaust or satanic domination, it implies the almost total destruction of an existing order and the selection of a few individuals worthy of passing over into a new order of things. Science fiction is a primary genre of this new myth because its very essence is the envisioning of a different social, natural, or technological order. Therefore, even when its central story is not an account of catastrophe, a work of science fiction is implicitly the account of a drastic transformation of the present human state of things. Finally, while the myth of racial temptation and conquest centers around social and cultural conflict, the myth of catastrophe tends to invoke the religious dimension of experience in its concern for ultimate transformations.

(3) The myth of effective individual action is increasingly being replaced by the myth of the violent avenger. Though there is a considerable similarity in structure between these two myths, it seems to me that most contemporary stories of violent vengeance are in effect a denial of the social efficacy of individual action. The traditional individual hero's primary role was to bring justice to society. Even when, as in many westerns, his original motive was vengeance, the hero's action became part of a larger narrative structure in which law and order were established or reaffirmed. In the myth of the violent avenger, however, this structure becomes attenuated. Society itself seems so pervaded with evil that it is irredeemable. That movement of the plot in which the individual hero's concerns became coordinate with society's need for justice simply does not take place. If the hero seeks to bring the forces of evil before the bar of justice he discovers that the law cannot touch them, or that, even worse,

they control the law. Thus his only moral satisfaction comes from destroying the leaders of the syndicate, or the muggers who have killed his wife, or the warlord who has kidnapped his sister. In this type of story attention is focused not, as in the traditional western, on the complex process by which the hero's individual actions become socially meaningful, but on the physical confrontation between heroes and the legions of evil. In such films, this climactic confrontation becomes an orgy of group combat rather than a carefully choreographed individual confrontation such as the classic western shootout. Kung-fu films consist primarily of such scenes of combat with cinematic devices like slow motion and freeze frames used to prolong and intensify the scenes of fighting. Similarly, in *The Wild Bunch*, Sam Peckinpah's highly successful western of the late 1960s, a film permeated by elements of the new popular mythology, the final shootout employed a similar cinematography to develop an unforgettable scene of transcendant vengeful slaughter. Though this kind of portrayal of violence is much criticized, its attraction to audiences is evident enough, and derives, I suspect, from an anxious erosion of the audiences' belief in the efficacy of traditionally justified individual violence. When it was possible to believe that the heroic individual could restore order to society by his actions, more controlled forms of violence were dramatic enough. With the decay of this perception of society, the act of violence itself, rather than its results, had to become the focus of emotional excitement.

All three of these new myths—erotic liberation and enslavement, catastrophe, and the violent avenger—reflect, in my opinion, a changing view of American society and its meaning and prospects. They suggest that important traditional ideologies—the belief in the family, in traditional sexual roles, in the power of the individual, in the certainty of social progress, and in the essential benevolence of technological and scientific advancement—have begun to decay and that the people are being attracted to new forms of mythology in order to understand and emotionally accept the more frightening world that they feel around them. Since these new myths now exist side by side with story forms that continue to express the traditional myths, we are not yet at the point where we can say that the new myths have prevailed. Therefore it is almost impossible to be certain about the long-term cultural significance of the new patterns of belief and emotion implicit in the popular story patterns I have attempted to analyze.

Some common thematic elements do seem to recur in these mythical shifts. One is the tendency toward transcendance as opposed to the secularity of the three main traditional popular myths. The myth of erotic liberation appeals to a fantasy of overpowering sexual experience in contrast to the synthesis of romance and social status in the myth of proper sexuality. The catastrophe myth elaborates terminal situations of danger, supernatural intervention, and total breakdown instead of the pattern of restoration of the social fabric set forth in the myth of racial temptation and conquest. Finally, the myth of the violent avenger embodies an image of uncontrolled violence, while the story of effective individual action stresses the harmonious balance between social order and individual moral action. An aura of basic insecurity pervades all three of the newer mythical patterns: the insecurity of personal relationships against the overpowering force of sexuality, the insecurity of the individual in a society on the edge of chaos, and the uncertain fate of the world itself in face of natural, supernatural, or technological catastrophe. In contrast, the traditional myths project an image of social and cultural stability strong enough to overcome the dangers of uncontrolled eroticism, localized corruption or deviance, and the challenge of alien cultures or races. Finally, the newer myths seem to center around the possibility of personal or social apocalypse, the transformative experience which disrupts the orderly process of society and changes everything. The traditional myths, on the other hand, usually affirmed the essential orderliness of society as a progressive regeneration or recreation of the values of monogamous marriage, law and order, and effective resistance to alien temptations.

It would surely be premature to say that the shifts in popular story patterns I have analyzed are evidence of a drastic shift in the American consciousness, yet they do suggest at least the hypothesis that the cultural disaffections and doubts that characterized small groups of radical young people in the 1960s have begun to expand into the broader popular consciousness. If these newer myths continue to develop, they may well signal the beginning of a final breakdown in that long-lasting American consensus of which Professor Bercovitch speaks in another essay in this collection. The doctrine of American mission that served to harmonize individual success and social good and to give a sacred dimension to the secular development of America found expression in the traditional myths of popular storytelling through the pattern of threat and regeneration. The newer imagining of disaster, the dangerous pursuit of erotic liberation, and the quest for vengeance may express profound doubts about the continuance of that mission and a search for new ways to mythologize a more threatening sense of reality.

13

Ball Four with Epilogue

William C. Dowling

James Barbour

More than fifty years ago in "America's Coming of Age," Van Wyck Brooks divided American culture into two presumably incompatible camps —"highbrow" and "lowbrow".[1] This division is readily apparent in our attitudes toward literature, especially autobiography, where there are a few canonically accepted works and a remaining preponderance of memoirs and life-histories, often gossipy and sensational, frequently "ghosted," and inevitably designed for an unsophisticated audience. Conspicuous even among the latter for its lack of literary merit has been the sports autobiography. From its beginnings with Christy Mathewson's *Pitching in a Pinch* (New York, 1912), this genre has been a "ghosted" melange of inside information and moral example designed for a juvenile audience and its intellectual equivalent, the sports bug. Over the last twenty years, however, the literary quality of sports autobiography has improved dramatically. Jim Bouton's *Ball Four*,[2] demonstrates the changes that have occurred. It deserves recognition for its popularity and notoriety, but even more, it deserves serious literary attention for the interesting and extremely complex autobiographical problem of identity—the nature and integrity of the self—that the book presents for the sophisticated reader.[3] An examination of *Ball Four* illustrates once again how a serious literary analysis often reveals the unsuspected and hidden depths of popular literature.

But before *Ball Four* is discussed, it needs to be placed in its proper context: that is, the significant recent changes in sports autobiography and the contemporary studies of self and time in autobiography. The transformation in sports literature is apparent if one begins with John McGraw's *My Thirty Years in Baseball* (New York, 1923). Manager of the New York

Giants, the feisty McGraw was rumored to have thrown games, either directly or by proxy, and was a part of the gambling crowd of New York City, which included Charles Stoneham, owner of the Giants, and the notorious Arnold Rothstein. McGraw's memoirs record none of his interesting associations or activities. Obviously he was observing a tacit understanding in sports journalism, which ignored the darker aspects of the national pastime.[4] Fred Lieb, long-time New York baseball writer, tells a story that illustrates the censorship surrounding the game and its heroes: the Yankees were on a spring training jaunt from Baton Rouge to New Orleans when Babe Ruth, pursued by an irate woman brandishing a knife, ran through a Pullman car full of newspaper reporters. No one said a word. Later, Bill Slocum of the *Morning American* remarked, "Well, if she had carved up the Babe, we really would have had a hell of a story."[5]

Sports autobiography has changed radically in the years since McGraw and Ruth. Much of the change is due to Jim Brosnan, relief pitcher with, among other teams, the St. Louis Cardinals and Cincinnati Reds. A talented writer, Brosnan in *The Long Season* and *Pennant Race*, made his life and profession his subject matter. He candidly presented his problems with management and an opinionated radio announcer (Harry Carey). He also was honest about his own drinking and his consuming concern with his own performance.

Soon a flood of mature personal histories began to appear. Some made their way to the best-seller lists. Jerry Kramer's *Instant Replay*, a "conversion narrative" moved to the football field, described how Vince Lombardi took a ragtag Green Bay team, gave them pride and self-confidence, and led them to the championship. A better book but ignored by the reading public was Pat Jordan's *A False Spring*, which recounted his loneliness as a teen-age bonus baby in McCook, Nebraska, and his furtive love affair at the end of the season with a haunted local girl; a year later he lost his "pitching rhythm" and closed down his dreams. Another kind of autobiography, of a type begun by Paul Gallico in the twenties, is the adventure-of-the-common-man-in-Wonderland, perfected and brought out in yearly installments by George Plimpton, whose classic misadventures were on the football field with the Detroit Lions in *Paper Lion*.[6] A different kind of autobiography (one mixed with reporting) is Roger Kahn's sensitive and nostalgic recollection of his family and the Brooklyn Dodgers of 1952–53 in *The Boys of Summer*.

Bouton changed all that. *Ball Four* reflects an absence of faith in people and in systems. Bouton's experience was the opposite of Jerry Kramer's. Whereas Kramer found a mentor and a moral and emotional leader in Lombardi, Bouton found a moral vacuum at the top in *Ball Four*. Ownership, management, managers, and coaches turn out to be self-serving, stupid, insecure people. A hero of wisdom and cunning during his playing days, Sal Maglie, when seen as pitching coach on Bouton's Seattle Pilots team, proves to have only a faint notion of his craft; Joe Schultz, the manager, summarizes his acquired knowledge in his favorite expression, "shitfuck," or variations thereof. The effect is deadly; there is nothing to believe in. And Bouton has no discretion. He names names and tells all: on the old Yankees, Bouton's original ball club, Yogi Berra and Elston Howard dragged their "charlies" [*sic*] across the cold cuts at the players' table, Joe Pepitone stuck a popcorn kernel under his foreskin and went to the trainer complaining of a possible venereal disease. Unlike the sports-writers of Lieb's day, Bouton neither overlooks nor spares his heroes: Roger Maris emerges as an incredibly withdrawn redneck, and Mickey Mantle (the latter-day Babe Ruth) drinks too much, is rude ("cruel" would be a more descriptive word) to children, and is an energetic leader of the Beaver Patrol (baseball peeping toms) on the roof of the Shoreham Hotel in Washington.

Ball Four recognizes none of the accepted rules and conventions, but its unforgivable transgression is to talk about the sexual activities of the team on the road. Bouton allows his sexual performers anonymity, but they are often onstage, peeping through keyholes at the "local talent," trysting in elevators, plunging away in such unlikely attire as baseball sox and shower clogs, playing tape recordings of the previous night's encoun-ter for the boys in the locker room, hiding in hotel closets with permission to listen to the amorous noises of a nearby roommate—the sounds of copulation are in the air everywhere in *Ball Four*.

Ball Four, however, is more than a book about baseball and baseball players. It is true that Bouton captures the world of the professional ballplayer, but he also presents portraits of himself within the frame of the "long season," and smaller snapshots taken in previous seasons, reaching back to a younger Bouton in the minors, and finally to the child going to the Polo Grounds with his brother. *Ball Four* presents the problem cen-tral to recent autobiographical studies of identity over time: the matter of self and the multiplicity of selves changing throughout time. James Olney in his remarkable study *Metaphors of Self* notes that "Time carries us away not only from others but from ourselves as well, and we are all continuously dying to our own passing selves."[7] The self changes, but there is also that something in the personality which is constant, unchang-ing. To press Olney's metaphor, there are breaks in the thread, but the thread remains the same:

> Like the elements, individual man never is but is always becoming: his self, as C. G. Jung will say some twenty-five hundred years after Heraclitus . . . is a process rather than a settled state of the being. The order that men seek is never static and out there but always going on, and going on within them, and always coming into being. Only with the coming of death must the self settle its accounts.

> Hence, the same man, according to Heraclitus, cannot step twice
> into the same stream, and this is doubly true; for the man and for the
> stream. But there is a oneness of the self, an integrity or internal
> harmony that holds together the multiplicity and continual trans-
> formations of being.[8]

The real self of Jim Bouton is not, for all the time he spends on stage,
easily captured. The author is evasive, consciously acting roles, being
"hard working" and "serious" for management, "friendly" and "fun-loving"
for his teammates—an old player has to play many roles in order to hang
on in the game. Bouton's intention is to reconstruct the external scene,
not to reflect upon it. Like an artist roughing in his sketch, Bouton carries
his notebook, makes jottings, and tapes his entries at the end of the day.
His book reflects his method. It is anecdotal, full of the briefest of observations as it skips among vignettes. *Ball Four* suggests "man talking," and
only infrequently "man thinking."

The matter of autobiographical form also adds to the complexity of the
book. There are two basic and distinct forms for personal histories. Each
has separate implications for the matter of self-in-time and the perception
of time. On the one hand there is the memoir, in which the narrator
reconstructs life from a fixed point in retrospective time perceiving it as a
simultaneous whole. Here is Benjamin Franklin in the opening lines of
his *Autobiography:* "I should have no objection to go over the same life
from its beginning to the end, only asking the advantage authors have of
correcting in a second edition some faults of the first. So would I also wish
to change some incidents of it for others more favorable." The metaphor
of life-as-book embodies the controlling perspective of existence as a story
which, even though it unfolds over time, is complete up to the moment of
its retrospective telling.

In formal counterpoint to the memoir, however, there has existed since
before Samuel Pepys another autobiographical tradition, the diary or the
journal. In such narratives the perspective is located at the opposite
extreme from the memorist's fixed and retrospective point of view. In the
journal or diary the existential drama of identity-over-time is imitated in
direct terms, so that the narrator's daily entries become small untidy
chapters in a story the outcome of which he cannot foresee. If the memoir
gives us an autobiographical perspective that is, so to speak, frozen or
spatial, the journal gives us a perspective that is fluid and temporal—the
form of a story with a plot that remains mysterious, except in its most
general outlines, to its narrator-protagonist.

The journal or diary tells a story, however, only in the limited sense
that existence may be viewed as a story, with events following on other
events. The apparent plotlessness of the conventional journal or diary
becomes a matter of narrative perspective, for the diarist is someone who

perceives his or her existence as a story worth the telling but is simultaneously aware that its plot is something beyond the comprehension of anyone imprisoned within the horizon of daily experience.

Ball Four is obviously a journal. It has daily entries and follows the progression of human time. But the fact that the entries begin on 26 February and end on 2 October indicates that a sports time scheme controls the narrative. The baseball journal conforms to the season, beginning with spring training and ending in early autumn. The history of Bouton's encounter with the 1969 Seattle Pilots is dominated by the baseball year and only incidentally by human time; the tension of success and failure is intensified by the compression of time, the rhythms of a different year with its own clearly defined clock—the midpoint at the Fourth of July, the eleventh hour at Labor Day.

But if *Ball Four* has one calendar within another, it also contains one form within another. The book, as we have said, is a journal, but it at times sounds the tone of the memoir. Life is in flux for a ballplayer. Part of Bouton's life, however, exists beyond this change. The book is rich in memories, and they are islands in the flowing of time. Bouton's principles and ideals have been cultivated over time; now they, like the life of the memoirist, are complete, existing outside of time and impervious to it.

It is the journal form, however, that creates the tension in the book. The reader approaches the tale knowing it stretches for some three hundred pages, but the diarist or journalist is trapped in present time and knows little about the conclusion of his narrative. Bouton, who is in constant jeopardy as the last pitcher on the staff, is only dimly aware of, but is extremely interested in, the plot of his story. He would like to know how it ends. However, he is not in control of his tale—control belongs to those in the organization who make personnel decisions. Thus Bouton attempts to find out more about his plot, and plots, by attempting to impress his employers and by being a good fellow, so that he can remain in his story.

One of Bouton's recurrent metaphors equates dying with being released or sent down to the minors. (Chapter 3 is entitled, "And Then I Died.") The drama of *Ball Four* arises from this metaphorical life-and-death struggle. In writing the book Bouton is extending his life, just as his perfecting the knuckleball, performing well, and impressing the manager extend it. Time and character, then, are complex matters. On the one hand time is completed in terms of character, for Bouton's attitudes are fixed. Simultaneously, for Bouton the character in his own story, nothing is fixed and everything is fluid. And there is also the significance of time as imposed by the season. Each season recalls seasons past, and for Bouton there have been many seasons. The author is trapped at the opposite ends of the same time line. He is only twenty-nine years old, yet in baseball chronology he is an old-timer who is ready "to die." As an autobiographer he is an impossible anomaly: at once he is an old man dying out of the game and a young man, vigorous and energetic, playing the game.

II

In the brief retrospective conclusion to *Ball Four*, written in the winter of 1969–70, Bouton reviews the past season—his newfound pitch, the knuckleball, new friendships, laughter in the back of the team bus and in the bull pen, all mixed with increasing rebuffs from his teammates— and concludes that writing his book "taught me a great deal not only about others but about myself." ("I am not sure I liked everything I learned, but learning is often a painful experience." [p. 368]) Bouton, who began his book in order to capture for his reader the foreign and unknown world of professional baseball, claims to have discovered along the way a higher good, self-knowledge. Thus he finally shapes his book in the outline of classical autobiography. It begins as an outward journey and concludes in describing an inward terrain. Bouton's final reflection places his book in the autobiographical tradition of Augustine, who pleaded that God through his *Confessions* might show "my full self to myself."

Bouton's assessment of his autobiographical experience is interesting—it is a pity that it is not also true. (It is very much like the ending which contradicts the fiction and indicates that the author didn't understand his story.) The distinguishing feature of *Ball Four* is precisely the author's inability to "see" himself and understand the effect he has upon others. He fascinates as would the perceptive tour guide who consistently walks into walls. Clearly there is something missing in his vision. It is that "something missing" which in *Ball Four* invites commentary—the reader must fill the silences where the author avoids reflection, peer a little longer at his behavior, look beneath his disguises, and rummage through the closet where his old selves are hidden.

Bouton's tour through the land of baseball may be read as a modern-day *Typee:* the author is the civilized guide among perpetually adolescent natives. For most of the inhabitants it is a land of heart's desire, a fantasy come true, and, more important, an experience that tragically perpetuates childhood and innocence and crowds out maturity. It is also for the author a descent into the regions of Neanderthal thought (p. iii). For Bouton baseball finally represents a schizophrenic experience. He is both the rational cicerone and, at the same time, one of the natives. The real world and the world of baseball are in constant conflict in *Ball Four* and, needless to say, in Bouton's mind. The real world is meaningful and important and one's participation in it is significant—there one "changes the world" and has an influence on "other people's lives." The other is something one does for one's self.[9] The problem for Bouton is that he sees himself as being on the fringes of both worlds: a player of games in a serious world and too serious-minded for the world of games. He enjoys the recognition and popularity that come with being a ballplayer. At the same time his sense of self-indulgence and contrition is frequently overwhelming, as on his return from a baseball clinic for underprivileged children in Washington, D.C.: "And once again I wished I had the guts to chuck baseball and go out and do something for somebody beside myself. And getting mad at myself for not being able to do it, I look for somebody else to blame . . ." (p. 188).

One dilemma confronting the author is that of self-esteem. As a baseball player he must escape his own value system, and this he accomplishes by identifying with others on the fringe of the real world who contribute to it or believe in the right things—they agree with his "liberal" ideas—but who, like Bouton, are shunned by society. They, in effect, are projections of the self, doubles through whom he expresses attitudes about himself.

This sense of self is illustrated in two virtually identical scenes set outdoors. The first takes place in Pershing Square in Los Angeles, which Bouton and his roommate, Gary Bell, have visited to observe and rap with the speakers. Bouton moves from a group of, as he says, "old ladies in sneakers" preaching about the Second Coming of Jesus to a group of chanting hari krishnas, one of whom explains "that their religion simply was to reaffirm love of God regardless of the particular religion and I thought that was fair enough and we hung around enjoying the chanting and sitar music" (p. 101). The scene concludes with a passing middle-aged priest telling one of the chanters that they should go back where they came from. "He said we already had enough religions in this country" (p. 101). This is a drama of choices and consequences. As an unbeliever (his teammates will later place him on the all-agnostic team), Bouton acknowledges that he is beyond salvation after listening to the old ladies. His sympathy for the krishnas, then, is a matter of identification—in their separateness (their robes and chanting) he sees something of himself and his relationship to society, which, like the priest, rejects the unconventional although it may be nobler (it is significant that the krishnas preach the love of God, whereas the "old ladies" are preaching judgment).

The scene is essentially repeated three weeks later, when Bouton and Bell move on to Berkeley, California, to take in the student protestors: "[we] walked around and listened to speeches—Arab kids arguing about the Arab-Israeli war, Black Panthers talking about Huey Newton and the usual little old ladies in tennis shoes talking about God. Compared with the way everybody was dressed Bell and I must have looked like a couple of narcs" (p. 136). But, Bouton observes, the protesters "are concerned about the way things are and they're trying to change them. What are Gary and I doing beside watching?" (p. 137) The reference to himself as a "narc" suggests Bouton's divided self-image: his appearance, with crew cut and spring-training tan, belies his sympathies. The reference also captures Bouton's sense of disguise and alienation, for there is a suggestion of guilt, not only for "spying" on the protesters, but for the notebook and journal he has been keeping. The remaining entry for 2 May, this most revealing of days, is flush with self-revelation. The umpire behind the plate for the game that night is Emmett Ashford, the first black umpire in the major leagues. Ashford is another analogue of Bouton's self. He is alone in a white world (metaphorically another "narc"), rejected by his peers for showboating, and maliciously and mindlessly ridiculed by white umpires and players alike. Ashford is a dark reminder of a past and an earlier self and perhaps a future fate which Bouton hopes to avoid: "I know about lonely summers. In my last few years with the Yankees I had a few of them. You stand in a hotel lobby talking with guys at dinnertime and they drift away, and some other guys come along and pretty soon they're gone and you're all alone and no one has asked you what you're doing about dinner. So you eat alone. It must happen to Ashford a lot. And it's one of the reasons I can't bring myself to argue with him" (p. 137).

The entries for the day conclude with a pertinent but brief scene in which one of the author's teammates accuses him of bringing the radical *Berkeley Barb* into the clubhouse. The scene repeats the pattern first recorded in Pershing Square: identification with social outcasts and a subsequent rejection, first by a representative of the real world and then by someone from the world of baseball. It is Bouton who plants the *Barb* in the clubhouse to be found, thus engineering his own exposure and, ultimately, his rejection. He shapes his life in this pattern: it occurred previously in New York (probably it antedates the history in the book) and will inexorably and unconsciously be the future Bouton fashions in *Ball Four*.

The land of baseball that Bouton reveals is a bittersweet realization of his childhood dreams. His earliest memories are of watching his ballpark heroes play in a distant and magically enclosed circle. Walking out to the bullpen in Seattle, the veteran remembers "sitting up in the left-field stands in the Polo Grounds as a kid and thinking to myself, 'Cheez, if I could only run out on the field and maybe go over and kick second base, or shag a fly ball—God, that would make my year. I'd never forget it as long as I lived if I could just run across that beautiful green outfield grass.' And now sometimes I forget to tingle" (p. 238). Bouton recalls once sailing a Dixie cup out of the upper deck onto the infield of the Polo Grounds. Johnny Antonelli, pitching star for the Giants, bent over and picked up his flying saucer: "I got a huge kick out of that. Imagine, Johnny Antonelli picking up the cover of my Dixie cup" (p. 269). But the boy matures, the distance collapses as the circle is approached, and the glimmer of romanticism is snuffed by the presence of the cruel and insensitive hero. Bouton remembers himself in adolescence after his family had moved to Chicago, leaning over the dugout in Wrigley Field, "trying to tell Al

Dark how great he was and how much I was for him and, well, maybe get his autograph too, when he looked over at me and said, 'Take a hike, son. Take a hike' " (p. 112).[10]

Through such memories *Ball Four* tells the tale of man who falls from innocence into experience—in this case, the child who becomes the professional and finds his heroes to be venal and crude. The magical world viewed from the inside is discovered to be controlled by countless Calibans. The game of baseball, the veteran Bouton observes, "is foolishness too, grown men being serious about a boy's game. There's pettiness in baseball, and meanness and stupidity beyond belief, and everything else bad that you'll find outside of baseball. I haven't enjoyed every single minute of it . . ." (p. iii).

Much of the stupidity in baseball, and much of the humor in *Ball Four*, derives from the unflagging and unsuccessful attempts by managers and coaches to control the randomness that is the essence of the game. Failure in baseball occurs with great frequency.[11] Ty Cobb, for example, the greatest hitter in the history of the game, made an out .633 percent of the time, which suggests that the nature of the game will out—it refuses to yield totally to skill or force; accident will impose its own intractable shape. As Roger Angell observes in *The Summer Game*, "the patterns of baseball, for all the game's tautness and neatness, are never regular. . . . The surprise, the upset, the total turnabout of expectations and reputations —these are delightful common places of baseball."[12]

The baseball scenes in *Ball Four* offer innumerable absurd variations on the theme of control. The Seattle Pilots—castoff players, uncommunicative coaches, and a semiliterate manager—meet incessantly in attempts to control the randomness of the game, endlessly discussing how to pitch to hitters, how to "defense" them. Members of the rag-tag pitching staff are physically inadequate to the near impossible demands of their profession —they cannot blow the ball by hitters, they get their pitches up, hang pitches which do not break (or, in Bouton's case, do not knuckle), and the randomness that begins with the striking of the ball prevails.

Frustrated in their attempts to control the game, the manager and his coaches, to justify their existence, resort to an ersatz control. They regulate dress, assign roommates on the road, determine the number of balls that can be taken out of the ball bag (one to a player), and require that everyone be quiet and appropriately remorseful after a losing game. In this charade the pitching coach plays an important role, for control over the game begins (and more frequently ends) with the pitcher. The coach who instructs the pitcher and, by tutelage, controls the pitches, is the shaman who must eternally assert the possibility of control, even as the ball bounces uncontrollably about the field. When accident overwhelms the game, as is often the case, the pitching coach is forced to establish control *post factum*. This he does by identifying the pitcher's mistake, suggesting thereby that were the pitch what or where it should have been, order would have been maintained. By declaring the untoward event to have been caused by "pilot's error," the coach restores order to the game and upholds the sunlit verities of the sport (keep it low and away that it may go well with thee).

This innocent longing for control and the ready desire to fix blame for its absence results in a fallacy which Bouton recalls vaguely from an old philosophy course (*post hoc ergo propter hoc:* after this, therefore because of this) which fuels most of the thinking, or what passes for thinking, in baseball. When Bouton questions, for example, why the starting pitcher for the next series is not sent on ahead of the team in order to get his rest, he is told that it was tried and the pitcher was knocked out early. A similar episode involves Sal Maglie, the pitching coach, in a discussion of a change-up thrown on a full count. Steve Barber, the Pilot pitcher, had thrown the pitch and badly fooled the batter, but as the playful gods of the diamond would have it, the hitter plopped the ball into the opposite field and knocked in two runs. Maglie's immediate response in the dugout is to snap his fingers and mutter, "Son of a bitch—the 3-and-2 change. That goddam 3-and-2 change." In a world of fossil thought where fallacy is king and precedent remains unchallenged,[13] Bouton skips to a different and very personal melody. He believes little (nothing stated by management), opposes much, and questions everything. In a conservative world, Bouton is a radical in his thought and behavior. In a world that worships control, Bouton exhibits a disconcerting lack of control. The metaphor that best describes him is the pitch he throws, the knuckleball.

Among baseball pitches, the knuckleball is unique; it alone is gripped with the fingertips—usually three, but sometimes two—and not with the fingers. The pitch by design eludes the control of the pitcher. As Bouton explains it, the "air currents and humidity take over and cause the ball to turn erratically and thus move erratically" (p. 19). On occasion it moves not, but only "turns over" on its way to the plate, obedient only to its own inconsistency. As Bouton attempts to master the knuckleball, the pitch begins, in a strange reciprocity, to define the author: Bouton grips the pitch with his five fingertips (an unusual grip on this unusual pitch), which finally leads him to observe at the end of the Seattle experience, "they think I'm weird and throw a weird pitch" (p. 275). The author's dedication to the knuckleball (he tries to attain an identical release on each pitch, so that the ball will respond to the atmospheric conditions and not "turn over") demands constant throwing practice, and, sadly, it requires someone to catch the ball, or, after a good knuckler, capture and retrieve it. The pitch forces Bouton to argue with his manager and coaches, who do not want to understand its subtle requirements and view the necessity of his constant throwing as irrational; his need for a catcher (who invariably is hit by the baffling pitch) meets, understandably enough, with growing resistance. Bouton, in the end, is viewed by his peers as an extension of the one pitch he throws—unconventional and erratic. In a game in which pitchers labor for years to control their pitches, Bouton practices to perfect the one pitch in which direction is surrendered to the vagaries of moisture and air currents.

The trajectory of the knuckleball is also analogous to Bouton's misadventures during the 1969 season. Both pitch and author begin by moving in a straight line, but a little way out, losing momentum and resolve, they begin to veer and wiggle. Knuckleballs are all idiosyncratic, but the best appear to swing in wide arcs, deviating from the line as they move forward, and at the last moment, almost on top of the plate, break capriciously toward the ground. Thus Bouton's behavior in *Ball Four* mimics the movement of the knuckleball, oscillating erratically as the season ages, and finally departing absolutely from its chosen path as his hopes collapse. The intended movement of the narrative line is simple, albeit somewhat wishful. Bouton hopes to hustle and impress management, to perform well, to make the playing roster of the Seattle Pilots, and, as in his dreams, cap the season with a shining achievement or an award of considerable recognition (Bouton confesses that he lives in his fantasies). Bouton's private aspirations are of greater significance, for he is aware of the metaphorical meaning of the new season with the newly formed expansion team. It uniquely allows for the fashioning of a new self, the chance to slough off old skin and shape a self more acceptable to himself and his teammates, the hope of escaping past loneliness by being one of the boys. But being one of the boys is a chasm he cannot leap, and the self he creates to jump it appears with greater infrequency and then disappears altogether.

Bouton's ideal self, were he to succeed in fabricating one, would be patterned after Ruben Amaro, an ex-teammate on the Yankees, whom Bouton encounters during a spring training game with the California Angels: "Ruben Amaro is here with the Angels and I was happy to see him. We were good friends in New York. He's the kind of guy, well, there's a dignity to him and everybody likes and respects him. He's outspoken and has very strong opinions but he never antagonizes people with his positions the way I sometimes do. I wish I could be more like him" (p. 49). The self Bouton shapes, however, is a mindless clown, modeled after his perception of "the boys". This self eschews reading (books separate one from the group), joins in small talk, plays card games, listens to country music, and participates in the lewd and boisterous remarks from the back of the bus (an activity he admittedly relishes). Making the team may be facilitated by being part of the team, and Bouton's creation is designed to fit in with the group. This clownish self emerges completely late in spring training in a bar in Yuma, when Johnny Podres, another fading veteran, gives Bouton advice about his pitching motion and has him practice it before the patrons and his teammates. He says, "I was pleased that Podres should care and that he remembered my old motion and that there was that little stirring in my belly that maybe he was right, maybe I could still find the old magic. But then I remembered baseballs disappearing into clouds, and I smiled and tried to sit down. 'One more time,' Podres said. And all the guys said, 'Yeah, one more time, Bouton, and this time get it right.' So I did it one more time, wishing I could drink beer faster and get drunker" (pp. 80–81).

Bouton's reaction to his performance is ambivalent (wishing to drink faster and get drunker), but his success in playing the role is apparent—four days later he loses to his roommate Gary Bell, a popular player destined to be Bouton's go-between with the team, by one vote in the balloting for alternate player representative (p. 89). This is the high point from which Bouton's popularity declines precipitously: six weeks later, on 21 May, he is among three players nominated as alternate and receives one vote (p. 161); again on 9 June he is nominated "and everybody laughed. I declined on the spot. I refuse to give them another chance not to vote for me" (p. 195).[14] Once Gary Bell is traded, Bouton's descent is measured by the often violent response of his teammates. ("Gary was my link to most of the other players. Despite my efforts to be one of the boys, the fact that I was Gary's roommate is what helped most." [p. 189]) Bouton's flaws become more apparent. He, for example, talks too much: he expresses the wrong ideas to the wrong people at the wrong time. Marvin Milkes, the general manager of the Pilots, tells Bouton in their first meeting, "we're going to let bygones be bygones and whatever has been said in the past—and I know you've said a lot of things—we'll forget all about it and start fresh" (p. 12). This reputation stalks Bouton throughout the book. Milkes later in the season observes that Bouton is known for doing imitations and giving speeches, that he was told by New York that Bouton was "kind of crazy and silly" (p. 259).

Bouton also exhibits little sense of propriety. As a young pitcher on the Yankees he sings the Howdy Doody theme song to Bob Smith, the creator of the show, at the counter of a Rexall Drug store in Ft. Lauderdale. He tells his bullpen mates in New York that Billy Graham is a dangerous character for claiming Communists were responsible for the riots in the black ghettoes (no one would speak to Bouton for three days). He irritates his teammates on the Pilots with trivia questions and discussions of cryogenics and similarly recondite matters. Bouton also lacks an internal censor, or at least his is off-duty much of the time. For example, when an older pitcher quits because he is occupying room on the roster that should go to a younger man, the manager announces the retirement in a clubhouse meeting, observing that "It takes a lot of courage for a guy to quit when he thinks he can't do the job anymore." Bouton responds by saying the unsayable on an expansion team devoid of talent: "So I opened my big yap and said, 'If that's the case a lot of us ought to quit' " (p. 94).

As the season moves into late May and early June and the antagonisms mount, Bouton begins to use the word "weirdo" to describe his team-mates' perception of himself. Yet he means "weird" and "flaky" as words of approbation setting him and his friends apart from the mindless world of baseball. As Bouton is rejected, he begins to identify with the flakes, the hari krishnas of the baseball world, particularly with Marshall, who has a master's degree in physical education from Michigan State University,[15] and with Steve Hovley, the true eccentric and intellectual on the team. Bouton's entry of 26 June, occasioned by Hovley's recall from the minors, marks Bouton's rejection of the boys and his identification with the weirdos, meaning those who play chess, read Dostoevsky, and understand the principle of randomness as applied to pitching patterns.

> Just before Hovley rejoined the club we were talking about him in the bullpen. I count him as one of the most intelligent men, the closest to a real intellectual, I've ever met in baseball. So I volunteered that he was a pretty bright fellow. "Yeah, but does he have any common sense?" Talbot said.
>
> "I know just what you mean about not having any common sense," O'Donoghue said. "He doesn't."
>
> I asked him what he meant by that.
>
> "Well, one time we were sitting in a restaurant," O'Donoghue said, "and Hovley was walking down the street with ski cap pulled down over his face and he came past the restaurant and stood outside on the sidewalk peering in at us."[16]
>
> Oh.
>
> Another reason Hovley has no common sense is that he may wear the same shirt five days in a row and the same sportscoat and he doesn't dress the way most players do.
>
> Sometimes I think that if people in this little world of baseball don't think you a little odd, a bit weird, you're in trouble. It would be rather like being considered normal in an insane asylum. (p. 218)

Of course, Hovley is wearing his ski mask in the late spring or early summer (when else would two pitchers be eating together?), and it *is* unusual to wear a single garment all week. The passage reveals the distortions of Bouton's perceptions—in his distaste for conformity and the baseball mind he has missed Hovley's eccentricity entirely. Bouton has compartmentalized his world into good and bad, right and wrong, and has fallen into dogmatism and righteousness, the faults about which he complains.

The team's rejection of Bouton explodes violently on 15 July. Events leading up to the incident have prepared him for the repudiation. On 6 July, Bouton is silenced by Gene Brabender, a man of enormous strength, while singing "The Lord's Prayer" during a stormy flight (p. 229); on 8

July a bullpen catcher makes no effort to catch the knuckleballs which don't fall into his mitt; on 11 July the manager denounces the player who leaked an untrue story as a "nogood cocksucker"—"At that point," the innocent Bouton observes, "I felt a lot of eyes on me" (p. 237); on 13 July, when he begins talking about *Psycho-cybernetics* prior to a stag movie, a teammate remarks, "Get him the fuck out of here" (p. 241). The entry for 15 July is overwhelming:

> When I got to the clubhouse tonight I found that my two pairs of new baseball shoes had been nailed to the clubhouse floor. Used for the operation were square cement nails. They tore huge ugly holes in the soles. Also the buttons were torn off my sweatshirts, my Yoo-Hoo T-shirts were ripped to shreds and several jockstraps were pulled permanently out of stretch. . . . In fact I can't imagine why anybody would want to do that. I think it was a prank. I think it was funny when I tried to pick up the shoes that were nailed down. I think it was supposed to be funny. I think (pp. 243–44).

A more honest evaluation comes at the end of the season: "The pettiness and stupidity were exasperating, sometimes damaging. And it's going to be a long winter before I can enjoy having my shoes nailed to the clubhouse floor" (p. 368). But the violence here transcends traditional locker room comedy. Shoes are nailed to the floor, but not with giant cement nails, and not two pair, and not new shoes—and the gratuitous destruction of shirt and jockstraps is a grotesque revelation of the hatred of his teammates. The rejection is total, terrible, and devastating. The season that began with the projection of an ideal self in Ruben Amaro culminates in the symbolic violence wrought on Bouton's effects. The remaining months of the season take Bouton to Houston and another league (the rumor is that Milkes wanted to get rid of him) where Bouton chums with the black players on the Astros (identification, once again, with outsiders), and then, in his final rejection, he asks Tommy Davis, a black veteran who followed Bouton from the Pilots to the Astros, to share an apartment for the last two weeks of the season. The response is noted parenthetically and thereby, perhaps, less painfully: "(Tommy Davis, by the way, has decided against having a roommate. I'm sure it's not because I'm white)" (p. 350).

In *Ball Four* Bouton presents a child's vision (and version) of a one-dimensional world of good and evil, in which the child, without reason, is terribly wronged. Bouton in his fairy tale plays the role of Cinderella who suffers at the hands of her sisters and stepmother (teammates, coaches, and manager) because of her beauty and goodness (honesty, intelligence, and virtue—qualities which set him apart). And as the reader is introduced to the crude and comic world that seems to surround and threaten Bouton, he sinks into and accepts the vision that holds it together. But there is at the beginning of the narrative the corrective figure of Ruben Amaro, the man the narrator would like to emulate; outspoken, with strong beliefs, but with dignity, who, unlike Bouton, is universally liked. Amaro thrives in the same world that disdains the narrator, indicating that Bouton is rejected not because the world of baseball is incredibly stupid and conservative (as it may well be) but because of a radically flawed personality of which he remains oblivious.

A scene in the bullpen at the end of the Seattle experience reveals the essential self of the narrator. Bouton has suffered a bad outing and wants to throw on the sidelines, a request which meets with resistance from the coach (O'Brien), the catchers in the pen, and is parodied by another pitcher (Gelnar) who claims he also wants to throw. After checking with the manager, O'Brien allows Bouton to throw, which he does for about forty pitches and then stops to deliver a speech:

> "You know something? There are going to be better days for me, but it's going to be hard to forget what people on this bench were like when things were bad. O'Brien, you've been nice to me lately and I thought it was because you were changing. Now I realize it was only because I was pitching well. You're the same old guy just waiting for the right moment to come out and be yourself."
>
> "You're making an ass out of yourself," Pagliaroni said.
>
> "Well, maybe I'll apologize tomorrow," I said. "But I think I said something that needed to be said."
>
> "Yeah, and how about the night you said, 'The hell with the rest of the guys. They don't pay my salary,' " Pagliaroni said.
>
> I said I didn't know what the hell he was talking about.
>
> "You know, the day we had that extra-inning game," Pagliaroni said. "You left in the ninth inning and when somebody asked you where you were going you said home, and he asked you what about team spirit, and you said, 'The hell with the rest of the guys. They don't pay my salary.' "
>
> "Pag, that actually happened," I said. "But it was meant to be funny. I was smiling when I said it and it was supposed to be a joke. Anyway, it's unfair of you to bring that up now. You're just jumping on a guy when he's down. You're taking something you heard third-hand and was misinterpreted in the first place and you're trying to tell me you're using that as an excuse not to catch me."
>
> There must have been steam coming out of my ears by now, because O'Brien said, "Go take a shower."
>
> "Okay, I'll take a shower," I said. "Only I want you guys to think about what I said."
>
> "I'll think about it," Pagliaroni said. "My whole life revolves around Jim Bouton."
>
> "I guess you won't think about it much at that," I said (pp. 283–84).

Later in the clubhouse Bouton apologizes—"I suddenly remembered something Mike Marshall once told me: " 'It doesn't hurt to say you're sorry,' Marshall said, 'even if you don't mean it' " (p. 284). Bouton apologizes not because he is wrong or has acted foolishly, but because he believes he has damaged himself. The judgment of Pagliaroni, a perceptive and witty man, cuts to the heart of the matter: Bouton is self-centered, concerned and utterly absorbed with himself. Pagliaroni finds an element of truth in the remarks which Bouton claims were made in jest: "The hell with the rest of the guys. They don't pay my salary." The essential self, which emerges after the early presentational ones have been paraded and retired, is willful, self-righteous, sensitive about himself but insensitive about others (he delights in practical jokes and relishes the discomfort they cause), an exhibitionist who demands attention (when the Pilots play on national TV he spends the game warming up for the cameras). Bouton's essential self is the child out of control, refusing to cooperate with the scheme of things, and recoiling in incomprehension and then damning an unyielding world.

And the answer to the question of why it was Bouton and not someone else who lifted the veil of secrecy from clubhouse and off-field activites in baseball lies in his character as narrator. It was a forbidden act in which a disobedient child broke the rules of a game of which he was never really a part. As Bouton remarked when he was sent down to the minors: "I'm in business for myself" (p. 110).

EPILOGUE

> "Thus saith the Lord God unto these bones: Behold, I will
> cause breath to enter you, and ye shall live."
>   Ezekiel 37:5

The last story Bouton tells in *Ball Four* is the saga of Jim O'Toole, still another veteran who started out even with him in spring training and concluded the season pitching for Ross Eversoles in the Kentucky Industrial League. The narrator then asks, "Would I do that? When it's over for me, would I be hanging on with Ross Eversoles?" (p. 369).

Bouton "died" the year *Ball Four* was published; his concentration, necessary for the mastery of the knuckleball, was destroyed by the public appearances he made in promoting the book. The knuckleball straightened out and the Astros released him. As he adjusted to civilian life he spent weekends pitching for the Trenton Pavers in New Jersey. In the summer of 1975 he began a comeback which was interrupted by the ABC adaptation of *Ball Four*, a comedy series for which Bouton wrote and in which he acted. Then, seven years after being released, he began to search for a new life by entering the old one—he placed his knuckles on the ball (a mystic grip to cure the mid-life crisis) and began a comeback with scenic stopovers in Knoxville, Durango (Mexico), Portland, Savannah, and, finally, on 10 September 1978, Atlanta, where at the age of thirty-nine, he started against the Los Angeles Dodgers—ten years after the publication of *Ball Four*, Bouton was back from the dead. To finance his impossible quest he cashed in his children's college savings accounts,[17] and after the 1978 season ended he separated from his wife.[18] The family financed the high cost of his resurrection. As Bouton observed in recounting his sojourn to Atlanta, "ballplayers reflect society."[19] Certainly Bouton, in his baseball knickers, is a strange mirror of our times: a man-child who believed in the right things in the liberal Sixties, and a narcissist in the Seventies, an age which "demands immediate gratification and lives in a state of restless, perpetually unsatisfied desire."[20]

NOTES

1. Van Wyck Brooks, *Three Essays on America* (New York, 1934), p. 17.

2. Jim Bouton, *Ball Four* (New York, 1970). All references will be taken from this edition and cited parenthetically within the text.

3. Bouton claims in "Son of 'Ball Four' " (*Sports Illustrated*, 9 April 1979, p. 92) that *Ball Four* sold "over 200,000 copies in hard over, is still going strong in paperback, and just got translated into Japanese. It's the largest selling sports book ever." Since then the paperback edition has gone out of print.

4. For complete information see Harold Seymour, *Baseball: The Golden Age* (New York, 1971) and Lee Allen, *The National League Story* (New York, 1965).

5. Fred Lieb, *Baseball As I Have Known It* (New York, 1977), p. 159.

6. Plimpton has also written about golf, hockey, boxing, and even about performing in the circus, but his heart remains with the old gang from the Detroit Lions who reappear in subsequent books: *Mad Ducks and Bears* (New York, 1973) and *One More July* (New York, 1977).

7. James Olney, *Metaphors of Self* (Princeton, 1972), p. 29.

8. Olney, *Metaphors of Self*, p. 6.

9. Bouton divides life into two halves, half for himself, the other half, which comes second, for society—"You can always be a teacher or a social worker when you've reached thirty-five" (p. ii). In the summer of 1978 Bouton reached the advanced age of thirty-nine and was still playing baseball.

10. The story is pertinent because Al Dark had the reputation for being a saint, which in baseball circles means one doesn't drink or curse; being a Baptist, Dark did neither. The reputation says nothing, however, about kindness or cruelty.

11. The best of football teams, both professional and college, have had perfect records for a season, and some college teams have been unscored upon; baseball, however, is an impossible game to dominate consistently—consider the record of the 1927 Yankees, reputed to be the best baseball team of all time: 110 wins and 44 losses. In contrast the worst team, possibly, in baseball history, the 1916 Philadelphia Athletics, won 36 and lost 117, which indicates that even the worst team in baseball can contrive to win .236 percent of the time.

12. Roger Angell, *The Summer Game* (New York, 1972), p. 296.

13. In clubhouse meetings all advice on pitching to hitters is recorded—and never erased. Thus when Gary Bell offered the same advice for pitching to every Washington Senator—

"smoke 'em inside"—it was duly recorded and presumably passed on to future generations of Pilot pitchers. So much for precedent.

14. The reason there are so many elections for alternate is that the Pilots continue to trade away their player representative, hence the alternate is advanced and an election held to fill the vacancy.

15. Marshall was granted a Ph.D. in Education from Michigan State University in 1979.

16. Hovley could have been arrested as were three men in Council Bluffs, Iowa, who put paper sacks over their heads and peered in the windows of a pancake house, frightening the customers—another example of how life imitates literature. See *Albuquerque Tribune*, 10 April 1979.

17. Terry Pluto, *The Greatest Summer* (Englewood Cliffs, N.J., 1979), p. 134.

18. Bouton, "Son of 'Ball Four'," p. 104.

19. Bouton, "Son of 'Ball Four'," p. 102.

20. Christopher Lasch, *The Culture of Narcissism* (New York, 1979), p. 23.

14

God and Man in Bedford Falls: Frank Capra's *It's a Wonderful Life*

Robert Sklar

Frank Capra yearned for freedom, Frank Capra quoted Patrick Henry. On the Fifth of May 1946, Frank Capra issued his declaration in the New York *Times*. Some Hollywood producers and directors, he wrote, "have decided to break away, take the gamble, and strike out for themselves. . . . They are men willing to gamble their hard-earned savings to gain independence." Yes, of course, Frank Capra led the gamblers' vanguard. Already in April 1945, more than a year before his manifesto was fit to print, he had formed a new company (with fellow directors George Stevens and William Wyler) to produce films independently from the studio factory system. Frank Capra, who had created idealized myths of social order in his popular films of the 1930s, aimed now to embody an American myth on his own: to be free, to be independent, to be his own boss. As the new company's organizer, president, and chief stockholder, Frank Capra called it Liberty Films.

And how did Frank Capra use his new-won liberty? He made a film for release at Christmas 1946, about a man who never got a chance to break away, take a gamble, strike out for himself; a man constantly prevented from fulfilling his desires, developing his ideas, putting his dreams into practice; a man bound by small-town horizons, a struggling business, an implacable enemy; a man ultimately so humiliated, so pressed to the wall, so despondent, so defeated, that he leaves his family on Christmas Eve and tries to take his own life. Indeed his suicide would be successful if God did not directly intervene with a miracle that saves him, though it also puts him through an ordeal even more harrowing and humiliating than anything in life itself. And with no irony intended, Capra titled this film, *It's a Wonderful Life*.

The fascination of *It's a Wonderful Life* begins with what it suggests about a famous motion picture director's state of mind when, at forty-nine, after two decades of Hollywood studio employment, he took the gamble of his life. For Frank Capra, in his moment of self-testing, chose to make a film about a man who saw himself a failure; chose to make a film with the message that life offers more important rewards than wealth, worldly success, and the opportunity to fulfill one's dreams; chose to make a film that might solace and uplift those who feel humiliated, frustrated, defeated by life.

It is possible to raise the question whether *It's a Wonderful Life* served as an expression of Capra's own doubts and fears about his enterprise, as a premonitory consolation for the possibility of his own failure. For Liberty Films did not succeed as an independent company; after making one more film under the Liberty banner, *State of the Union* (1948), Capra persuaded his reluctant partners to sell their assets to Paramount Pictures and join the studio as contract directors (Stevens had directed the only other Liberty production, *I Remember Mama*, in 1948; Wyler never made a picture for the company). And Capra, in his autobiography a quarter century later, marked Liberty Films' dissolution as the beginning of the end for his creative drive. Patrick Henry's famous declaration, one may recall, was "give me liberty or give me death." Capra fully grasped the polarity. Speaking of himself in the third person, he looked back on Liberty Films' demise and wrote, "part of what had made him great was dying."

There is yet another way *It's a Wonderful Life* fascinates for the light it sheds on Capra's quest for independence, for freedom, for the right to speak as a filmmaker solely with his own voice—a way that serves to expose the film's formal and structural elements as well as its explicit and implicit stories. For Capra is not, in a manner of speaking, the only filmmaker at work in *It's a Wonderful Life*. The other filmmaker is the Deity. God is not only a performer (of miracles) in the film, He is also the maker of a film within the film: the story of George Bailey's life from the day he saves his brother from drowning (and loses his hearing in one ear as a result) to the day when his travail becomes so overpowering that he wants to end his own life.

Capra's remarkable invocation of God as codirector may be seen almost as an act of hubris on the filmmaker's part, linking his godlike capabilities—to be omniscient, to move freely across space and time—with the Deity Himself. But it is also, clearly, an act of faith, perhaps an effort to reinforce religious belief in the face of postwar secularism, by depicting God as committed to human welfare and capable of using His powers to fulfill that commitment. And it may also be an act of desperation, reaching out to divine intervention and the miraculous to provide a resolution and an uplifting ending that his own human ingenuity could not achieve. Finally, it is a way for Capra to demonstrate filmmaking techniques in God's film-within-a-film that he might have been reluctant to use without the cover of divine collaboration. As a result, *It's a Wonderful Life* stands as the only one of Capra's motion pictures as inventive in its film form as in its myths of social relations and leadership in American Life.

God is not the only collaborator in shaping the story of *It's a Wonderful Life*. As in Capra's social fables of the depression era, "the people" also create moral meaning, instigate moral action. In the earlier films, their interventions on behalf of beleaguered heroes come at the climax; in *It's a Wonderful Life*, they set the film in motion. Indeed, there are two miracles in *It's a Wonderful Life*, one divine and one human, or social. The social act (collections of many individual acts) frames the supernatural, calls it forth, and then completes it; the two are so entwined in the film's structure that one could not occur without the other.

It's a Wonderful Life opens by introducing the viewer to a community: You Are Now in Bedford Falls, so a sign tells us; it is winter, it is Christmas time; it is old-fashioned small-town America, and voices are being lifted up to Heaven not in praise of God's Son, but to succor one of their own. George Bailey is in trouble, Lord, say the voices, each in its own way, and the filmmaker, Frank Capra, performs his own minor miracles of omnivision: he points his camera heavenward and by the wonderful power of cinematography shows us that God has heard and will respond.

What does God do? He calls upon one of his heavenly host, an angel (second class) named Clarence Oddbody, interrupting the fellow's reading of Mark Twain's *Adventures of Tom Sawyer*, to acquaint him with the adventures of George Bailey. It seems that God has been recording George Bailey's life on film, and He has edited the highlights to inform angel Clarence about the man he will soon be asked to help. The image turns gray, then gradually comes into focus, and we encounter George Bailey at the age of twelve, about to ride a shovel down a snow-covered slope.

We are now spectators not of one but of two films. The primary image, the film we see, is God's biography of George Bailey. But God's film is a film within Frank Capra's film, and lest we forget that, Capra reminds us periodically by showing that the film-within-a-film is also a *projected* image within a film. It begins, as noted, out of focus; there are occasional voice-over comments on the scene; at one moment, when the mature George Bailey makes his first appearance, the frame is frozen, and the voice-over becomes a dialogue between the presenter and the spectator of the film within Frank Capra's film. These breaks in the seamless web of verisimilitude violate the cardinal Hollywood principle that films—even fantasy films—are not to undermine the illusion of reality by calling attention to their own devices. They are Capra's method of telling us that while the subject of God's film is George Bailey, the subject of *his* film is not only George Bailey's destiny but also God's hand in that destiny—in a larger sense, God's overseeing of the world.

God does not openly play his hand until the end—at least the *willed*

end—of George Bailey's biography, so the first task is to discover the kind
of man George Bailey grew up to be. After that first episode of sliding on
the ice, God presents a few more exemplary and critical moments in
George's journey through life. Still a youth, George works in Mr. Gower's
drugstore and prevents a tragedy when he sees the pharmacist, distraught
after learning of his son's death in the post–World War I influenza epi-
demic, drunkenly mixing poison in a prescription. In the late 1920s, after
a long delay, George is preparing to leave for college ("I'm shaking the
dust of this crummy little town off my feet") when his father's fatal stroke
compels him to remain and run the family's building and loan association.
In the depths of the Great Depression he marries and aims to spend his
honeymoon in New York and Bermuda when a run on the banks forces
him to use his personal savings—and travel money—to rescue the building and loan.

A fews years later, he opens a small subdivision for building and loan
subscribers, ever cognizant, however, that his brother and his classmate
Sam, both on the road to wealth and cosmopolitan experience, have left
him in the small-town dust. Even World War II does not take George out
of Bedford Falls, for that long-ago loss of hearing renders him unfit for
service. And finally, on Christmas Day 1945, when brother Harry is about
to return triumphantly with a Congressional Medal of Honor, comes the
crisis that evokes the prayers for God to intervene.

As George's story unfolds, it becomes clear that the shovel on which
young George sits and slides in that first glimpse of him is symbolic of his
role in life. George is a man who moves the earth. George is a builder.
George has many other rich and varied parts to play, as son, brother,
husband, father, nephew, friend, and more, but fundamentally he is cast,
in his own mind, and in the community's eye, in a quintessential male
role: the shaper of new spaces, he who constructs.

In his innermost self, George yearns to be a man who soars, and whose
ideas and creations also soar. He dreams of building airfields, skyscrapers
a hundred stories high, bridges a mile long. At his deepest moment of
despair we get a quick look at his workshop, his table in a corner of the
living room, as he smashes his model bridges and skyscrapers, admitting
that the dream is dead. Nevertheless, he is a builder of another kind, the
son who takes over his father's business, Bailey Bros. Building & Loan,
and helps other people fulfill their more modest dreams of freedom: to
own their own home. His own actual accomplishments do not soar for him
but soaring, be it remembered, is a relative thing. When Bailey Park
opens, his new subdivision of tidy, small, detached houses (in the film an
incongruous postwar tract, with Southern California mountains in the
background, meant to stand for 1930s housing in upstate New York), it is
no coincidence that among the new homeowners Capra focuses on people
from his own country of origin, the Martini family of Italian immigrants.

Though Bailey himself may be immobile, he serves as an aegis for the American dream of freedom and mobility. When Martini and his wife cross themselves as they take possession of their new home, God's film-within-a-film clearly implies there is religious as well as secular value in George Bailey's work as a builder.

As a builder, and as an immobile man, George Bailey is different in several ways from heroes in Capra's depression-era social fables—Longfellow Deeds in *Mr. Deeds Goes to Town* (1936), Jefferson Smith in *Mr. Smith Goes to Washington* (1939), Long John Willoughby in *Meet John Doe* (1941). All three of those prewar heroes were small-town men who did have mobility, who brought their small-town values to the city, in fact, and confronted the urban centers of power. They all had elements of the builder in them, Deeds with his plan to help the farmers, Smith with his project for a wilderness boys' camp, Willoughby (John Doe) with his less specific but nevertheless similar goals of neighborliness and community organization. Yet they were all, in a sense, fish out of water. The metropolis was not their true milieu. They had been pulled away from their roots, and they made their efforts in alien territory.

To be sure, their struggles encompassed the national issues of their time: the economic collapse of the Great Depression, the challenge to democratic institutions by corrupt and power-hungry individuals in government and the press. They dealt with masses of men and women— Jefferson Smith with his fistfuls of telegrams on the Senate floor, John Doe behind a forest of microphones, peering at a sea of anonymous faces. The small town is a neighborly place, where everyone knows everyone. Capra's 1930s heroes had moved beyond that sphere of knowledge, and this was one factor contributing to the heroes' growing crises in the years before the war: the shift from vindication for Mr. Deeds to an ambiguous denouement for Mr. Smith to defeat for John Doe, and the deeper range of their humiliations along the way.

George Bailey is pointedly excluded from the larger world: he serves his country as an air-raid warden, seeing that blackout shades are pulled tight. Never does he move beyond the community sphere, never beyond the range of those he knows by name. Though he has clear continuity with Deeds and Smith and Doe, particularly in the increasing severity of his personal crisis, Bailey's situation also bears more direct comparison to an earlier Capra hero, Tom Dickson (played by Walter Huston), a New York banker in the 1932 film *American Madness*.

Dickson's struggle is against a conservative board of directors who oppose him because he makes business loans on his judgment of an applicant's character—and many of the people he approves are upward-striving immigrants much like Martini in *It's a Wonderful Life*. Dickson knows his community and his customers, but, like the later 1930s heroes, his threatened downfall is due to the unknown mass: his bank is robbed, and a rumor spreads about the bank's cash loss that brings depositors swarming to retrieve their holdings. It is a crisis of confidence, and Dickson, beset by marital problems, has lost his own confidence. His assistant, however, calls upon the men to whom Dickson had made loans: he helped you, now help him. They come into the bank waving dollars, ostentatiously make deposits, and sway the surging mob back toward confidence in the bank.

Besides the obvious connections between Bailey and Dickson—both help others fulfill their dreams by making loans on the basis of character; both come to require the assistance of others in return for their trust— there is another link that is something of a surprise. Both men are sophisticates, or rather, the small-town man, tethered by responsibilities that never let him pass beyond the town depot, is as urbane in his way as the city banker is in his.

This complex charm lies at the heart of George Bailey's character, and it is most obviously a creation of James Stewart's performance in the role (the favorite of his acting career). *It's a Wonderful Life*, for all its pathos, is frequently a funny film, and Bailey carries the comedy. George is witty and worldly-wise; he can dance the Charleston, banter the language of love-play with his wife-to-be, Mary (Donna Reed), and conquer his ambivalence about love with a direct amorous gesture. In this he is at his farthest removed from the prewar Capra hero, the naive, often passive man-child that Gary Cooper portrays with Deeds and Doe, and Stewart himself plays (perhaps to a lesser extent than Cooper) in Jefferson Smith. These three are men with small-town horizons who are led to apply their values in a wider world; Bailey is a man with vast horizons who is forced to accommodate them to the narrow small-town realm. His worldliness, his comic creativity, only add to the poignancy of his frustration at operating in a diminished sphere.

For the thematic purposes of *It's a Wonderful Life*, Capra had reasons to make George Bailey a stronger, more clever hero than his counterparts in the 1930s films. Bailey's leadership differs from theirs. He is a man on whom a community's fate rests. He is not, as were Deeds and Smith and Doe, involved in individual acts symbolizing national or international political conflicts. He is engrossed in shaping a community's character and individual lives within it. Nor is his adversary representative of large social forces: Potter the banker (Lionel Barrymore) is a member of the same community, directly contesting for the power to determine destinies.

In critical writings on *It's a Wonderful Life*, Potter is often regarded as a Victorian survival, a Dickensian anachronism in a mid-twentieth-century tale. Though this may be the case, the exaggerated nature of Potter's characterization serves to make the struggle between two kinds of community leadership, indeed two kinds of capitalist enterprise, unmistakably clear. Potter's leadership destroys human hopes; Bailey's builds them.

The land where the Bailey Park subdivision went up was once used as a cemetery; the slums the banker owns are called Potter's Field, the common name for a paupers' burial ground. The polarities with which Capra was struggling in his personal career are curiously embedded in the conflict between Bailey and Potter. On one side is liberty; on the other, death.

But the anxieties and hopes of Capra's quest—and the anxieties and hopes of the Bedford Falls community—are not available to George Bailey in his own right. His is not a choice between liberty and death, it is a choice between, on the one hand, service, self-denial, and a blunt recognition that he will never fulfill his dreams, and, on the other, ending this seeming death-in-life with self-annihilation. George comes to this despairing point when his Uncle Billy inadvertently puts a Building & Loan deposit in Potter's grasping hands. Billy's stupidity, Potter's malevolence, his own helplessness—these are not isolated instances, they are the past and likely future pattern of George Bailey's days. His frustration and anger erupt at his wife, his children, his home, his futile model constructions, his car, his neighbors, and ultimately at himself. At the end of his rope, he turns to God as did his family and community when the film began, asking to be shown the way. And then, in Martini's restaurant, a stranger slugs him, the husband of a teacher he has insulted. There is to be no surcease from his hell on earth. Potter had cynically told George he was worth more, with his insurance policies, dead than alive. All right then, his last act of community service will be his own self-sacrifice.

George stumbles to the bridge and prepares to jump into the icy river. Here ends God's screenplay of George Bailey's story. Clarence Oddbody now knows all there is to know. It is time for divine intercession. The spectator at God's film-within-a-film will himself enter the frame. And God's role as Frank Capra's collaborator shifts from codirector to leading performer.

Clarence lands in the water as George prepares to jump; the timing is deliberately ambiguous. Ever the man of service, George saves the angel instead of carrying out his own plan. Yet his despair is in no way mitigated. He tells Clarence, "I wish I had never been born," a desire strikingly more extreme even than suicide, for it entails not simply an extinction but a negation: George Bailey wiped from the face of the earth, nothing left behind, no memory, no heirs, no contribution to other lives. George's remark gives Clarence an idea. He confers with God, who makes His presence known with a whistling wind. God will grant George his wish: He will show him a world in which he had never been born.

Now God becomes not the maker of a film within Frank Capra's film but the maker of a fiction within Frank Capra's fiction. For it is a story that God is about to tell George Bailey. Since it did not happen, God is making it up from scratch. Deciding to invent a fiction, of course, the Deity could have told any sort of tale. He might have given George some

consolation, for example, that human beings are capable of attaining comfort or a measure of happiness by their own devices, without the need for
his support. Perhaps He could have made George a little jealous of the
pleasures others would have enjoyed, with his family and friends, had he
not lived to share in them. Instead, he concocts a tale of unmitigated
bleakness: if you had not lived, God tells George Bailey, life for those you
love would have been an even greater hell on earth than the hell on earth
that you believe you've lived.

God punishes George not once but twice for his prideful wish to escape
his destiny. George first must witness the degradation of all he has known
and loved: in the absence of his freedom-giving leadership, Potter's
thanatos holds sway. Bedford Falls changes into Pottersville. The bucolic
main street becomes a honky-tonk gauntlet of neon, sex, and booze. What
was Martini's restaurant turns into a gangster hangout, and Martini is
nowhere to be found; with no Bailey Park to live in, he's down in Potter's
Field, where Ernie the cab driver also remains, deserted by his wife and
child. Without George, Gower the druggist poisoned a customer and
went to jail. George's home remains the wrecked shell it was before he
and Mary took it over. His brother Harry died as a youth; nobody saved
him when he fell into the icy pond. The Building & Loan has folded,
Uncle Billy has been committed to an asylum, Ma operates a boarding-
house. And worst of all, wife Mary, without him, has lived out her lonely
days as a bespectacled spinster librarian (what does George's never having
been born have to do with her eyesight?).

Yet such knowledge of the consequences arising from his absence is not
all George is made to suffer in witnessing God's fiction. He must also
learn what it feels like to be nobody. Seeing the debased lives which the
community, his family, and friends lead without him, George must also
experience their rejection of him. His corporeal self, in God's miracle,
encounters the people he knows, in this created world which is not his
world, and one and all, friends, mother, wife, they deny him. Humiliated
by life, George is even more deeply humiliated by not-life. "You really had
a wonderful life," Clarence assures George, and the man is in no mood to
quibble over adjectives. Even a life that seemed so hard to bear is better
than this version of hell that God has molded for him—observing his
loved ones living a different, more difficult, life without him. "Each man's
life touches so many other lives," Clarence sums up God's lesson. The
Deity impresses the lesson on George by showing him a world of people
known to him, but which he cannot touch. George prays God to be
restored to life.

In later years, Capra has spoken of the film's message as one of comfort
and renewal for the "little man"—that *every* life, even the most humble,
may have its priceless value in the qualities of friendship and family love it

brings forth. The meaning of *It's a Wonderful Life* thus translates into Life *Is* Wonderful. And doubly to prove the point, the people's miracle follows closely upon God's: in hatsful and basketsful of money, those whom George has aided and befriended return the favor, making up the loss suffered when evil Potter sequestered Uncle Billy's strayed deposit.

But George is hardly an example of a "little man." However humble his life may be, compared to his hopes and expectations, he is a man whose powers range beyond the sphere of friends and family: he is a community leader and molder, a man upon whom many people depend. God stacked the deck of His fictional miracle to drive home the point to George that his dereliction from duty can have only the most awful consequences for himself and all those others. George must reaffirm his role as one who serves others rather than himself, however he may groan under the burden of responsibility.

In the evolution from Deeds through Smith to Doe, the prewar Capra hero had come to resemble more and more a Christ-like figure. In George Bailey the identification of the hero as suffering savior is all but complete. God's miracle for George occurs on Christmas Eve: the people whose money saves George sing in praise of the new-born King to accompany George's rebirth into life—one might almost say his resurrection.

"Remember, no man is a failure who has friends," is the oddly muted coda to this fable—inscribed on Clarence Oddbody's copy of *The Adventures of Tom Sawyer* left behind by the departed angel who, in saving George from suicide, had earned his wings. That may be sufficient consolation for a "little man," in Frank Capra's ideology, but can we believe that it alleviates George Bailey's sense of defeat and despair? From the evidence of Capra's feelings about the failure of Liberty Films, it is unlikely that the director, in every sense a leader in the Hollywood filmmaking community, would have accepted such consolation for himself. His sale of the independent company turned out to be a kind of creative suicide, and henceforward he worked in a setting not unlike the hell God envisioned for George Bailey: a place where he could exist, but no longer touch the lives of motion picture audiences.

NOTE

This essay is a revised version of a lecture delivered at the University of New Mexico on January 31, 1980. I would like to thank Professors Sam Girgus and Ira Jaffe for their comments on the lecture, as well as members of the audience for their questions and responses, which have helped me in revising the lecture.

Frank Capra's article in the New York *Times* of 5 May 1946 was called "Breaking Hollywood's 'Pattern of Sameness.' " It is reprinted in *Hollywood Directors, 1941–1976* ed., Richard Koszarski, (New York, 1977), pp. 82–89. Capra's autobiographical comments on Liberty Films and *It's a Wonderful Life* appear in his *The Name Above the Title: An Autobiography*

(New York, 1971). See especially pp. 375, 399–403 and passim. Capra's films of the Depression era are analyzed in Robert Sklar, *Movie-Made America: A Cultural History of American Movies* (New York, 1975), pp. 205–14. For additional interviews, reviews, and essays on the director, see *Frank Capra: The Man and His Films,* ed. Richard Glatzer and John Raeburn (Ann Arbor, 1975).

It's a Wonderful Life was a production of Liberty Films, distributed by RKO Radio Pictures. Produced and directed by Frank Capra, from a screenplay by Frances Goodrich, Albert Hackett, and Frank Capra, with additional screenplay material by Jo Swerling, based on a story by Philip Van Doren Stern. Music by Dimitri Tiomkin. Cinematography by Joseph Walker. Leading players: James Stewart, Donna Reed, Lionel Barrymore, Thomas Mitchell, Henry Travers, Beulah Bondi, Frank Faylen, Ward Bond, Gloria Grahame, H. B. Warner, Todd Karns, Samuel S. Hinds, Mary Treen, Frank Albertson, Virginia Patton.

15

The Penitente Brotherhood in Southwestern Fiction: Notes on Folklife and Literature

Marta Weigle

The Brotherhood of Our Father Jesus, commonly known as the Penitente Brotherhood, is a lay religious society of the Roman Catholic Church. Its greatest strength lies in Hispano northern New Mexico and southern Colorado. Local chapters, called *moradas*, a term also applied to the meetinghouse itself, are governed by elected officials headed by an *Hermano Mayor* or "Elder Brother." Often, moradas are associated with one another in various larger councils. Since 1947, many have affiliated with the Archbishop's Supreme Council, but some remain independent of this rather loose organization.

The Brotherhood's origins are uncertain, but it probably began in the early 1800s as a creative response to inadequate Church ministrations and still-perilous conditions in the Hispanic settlements along the isolated northern border of New Spain. There is a strong Franciscan element, and some influence from Spanish and Mexican penitential confraternities which use the name Our Father Jesus Nazarite.[1]

Bishop Zubiría of Durango, Mexico, first denounced the Brotherhood in a letter from Santa Cruz dated 21 July 1833. After 1851, Bishop (later Archbishop) Jean Baptiste Lamy attempted to formalize and direct the Brothers, but it was his successor, Archbishop Jean Baptiste Salpointe, who engaged in the most public controversy with the Brothers. This was a difficult period for the new United States territory and especially for the Catholic Church. Basically, Lamy, most of his fellow priests and nuns,

An earlier version of this paper was delivered at the fourteenth annual meeting of the Western Literature Association in Albuquerque, New Mexico, on 5 October 1979.

and his next four successors (Salpointe, Chapelle, Bourgade, and Pitaval) were French clergy attempting to establish an American Catholic Church administration in a Mexican Catholic country which had only recently declared its independence from Spain in 1821. Willa Cather's 1927 novel, *Death Comes for the Archbishop,* depicts this effort from the French point of view, accurately indicating Lamy's caution about confronting the Brotherhood and suggesting Padre Martínez' involvement with Brothers in the Taos area, while at the same time denigrating the Penitentes by associating them with the Padre's stupid, stupefied, and thoroughly unsavory student-secretary, Trinidad Lucero.[2] Elliott Arnold's historical novel describing the same period, *The Time of the Gringo* (1953), also refers to "fanatical" Brotherhood penitential rites when depicting events in Taos.

Penitente Brothers are generally men of Hispanic descent who have committed themselves to a humble Christian life based on mutual aid, community welfare, and Lenten and Holy Week devotions centered around penance and the Passion of Jesus. These devotions, which formerly involved public self-discipline such as flagellation and cross bearing, proved controversial for Church officials and attracted undue and unwelcome attention from Anglo visitors and settlers. A bibliography of over a thousand items wholly or partially devoted to the Brotherhood attests to the fascination experienced by such newcomers to the Hispanic Southwest, whether in the nineteenth or the twentieth century.[3]

One of the earliest references to the Brotherhood is in Santa Fe trader Josiah Gregg's 1844 *Commerce of the Prairies,* an account of his travels and experiences living in New Mexico during the 1830s.[4] Gregg's description of Penitente rites at Tomé, New Mexico, was followed by numerous reports from army personnel, Protestant missionaries, and other Anglo visitors. However, none of these stirred the popular imagination as much as Charles F. Lummis' journalistic and photographic exploits during the 1880s and 1890s.

From September 1884 through January 1885, Lummis walked 3,507 miles from Ohio to California, forwarding a weekly letter describing his journey to the fledgling *Los Angeles Times.* His "first acquaintance with those astounding fanatics, the Penitentes . . . ignorant perverters of a once godly Brotherhood . . . [whose] astounding barbarities are still practiced by citizens and voters of the United States" came through the Manuel Chaves family of San Mateo, New Mexico.[5] In February 1888, Lummis returned to the Chaves ranch to recover from a paralyzing stroke. There, on 29 and 30 March, accompanied by Ireneo Chaves and "a peon," *both of whom carried cocked six-shooters,* Lummis photographed several Brotherhood rites, including flagellants, cross bearers, and a simulated crucifixion.[6] He prepared an embellished account of his experiences in an illustrated article whose history he described in his unpublished memoirs, "As I Remember":

> But so unknown was the Brotherhood then, every magazine in the
> United States [some seventeen] returned the article I wrote about
> it. They deemed it a fake. It was only when John Brisben Walker
> ventured with his old time *Cosmopolitan* that the matter saw the
> light for the first time. Since then the pictures of this medieval
> ceremony have figured in several of my books and the cult of the
> Penitentes is known the world over. [7]

Lummis' claim is not exaggerated, for the 1889 *Cosmopolitan* article
was reprinted with few alterations in several magazines and the various
editions of his "See America First" books—*Some Strange Corners of Our
Country: The Wonderland of the Southwest* (1892), *The Land of Poco
Tiempo* (1893), and *Mesa, Cañon and Pueblo: Our Wonderland of the
Southwest* (1925).

Lummis claimed later to have been shot at by Brothers angry at his
disclosures, and this legendary motif of the grim dangers associated with
writing about and photographing Brotherhood rites can thus be traced to
him. To this day, it remains a cherished belief-legend which received
fresh impetus when free-lance writer and University of New Mexico instructor Carl N. Taylor was murdered at Cedar Crest in the Sandia Mountains on 5 February 1936. Since Taylor had just completed an article on
the Brotherhood for *Today Magazine*, its editor and his literary agent
suggested that "Taylor may have been the victim of some strange Penitente
plot." Although Modesto Trujillo confessed to the killing to rob Taylor
and the district attorney's investigations absolved the Brotherhood entirely, scores of newspapers printed erroneous versions under lurid titles,
and a so-called documentary, "The Penitente Murder Case," was filmed
in Hollywood and banned in New Mexico by Governor Tingley. At the
time, this publicity was particularly unwelcome because Archbishop Gerken
and several Brothers were working closely to reorganize and recognize
the Brotherhood, a long overdue reaffirmation which was then delayed
until January 1947. [8]

Both fiction and nonfiction writers have responded to this mystique of
danger and dark fanaticism with zeal. In fiction, this has often produced
sheer lunacy such as Albert B. Reagan's 1914 novel, *Don Diego: Or The
Pueblo Indian Uprising of 1680*, in which the Indians are full-blown
"Penitenties" [sic] at that early date, or Harold Heifetz's 1968 novel,
Jeremiah Thunder, in which a black man is crucified during a peyote
ceremony to bring rain at a western Indian pueblo rather like Acoma. The
pulps include John M. Burwell's 1912 dime novel, *The Secret of La Gran
Quivira*—"A Tale of the Soul of Kit Moonlight of Bro Way and P'ee-K'oo,
Who for Love of Her Became a Penitente"; Alice Eyre's 1942 *Torture at
Midnight: The Mystery of the Penitentes*, in which "Jack Ogarrity, a de-
tective in Albuquerque, runs afoul of the wrath of the *Penitentes* when he

is called in by his close friend, Father Hernandez, to solve the mystery of the disappearance of the Mission bell" and eventually manages to solve "the many hideous secrets of the Penitentes," among other feats; and Mona Farnsworth's (Muriel Newhall) 1972 Gothic novel, set in a very fictional Taos, *A Cross for Tomorrow*, in which the heroine manages to get herself tied to a cross next to her childhood friend's husband, whose adulteries have been curtailed by the forty days' continence supposedly required of the Brother who plays Christ. Even more respectable fiction like Hervey Allen's 1933 novel, *Anthony Adverse*, or Joseph Dispenza's 1978 novel, *The House of Alarcon*, depict the Brothers as sinister and somehow aberrant, although indispensable to showing the "strange corners" of the Hispanic Southwest.

The first novel about the Brotherhood, Louis How's *The Penitentes of San Rafael: A Tale of the San Luis Valley*, was published in 1900. Although based on an actual incident when United States troops intervened to stop Brotherhood rituals, probably in San Pedro,[9] the book owes much to Lummis's earlier publications. The latter's alleged eyewitness report of the Brother calling out to be nailed instead of "dishonored" and bound to the cross stimulated a spate of fiction and near-fiction about the Brotherhood which unfortunately continues today. How is in many respects Lummis's literary counterpart, the founder of what may be termed the "overenthusiastic Oberammergau" school whose adherents suffer from literalism regarding passion plays and penance and fixate on the Brother who will play the Cristo and the continence and wilderness-wandering supposedly demanded of him. How's protagonist-Cristo, the hapless Paez, for example, goes into the "wilderness" of southern Colorado for forty days dragging a huge cross. (Incidentally, he dies before they can nail him to it.) Although there were certainly folk passion plays performed in some New Mexico and Colorado villages, these were not invariably associated with the Brotherhood, whose rites are generally more stylized and symbolic.[10] The Stations of the Cross, *not* all the details from the New Testament accounts of Christ's life and passion, form the basis for most observances. In any case, no one has succeeded in doing for either local passion play or Brotherhood ritual what Nikos Kazantzakis did in *The Greek Passion*.[11]

A "Brotherhood Kazantzakis" would have met and would still meet the serious criticisms and challenge issued by Kyle Crichton in "Cease Not Living," his 1935 essay on regionalism in the Southwest, which he concludes by suggesting "that New Mexico become less a part of the Southwest and more a part of the world . . . [and] also that the whole theory of regionalism be laid quietly away with the other relics of a period when it was felt that the way to live was to cease living."[12] After accurately observing that "what the literate visitor to New Mexico hastens to do upon his first visit is fashion an article on the Penitentes,"[13] Crichton, by then a "cure" from Albuquerque Methodist "San [atorium]" and an associate editor of *Collier's Magazine*, casts a jaundiced eye on his own earlier and his fellow writers' efforts:

> Over everything coming from the Southwest hangs that aura of triviality and amateurishness. Writers who have been living in the section for years are still so greatly influenced by the "romance" of it that even their most profound utterances have an unreal and fantastic sound. . . . When I speak of the fantastic quality of most Southwestern writing, I mean its substitution of myth for reason, its insistence on evading thought by considering everything strange as an isolated instance of individuality rather than a part of the pattern of life.[14]

Writings about the Brotherhood are used to justify his condemnation. Crichton claims:

> I have never read, for example, a sensible piece on the Penitentes. Aside from the information that the practice had been noted in Italy as early as the Fifteenth Century and was still prevalent in outlying districts of New Mexico, I know nothing of its background. More than that, I know *nothing about its meaning to the people who practice it. . . .*[15]

It is hard to disagree after reading Penitente novels full of blood, intrigue, and sex, such as W. P. Lawson's *The Fire Woman* (1925), set in Truchas; D. J. Hall's *Perilous Sanctuary* (1937), set in the Sandia Mountains; and O'Kane Foster's *In the Night Did I Sing* (1942), set in the Taos Valley. All three imply that penance is a cheap coin to pay for illicit sex, and that Brotherhood circumspection shrouds political machinations and even murder rather than protecting a genuine religious observance from desecration. Such novels represent what MacEdward Leach terms regional literature which "reconstructs a folk society, revealing its customs, beliefs, speech, etc. . . . [selectively], often arbitrarily, so as to establish a point."[16] Their "point" would seem to be that only the lash and the cross stand between the Hispano villager and adultery, anarchy, and worse.

Because of the distortions in such fiction, it is imperative to compare the ethnographic literature on the way the Brotherhood functioned in a community.[17] The Brothers performed year-round charitable acts, and local moradas served as welfare agencies for impoverished villagers. They also arbitrated village disputes and punished various transgressions both within and outside their membership. Mary Austin shows this important function in "Business at Cuesta La Plata" (1934), a "one-smoke" story involving a trial presided over by members of the morada.

However, two novels do convey a truer meaning of the Brotherhood to village and villager: Raymond Otis' *Miguel of the Bright Mountain* (1936) and Robert Bright's *The Life and Death of Little Jo* (1944). Otis' Truchas is a far cry from Lawson's bloodthirsty, lustful community. It is by no means "solidly Penitente"; Miguel's mother and other women, for example, do not entirely approve of the Brotherhood. Nevertheless, the Tinieblas (Tenebrae) service on Good Friday evening, *not* a simulated crucifixion, is portrayed as the dramatic high point of the villagers' year. This seems to have some "ethnographic reality," because the Tinieblas is indeed a time of intense emotion and generates a strong sense of village solidarity and continuity as the names of deceased relatives are called out to be prayed for.[18] Otis' combination of viewpoints in the opening chapter—the young Miguel's and his mother's—strongly suggests this genuinely moving and unifying power in Brotherhood ritual.

The concluding chapters of Otis' novel are less insightful. Miguel's one-shot penitential retreat to assuage his "gnawing" guilt about Maria—and presumably to eradicate his Santa Fe experiences—seems too facile, disturbingly like the old canard about confession-penance-sin-again which underlies so much writing about the Brotherhood. There is one important exception, however. Otis does not choose to make an easy identification of Brotherhood-home-village-Hispanic tradition, for Miguel does not in the end remain in Truchas. Instead, he retreats to the Pedernal Grant where he in effect works for the Anglos but at the farthest remove from their society. The village and the Brotherhood persist, but both are threatened not only by the paved road but by the inadequacies of Brothers such as Miguel's father Eliseo and his brother Pablo.

By contrast, Robert Bright's Talpa is more personalized and animated, in part due to the two authors' different life situations. Otis was but a frequent visitor to Truchas, while Bright resided in Talpa for several years before undertaking *The Life and Death of Little Jo*.[19] Personalities and local incidents are thus bound to give his book a unique flavor. Interestingly, the Brotherhood is portrayed as a less important symbol for all Hispanic village life. In fact, Little Jo's 1939 initiation at age seventeen is mentioned in a single line, while his personal penance in the morada graveyard is carefully motivated in terms of his own life within the village and effectively presented in three paragraphs. This sensible, sensitive treatment puts the Brotherhood in a perspective much closer to the "real" one.

In the final analysis, all such fiction remains the product of outsiders and must be supplemented by insiders' accounts such as Lorin W. Brown's Federal Writers' Project manuscripts, Cleofas M. Jaramillo's reminiscences, and Gilberto Benito Córdova's folk history of Abiquiú, New Mexico, as well as by fieldwork, ethnographic, and historical studies.[20] That is as it should be if one's goals are to understand the Brotherhood per se and the literary works about it more fully. However, a further understanding is indicated in fiction about the Brotherhood—a process of participation, observation, selectivity, and imagination which can and should inform both art and science, literature and ethnography.[21]

There is no question that the Brotherhood and its activities were an important part of Hispano folklife in northern New Mexico and southern Colorado. It was also a "fact" of Anglo life there. Lamentably, "Penitente hunting" was, and sometimes continues to be, almost a seasonal sport, as Curtis Martin shows in his 1943 novel, *The Hills of Home*. The Brotherhood was also ignored by some, accepted matter-of-factly by others, and even joined by a few more reverent neighbors. This range of attitudes is shared by nonmember Hispanos and some Indians in the area.

Actually, the social scientists, the folklorists, and the writers emerge as anomalous and unsettling. Are they voyeurs only? Gossips? Dupes? Desecraters? Participant-observers? What kinds of understandings do they seek? How do they finally express their comprehension? To whom? And why?

Oddly enough, one of the more garish Penitente novels, Harry Sylvester's *Dayspring* (1945), set in the Taos area, proves to be among the most heuristic in this respect. Its protagonist, an anthropologist doing fieldwork in Taos, converts to Catholicism and eventually joins the Brotherhood in Ranchos de Taos. In a sublimely ridiculous scene described in the thirteenth chapter, he drags the death cart during a public Good Friday procession witnessed by a number of Anglos, including his department chairman! (The use of the death cart here rather than the cross is insightful because of the complex of beliefs about Brothers being people of the dead hiding skulls beneath their hoods as well as similar legends used to keep nonmembers at bay while bolstering members' faith.[22]) The anthropologist sees himself for the "faker" he of course thoroughly embodies, but he also sees the other Anglo onlookers. Back in the morada, he falls exhausted to the floor and weeps—for himself, for his estranged wife, and "mostly and in what amazement he was capable of, for the icy vanity of his own people."

Obviously, *Dayspring* is not to be recommended above fiction by Otis, Bright, Harvey Fergusson, and others more reliable and restrained, but its theme is important for folklorists and fiction writers. The collector, the ethnographer, and the writer all have a grave responsibility to their subjects. In the case of the Brotherhood, relations between Church and parishioners, between villagers and politicians, within and between villages, and so on, have too often been strained by inaccurate, inflammatory, and unwitting prose of all kinds. There must be an awareness of the complex fabric of social reality which reminiscences, legends, stories, reports, accounts, and the like create. The inter- and intra-ethnic relationships between plural cultures in the Southwest since historic times and before demand evidence of that awareness and imaginative expressions of it from resident, writer, folklorist, and whomever. To date, that seems the most important and least heeded lesson to be learned from both fiction and nonfiction about the Brotherhood.

NOTES

1. Marta Weigle, *Brothers of Light, Brothers of Blood: The Penitentes of the Southwest* (Albuquerque, 1976), pp. 19–51.

2. Full bibliographical references for Cather's and all works of fiction mentioned in this article are appended. For a discussion of Cather's view of the Martínez-Lamy disputes, see Ralph H. Vigil, "Willa Cather and Historical Reality," *New Mexico Historical Review* 50 (1975): 123–34. For notes on "The Enigmatic Role of Don Antonio José Martínez" in the development of the Brotherhood, see Weigle, *Brothers of Light*, pp. 47–49. More recent studies include: Dora Ortiz Vásquez, *Enchanted Temples of Taos: My Story of Rosario* (Santa Fe, 1975); Guadalupe Baca-Vaughn, trans. and ed., *Memories of Antonio José Martínez by Pedro Sánchez* (Santa Fe, 1978); and Ray John de Aragon, *Padre Martinez and Bishop Lamy* (Las Vegas, N.M., 1978).

3. Marta Weigle, comp., *A Penitente Bibliography* (Albuquerque, 1976). This is an almost exhaustive listing through August 1975.

4. Josiah Gregg, *Commerce of the Prairies*, ed. Max L. Moorhead, American Exploration and Travel Series, no. 17 (Norman, Okla., 1954), pp. 181–82.

5. Charles F. Lummis, *A Tramp Across the Continent* (New York, 1892), pp. 189–90.

6. Turbesé Lummis Fiske and Keith Lummis, *Charles F. Lummis. The Man and His West* (Norman, Okla., 1975), pp. 44–45. Also see Marc Simmons, *Two Southwesterners: Charles Lummis and Amado Chaves* (Cerrillos, N.M., 1968); and Dudley Gordon, *Charles F. Lummis: Crusader in Corduroy* (Los Angeles, 1972).

7. Quoted in Fiske and Lummis, *Lummis*, p. 45. References to Lummis' publications are in Weigle, *Penitente Bibliography*, pp. 94–94.

8. Weigle, *Brothers of Light*, pp. 105–9.

9. Ibid., pp. 84, 255.

10. Ibid., pp. 30–31, 162–68, 171–73. Also see Thomas J. Steele, S. J., trans. and ed., *Holy Week in Tomé: A New Mexico Passion Play* (Santa Fe, 1976); and idem, "The Spanish Passion Play in New Mexico and Colorado," *New Mexico Historical Review* 53 (1978): 239–59.

11. Nikos Kazantzakis, *The Greek Passion* (1954).

12. Kyle Crichton, "Cease Not Living," *New Mexico Quarterly* 5 (1935): 76.

13. Ibid., p. 74.

14. Ibid., p. 75.

15. Ibid. Italics added.

16. MacEdward Leach, "Folklore in Regional American Literature, *Journal of the Folklore Institute* 3(1966):382.

17. Weigle, *Brothers of Light*, pp. 150–53.

18. Ibid., pp. 174–75. The Good Friday morning Encuentro—the enactment of the Fourth Station of the Cross, the meeting between Jesus and Mary on the way to Calvary—is another such visibly moving observance that is rarely mentioned in Penitente fiction. See, e.g., Weigle, ibid., p. 167; Lorenzo de Córdova [Lorin W. Brown], *Echoes of the Flute* (Santa Fe, 1972), pp. 16, 23, 44–45.

19. Marta Weigle, "Introduction" to the reprint edition of Raymond Otis, *Miguel of the Bright Mountain* (Albuquerque, 1977), pp. v–xxx; and idem, "Introduction" to the reprint edition of Robert Bright, *The Life and Death of Little Jo* (Albuquerque, 1978), pp. v–xiv.

20. Lorin W. Brown, *Echoes of the Flute;* idem, with Charles L. Briggs and Marta Weigle, *Hispano Folklife of New Mexico: The Lorin W. Brown Federal Writers' Project Manuscripts* (Albuquerque, 1978); Cleofas M. Jaramillo, *Shadows of the Past (Sombras del Pasado)* (Santa Fe, 1941); idem, *Romance of a Little Village Girl* (San Antonio, 1955) and Gilberto Benito Córdova, *Abiquiú and Don Cacahuate: A Folk History of a New Mexican Village* (Los Cerrillos, N.M., 1973).

21. See the issues examined by Audrey Borenstein in *Redeeming the Sin: Social Science and Literature* (New York, 1978).

22. Marta Weigle, "Ghostly Flagellants and Doña Sebastiana: Two Legends of the Penitente Brotherhood," *Western Folklore* 36(1977): 135–47; Thomas J. Steele, S. J., "The Death Cart: Its Place among the Santos of New Mexico," *Colorado Magazine* 55(Winter 1978):1–14.

BIBLIOGRAPHY

Unless otherwise noted, the titles are novels with plot or major themes focused around the Penitente Brotherhood and its observances.

Allen, Hervey. *Anthony Adverse.* New York: Rinehart, 1933. (Mention, chap. 68.)

Allison, Irl Leslie. *Through the Years.* New York: Schroeder and Gunther, 1925.

Arnold, Elliott. *The Time of the Gringo.* New York: Alfred A. Knopf, 1953. (Mention, chaps. 2, 8.)

Austin, Mary. "Business at Cuesta La Plata." In *One-Smoke Stories,* pp. 200–210. Cambridge, Mass.: Riverside Press, 1934. (Short story.)

———. *Starry Adventure.* Boston: Houghton Mifflin, 1931. (Mention, pp. 117–19.)

Barker, S. Omar. *Little World Apart.* Garden City, N.Y.: Doubleday, 1966. (Mention, pp. 169–77.)

Bradford, Richard. *Red Sky at Morning.* Philadelphia: J. B. Lippincott, 1968. (Mention, chap. 13.)

Bright, Robert. *The Life and Death of Little Jo.* Garden City, New York: Doubleday, Doran, 1944.

Burwell, John M. *The Secret of La Gran Quivira: A Novel.* Willard, N.M.: Quetzal Publishing, 1912.

Carr, Lorraine. *Mother of the Smiths.* New York: Macmillan, 1940. (Mention, chap. 9.)

Carr, Robert Spencer. *The Room Beyond.* New York: Appleton-Century-Crofts, 1948. (Mention, chap. 23.)

Cather, Willa. *Death Comes for the Archbishop.* New York: Alfred A. Knopf, 1927. (Mention, Book 5.)

Chavez, Fray Angelico. "The Fiddler and the Angelito." In *From an Altar Screen, "El Retablo": Tales from New Mexico,* pp. 22–29. New York: Farrar, Straus and Cudahy, 1957. (Mention, p. 25.)

———. "The Penitente Thief." In *New Mexico Triptych,* pp. 23–54. Paterson, N.J.: St. Anthony Guild Press, 1940. (Short story.)

Dispenza, Joseph. *The House of Alarcon.* New York: Coward, McCann & Geoghegan, 1978. (Mention, pp. 115–19.)

Eyre, Alice. *Torture at Midnight: The Mystery of the Penitentes.* New York: House of Field, 1942.

Fay H. Burton. "The Devil and the Penitent." *New Mexico Magazine,* April 1933, pp. 20–22, 48–49. (Short story.)

Fergusson, Harvey. *The Blood of the Conquerors.* New York: Alfred A. Knopf, 1921.

———. *The Conquest of Don Pedro.* New York: William Morrow, 1954. (Mention, chap. 11).

————. *Grant of Kingdom*. New York: William Morrow, 1950. (Mention, pp. 100–101, 288–91.)

Foster, O'Kane. *In the Night Did I Sing*. New York: Charles Scribner's Sons, 1942.

Hall, D. J. *Perilous Sanctuary*. New York: Macmillan, 1937.

Heifetz, Harold. *Jeremiah Thunder*. Garden City, New York: Doubleday, 1968.

Herrick, Robert. *Waste*. New York: Harcourt, Brace, 1924. (Mention, pp. 405–6, 425.)

How, Louis. *The Penitentes of San Rafael: A Tale of the San Luis Valley*. Indianapolis, Ind.: Bowen-Merrill, 1900.

Lawson, William Pinkney. *The Fire Woman*. New York: Boni & Liveright, 1925.

Martin, Curtis. *The Hills of Home*. Cambridge, Mass.: Riverside Press, 1943. (Mention, chap. 16.)

Newhall, Muriel [Mona Farnsworth]. *A Cross for Tomorrow*. New York: Pinnacle Books, 1972.

Otis, Raymond. "El Penitente." *Dial* 85(1928):406–13. (Short story.)

————. *Miguel of the Bright Mountain*. London: Victor Gollanez, 1936.

Reagan, Albert B. *Don Diego, or The Pueblo Indian Uprising of 1680*. New York: Alice Harriman, 1914. (Mention, pp. 76–80.)

Stevenson, Philip. "At the Crossroads." In *Folk-Say: A Regional Miscellany*, edited by Benjamin A. Botkin, pp. 70–82. Norman: University of Oklahoma Press, 1931. (Short story.)

Sylvester, Harry. *Dayspring*. New York: D. Appleton-Century, 1945.

Waters, Frank. *People of the Valley*. Denver, Colorado: Sage Books, 1941. (Mention, chaps. 4, 5.)

16

Mark Twain and the Mind's Ear

Walter Blair

I start by quoting a paragraph from Mark Twain's first block-busting book, *The Innocents Abroad*. This book, which established a worldwide reputation for Mark Twain, recounted in a humorous fashion the visit of Clemens and a charter group to Europe and the Holy Land. It made a great deal of fun of credulous and sentimental tourists. The company was an American Victorian crowd which believed that it ought to be terribly impressed by the Holy Land and which understood what it was expected to do when it got to places that the Bible celebrated: everyone should weep copiously. As a result, every time they were informed they had reached one of the proper places, they hauled off and soaked the earth with tears. Mark Twain every now and then in the book impersonated a dribbling pilgrim such as one he spoke of with great admiration: "He never bored but what he struck water." The tomb in which guidebooks authentically informed tourists Adam had been buried naturally called for large expenditures of tears. In his role of a mawkish innocent abroad, "Mark Twain" did what was required:

> The tomb of Adam! How touching it was here, in a land of strangers far from home and friends and all who cared for me, thus to discover the grave of a blood relation. True, a distant one, but still a relation! The unerring instinct of nature thrilled its recognition. The fountain of my filial affection was stirred to its profoundest depths, and I gave way to tumultuous emotion.
>
> I leaned upon a pillar and burst into tears. I deem it no shame to have wept over the grave of my poor dead relative. Let him who would sneer at my emotion close this volume here, for he will find little to his taste in my journeying through Holy Land. Noble old

man—he did not live to see me—he did not live to see his child. And I—I—alas, I did not live to see *him*. Weighed down by sorrow and disappointment, he died before I was born—six thousand brief summers before I was born. But let us try to bear it with fortitude. Let us trust that he is better off where he is. Let us take comfort in the thought that his loss is our eternal gain.

Read this aloud. I am reasonably sure that Mark Twain would say that you've just done something that a reader should do to learn or to demonstrate the qualities of his writings. You have caused it to reverberate in the mind's ear. I base my belief on things that Twain said about other writers and about himself over many years of a long career.

Writers have to be egoists. If they weren't, they wouldn't have the nerve to expect people to spend all the required time reading their books. So even when they talk about other authors, practically always they are talking about themselves. Do they praise an author for having good qualities? You can be sure that they think they themselves have those qualities. Do they condemn an author for having defects? You can be sure that nine times out of ten they are certain that they don't have those vile faults. So I look with great interest at what Twain says about one of his very dear friends and a really great author, William Dean Howells, in one of the few studies of individual authors that he ever wrote. He said of Howells, "He was in my belief without a peer in the English-speaking world." (Twain was of course being modest; he knew of at least one peer that Howells had.) A thing that strikes you is that he discusses Howells' writings as if they were talk. He praises not the flow of his writing, but "the easy and effortless flow of his speech." And his recipe for appreciating a great paragraph by Howells which he quotes and analyzes in detail is rather interesting. He says, "The thing you must do is examine it . . . . I don't mean in a bird's-eye way; I mean search it, study it, and of course read it aloud . . . . It is my conviction that one cannot get out of finely wrought literature all that is in it by reading it mutely."

One thing that Twain saw as a very fine quality of this same paragraph "after reading it several times aloud" was its wonderful compactness—"how simple" it is, "how unconfused by cross-currents . . . . how compressed." He talks about the impossibility of cutting down the passage in any way. And I think that when you turn to Mark Twain you'll find many remarkably compressed passages that read quite beautifully aloud. One is a passage that occurs in *Huckleberry Finn*, a passage that Bernard DeVoto called "one of the most blinding flashlights in all fiction." It's a brief paragraph that introduces a character who thereupon disappears forever. Like a great many characters in Shakespeare, this one has come alive in something like a hundred words. Huckleberry Finn has witnessed a brutal killing in a little riverside town. Poor drunken Boggs has been shot by the aristocratic Sherburn. Huck tells about the sequel:

Everybody that seen the shooting was telling how it happened, and there was a big crowd packed around each one of these fellows, stretching their necks and listening. One long lanky man, with long hair and a big white fur stove-pipe hat on the back of his head, and a crooked-handled cane, marked out the places on the ground where Boggs stood, and where Sherburn stood, and the people following him around from one place to t'other and watching everything he done, and bobbing their heads to show they understood, and stooping a little and resting their hands on their thighs to watch him mark the places on the ground with his cane; and then he stood up straight and stiff where Sherburn had stood, frowning and having his hat-brim down over his eyes, and he sung out, "Boggs!" and then fetched his cane down slow and to a level, and says "Bang!" staggered backwards, says "Bang!" again, and fell down flat on his back. The people that had seen the thing said he done it perfect; said it was just exactly the way it all happened. Then as much as a dozen people got out their bottles and treated him.

In addition to compactness, the passage illustrates another quality that Twain admired in old Howells—concreteness. Reading Howells aloud, he found his friend could "catch that airy thought and . . . reduce it to a concrete condition, visible, substantial . . . like a cabbage . . . translating the visions of the eyes of flesh into words that reproduce their sounds and colors." As I read that statement, I couldn't help but think of what Joseph Conrad said when he defined the task of an author: "By the power of the written word to make you hear, to make you feel . . . before all, to make you see—that and that only is the task of the author."

Twain worked to develop this skill quite early. The first short piece of his that won wide attention was a story that appeared when he was a very young man, "The Notorious Jumping Frog of Calaveras County." A paragraph it contained will show how he made things concrete. Notice how palpable to the senses every sight and movement is made, and how this vividness of detail adds to the fun. The speaker is an old mining rat who's talking about a prodigious gambler, Jim Smiley, who had a whole stable of wonderful animals. They were wonderful, that is, for a gambler because they all looked like Ziggies, as if they were always doomed to fail. Their looks caused people to bet against them, and then when the bets were down, they turned out to be something rather different. Wheeler's talking, for instance, with great admiration about Jim's mare:

Thish-yer Smiley had a mare . . . and he used to win money on that horse, for all she was so slow and always had the asthma, or the distemper, or the consumption, or something of that kind. They used to give her two or three hundred yards' start, and then pass her under way; but always at the fag end of the race she'd get excited

and desperate like, and come cavorting and straddling up, and scat-
tering her legs around limber, sometimes in the air, and sometimes
out to one side among the fences, and kicking up m-o-r-e dust and
raising m-o-r-e racket with her coughing and sneezing and blowing
her nose—and *always* fetch up at the stand just about a neck ahead,
as near as you could cipher it down.

Reading such a passage aloud made evident not only compactness and
concreteness; it also revealed meaning. It was a clarifying device: you
could see whether an author wrote lucidly or not.

Something that astonished many of Samuel Clemens' contemporaries
happened when he was in his fifties. He became an interpreter of—of all
people—Robert Browning. In those innocent days before Ezra Pound
and T. S. Eliot, among poets with a reputation of being obscure, Robert
Browning was a champion. Ladies who pursued culture—and sometimes
caught it—would attend meetings of clubs which would attempt to figure
out what Browning was saying, and Mark Twain became a leader of such a
group. His recipe for appreciating Browning was one that I think is predictable on the basis of what I've been saying about him. He said, "Put
me in the right condition, and give me room according to my strength,
and I can read Browning so Browning himself can understand." In other
words, read him aloud.

Well, the students in his Browning seminar agreed. One of them testi-
fied, "To him there were no obscure passages . . . no guessing at the
meaning. His slow deliberate speech and full voice gave each sentence its
quota of sound, and sense followed . . . easily."

Anyone who knows Mark Twain's biography and his writings at all well
really won't be astonished to find that Browning was a figure he greatly
appreciated. For the fact is that at their best Mark Twain and Browning
did very much the same thing. They had characters recite dramatic mono-
logues during the course of which they came alive for people who read what
they said or heard other people read what they said, aloud. "Experience
has taught me long ago," Mark Twain said on one occasion, "that if ever *I*
tell a boy's story . . . it is never worth printing . . . . To be successful and
worth printing, the imagined boy would have to tell the story himself, and
let me be his amanuensis."

I can't say why Browning got into the habit of writing dramatic mono-
logues, but I can guess with some assurance why Mark Twain did. Just
before his sixtieth birthday, Mark Twain wrote his chief critical discussion,
"How to Tell a Story." In it, he said, "I claim to know how a story ought to
be told, for I've been almost daily in the company of the most expert
storytellers for many years." And he quickly adds a significant qualification:
"Understand, I mean by word of mouth, not print." True enough, as you
read the account of Mark Twain's life you find he consorted with, one after

another, a parade of tremendous storytellers. His mother, first of all, "that obscure little woman with the enchanted tongue . . . the most eloquent person I met in all my days." Again there was Uncle Dan'l, the slave from whom Jim in *Huckleberry Finn* was copied. Clemens spent all his summers on a farm throughout his formative years. And he said,

> I know the look of Uncle Dan'l's kitchen as it was on privileged nights . . . white and black children grouped on the hearth, with firelight playing on their faces and shadows flickering. . . . And I can hear Uncle Dan'l telling the immortal [Brer Rabbit] tale. . . . And I can feel again the creepy joy which quivered through me when the time for the ghost story was reached—and the sense of regret, for it was always the last story of the evening . . . .

At eleven or twelve, Clemens became a printer's apprentice; for several years he associated with storytelling printers. When he was on the river he heard many stories told by Mississippi pilots. Later miners, prospectors, fellow reporters on newspapers, other comic writers and lecturers, with whom he lived or worked were raconteurs.

I think a very good case can be made for the claim that the crucial turning point in his career came when he was a newspaper reporter out in San Francisco and as a result of certain difficulties with the police department found it necessary to absent himself from San Francisco for a while. He went out to the Gillises in the gold country. He was aged twenty-nine. California was having some of its typical unusual weather, that is, it was raining cats and dogs and houses were sliding down hills. So he and several soggy pocket miners, day after day, night after night, huddled around stoves and fireplaces swapping stories. And one story was the one I mentioned a while back, the Jumping Frog story, which won him his first national fame, "the germ," he said, "of my coming fortune. It gave me a reputation throughout the world and paid me thousands and thousands of dollars."

From that time on, Mark Twain told in print many oral stories he'd heard. For example, at least eight stories, one of them the best short piece he ever wrote (I'll mention that a little later), were stories he heard told around the fires in Angel's Camp or at Jackass Hill. "I amend dialect stuff," he wrote, "by talking and talking it till it sounds right."

Like Browning, he loved to make the storyteller come to life. On occasion, he put the teller above the story he told. "The stories," he once said, "are only alligator pears. One merely eats them for the sake of the salad dressing." The salad dressing was the speaker, the storyteller. What he said and the way he said it made him known to the person who read or heard the story. He gave readers two helpings of humor: one was the enclosed story; the other was the framework. The funny monologue was

voiced by a funny monologist. As well as his frog story, the teller, Simon
Wheeler, was laughable, Simon was a funny character, typical of Mark
Twain's speakers in that he had no sense of humor whatever. One joke in
the framework of the jumping frog story was that a man without a sense of
humor told a funny story to a listener who had no sense of humor. Twain
described Wheeler this way:

> He never smiled. . . . All through the interminable narrative there
> ran a vein of impressive earnestness and sincerity which showed me
> plainly that, so far from his imagining that there was anything ridicu-
> lous . . . about the story, he regarded it as a really important matter,
> and admired its two heroes as men of transcendent genius. . . .

Another humorless old coot named Jim Baker told another story (one
that I regard as Mark Twain's second masterpiece) that Clemens had
heard on that visit to Angel's Camp. Baker had lived alone in the deserted
mining camp until he was a mite touched in the head, and as a result he
decided that animals were human. He knew they were human because
they were so ornery. They could talk and swear and tell lies and cheat.
"Why," he said, "a jay hasn't got any more principle than a Congress-
man!" He told about the prodigious ability of one jay to swear. This jay
somehow had got the notion that he'd like to fill up a knothole in a
deserted cabin with acorns. I don't know why—he never said. Just because it was there, I suppose. The trouble was that the hole was in the
roof of a completely hollow cabin, so as he dropped those acorns in they
just disappeared in a vast space. After he had dumped a number of into
that endless pit,

> he begun to get mad. He held in for a spell walking up and down the
> comb of the roof, and shaking his head and muttering to himself; but
> his feelings got the upper hand of him presently, and he broke loose
> and cussed himself black in the face . . . . When he got through he
> walks to the hole and looks in again . . . then he says, 'Well, you're a
> long hole, and a deep hole and a mighty singular hole altogether—but
> I've started to fill you, and I'm damned if I don't fill you if it takes
> me a hundred years!'
> "And with that, away he went. You never see a bird work so . . . .
> The way he hove acorns into that hole for about two hours . . . was
> one of the most exciting and astonishing spectacles I ever struck
> . . . . At last he could hardly flop his wings, he was so tuckered out.
> He comes a drooping down, . . . sweating like an ice-pitcher, and
> drops his acorn in and says, '*Now* I guess I've got the bulge on you
> by this time!' So he bent down for a look. If you'll believe me, when
> his head come up again he was just pale with rage. He says, 'I've

shoveled acorns enough in there to keep the family thirty years, and if I can see a sign of one of 'em I wish I may land in a museum with a belly full of sawdust in two minutes.

"He just had strength enough to crawl up on the comb and lean his back agin the chimbly, and then he collected his impressions and begun to free his mind. I see in a second that what I had mistook for profanity in the mines was only just the rudiments, as you may say."

Huck Finn, like Simon Wheeler and Jim Baker, had a lousy sense of humor. In that long book of his, he laughed only twice, I think, and saw only one joke—and it really wasn't a joke that was there at all. But he was a keen observer of scenes who set down sensuous descriptions of people and actions. He was interested in relationships, so he was impressed when one of the townspeople reenacted the death of Boggs, and he appreciated too a theatrical performance that had excellence. A man about whom he grew ecstatic—I think you'll see for good reason—was an under-taker who officiated at a funeral in a riverside town. Huck tells about his performance with typical solemnity and appreciation. The mortician is doing his best act, presiding at a funeral:

When the place was packed full, the undertaker he slid around . . . with his softy smoothering ways . . . getting people and things all ship shape and comfortable, . . . and making no more sound than the cat. He never spoke; he moved people around, he squeezed in late ones, . . . and done it with nods, and signs with his hands. Then he took his place over against the wall. He was the softest, glidingest, stealthiest man I ever see; and there warn't no more smile to him than there is to a ham. . . . Then the Reverend Hobson opened up, slow and solemn, and begun to talk; and straight off the most outrageous row busted out in the cellar . . . .only one dog, but he made a most powerful racket, and he kept it up, right along—the parson, he had to stand there, over the coffin, and wait . . . . It was right down awkward, and nobody didn't seem to know what to do. But pretty soon they see that long-legged undertaker make a sign to the preacher as much as to say, "Don't you worry—just depend on me." Then he stooped down and begun to glide along the wall, just his shoulders showing over the people's heads. So he glided along, and the pow-wow and racket getting more and more outrageous all the time, and at last, when he had gone around two sides of the room, he disappears down cellar. Then, in about two seconds we heard a whack, and the dog he finished up with a most amazing howl or two, and then everything was dead still, and the parson begun his solemn talk where he left off. In a minute or two here comes this undertaker's back and shoulders gliding along the wall again; and so he glided, and glided, around three sides of the room, and then rose up, and shaded his mouth with his hands, and stretched his neck out towards the preacher, over the people's heads, and says, in a kind of a coarse whisper, *"He had a rat!"* Then he drooped down and glided along the wall again to his place. You could see it was a great satisfaction to the people, because naturally they wanted to know. A little thing like that don't cost nothing, and it's just the little things that makes a man to be looked up to and liked. There warn't no more popular man in that town than that undertaker was.

I hope that reading of passages by Twain aloud has shown in addition to other qualities what might be called "poetic techniques." The way he played with that word "glided" was really a poet's trick, you know. Twain praised Howells' style, his prose style mind you, in terms that were applicable to poetry. Not only was it—like the best poetry—concrete and compact, it was also, Twain said, "limpid, fluent, graceful and rhythmical." He talks about Howells' prose as if it were poetry, "unvexed by ruggedness, clumsiness or broken meters." And he's keen on the way emotion permeates the writings of Howells, particularly his humor: "I do not think anyone else can play with humorous fancies so gracefully and delicately and deliciously as he does, nor . . . can come so near making them look as if they were doing the playing themselves . . . . His is a humor which flows softly all around about and over and through the mesh of the page, pervasive, refreshing, health-giving . . . ." To illustrate the fact that as usual when Mark Twain spoke of an achievement of Howells he was praising something he himself did, let me read a paragraph in Huck's book that I guess is my favorite. I find that (again quoting Twain on Howells) it is "full of photographs with feeling in them and sentiment, photographs taken in a dream." What's more, it's got rhythm, no "broken meters" here. It's Huck telling how he and Jim on their raft drifted down the Mississippi River at night:

Sometimes we'd have the whole river all to ourselves for the longest time. Yonder was the banks and the islands, across the water; and maybe a spark—which was a candle in a cabin window— and sometimes on the water you could see a spark or two—on a raft or a scow, you know; and maybe you could hear a fiddle or a song coming over from one of them crafts. It's lovely to live on a raft. We had the sky, up there, all speckled with stars, and we used to lay on our backs and look up at them, and discuss about whether they was made, or only just happened—Jim he allowed they was made, but I allowed they happened; I judged it would have took too long to *make* so many. Jim said the moon could a *laid* them; well, that looked kind of reasonable, so I didn't say nothing against it, because

I've seen a frog lay most as many, so of course it could be done. We
used to watch the stars that fell, too, and see them streak down. Jim
allowed they'd got spoiled and was hove out of the nest.

If I have convinced you that reading Twain aloud is the key to appreciating him, I'm very happy. If not, I still have a couple of escape hatches,
so I still can recommend this procedure. I have not followed Twain's
recipe. He said, "Never *read* a passage. Memorize it." And most of us are
too lazy to do that. He had a reason for memorizing: so one can watch that
audience and know how long to pause between bits of reading.

There's another error easily made. I recall a story Twain told several
times about an event in the early years of his marriage. He won his
aristocratic wife, Olivia, by telling her she could reform him. She believed
him, and she started to work on a large number of very bad habits he had.
One was to carry on the way that bluejay did. Clemens was a superb, a
fluent, and an unceasing user of profane language. Almost anything would
cause him to soar into eloquent expression. Frequently in the morning,
for some reason or other, a calamity occurred—he found a button was off a
shirt, or something else, especially at that hour of the day, was very
provoking. Livy noticed this tendency—she could hardly manage not to.
She asked some kind neighbor what you did about a man who carried on
that way. The neighbor said, "Well, the thing to do is listen carefully,
then repeat exactly the words that man has used." So, on one occasion,
when Clemens, as he described it, was "doing his devotions" because of
some horrible calamity, he looked around, and there was a big hunk of
silence in the corner of the room, and in it was Livy. Livy believed that if
she uttered those awful words, coming from her innocent lips they would
so horrify her husband that he would reform. So, to the best of her ability,
she repeated verbatim those commentaries of his. To her astonishment
and distress, instead of saying, "By God, I'll reform," he lay down on the
bed and howled with laughter. She said, "What's the matter?" He said,
"Oh, Livy! You got the words, but you ain't got the tune." If I've rendered
Twain's words not quite in tune—somewhat off-key—I'm sorry. But I still
hope that even an off-key rendition may help you appreciate Mark Twain's
writings by storing them in your mind's ear.

17

American Studies:
The Myth of Methodology*

Joel Jones

> He [Emerson] was in reaction against the formal logic of the eigh-
> teenth century, since he believed it not merely to confine but to
> distort; yet he insisted that "we want in every man a logic, we
> cannot pardon the absence of it." What he wanted could not be
> measured by propositions; it was to be "a silent method," "the
> proportionate unfolding of the intuition." (F. O. Matthiessen, *Ameri-
> can Renaissance*[1])

The elemental and essential function of the American Studies movement in higher education—as it has taken programmatic shape at either
the undergraduate or graduate level—has been to perpetuate the spirit
and substance of the ideal of "scholar" as embodied in the lives and
writings of Emerson, William James, and F. O. Matthiessen. For people
who identify with this vein of thought in American intellectual history,
pragmatism conjoins easily with idealism, and knowledge is seen as inherently both personal and political. For some of us the touchstone of the
American Studies movement (as it has manifested itself in both teaching
and research) is Emerson's essay of 1837, "The American Scholar." One
need not expound extensively on that essay now, other than to say that its
basic tenets unfortunately run contrary to much of the practice of American scholarship as witnessed in the contemporary American university.
The same can be said for the ideals regarding teaching and research found
in the writings of both William James (e.g., the "Ph.D. Octopus") and F.
O. Matthiessen (the preface to *American Renaissance* and several essays

---

*Reprinted from Joel Jones, "American Studies: The Myth of Methodology," *American Quarterly* 31(1979):382–87. Copyright 1979, Trustees of the University of Pennsylvania.

in *The Responsibilities of the Critic)*. These three men *professed* in their lives and their work an acute understanding of both the *politics of knowledge* and the *personal nature of knowing*. Whatever else one might say about the significance of American Studies—the necessity for nurturance of the interdisciplinary, the need for connection and synergy, holism and heurism, eclecticism and experimentation, pluralism and principled opportunism, authenticity and authority in teaching and research—one will come back, finally, to the basic premise: that knowledge is inherently both political and personal. To attribute this significance to the American Studies movement is to raise, simultaneously, serious questions about the movement's rather self-conscious concern regarding its own "methodology."

Several of the first pieces that I published as a young professor in American Studies nearly twelve years ago dealt with the movement's compulsive search for a method—and were, in fact, reflections themselves of that professional compulsion and philosophic compunction to articulate a methodological consensus for American Studies. At the time I was favorably impressed by the rapid appearance of several anthologies that collected some of the movement's introspective attempts and established a common base of referential material for those of us engaged in and committed to American Studies: *Studies in American Culture, American Character and Culture, American Studies in Transition, New Voices in American Studies*, and *American Studies: Essays on Theory and Method*, to name several. In 1969, just when I was beginning to wonder if one could make a career out of discussing the problems of methodology and subject matter in American Studies, an anthology was published that addressed itself to those same problems and contained among its thirteen essays nine that had also been published in the earlier anthologies. One could only see this as an indicator that the compulsion for introspection had perhaps gone as far as it fruitfully could at that point. One might be better off just *doing* American Studies for a while and worrying less about the theory of our so-called area of study.

Too many practitioners of American Studies had, in fact, become encaptured, enraptured, and enthralled by what I would like to call *the myth of methodology*—The sense that without method we could have no legitimacy, no meaning. My own attempt at that point became, on the one hand, to encourage graduate students in American Studies to acquaint themselves with the literature of that search for methodology (an acquaintance which, hopefully, would build in them the confidence that they were involved in an academic area that did have some legitimate sense of itself), and on the other hand, to encourage them to cut behind the myth of methodology and be more concerned about establishing a mode of research and teaching that would revolve around personal voice and political vision, a style ("method," if you will) for teaching and research that would be characterized, in the William Jamesian sense, by pragmatic authenticity. First comes the person, next the problem, then the process (the method) for seeking an understanding. The obsessive quest for a singular methodology can subvert both the substance and the significance of this dynamic.

A primary role for American Studies in the forty-plus years of its existence has been to create some "space" in academia for those scholar-teachers who would develop a style of teaching and research responsive, as Emerson suggested, to one's experiential and existential context. As Gene Wise, chairperson of American Studies at the University of Maryland, commented to me in a letter of several years ago (quoted here with his permission), "What American Studies has *distinctively* going for it is its flexibility and its sensitivity to new and different problems. This means that for most people in American Studies formalized research scholarship is a by-product of their curiosity and receptivity to the world of ongoing experience." In an increasingly restricted and restrictive academic marketplace, in an academic ethos increasingly marked by caution and conservatism, American Studies must continue to support the scholar who would transcend the rigidity and routine which too often characterize the methodological training (ironically true more in the humanities and social sciences than in the natural or hard sciences) of both the doctoral candidate and the young professor. American Studies must continue to proffer the necessary encouragement and support for those who would risk the leap beyond methodology (insofar, at least, as method is traditionally defined in disciplinary or even interdisciplinary terms).

One realizes that in order to encourage American Studies scholars to move beyond the myth of methodology one should rally a few allies from both within and outside the American Studies fold. Let us, then, consider briefly statements by two philosophers (both from Harvard, though separated by several generations), a computer programmer, a physicist, a literary critic, a feminist, and two cultural historians. In his rather prophetic and incisive essay of over a half-century ago, "The Ph.D. Octopus," William James warned us of the dangers in store for academia as the emphasis on graduate study took shape at institutions like his own Harvard and elsewhere. He spoke of the negative effects that specialization and the obsession with methodology might have on scholarship and teaching insofar as vision (imagination) and voice (integrity) were concerned. Much closer to our own time, in *The Predicament of the University*, which provides perhaps as substantive and incisive a critique of higher education as any of the plethora of studies to emerge in the last decade, Henry David Aiken (who left the Philosophy Department at Harvard after twenty years to go to Brandeis) warns us of what he calls "that fatal sin of methodolatry, the worship of the procedure or routine, which itself can stultify the advancement of learning." In a totally different sort of study, though of equal substance and insight, Mary Daly in *Beyond God the Father: Toward a Philosophy of Women's Liberation*, attacks specifically "the tyranny of methodolatry" that "hinders new discoveries" and "prevents us from raising questions never asked before and from being illumined by ideas that do not fit into pre-established boxes and forms."[2]

Two other critiques of traditional methodology that articulate a similar metaphorical alternative are Edward De Bono's *Lateral Thinking* and Robert Pirsig's *Zen and the Art of Motorcycle Maintenance. Lateral Thinking* is a rather prosaic (almost workbooklike) conceptualization of an interdisciplinary (or transdisciplinary) approach to problem solving and creative thinking; lateral thinking is juxtaposed to the more traditional, specialized, disciplinary "vertical" mode of thinking. In *Zen*, Pirsig has the protagonist of his novel-treatise suggest (when reflecting upon his difficulties as a student at the University of Chicago) that, "drifting is what one does when looking at lateral truth. He couldn't follow any known method of procedure," for "instead of expanding the branches of what you already know, you have to stop and drift laterally for a while until you come across something that allows you to expand the roots of what you already know."[3] In my mind both of these works should be seminal reading for students and scholars in American Studies, for they reflect in their respective statements the ideal of scholarly synopsis, synthesis, and seeking which the American Studies movement should continue to sustain in the context of an academic world increasingly committed to and characterized by tight structure and narrow specialization.

Also, in critiquing the myth of methodology, one might cite the cultural historian, Henry Glassie, who, in his lengthy essay, "Meaningful Things and Appropriate Myths: The Artifact's Place in American Studies," contends, "The annihilation of self in methodology and the endless counting of sensate phenomena represent a failure of nerve, not its reverse, a shying from essentials." Glassie insists (echoing William James's concern) that "graded on mechanical performances rather than venturesomeness of thought, developing scholars are coerced into intricate specializations within constricted disciplines." One should not belabor this attack on methodology; nor should one overstate the case. Obviously, a methodological sense and sensitivity is finally necessary for significant scholarship. Those of us committed to American Studies should agree, though, with Wylie Sypher, who, while serving as chairman of the English Department at Simmons College, wrote, "My plea is that methods should not become programmatic, that criticism should not become official, since the official is the pedantic. We should distrust any system whatever. The evil comes when method is used (or abused) technologically—that is, when it is beguiled by its own mechanism."[4]

To conclude this chorus of (admittedly disparate and possibly discordant) voices in opposition to the primacy of methodology, let me turn to a scholar most closely identified with the American Studies movement—Leo Marx. In 1969 Professor Marx responded to the now classical challenge of his mentor, Henry Nash Smith, in 1957 regarding the viability of *a* method for American Studies by suggesting that for "the humanist working in American Studies, . . . considerations of method are secondary," and we will define our "purpose without reference to any methodological restrictions, but rather in relation to a vast, apparently limitless subject matter."[5] Professor Marx's position, in fact, echoes and expands that of Smith in his seminal essay. It should be noted, though, that many in the American Studies movement have felt uncomfortable with this proclivity to personal voice and pluralistic eclecticism or principled opportunism in method. Robert Sklar, for example, criticizes for *A.Q.* readers what he sees as a "strong antipathy among some sectors of the American Studies field toward efforts to move beyond individualistic, idiosyncratic and impressionistic modes of scholarly procedure . . . to the goal of clarifying an 'American Studies philosophy.' " Professor Sklar attributes this "antiphilosophical" consciousness, as he calls it, to "the need to survive in specific academic settings by incorporating any and all interdisciplinary urges with favor to none." He suggests that American Studies scholars of this bent need to be "better able to grasp the relation between expression and social context in their scholarly pursuits."[6] And yet he dismisses as inadequate two of the more concerted and committed attempts to articulate a coherent methodology—the 1973 *A.Q.* statement on American Cultural Studies by Mechling, Merideth, and Wilson, and Cecil Tate's book of the same year on *The Search for a Method in American Studies*— not recognizing himself that very pointed philosophic position statements such as these, as well as his own commitment to a methodological conscousness, are themselves quite specific reflections of the material and mythical realities of academia.

To discern a myth is not to decry it—I simply want practitioners of American Studies to recognize the power of this particular myth in academia and to appreciate the fact that a central significance of American Studies has been and must continue to be the protection of individual voice and vision (Emerson's method of "silent intuition") against the collective routinization or mechanization of inquiry which too often guises itself as methodology.

In closing, I would stress that this critique of methodology and espousal of the transmethodological impulse in the American Studies movement should not be seen either as an uninformed attack on scholarship nor as an uninitiated utopian view of academia. Regarding the latter, as a central academic administrator in a large state university I deal with "hard-core" academia every day, and, as for the former, as I recently wrote in another context, there need be "no conflict or contradiction between new criticism and American Studies, between careful textual analysis and creative contextual conjecture. One cannot move to the cutting edge of ideas unless one begins at the bedrock."[7] Be creative, but be concrete; do not hesitate to make the intellectual leap, but be certain that you start from solid ground. Substance first, then synthesis and synopsis. To criticize the compulsive concern for methodology is *not* to criticize a commitment to scholarship. In American Studies the most exciting teaching and research moves beyond subject-specific scholarship to speculative synthesis. However, as the best American Studies scholars always make clear, in precept and practice, without scholarship, there can be no synthesis. Finally, though, the mastery and the meaning (the magic, if you will) come not from methodology (unless defined in the Emersonian sense) but rather from the presence of the scholar, from the voice and vision of the individual.

NOTES

1. F. O. Matthiessen, *American Renaissance: Art and Expression in the Age of Emerson and Whitman* (New York, 1941), pp. 3–4.

2. Henry David Aiken, *The Predicament of the University* (Bloomington, Ind., 1971), p. 234; Mary Daly, *Beyond God the Father: Toward a Philosophy of Women's Liberation* (Boston, 1973), p. 11; William James, "The Ph.D. Octopus," in *Memories and Studies*, ed. Henry James, Jr. (New York, 1911), pp. 329–47.

3. Edward De Bono, *Lateral Thinking: Creativity Step by Step* (New York, 1970), pp. 9–10; Robert M. Pirsig, *Zen and the Art of Motorcycle Maintenance: An Inquiry Into Values* (New York, 1974), pp. 122, 170.

4. Henry Glassie, "Meaningful Things and Appropriate Myths: The Artifact's Place in American Studies," in Jack Salzman, ed., *Prospects: An Annual of American Cultural Studies* (New York, 1975); Wylie Sypher, "The Poem as Defense," *American Scholar* 37(Winter 1967–68):88.

5. Leo Marx, "American Studies—A Defense of an Unscientific Method," *New Literary History* 1(October 1969):77.

6. Robert Sklar, "The Problem of An American Studies Philosophy: A Bibliography of New Directions," *American Quarterly* 28(August 1975):262.

7. Joel M. Jones, "Scholarship and Synthesis: George Arms at New Mexico," *American Literary Realism* 10(Summer 1977):229–30.

Index

Adams, Henry, 33, 44, 115, 122
Adler, Felix, 90–91
Afro-American literature, 3, 125–42
Aiken, Henry David, 242
American Renaissance, 28–29
American Studies, 1–4, 6, 240–45
American Studies Association, 1
Antin, Mary, 108
autobiography, 58, 108, 193–209

Barthes, Roland, 6
Beadle, Erastus, 171
Beall, Dorothy Landers, 65–66
Bellamy, Edward, 32
Bellow, Saul, 113
Bercovitch, Sacvan, 105–06, 112, 192
Blavatsky, Madam Helena P., 100
Bolivar, Simon, 17
Bouton, Jim, 4, 193–209
Brann, William Cowper, 91, 92
Bright, Robert, 226
Brooks, Van Wyck, 66–67, 68–69, 193
Browning, Robert, 234

Cahan, Abraham, 113, 118
Capone, Al, 151
Capra, Frank, 3–4, 211–19
Civil War, 7, 27, 28, 34, 45–46, 112
Cotton, John, 9
Cooper, James Fenimore, 19
cowgirls: 168–80; in dime novels, 171–73; in Western literature, 173–76; in film, 176–77; in rodeos, 178
Crane, Hart, 58–74
Crèvecoeur, J. Hector St. Jean de, 15
Crichton, Kyle, 224–25
crime, organized, 144–53, 185–86, 187, 190–91

Daly, Mary, 242–43
DeBono, Edward, 243

Degler, Carl, 8
dime novels, 171–73, 185
Donnelly, Ignatius, 32
Dunbar, Paul Laurence, 126–42

Edwards, Jonathan, 12
Emerson, Ralph Waldo, 30–32, 33–34, 62, 112, 121, 240
Evans, Walker, 71, 72–73

families: 187–88; frontier, 155–64
feminist movement, 21, 22
Fiedler, Leslie, 114, 119
Fiske, John, 82
Fox, George, 79
Frank, Waldo, 67–68, 107
Franklin, Benjamin, 196
French and Indian War, 11, 12
frontier: 24, 115–17; Canadian, 23–24; families, 155–64. See also women in the West

Glassie, Henry, 243
Goodman, Paul, 5–6
Great Awakening, 11, 12
Gregg, Josiah, 222
Grey, Zane, 175

Hawthorne, Nathaniel, 19
Hidalgo, Padre Cura Miguel, 17
Higham, John, 27, 122
Hill, Christopher, 8
Hobsbawm, Eric, 8
How, Louis, 224
Howells, William Dean, 2, 43–55, 76–85, 113, 232, 238
Hubbard, Elbert, 91–92
Huizinga, Johan, 59, 60

Ideology, American, 2, 6, 8, 10, 19, 28, 34, 40n, 46, 54, 105, 106, 110
Ingersoll, Robert G., 92–93

James, Henry, Jr., 54–55, 78
James, Henry, Sr., 78
James, William, 76, 81, 83, 84–85, 87n, 240, 242
Jefferson, Thomas, 18
Jewish experience: in Hollywood, 110–11; leftist politics, 109–11, 117–18; in literature, 3, 106–22

Kazin, Alfred, 116
King Lear, 131–32
King, Martin Luther, Jr., 6, 121
knuckleball, 202–03, 208

Lamy, Archbishop Jean Baptiste, 221–22
Lazarus, Emma, 121
Lewis, Sinclair, 43
Luciano, Charlie "Lucky", 147, 148, 149, 153
Lummis, Charles F., 222–23, 224

Mailer, Norman, 108–09, 113
Malamud, Bernard, 118, 120–21
Marin, John, 63, 64, 66, 71
Marx, Leo, 243–44
Marxism, 79, 80
Matthiessen, F. O., 240
Melville, Herman, 33, 35, 198
Methodism, 78–79
Miller, Perry, 25
Modernism, 58–74 *passim*, 113, 155–64 *passim*
Mumford, Lewis, 63, 64
myth: 1, 2, 105–22, 125, 211; of American West, 116–21, 173, 186–87; defined, 124–25; popular, 184

narrative structures: 106, 112–14, 182–92; detective story, 183, 185–86; romance, 183, 184; science fiction and fantasy, 183, 187; spy story, 183; westerns, 171–73, 183, 185, 186–87, 191. *See also* pornography
New Left, 6
New Thought, 97–99

Olney, James, 195–96
Oriental religion, 99, 100–01
Otis, Raymond, 226

Paine, Thomas, 18
Parkman, Lester Shepard, 173
Patch, Sam, 47–48

Penitente Brotherhood, 4, 221–28
Pepys, Samuel, 196
Pirsig, Robert, 243
plantation tradition, 128, 137, 140, 141, 143n
Poole, Ernest, 65
pornography, 184, 188–89
Porter, William Sydney (O. Henry), 175, 176
Protestantism, American, 88–99, 101–02, 105–22 *passim*
Puritan culture, 2, 7–13, 20, 105, 107
Pyle, Howard, 78, 82–83

Quakerism, 79

Ravage, Marcus, 117–18, 119
realism: cinematic, 111; literary, 43, 45, 46–47
Revolution, American, 12–14, 112
Rhodes, Eugene Manlove, 174
Roebling, John A., 65
Romanticism, 28–29, 30, 60
Roth, Henry, 113

Schaff, Philip, 26–27
Schlatter, Francis, 94
Sinclair, Bertha "Muzzy", 174, 176
Sklar, Robert, 244
Slotkin, Richard, 111–12, 173, 176, 186–87
Smith, Henry Nash, 243–44
spiritualism, 96–97
Stanton, Elizabeth Cady, 21, 29
Stella, Joseph, 61–62, 71, 72
Stevens, Wallace, 59–60
Swedenborgianism, 77–78, 82
Sylvester, Henry, 227
Sypher, Wylie, 243

Teresa, Vincent, 147–48
Theosophy, 99–100
Thomas, Keith, 8
Thoreau, Henry David, 29
Tocqueville, Alexis de, 7–8, 19, 20
Tolstoi, Leo, 79, 80, 81, 84
Transcendentalism, 79
Turner, Frederick Jackson, 24, 115, 122
Twain, Mark (Samuel Clemens), 4, 48, 78, 82, 83, 231–39

Van Dyke, Henry, 83, 93
Victorian culture: 231; female stereotypes, 161; ideology, 156–59, 160, 161–64

Weber, Max, 8
West, Nathanael, 113, 118

westerns, 183, 185, 187, 191
Wheatley, Phyllis, 126, 127, 142n
Wheelwright, Philip, 112
Whigs, 12, 13, 16
Whitman, Walt, 29, 32–33, 44–45
Williams, William Carlos, 59
Winthrop, John, 35, 106

Wise, Gene, 242
Wister, Owen, 175
Wittgenstein, Ludwig, 129–30
women in the West: "Amazon" characters,
    171–72, 173, 179; frontier, 3, 155–64,
    166–80; "Pard" and "Sport" characters,
    172–79